THE ITALIAN DICTATORSHIP

THE ITALIAN DICTATORSHIP

Problems and perspectives in the interpretation of Mussolini and Fascism

R. J. B. BOSWORTH

Professor of History, University of Western Australia

A member of the Hodder Headline Group
LONDON

First published in Great Britain 1998 by
Arnold, a member of The Hodder Headline Group,
338 Euston Road, London NW1 3BH

http://www.arnoldpublishers.com

Co-published in the United States of America by
Oxford University Press Inc.,
198 Madison Avenue, New York, NY 10016

The advice and information in this book are believed to be true and accurate
at the date of going to press, but neither the author nor the publisher can
accept any legal responsibility or liability for any errors or omissions.

British Library Cataloguing in Publication Data
A catalogue entry for this book is available from the British Library

Library of Congress Cataloging-in-Publication Data
Bosworth, R. J. B.
    The Italian dictatorship: problems and perspectives in the
interpretation of Mussolini and fascism/R.J.B. Bosworth
    p.   cm.
    Includes bibliographical references and index.
    ISBN 0–340–67728–7 (hb). — ISBN 0–340–67727–9 (pbk.)
    1. Fascism—Italy—Historiography.   2. Italy—Politics and
government—1922–1945—Historiography.   3. Mussolini, Benito,
1883–1945.   4. Historiography—Italy—History—20th century.
I. Title.
DG571.16.B67   1998
945.09'072—dc21   98–14742
                                                            CIP

Production Editor: Liz Gooster
Production Controller: Rose James
Cover Design: Terry Griffiths

ISBN 0 340 67727 9 (pb)
ISBN 0 340 67728 7 (hb)

for Jonathan Steinberg

'The prince wants and must want his subjects to be blind, ignorant, spiritless, deceived, and oppressed; because, if they were anything else he would immediately cease to exist.'

(V. Alfieri, *The Prince and Letters*, Toronto, 1972, p. 15)

Contents

List of Abbreviations

ANC	*Associazione Nazionale dei Combattenti* (National Returned Soldiers Association)
ANI	*Associazione Nazionalista Italiana* (Italian Nationalist Association)
BR	*Brigate Rosse* (Red Brigades)
DC	*Democrazia Cristiana* (Italian Christian Democracy)
EUR	*Esposizione Universale Romana* (Rome's Universal Exhibition)
FDP	German Free Democratic Party
GeL	*Giustizia e Libertà* (Justice and Liberty)
GUF	*Gruppi Universitari Fascisti* (Union of Italian Fascist University Students)
ISPI	*Istituto per gli Studi di Politica Internazionale* (Italian Institute for the Study of International Policy)
KPD	German Communist Party
LUCE	*L'Unione Cinematografica Educativa* (Italian Educative Film Union)
MSI	*Movimento Sociale Italiano* (Italian Social Movement: neo-Fascists)
NATO	North Atlantic Treaty Organisation
PCI	*Partito Comunista Italiano* (Italian Communist Party)
PDS	*Partito Democratico della Sinistra* (Democratic Party of the Left)
PNF	*Partito Nazionale Fascista* (National Fascist Party)
PSIUP	*Partito Socialista Italiano di Unità Proletaria* (Italian Socialist Party of Proletarian Unity)
RAI	*Radiotelevisione Italiana* (Italian State Radio and TV)

(*Note:* Throughout this text Fascism with a capital F signifies the Italian regime and ideology; fascism with a small f means the more generic variety.)

Preface

As an Italianist, I have spent my career doubly detached from my subject matter. I was born and, throughout my academic life, I have lived in Australia, that curious part European and part utterly non-European country. The realities of Australian university life, especially as braced for two decades against the continuous cold and hostile winds of economic rationalism, have also meant that I have most often taught European and not specifically Italian history. My detachments I have had to allow for and try to circumvent.

One way an Australian can overcome the 'tyranny of distance' is by working as a historiographer as much as a historian, and this I have regularly done and do again in this current book. Even so, I remain heavily dependent on being able to speak and listen to a world beyond my part of the Antipodes. In the 1990s ventures into cyberspace make such discourse easier than before; but conversation grows with usage, and I am very aware that my written history is the product both of my own mind (and its limitations) and of those with whom I converse. Those whose talk has enlivened me and rescued me to some extent from the enormous condescension of geography include Michal and Mary Bosworth, Glenda Sluga, Nick Doumanis, Graham White, Shane White, Loretta Baldassar, Lorenzo Polizzotto, Roger Absalom, Keith Robbins, Tony Cahill, Rob Stuart, Jonathan Steinberg, Giovanna Rosselli, Patrizia Dogliani, Luciano Tosi, Enrico Serra and many another in Italy, Australia, the USA and the UK. I am, of course, hopelessly in their debt as I have sought to harness their words to my usage.

For the appearance of *The Italian Dictatorship* I am also grateful to Christopher Wheeler of Arnold. It was Christopher who originally suggested to me that I write this study, and it has been Christopher who has so courteously and effectively seen it through to completion. I am heavily indebted to him and to Liz Gooster, Christina Malkowska Zaba and Barbara Massam for thier work on my prose style and presentation. Much of the writing I did in my office at the University of Western Australia, with its wonderful students and lovely campus, set beside shimmering water, adorned with majestic trees and enlivened by the raucous cries of parrots, and with so many of its buildings hinting at a Fascistoid architecture – this Antipodean seat of academe runs to colonnades, a campanile and slogans worthily carved on walls. Much of my collecting of information was done on my regular visits to Italy, a country which I have sought to see from Lecce to Cuneo and from Trieste to Siracusa, even as, from time to time, I have locked myself in this or that library. The last touches of the book were put into place while I was a Visiting Fellow at Clare Hall, Cambridge. In other words, my comment in the preface to my last book, *Italy and the Wider World* (1996), that I live both a fortunate and a translated life continues to hold true. Who, I still ask myself, would not be a historian and a teacher, and especially a historian of modern Italy, if they had the chance? Who would not delight in a discipline and a subject-matter of infinite variety and unending contradiction as it seeks to explore the frail but stubborn beauty of humankind?

R. J. B. Bosworth
Nedlands (WA) and Cambridge
1997–8

Introduction

Fascist Italy's largest concentration camp[1] was situated at Ferramonti di Tarsia in Calabria. Its regulations having been promulgated on 10 July 1940 before the site was actually ready, the camp expanded until, in 1943, it was housing many thousands of Jews, Greeks, Yugoslavs and other enemies of the Fascist State. On 8 September 1943, the eventual fate of its Jews remained uncertain, but, in the end, they were saved by the arrival of the US Army. The Americans' timely presence prevented the inmates from falling victim to the Verona Manifesto, issued by the Salò Republic on 14 November that year and proclaiming Jews the 'enemy number one of the nation'.[2]

Now the remains of the Ferramonti camp are buried under the Salerno–Reggio Calabria motorway. Its physical existence and perhaps its memory thus obscured, Ferramonti scarcely joins Auschwitz, Belzec, Treblinka and the scores of other death camps scattered around fascist Europe in the annals of human infamy. None the less, conditions at Ferramonti from 1940 to 1943 were often harsh. Inmates died there, especially during the lengthy construction phase when typhus, assisted by the lack of clean and readily available water, swept the site.[3] Those initial regulations also had some harsh features, demanding, for example, that there be three daily roll calls of prisoners assembled outside their huts.

These roll calls deserve examination for a moment. The historian of Ferramonti has noted that the mustering of inmates soon created difficulties.

1 This 'good' camp is contrasted effectively in its history and recollection in J. Walston, 'History and memory of the Italian concentration camps', *Historical Journal*, 40, 1997, pp. 169–83. See also Chapter 8 below.
2 Cited by C. S. Capogreco, *Ferramonti: la vita e gli uomini del più grande campo d'internamento fascista (1940–1945)*, Florence, 1987, p. 30; cf. also his 'I campi di internamento fascista per gli ebrei (1940–1943)', *Storia contemporanea*, 22, 1991, pp. 663–82. Between 1940 and 1943 there were more than 50 camps spread across the country (p. 672).
3 C. S. Capogreco, *Ferramonti*, pp. 49, 85.

Guards had trouble pronouncing foreign names and comprehending foreign replies. The parades became confusing and lengthy, sometimes lasting more than two hours. The likely consequences had this been a Nazi camp are not hard to imagine. But, in Fascist Italy, what happened? The camp commandant grew impatient at his juniors' lack of culture. The juniors shrugged their shoulders at the impossibility and irrationality of the task which officialdom had set them. Both the senior officer and his subordinates knew that it was unpleasant to stand for hours in the sun or the rain. Each understood that the prisoners, human beings too, were reluctant to do so. Each began to disobey the letter of the law. The number of roll calls was reduced from three, to two, to one, to one every second day.[4] Humanity, decency, obfuscation, procrastination, 'corruption' and life began to triumph over uniformity, 'modernity', 'efficiency', terror and death.

A similar story can also be told concerning the camp's relationship with the inhabitants of Tarsia, the nearest small town or *paese*. The inhabitants of Tarsia defined themselves, as *cittadini* might, against the peasants who lived in smaller settlements outside the *paese*. However, the opening of the camp brought a third party into the equation. The prisoners, it was soon clear, possessed the kind of glamour which all locals assumed must belong to the wider and more modern world. Prisoners had, or seemed to have, familiar and even confident dealings with the state, that usually distant, menacing and imponderable entity – thus, by 1942, only 10 per cent of local postal traffic went to Tarsia *città*; the rest went to the camp. Prisoners were 'cultured'; with seeming effortlessless, they had mastered the culture of the great world.[5] The camp library held 2000 books, classical music was played there, and an artist painted (and eventually could be persuaded to exhibit his latest daubings in Tarsia). Moreover, the prisoners seemed rich. Even if they had to depend on charity for survival, it was rumoured that they consumed sugar. Indeed, by 1942–3 they were acquiring the ration of virtually the whole *comune*, a situation made possible by the fact that peasants did not take up their allotted share of so unfamiliarly urban a product, one which represented a modernity that had still not intruded into peasant lives.[6] In Calabria, it seems, when the liberating Americans arrived, existence was divided into different time zones; the prisoners, some officials and members of the town bourgeoisie might comprehend the meaning of '1943' but, for many of the peasants, the calendar might as easily have been set at 1443 or 993.

Nor were these divisions confined to the deepest south. In his finely textured account of the Northern Italian peasants' reception after 8 September 1943 of escaped British and Commonwealth prisoners, Roger

4 C. S. Capogreco, *Ferramonti*, p. 47.
5 The camp authorities even tolerated the establishment of two synagogues, one more liberal than the other, for the Jewish inmates, and generally favoured 'religious freedom'. K. Voigt, *Il rifugio precario: gli esuli in Italia dal 1933 al 1945*, Florence, 1996, ii, pp. 227–8.
6 C. S. Capogreco, *Ferramonti*, p. 178. For comment on the regime's representation of sugar, see K. Pinkus, *Bodily regimes: Italian advertising under Fascism*, Minneapolis, 1997, pp. 88–95.

Absalom has told a similar tale of self-interested and 'realistic' *paesani* charity and love, and of ideals and ambitions belonging to an early modern world.[7] Such ideals had a violent strain, too. Listen, for example, to a conversation between an escaped English POW and a sharecropper in Tuscany (the sharecropper surmised that England might be near 'Africa'):

'Are you Catholics?'
'No.'
'Do you believe in God?'
'No.'
'Do you hear that, Maria? Educated men and they don't believe in God.'
'Maybe that's their custom.'
'I always told you there was no God. Why don't the Allies bomb the Vatican?'
A pause.
'Why should they?'
'They'd get rid of the priests. They won't have another chance like this.'[8]

What message can be read in such an exchange? For some, the answer is simple. Even when they display a certain peremptory judgement against the rich and powerful, the Italians are nice people – *italiani brave gente*. They cannot be imagined as 'Mussolini's willing executioners'; they embody the 'banality of good'.[9] If 'Auschwitz' represented the ultimate degradation of the human spirit[10] and made plain the final contradiction of modernity,[11] then the Italians had no real part in it. Fascism might be a word which spread from Italian into other languages, but Italians themselves lacked a 'fascist personality';[12] they were too charming and too individualist to transmogrify into the 'beast from the abyss', too feckless and too 'civilised' to act as the agents of 'the barbarisation of war' on the Eastern front or of the barbarisation of peace at home.

Perhaps. And yet, whatever might be assumed to be the Italian 'national character', it is only too easy to unearth brutality and murder in the policies of the Italian Fascist regime. In 1930–1, under Mussolini's leadership but

---

7 See R. Absalom, 'Hiding history: the Allies, the Resistance and the others in Occupied Italy 1943–1945', *Historical Journal*, 38, 1995, pp. 111–31 and, at greater length, his *A strange alliance: aspects of escape and survival in Italy 1943–45*, Florence, 1991.

8 S. Hood, *Pebbles from my skull*, London, 1963, pp. 32–3. An extended edition of this work is available as *Carlino*, Manchester, 1985.

9 See J. Steinberg, *All or nothing: the Axis and the Holocaust 1941–1943*, London, 1991 and D. J. Goldhagen, *Hitler's willing executioners: ordinary Germans and the Holocaust*, New York, 1996. There is further comment below in Chapter 4 about these matters.

10 Perhaps the most moving and humane of all accounts of Auschwitz is that by the Italian anti-Fascist and Jew Primo Levi, *If this is a man*, London, 1966. See further, Chapter 8.

11 See Z. Bauman, *Modernity and the Holocaust*, Oxford, 1989.

12 Indeed, the classic psychological explorations of fascism by Fromm, Reich and others rarely mention Italy. See further, Chapter 9.

with the agency of the professionals of the Royal Italian Army, at least 100 000 Libyans were deported from their homes in the interior of their land and left to starve to death in a concentration camp, victims of a policy defined by its historian as possessing 'the nature and extent of an authentic genocide'.[13] After the conquest of Addis Ababa in May 1936, Mussolini cheerfully ordered the liquidation of the Ethiopian intelligentsia, and his officers, again as likely to be from the army as from Fascist squads, readily adopted fire and sword tactics and sought to extirpate the remains of an Ethiopian national history, preserved in the holy city of Aksum.[14] Similarly, Mussolini and his army must bear responsibility for the Fascist deployment of poison gas both during the actual war in Ethiopia and, on occasion, in the pacification which followed.[15] Even before Fascism, eminent figures like the publicist Matteo Pantaleoni and the sometime Governor of Eritrea and Minister of Colonies Ferdinando Martini preached what might be interpreted as genocide as the proper fate for native peoples.[16] The Slovenes of north-eastern Italy and the Yugoslav border territories also had few reasons to look back favourably on Fascism – during the regime they could expect repression; in war they endured 'ethnic cleansing' and a civilian death toll of more than 10 000.[17]

Perhaps all imperialists from time to time thought or behaved this way, but the Fascist regime was not soft in its domestic dealings either. The Salò Republic, which some historians view as 'real' Fascism, forgot the banality of good and assisted its German allies in the killing of more than 7500 Jews who had been resident in Italy and its empire.[18] In Trieste the *Risiera di San Sabba* acted as a distribution point for Auschwitz, and thousands died in the camp itself – officially the Nazis were in control, but they could not have functioned without local Italian assistance.[19] Moreover, though doubtless not equalling the death-toll of Nazism or Stalinism, Fascism had imposed a tyranny on Italy for two decades before 1943. The most notorious victims of this tyranny were those who dared publicly to dissent from it – the moderate socialist Giacomo Matteotti, killed in 1924 by Amerigo Dumini, a Fascist squadrist with experience in Chicago;[20] the liberal democrat Giovanni Amendola, who died in exile less than 12 months after a Fascist

---

13 A. Del Boca, *Gli italiani in Libia dal fascismo a Gheddafi*, Bari, 1988, p. 183.

14 For an introduction see D. Mack Smith, *Mussolini's Roman Empire*, London, 1976, pp. 78–80.

15 For the detail see A. Del Boca (ed.), *I gas di Mussolini: il Fascismo e la guerra d'Etiopia*, chapters by Del Boca and Giorgio Rochat.

16 For such examples, see R. J. B. Bosworth, *Italy and the wider world 1860–1960*, London, 1996, pp. 99, 104.

17 J. Walston, 'History and memory of the Italian concentration camps', p. 170.

18 Out of a total of some 44 500 Italian and foreign Jews. See M. Michaelis, *Mussolini and the Jews: German–Italian relations and the Jewish question in Italy 1922–1945*, Oxford, 1978, p. 392.

19 G. A. Sluga, 'The Risiera di San Sabba: Fascism, anti-Fascism, and Italian nationalism', *Journal of Modern Italian Studies*, 1, 1996, pp. 401–12.

20 For his unrepentant post-war memoirs, see A. Dumini, *Diciassette colpi*, Milan, 1958.

beating;[21] the Catholic priest Don Giovanni Minzoni, murdered by vengeful squadrists almost a year after the Fascists had taken government;[22] and Antonio Gramsci, the humanist Marxist leader of the Italian Communist party, who was gaoled after a Fascist trial in which Mussolini ordered the judge to stop Gramsci's mind working for 20 years. Gramsci, who, to add to his woes, had Pott's disease, lasted 10.[23]

Other victims were less public – Slovenes and any of those who resisted the 'Italianisation' of the border territories; women who died after back-street abortions or in childbirth while the regime trumpeted its gains in the 'Battle of the Births'; workers whose pay and conditions were severely cut by the regime and who, as a result, could do little more than aim to survive from one day to the next and who did not always succeed; peasants left prey to disease and their landlords in a world in which *marasmus*, that is, simple starvation, exacted a regular tithe of lives; soldiers sent off to kill and to die in ill-equipped and poorly led Fascist forces, and in battles fought more for glory or for an alleged tactical advantage than for any sensible reading of national interest. By most standards the Fascist regime was a vicious one, and its cruelty and its failure should not be forgotten, even in that present which is complacently defined as living after the 'end of history'.

It is in this and some other senses that I have chosen to entitle this book *The Italian Dictatorship*. The two key words in the title carry equal weight. Better than 'Mussolini's Italy' or 'the Fascist regime', 'the Italian dictatorship' expresses the sense in which the politics of Italy from 1922 to 1945 abandoned what is best in humankind, but did so in a way which was decidedly coloured by history, whether national or non-national. An understanding of Fascism must reckon with 'Italy', that is, with the state created in the Risorgimento of the mid-nineteenth century, and with the 'Italies', that is, with those parts of society indifferent to the nation state. My title also puns on the classic account of Nazism, written by the moderate conservative political scientist Karl Dietrich Bracher.[24] It does so in an upside-down way, because Bracher asserted the primacy of politics in the history of Nazism and I shall be less sure of that assumption in relation to the history of Fascism. None the less, in the pages which follow I shall endeavour to be as aware as possible of concepts which have been, or might be, usefully borrowed from the more developed historiography of Nazism

21 The standard English-language introduction to the history of the Resistance in Italy remains C.F. Delzell, *Mussolini's enemies: the Italian Anti-Fascist Resistance*, Princeton, 1961. See further, Chapter 8.
22 For an introduction see P. Corner, *Fascism in Ferrara 1915–1925*, Oxford, 1975, pp. 255–6. Italo Balbo, sometimes regarded as one of the more respectable and charming of the Fascist chiefs, was directly involved in the murder.
23 For a still useful, straightforward introduction to his ideas, see J. Joll, *Gramsci*, Glasgow, 1977.
24 K. D. Bracher, *The German dictatorship: the origins, structure, and effects of National Socialism*, Harmondsworth, 1973. (The original German edition, *Die deutsche Diktatur: Entstehung, Struktur, Folgen des Nationalsozialismus*, was published in 1969).

and Germany, all the more so because the aim of this book is not to write a history of Fascism, or at least not to do so directly. Instead, I shall narrate the history of attempts to account for Fascism.

What, then, are the basic issues which have preoccupied those who have endeavoured to comprehend the Fascist experience? One major question for historians of Fascism is that of origins. Just as Germanists have debated whether Nazism (or, indeed, 'eliminationist anti-Semitism') can be detected in Imperial Germany, in 1848, in the Lutheran Reformation or even in the earliest Germanic times, so Italianists have asked whether Fascism was or was not the 'revelation' of Italian history, the 'photograph' of Italian society. Especially they have wondered whether the recourse to dictatorship flowed naturally and inevitably from the limitations and inadequacies of the Risorgimento, that time of national unification and of the construction of the Liberal state. From an awareness of this issue have sprung other questions: how liberal was Liberal Italy? In what sense was it or was it becoming a nation? How did its institutions fare under the severe 'test' of the First World War? To what extent, by 1919, did Fascism offer the only current means to hide the continuing gap between politics and society, rhetoric and reality in post-Risorgimento Italy?

Or, by contrast, were the short-term causes of Fascism's rise much more significant than anything which came from the more remote past? The *fasci di combattimento* were inaugurated in a meeting at the Piazza di San Sepolcro (The Square of the Holy Sepulchre) in Milan on 23 March 1919; Mussolini took power on 28 October 1922. The appearance of Fascism thus occurred in the immediate aftermath of the First World War, after its conclusion in Western Europe, then being made concrete in the provisions of the various treaties signed at Versailles and elsewhere, and following the cessation of that rather different and sometimes forgotten conflict in Eastern Europe which coincided with the Russian Revolution and was not given some finality until the Bolshevik victory in the subsequent Russian Civil War. Was Fascism the ideology and experience of the trenches brought to political authority? Was it in that sense a 'Revolution', a contagion caught by Italians during the war and only then? Did the regime mark, as the great liberal philosopher historian Benedetto Croce would eventually claim, a 'parenthesis' in the otherwise positive national history of Italy? And what is to be made of Croce's dismissive comments that Fascism scarcely deserved much historical attention? It occupied a soulless period of time, he said, which induced *fastidio* (that is, boredom and disgust) in all who thought about it; its leader, moreover, was vain, ignorant and tasteless.[25]

If the special history of Italy as a nation raises many unresolved questions in regard to Fascism, what about class? Croce, with that self-interest

25 See B. Croce, *Croce, the King and the Allies: extracts from a diary, July 1943–June 1944*, London, 1950, pp. 43–4, and cf. R. De Felice, *Le interpretazioni del fascismo*, Bari, 1971, pp. 29–30.

frequently displayed by liberals anxious to lift any responsibility for the 'crisis of the twentieth century' from their own ideas and social grouping, was certain that Fascism was an inter-class movement. In so concluding, Croce disagreed with Marxists who, already before 1922 and while the direct objects of Fascist assault, sought to understand the new ideology in class terms, as a superstructural gloss on an economic and social 'reality'. Ever since these first days, historians have argued over whether or not Fascism had a 'mass base'. Was it just some sort of 'white guard', manipulated by finance capital, or by other sections of the rich and powerful, in their own cause? If it did have a mass base, who constituted it – the petite bourgeoisie, destined, according to classic Marxism, to become 'unhistorical', and thus to die out in a contest between bourgeoisie and proletariat? Or, as has been frequently argued over the last three decades, did Fascism express the hopes and ideals of an 'emerging middle class', which, either materially or psychologically or both, had done well out of the First World War and those other events and ideas which were hastening the modernisation of Italy and the nationalisation of its masses?

What, too, of gender? To what extent was Fascism a boys' ideology and practice? Much of its rhetoric and some of its deeds were pronouncedly patriarchal. Mussolini's myth emphasised both that the *Duce* was a man with balls, and that he could and did 'break the balls' of his opponents. A sceptic might point to the evidence that the domestic Benito was somewhat hen-pecked both by his enduring wife, Rachele,[26] and by his final mistress, Claretta Petacci.[27] The more serious question, however, is one about the originality of Fascist sexism. In its women's policies, did Fascism lead, or did it follow the long-standing assumptions of the Roman Catholic Church or of the Italian family?

Ethnicity, class and gender have all prompted debates about the nature of Italian Fascism. They do not, however, complete a list of basic approaches to the subject. In the scholarship on Nazi Germany[28] and, to some extent, even in work on Stalinism, one of the great contests has been that between 'intentionalists', who ascribe to Hitler mastery in his Reich, and 'functionalists', who aver that the most obvious characteristic of the Nazi regime was its 'institutional Darwinism'. For functionalists, tracing the way

---

26 In the crisis of July 1943 Rachele is thought to have advised Mussolini to liquidate his opponents and critics, but the *Duce* was, by then, not man enough (goak) to take her advice.

27 In April 1945, she would insist on dying with him. For a marvellous insight into Claretta, *piccola borghese*, see the description of her taste in furnishing 'like that in an American film set' and of especially bad taste, running to a black marble bathroom; her tomb which can still be located in the Campo Verano in Rome is similarly a study in excess. For the marble, see R. De Felice, *Mussolini l'alleato 1940–5: I. L'Italia in guerra 1940–1943*, Turin, 1990, p. 1537. An intrepid tourist will find the tomb.

28 For a splendid introduction to the historiography on Germany, see I. Kershaw, *The Nazi dictatorship: problems and perspectives of interpretation*, London, 1985 (and subsequent editions).

in which a Nazi policy, however banal, is given practical expression becomes a complex and salutary activity, and one likely to indicate that, within the bounds of the dictatorship and of the *Führerprinzip*, quite a degree of free will was left to most Germans. Though the 'Stalin revolution' is still deemed, in the final analysis, to have come from 'above', a 'new cohort' of 'social historians' assures us that even peasants at the bottom of the Soviet heap doggedly sought to redefine the regime's policies to suit their own ends, and, despite the terror and the purges, could craft some victories against official Soviet power.

These debates have only feebly visited the historiography of Fascist Italy. It is typical that Renzo De Felice[29] and Denis Mack Smith,[30] the most renowned of 1970s and 1980s Italian and non-Italian historians of the Fascist period, have both written biographies of Mussolini. Though they scarcely agree on a definition of biography and, indeed, preach radically diverse interpretations of Fascism, each explicitly or implicitly endorses the view that Mussolini himself defined his own regime, and each offers an account of 'Mussolini's Italy'. Paradoxically, both historians also provide Mussolini with a character reading which emphasises his timorousness as much as his courage, his adroit and even intuitive insight into his contemporaries' minds as much as his originality. Thus, even though De Felice and Mack Smith have continued to argue a Great Man line, Mussolini, a leader with certain skills as a machiavellian manipulator once he caught the drift of a particular situation, does seem a historical character ready for some deconstruction. What is to be made of evidence that, for example, he left considerable autonomy to his ministers so long as they remembered to consult him regularly and respectfully; or that the *Duce*, when troubled by decision-making, might remark meaningfully, 'This won't please the Fascists'?[31] Should a historian of Fascism compose a book entitled 'The Limits of Mussolini's Power'? After all, exactly how were Fascist policies implemented? Did they always originate from 'above', or could they be changed, challenged and even initiated from 'below'? Similarly, how Darwinian were the institutions of the Fascist state? How much did Mussolini lead and how much did he follow 'party' or 'élite' or 'public opinion' (but please define)?

Many of these questions, so familiar in regard to Nazi Germany, have scarcely been asked of Fascism. If the historiography of twentieth-century Italy exhibits a certain 'backwardness', the Fascist regime has inevitably been measured against the great models through which scholars have sought to

29 Successive volumes of this biography have appeared regularly since the publication of R. De Felice, *Mussolini il rivoluzionario 1883–1920*, Turin, 1965.
30 D. Mack Smith, *Mussolini*, London, 1981 and cf. his similarly 'intentionalist' *Mussolini's Roman Empire*, London, 1976.
31 For such insights see F. Suvich, *Memorie 1932–1936*, Milan, 1984, pp. 4, 10. Suvich added that he and his colleagues ignored the *voi* campaign and went on addressing each other and Mussolini in the respectful third-person *Lei* form (p. 12).

understand twentieth-century history. What, for example, is to be made of the model of fascism which links Fascist Italy, Nazi Germany and such other movements and regimes as Action Française, the British Union of Fascists, the Legion of the Archangel Michael in Romania, Franco's Spain and Peron's Argentina? Were these last movements and regimes just 'false fascisms'?[32] Was Italian Fascism only accidentally allied with German Nazism in the Second World War? Was Fascism, in its ideology and practice, *sui generis*? Was its Corporate State a specific creation, or did it parallel social and economic planning in other societies, whether fascist themselves or merely subject to a bourgeois 'recasting'?[33] Was Fascism's international aggression – as directed against Greece, Albania, Ethiopia, the peoples of its existing empire and the Allies in World War II – all its own making, or was it simply occasioned by the 'brutal friendship' with Nazi aggressors? Was Fascist racism, and especially Fascist anti-Semitism, 'native' or or did it, too, spring from a mimicry of Germany?

If the model of fascism raises as many questions as it provides answers, so, too, does its chief rival, the usually more conservative model of 'totalitarianism'. This word, now so familiar in every language, actually originated in 1920s Italy. First employed as a critique of the Fascist intrusion into 'free' society, it was adopted as a creed or variety of advertising slogan by the regime. A totalitarian state, in which everything was in the state, nothing was against it and nothing outside it, became, by 1926–7, the definition of the 'Fascist revolution'. Mussolini and his aides then proclaimed that the economy was wholly harnessed to the national cause and boasted that all Italians, both within Italy and even in the emigrant world, drew their identity from the national Fascist regime and its ideology.

These assertions of control, both direct and indirect, soon occasioned dispute, however, and have continued to do so, especially in the light of what have seemed the more fanatical, more powerful, more successful and more intrusive 'totalitarian' regimes of Nazi Germany, the Soviet Union and Communist China. None the less, historians can still be found who chart an 'Italian road to totalitarianism',[34] or who suggest that only the weakness of the Italian economy or the traditionalism of much Italian society held Mussolini back from 'truly' totalitarian deeds. Another important debating-point has been the extent of a 'totalitarian' legacy. Was the Italian Communist party (PCI), for example, likely to (re-)introduce totalitarianism into Italian society, if, in the post-war period, it was ever admitted to power,

---

32 For this usage see M. Ambri, *I falsi fascismi: Ungheria, Jugoslavia, Romania 1919–1945*, Rome, 1980. See further, Chapter 9.

33 I refer here to the massive study of 1920s France, Weimar Germany and Fascist Italy by C. Maier, *Recasting bourgeois Europe: stabilization in France, Germany, and Italy in the decade after World War I*, Princeton, 1975. See Chapter 9.

34 See e.g. E. Gentile, *La via italiana al totalitarismo: il partito e lo stato nel regime fascista*, Rome, 1995.

and to do so because of intellectual and political structures left over from Fascism? Some say yes to this question.

In earlier books I have written of my doubts about the totalitarian model and my awareness of the conservative political intent which has usually lain behind its deployment, at least since the 1950s.[35] This scepticism may display political bias on my own part, but in this book I shall contend that certainly the model of totalitarianism and perhaps the more credible model of fascism find their utility primarily in the questions they raise. After all, in a democratic or postmodern world, asking definite questions and providing tentative answers is the essence of the historian's task.

This introduction has roamed widely, and most of the issues which it has touched upon will reappear in the main body of the text. There, the starting-point is, as it must be for all historians, the present (and the future). Until very recently the history of fascism seemed of self-evident significance because of 'Auschwitz' and because of the resultant clichéd determination that 'it must never happen again'. Indeed, to a considerable degree, post-unification Italian history 'mattered', and Italian Fascism found a place in many a university course outside Italy, because of the possible connections between Mussolini's regime and German Nazism and its horrors. Even within Italy, it seemed important to many to examine the national past, particularly because the Fascist state had been Nazi Germany's premier ally. 'Fascism, never again' was a fundamental Italian slogan, too.

The fall of the Berlin Wall and the collapse of the communist empire in Eastern Europe and the territories of the Soviet Union in 1989–92, however, have somewhat altered this situation. In its last days, the USSR was very much a society still locked in its own myth of the Second World War experience and its constructed memory of a time when the anti-fascist alliance had extended to embrace even Marshal Joseph Stalin. In the 1990s it has become apparent that, despite the evils of the Soviet system and its evident inability, by the 1980s, to cope with the latest technological revolutions, the existence of a Soviet state, the survival in even the tiniest and most unrepresentative degree of the myths and hopes of the Russian Revolution, had conditioned many aspects of life outside the USSR. This is not the place to wonder about the effect of the liquidation of the USSR on the pay and conditions of ordinary men and women in the first and third worlds. But, in the little universe of history writing, a question can be asked. Is the history of Fascism still significant? After all, it should be admitted that Fascism presently does not matter in the same way or to the extent that it once did either in an Italy which has lost a soul and not yet found a reliable place in the new world empire, or to those outside Italy, who find instruction about the human condition in that nation's past. As a fresh millennium dawns, the horror of 'Auschwitz' and the 'long Second World

---

35 See especially R. J. B. Bosworth, *Explaining Auschwitz and Hiroshima: history writing and the Second World War 1945–1990*, London, 1993.

War'[36] fades from memory, and Fascism becomes another of those creeds which designed a welfare state, for its own people at least, and so to some seems no more than a dated residue of a dim past rumoured to have existed before the market conquered all. None the less, there are major reasons to doubt that we shall for evermore live after the 'end of history'. In this more hopeful, positive and nuanced view, we, the heirs of humankind, shall still need to measure our responsibility for Italian Fascism no less than for those other crimes, follies and tragedies of the past, both in time immemorial and in the twentieth century's 'age of violence'.

36 In both cases the terminology is mine in *Explaining Auschwitz and Hiroshima*.

1

The Italian 'Second Republic' and the History of Fascism: Finding (and Losing) a Usable Past?

In the politics of late-1990s Italy, names have had an unfamiliar ring. In the most recent national elections in April 1996 the winners were not called socialists, liberals, conservatives, communists, fascists or even democrats, but members of the 'Olive Tree alliance'. In 1998, Prime Minister Romano Prodi, an economist by training, still heads the resultant *L'Ulivo* ('the Olive Tree') government. His chief opponent, the narrow loser in 1996, was Silvio Berlusconi, a media magnate, whose group was denominated the *Polo della Libertà* or 'Liberty Pole'. Among Berlusconi's allies was Gianfranco Fini,[1] who, in the late 1980s, had become the youthful secretary of the neo-Fascist *Movimento Sociale Italiano*, whose lineage went directly back to the Fascist True Believers of the Salò Republic.[2] In November 1993 Fini had redefined himself as a 'post-fascist', and his party had adopted the bland enough name of National Alliance (*Alleanza Nazionale*).[3] Among the branches of the Olive Tree, by contrast, the biggest was the Democratic Party of the Left (*Partito Democratico della Sinistra*). In 1989, its supporters still rallied to the cause of the *Partito Comunista Italiano* (Italian Communist Party) but, after the fall of the Berlin Wall, they had transmogrified into the new organisation, even if, in their first campaigns, they archly proclaimed that, under their banners at least, 'the future has ancient roots'.[4]

---

1 For a biography, see G. Locatelli and D. Martini, *Duce addio: la biografia di Gianfranco Fini*, Milan, 1994.
2 For a clear introduction, see P. Ignazi, *Il polo escluso: profilo del Movimento Sociale Italiano*, Bologna, 1989.
3 For an English-language introduction, see A. Carioti, 'From the ghetto to *Palazzo Chigi*: the ascent of the National Alliance', in R.S. Katz and P. Ignazi (eds), *Italian politics: the year of the tycoon*, Boulder, Colo., 1996, pp. 57–78.
4 See e.g. *L'Espresso*, 37, 24 February 1991.

Separate from the two main blocs but similarly new in its rhetoric and name was the *Lega nord* (Northern League), headed by Umberto Bossi. Support for this movement stemmed from a reluctance to pay taxes; its sympathisers called the national capital *Roma ladrona* – 'Rome, the big thief'. At a minimum, the League demanded greater autonomy for the area north of the Apennines. In September 1996, after he and some of his 'Green Shirts' journeyed from the source of the Po river to its outlet on the Adriatic, Bossi actually declared the independence of what *Lega* propagandists called 'Padania'.

What's in a name; or rather, what message can be drawn from all these names?[5] Bossi may, for example, have proclaimed the creation of Padania and the establishment of a Padanian 'assembly' in Mantua and a Padanian 'capital' at Venice; but, except for Italian journalists, no one else seemed much to have noticed or cared. As its governments fell and its politicians pirouetted, Italy may have lurched from one 'crisis' to the next, but the national economy has continued to flourish and the standard of living of many Italians has at least held its own. Can it be that, when Carlo Emilio Gadda wrote his wonderfully scabrous murder-mystery-without-an-end, *That awful mess on the Via Merulana*,[6] he was prefiguring the whole history of Republican Italy, which has always seemed an 'awful mess', with the final collapse on the horizon, and yet which has never slipped into catastrophe?

Perhaps. But, setting aside the reality or otherwise of Italy's 'permanent crisis', something else can be learned from such unfamiliar or kitsch names as the olive tree, the pole or Padania. The political movements of Prodi and Berlusconi are not parties in the normally understood sense of the term. They lack caucuses, local branches, programmes and ideological traditions. *L'Ulivo* constitutes little more than an umbrella of convenience under which a coalition government can shelter, and includes surviving parties, such as the PDS, and politicians like Prodi himself, who, in the 'First Republic', the one which existed before *Tangentopoli* (Bribesville), would probably have been a member of the governing Christian Democrats. In many ways the Olive Tree is a name to adopt because other older, more familiar, more 'historical' names are best forgotten.[7] It is, and is meant to be, a sound of silence.

The designing of a name to hide rather than to give 'meaning' is even more evident in other political arenas. The *Polo* has been defined neatly as a 'virtual party', that is, one made by and for TV, and with no other serious

5 For a rather superficial English-language exploration of some of the ramifications, see D. I. Kertzer, *Politics and symbols: the Italian communist party and the fall of communism*, New Haven, 1996.
6 C. E. Gadda, *That awful mess on the Via Merulana*, London, 1985, first published in Italian, 1957.
7 Olive trees are doubtless old, 'Mediterranean' and green, and produce nourishing fruit (if treated with care and while the frost is not too severe).

or compelling area of operation.[8] Berlusconi seeks to be an 'image' politician, where the sleekness of his appearance is the main message for voters. Neither Berlusconi (himself Prime Minister in 1994–5), nor Prodi, nor the other two recent Prime Ministers, the bankers Lamberto Dini (1995–6) and Carlo Azeglio Ciampi (1993–4), have, in any established sense, possessed a 'mass base'. Defining democracy is, to say the least, a much-contested matter, but ever since the 'First Republic' withered away the summit of Italian politics has remained of dubiously democratic character.

Many commentators cheerfully assume that the lack of roots evident in contemporary politics is merely proof that the country is in a phase of transition, experiencing its own variety of 'velvet revolution'[9] while it passes from the 'corruption' of the First Republic to the new world order of the Second. After all, as liberal guru Lord Ralf Dahrendorf, frequently summoned as a pundit by the Italian press, has remarked, in these days 'it is not the political colour of a government which matters but only its efficiency' in downsizing the social state and in pressing through those other 'reforms' required under the hegemonic principles of economic rationalism.[10] It might be wondered whether Dahrendorf is preaching thereby his own version of virtual democracy; the parties he himself has been closest to, the FDP in Germany and the Alliance in England, also never managed to acquire mass support. But rather than being diverted into an account of the unpopularity or unrepresentativeness of liberalism outside Italy, we should return for a moment to contemplate 'Padania'. Though the standards of the *Lega* carry the image of a victorious Lombard knight from the battle of Legnano in 1176, the word Padania is a neologism. Bossi has never been very clear as to what the exact borders of this hypothetical republic might be and, whatever its span, Padania has never existed before. It is a place without history.

A certain pattern is emerging. This absence of history is something which the *Lega nord*, *L'Ulivo* and the *Polo* all share. If Italy is experiencing some form of political and cultural revolution, it is one emphatic in its novelty. In the past almost all revolutionaries, and certainly the French and Russian ones of 1789 and 1917, have been painstaking in linking themselves to a history, preferably one of alleged longevity and glamour. Typically,

---

8 For some English-language introduction, see S. Gundle and S. Parker (eds), *The New Italian Republic: from the fall of the Berlin wall to Berlusconi*, London, 1996; P. McCarthy, 'The overwhelming success and the consequent problems of a virtual party', in R. S. Katz and P. Ignazi (eds), *Italian politics: the year of the tycoon*, pp. 37–55.

9 See e.g. the *Economist*'s happy endorsement of an Italian 'revolution' in its issues of 20 February and 3 April 1993, in the latter case speaking cheerfully of tumbrils and guillotines. Before too long, however, this authoritative journal of liberal capitalism had become troubled by Berlusconi, on 4 March 1995 remarking of the tycoon's control of TV and information: 'Such an arrangement might seem out of place in Madagascar; in a modern western democracy, it is bizarre'.

10 C. Valentini, 'Scordatevi le riforme' [an interview with Dahrendorf], *L'Espresso*, 42, 14 November 1996, p. 74.

revolutionary claims to improve the present and to see the future have
gained their legitimacy through accounts of the past. Revolutions failed
when this new/old history lacked credibility. As I have noted elsewhere, the
final crisis of the USSR became evident when, in 1987–8, its history lost any
conviction; here was a regime which sloughed off its past just before it
became apparent that it had no future.[11] In the 1990s, which lack the stolid
certainties of Soviet times, it has been remarked that the Russian 'past
cannot be predicted'.[12] No doubt the future of the Second Republic in Italy
is somewhat more predictable than the future of 'democratic' Russia, and,
in any case an escape into United Europe seems to Italians of many political
stripes an ideal solution to the national problem. Perhaps they are right, but
present-day Italy is certainly experiencing an unmooring from the past and,
to an onlooker, this deprivation of history seems disconcerting.

Which past has Italy most particularly lost? With this question we reach
the nub of this book. The First Republic, at least from 1968 or thereabouts
(far too many current commentators assume that what was true in the
1970s had existed since the foundation of the Republic in 1946), did
become a regime with a very definite 'usable past'. At a particularly crisis-
ridden moment, the First Republic was underpinned by the history or the
'myth' of the Resistance. The full nature of this underpinning will be
explored later;[13] suffice it for the moment to note that, during the 1970s, it
came to be almost automatically assumed, at least in public, that all good
Italians were anti-Fascists. The most obvious incarnation of this purity of
the anti-Fascist past was Sandro Pertini, president from 1978 to 1985 and
an independent left-socialist, who had resisted Fascism with almost painful
honesty and obduracy, who, as a result, spent most of the regime in prison[14]
and who had been directly involved in the execution of Mussolini.[15] 'I have
never made the error of betraying liberty and democracy,' Pertini could
boast as he recalled a life devoted 'yesterday, today and always [to] the
Resistance'.[16] Girt with this righteousness drawn from the recent past,
Pertini was hailed as the most popular president in national history, the
nonno (grandfather) of all Italians.

Pertini acquired the presidency in 1978, at a moment in which the days
of the Republic seemed numbered. In March that year the Red Brigades
(BR), a left-wing terrorist group grown steadily more daring as the decade
wore on, had kidnapped Aldo Moro, seven times Prime Minister, then

11 R. J. B. Bosworth, 'Nations examine their past: a comparative analysis of the historiography of the "long" Second World War', *The History Teacher*, 29, 1996, pp. 509–12.
12 Cited by A. Wood, 'The Bolsheviks, the baby and the bathwater', *European History Quarterly*, 22, 1992, p. 494.
13 See Chapter 8.
14 There, again appropriately, he met and allegedly helped an ill and lonely Gramsci. See R. Uboldi, *Il cittadino Sandro Pertini*, Milan, 1982, pp. 105–6.
15 For his autobiography, see S. Pertini, *Sei condanne, due evasioni*, Milan, 1978.
16 R. Uboldi, *Il cittadino Sandro Pertini*, p. 45.

Christian Democrat party secretary, and the great middleman of national politics. In May the BR murdered him and left his body in the boot of a Renault 4, symbolically parked halfway between Christian Democrat and Communist Party headquarters. In June President Giovanni Leone, a Neapolitan Christian Democrat who had been given his position after losing out in factional conflicts among his party colleagues,[17] resigned over allegations of corruption. Pertini, by contrast, seemed clean in deed and word. Now, it was thought, his version of the Resistance[18] would save Italy's soul (and body) just as it had done at the end of the Fascist dictatorship.

A decade and a half later, however, much has changed in Italian political and historical discourse. Silvio Berlusconi himself highlighted the change. The forty-ninth anniversary of the end of Italy's Second World War fell on 25 April 1994, just after Berlusconi had won what seemed a sweeping electoral victory. This resultant opportunity for political change, Berlusconi urged, was the occasion to make peace between Fascists and anti-Fascists; their past conflicts should be redefined as only 'a piece of history'. Henceforth, 25 April should instead be celebrated by all as the beginning of a 'new era'.[19] Italians should look to the future and forget the divisions of their past. The history of Fascism and anti-Fascism, in Berlusconi's view, should become just another part of a cheerful and marketable[20] heritage, along with the history of the Roman Empire, Renaissance and A. C. Milan (the often-victorious football club which Berlusconi owned).

In 1994 Berlusconi imagined that he was destined to govern Italy for a considerable period. In fact, unable to manage Bossi and the *Lega*, his government fell apart after little more than a year, and, by 1998, his political course seemed near its end. Moreover, though a Berlusconian 'revisionist' reading of history is now more common than a Pertinian one, Berlusconi's understanding of a usable past has not won full suzerainty in an Italy in which free and contested historical debate survives. Nevertheless, certain questions require answers. What had occasioned this latest version of revisionism and why did it often seem convincing? What were the links between the politicians' deployment of history and that of academic historians? Who was translating messages from the archives to the press and TV, how, and with what effect? What, late in the 1990s, is the state of Italian (and non-Italian) scholarship about Fascism and anti-Fascism?

17 For a critical biography, see C. Cederna, *Giovanni Leone: la carriera di un presidente*, Milan, 1978.
18 In July 1979 he invited the Italian people to join in a 'New Resistance'. R. Uboldi, *Il cittadino Sandro Pertini*, p. 186.
19 See R. Ben-Ghiat, 'Fascism, writing, and memory: the realist aesthetic in Italy, 1930–50', *Journal of Modern History*, 67, 1995, p. 629.
20 For an English-language account of the first signs of Fascist history turning into heritage, see T. Mason, 'The great economic history show', *History Workshop*, 21, 1986, pp. 3–35. On the history of history on television in Italy, see G. Crainz, 'The representation of Fascism and the Resistance in the documentaries of Italian state television', in R. J. B. Bosworth and P. Dogliani (eds), *Italian Fascism: history, memory and representation* (forthcoming).

Until his death in May 1996, the most professional historian of Fascism, the most determined 'archive rat',[21] the scholar who 'knew' most about the subject and who had his expertise most widely recognised outside Italy[22] was Renzo De Felice. So complete was De Felice's comprehension of the history of Fascism that, when he compiled an 'introductory' bibliography on the subject, it ran to 12 208 items. Such a list, he noted disarmingly and characteristically, was, moreover, not directed at 'specialists' but only at 'people of a certain culture, journalists, those interested in some sense in the present age and in its various special features, and university students getting ready for an undergraduate degree or a doctorate'.[23] This bibliography, his multi-volume biography of Mussolini which had marched past 6000 pages and would never reach its end, his numerous editings of diaries and other primary sources from the Fascist period, his control over the important journal *Storia contemporanea* and his presence on the editorial board of the *Journal of Contemporary History* – all these seemed impregnable castles of historical knowledge destined to overawe any others who trespassed on the field. If a baron ruled over the Fascist segment of the Italian past, it was Renzo De Felice.

A few months before his death, this master of empirical detail gave an extended interview to a journalist, Pasquale Chessa, from Berlusconi's weekly, *Panorama*.[24] He did so on the twentieth anniversary of an earlier interview[25] conducted by the young American postdoctoral student, Michael Ledeen,[26] which, it is now apparent, had both launched De Felice as a historian of international fame and signalled the commencement of a damaging assault on the myth of the Resistance. The discussion between Ledeen and De Felice will be reviewed later in this book,[27] but now is the time to ponder De Felice's conclusions in 1995, in what might be regarded as his historiographical last will and testament.

The immediate occasion of the talk with Chessa was the prospect that De Felice would soon actually finish his biography of Mussolini and thus would publish the volume or volumes dealing with the last 22 months of the *Duce*'s life. However, De Felice also took the opportunity to remind his readers of matters which he had raised over the last two years in a series of articles in *Panorama* and in the moderate conservative daily papers, *Corriere della*

---

21 This is Stalin's celebrated definition of a historian. Quoted by R. J. B. Bosworth, *Explaining Auschwitz and Hiroshima: History Writing and the Second World War 1945–1990*, London, 1993, p. 146. See further Chapter 5.

22 For typical evidence of this recognition, see B. Painter, 'Renzo De Felice and the historiography of Italian Fascism', *American Historical Review*, 95, 1990, pp. 391–405.

23 R. De Felice, *Bibliografia orientativa del fascismo*, Rome, 1991, p. vii.

24 R. De Felice, *Rosso e nero* (ed. P. Chessa), Milan, 1995.

25 The English translation appeared as R. De Felice, *Fascism: an informal introduction to its theory and practice*, New Brunswick, NJ, 1977; the Italian edition was published as *Intervista sul fascismo*, Bari, 1975.

26 For an introduction to Ledeen and his own decidedly political career after the interview, see R. J. B. Bosworth, *Explaining Auschwitz and Hiroshima*.

27 See Chapter 5.

Sera of Milan and *La Stampa* of Turin. All in all, he had three great messages to convey. The first concerned the inferiority of the historical writing of any who disagreed with his own interpretations. The problem here was simple. De Felice stood for 'science', for reporting 'what actually happened' in the past. Others had instead composed a 'vulgate' about Fascism and anti-Fascism, counting 'above all on the political and ideological effects which they could draw' from the past. 'The problem of Mussolini today,' De Felice urged, 'should involve only the specialists of the history trade. However, the reverse is true. Italian historians continue to circle around the case of Mussolini, without having the will to confront it and resolve it definitively. The result is that the field stays open and exposed to the incursions of journalists, amateurs, money-grubbers, antiquarians.'[28] In his own eyes De Felice, was, by contrast, above reproach. With appropriate deference, his interviewer agreed. As Chessa remarked at the end of their discussion, 'It is impossible to put any ideological brand at all on [De Felice]. For him, the primacy of history is both an intense moral conviction and a regular way of going about his daily business.'[29]

De Felice's second message was more directly linked to the last days of Fascism between 1943 and 1945; that is, it involved an interpretation of the months of the Salò Republic and of the so-called 'armed Resistance' in Northern Italy, as well as of the 'Kingdom of the South' in those parts of the peninsula liberated by Anglo-American forces. Regarding this period of national history and the bitter ideological divisions which were then being fought through, De Felice had come to some clear, if not necessarily wholly convincing, conclusions.

The most basic was that Italian communists, even if now renamed the PDS, could not credibly claim a usable anti-Fascist past. The pretensions of the Communist party to have led the Resistance, and thus to have acquired national and moral credentials which might separate its history from the worst aspects of the history of the Soviet revolution, were peremptorily refuted: 'The Communist party of Togliatti had always been a Stalinist party. It was neither revolutionary, nor reformist, but part of the world system of power of the USSR.'[30] The communists were not, however, the only ones who needed their moral titles to be redimensioned. The Resistance as a whole, or rather that complex of struggles which went on after 8 September 1943, was better defined as a 'civil war', even if quite a lot of Italians were not enamoured of either contestant, preferring simply to wait out the conflict. For all this *attentisme* and, indeed, because of it, De Felice continued, the period from 1943 to 1945 witnessed the greatest of civil wars: then Italy 'knew a civil war of a size and drama unknown in other

28 R. De Felice, *Rosso e nero*, pp. 7, 135.
29 R. De Felice, *Rosso e nero*, p. 166.
30 R. De Felice, *Rosso e nero*, p. 73. See further Chapter 8.

countries'. The Italian case was 'unique in world history for its dimension and character'.[31]

In thus arguing, De Felice may have been exhibiting an ignorance about foreign histories, and most obviously about those of the Balkan countries which were neighbours of Italy and which fascist policies had so greatly damaged, but his real purpose in mounting this case was a contemporary one. Presumably avoiding the dangers of politicised journalism and amateurism, De Felice adjudged the last years of the war as a sad time in which the 'Italian bourgeoisie had failed its historic task'.[32] All of the weakness and imperfections of the First Republic after its foundation in 1946 had originated with what had been permitted to become the historical reading of these years, a history which was in fact a misreading. The misinterpretation of the Resistance had entailed a fundamental drying up of the national spirit. Borrowing an idea from the great and politically very conservative historian of the Risorgimento,[33] Rosario Romeo (died 1987),[34] De Felice stated that 8 September 1943 had become 'the symbolic date of everything wrong with Italy' (*il male italiano*). This anti-history had spread the false view that Italy was 'a country irredeemably mistaken'.[35] As a consequence, he concluded,

the drama lived by Italians from 8 September to 25 April [1945] has been put out of kilter by a historiography which reduced the Resistance to a cult-object. Rather it was a fundamental page in Italy's history which needs to be studied in a fully scientific manner in order to understand how the national moral thrust was used up in those two years and the reasons why that thrust was never restored

in that post-war period, in which the political parties of the Second Republic had lacked any proper 'patriotic sense'.[36]

De Felice was thus preaching a neo-Rankean message for a country which, in his view, had too long believed that 'all history is contemporary history'. Though his now-conservative and even nationalist politics kept peeping out, in De Felice's exhortations, historians, rather than seeking to provide clear moral lines which still carried messages for the present, should work empirically and 'scientifically'; they should commit themselves to an objective study of the past on its own terms. Only if they worked hard and thoroughly enough, and possessed the interpretative skills of De Felice

31 R. De Felice, *Rosso e nero*, pp. 22, 44.
32 R. De Felice, *Rosso e nero*, pp. 32–3.
33 For a collection of his political writings, see R. Romeo, *Scritti politici 1953–1987*, Milan, 1991.
34 For typical eulogies, see R. De Felice, 'Rosario Romeo: il grande storico, il grande amico', *Nuova Antologia*, f.2162, April–June 1987, pp. 9–11; P. Bonetti, 'Un liberale per il nostro tempo: Rosario Romeo', *Nuova Antologia*, f. 2201, January–March 1997, pp. 227–38.
35 R. De Felice, *Rosso e nero*, pp. 9–11, 31–2.
36 R. De Felice, *Rosso e nero*, pp. 60–1, 108. For further detail on the historiography of the Resistance, see Chapter 8.

himself, could they aspire to understand the past and come up with its proper interpretation. For De Felice and his acolytes, rather as for Geoffrey Elton in England,[37] the best historians simply told the truth through their empathy with the past. In so saying, De Felice showed no interest in the links between history and literature exposed by such postmodernist theorists as Hayden White,[38] or even in the relativism of those liberal and social democrats who, ever since the end of the Second World War, had argued that history was 'an argument without end'.[39] Ignoring the fact that the great majority of his critics lay to his Left, and that his words were hailed by a Right[40] which ran from Berlusconi to Fini, De Felice went to his grave maintaining that Fascism, when it was read 'historically', must be read apolitically.

De Felice's inheritance, however, was disputed. The so-called 'De Felice school' in practice contained a number of factions and, after their master's death, his pupils soon fell into open conflict. Publication of the journal *Storia contemporanea* ceased, to be succeeded in 1997 by *Nuova storia contemporanea*, a publication which placed itself further to the politicial right than De Felice might have preferred. Naturally, its sponsors took to constructing their own De Felice, a historian who, it was now explained, for all his commitment to 'science' and objectivity, was actually driven by a desire for a stronger national state, one which sometimes seemed of a type that the Fascist philosopher Giovanni Gentile[41] would have endorsed.[42]

These bickerings did not lessen the domination of what some commentators called the 'anti-anti-Fascist orthodoxy' in the interpretation of Mussolini's regime.[43] The leading figure among the new generation of

---

37 See his own neo-Rankean theorising, G. R. Elton, *The practice of history*, Glasgow, 1969; *Return to essentials: some reflections on the present state of historical study*, Cambridge, 1991.

38 See e.g. H. White, *Metahistory: the historical imagination in nineteenth-century Europe*, Baltimore, 1975; cf. the slightly more muted arguments of White in an article in the journal on which De Felice still figured as a member of the editorial board, H. White, 'Response to Arthur Marwick', *Journal of Contemporary History*, 30, 1995, pp. 233–46.

39 The best theoretical statement of this sort of relativism is E. H. Carr, *What is history?* Harmondsworth, 1964, although it was the rather conservative liberal Pieter Geyl who had learned from his Second World War that history could only be a debate. For an analysis of the context, see R. J. B. Bosworth, *Explaining Auschwitz and Hiroshima*, pp. 8–30.

40 Cf. also De Felice's common praise of the anti-Communism of French historian François Furet and, indeed, his eventual endorsement of the 'totalitarianist' thesis that, for all Italy's uniqueness, there were threads uniting Fascism, Nazism and Communism, both Soviet and Italian. See e.g. R. De Felice (ed.), *Mussolini giornalista*, Milan, 1995, p. x. Typically, De Felice also took the opportunity in this introduction to deride anti-Fascist attempts to deny a connection between Mussolini, the editor of the socialist *Avanti!* up to 1914, and Mussolini, the editor of *Il popolo d'Italia* from then on (p. ix).

41 Giovanni Gentile was assassinated by partisans in 1944 and thus has remained, in some eyes, a classic 'victim' of anti-Fascism.

42 See especially F. Perfetti, 'Democrazia, Stato e nazione nel pensiero di Renzo De Felice', *Clio*, 32, 1996, pp. 545–53.

43 See e.g. M. Knox, 'The Fascist regime, its foreign policy and its wars: an Anti-Anti-Fascist orthodoxy?', *Contemporary European History*, 4, 1995, pp. 347–65; S. Neri Serneri, 'A past to be thrown away? Politics and history in the Italian Resistance', *Contemporary European History*, 4, 1995, pp. 367–81.

neo-Rankean anti-anti-Fascists was Emilio Gentile, one of the more moderate of the De Feliceans, indeed one who stubbornly denied a political intent in De Felice's or his own work, rather defining the historian's task as the simple one of a 'continous acquisition' of facts.[44] Already before De Felice's death, Gentile had joined him by securing a chair at the University of Rome and a place on the editorial boards of *Storia contemporanea* and the *Journal of Contemporary History*.[45] From the beginning of Gentile's career[46] his work possessed some evident De Felicean characteristics. Gentile was very much another archival historian, the editor of Fascist papers,[47] careful and devoted not in writing a biography of Mussolini but instead in piecing together from a highly fragmented documentary base the history of the Fascist party (the PNF, *Partito Nazionale Fascista*).[48] In such work and in articles translated with increasing regularity into English, Gentile concurred with De Felice in emphasising the need to deal with Fascism on its own account.[49] He also agreed in treating its texts very seriously (and, his critics would claim, very literally).[50] For Gentile, Fascism had installed a totalitarian regime, bent on forging new men and women. It was 'the first political movement of this century which had carried mythical thought to power'. By 1939, 'the Fascist party, with its huge organisational base, dominated the Italian scene, exercising a virtually unlimited power and control over every sector of national life'. Such control was what defined the *via italiana al totalitarismo* (the Italian road to totalitarianism).[51] In 1995 Gentile felt confident enough to come up with

44 E. Gentile, 'Renzo De Felice: a tribute', *Journal of Contemporary History*, 32, 1997, p. 151.

45 Gentile even received the major accolade of being published in the *Annales*, 'the most famous history journal in the world'. E. Gentile, 'Le rôle du parti dans le laboratoire totalitaire italien', *Annales ESC*, 43, 1988, pp. 567–92. Marc Ferro, one of the editors of the *Annales*, was on the board of the *Journal of Contemporary History*.

46 See e.g. such early articles as E. Gentile, ' "La Voce" e l'età giolittiana', *Storia contemporanea*, 2, 1971, pp. 315–49; 'La politica di Marinetti', *Storia contemporanea*, 7, 1976, pp. 415–38.

47 E.g., G. Giuriati, *La parabola di Mussolini nei ricordi di un gerarca*, ed. E. Gentile, Bari, 1981.

48 See especially E. Gentile, *Storia del Partito Fascista 1919–1922: movimento e milizia*, Bari, 1989; *La via italiana al totalitarismo: il partito e lo stato nel regime fascista*, Rome, 1995. See also his early English-language article, E. Gentile, 'The problem of the Party in Italian Fascism', *Journal of Contemporary History*, 19, 1984, pp. 251–74.

49 See notably E. Gentile, 'Fascism in Italian historiography: in search of an individual historical identity', *Journal of Contemporary History*, 21, 1986, pp. 179–208. Cf. the very similar theses of a more junior De Felicean, N. Zapponi, 'Fascism in Italian historiography, 1986–93: a fading national identity', *Journal of Contemporary History*, 29, 1994, pp. 547–68.

50 For a striking example of such literalness, see E. Gentile, 'La politica estera del partito fascista. Ideologia e organizzazione dei Fasci italiani all'estero (1920–1930)', *Storia contemporanea*, 26, 1995, pp. 897–956, a lengthy piece which totally fails to grapple with the difference between words and deeds.

51 E. Gentile, *La via italiana al totalitarismo*, pp. 104, 130, 150, 225. In using this expression Gentile was of course punning, archly, on Togliatti's claim that the PCI was following 'the Italian road to socialism'.

his own definition of Fascism, one that he put in italics to give it extra conviction. Even if he admitted there could always be some gaps between theory and practice, Fascism, he concluded, amounted to '*totalitarian caesarism*', that is,

> a charismatic dictatorship of the Caesarian kind, integrated into an institutional structure based on a single party and on the mobilisation of the masses. It was in permanent development to make it conform more nearly to the myth of the totalitarian state, self-consciously adopting that model as a way of organising the political system, and, in a concrete manner, working as the fundamental code of belief and behaviour for the individual and the masses

throughout the country.[52]

Not a media personality in the sense that De Felice, whether willingly or not, had become, Gentile, as usual, avoided overt political moralising. Indeed, it is arguable that, apart from its almost automatic anti-anti-Fascism, the key to his work lay outside Italy. Though Gentile was always respectful of De Felice's achievement and accepted many of his arguments,[53] his real intellectual debts were accrued in the United States. As his use of the phrase about the nationalisation of the masses above hints, Gentile essentially translated George Mosse's ideas on 'Nazi culture'[54] into the history of Fascist Italy.

Gentile had begun his career as a student of Liberal Italy, especially scrutinising the minds of those intellectuals who may have been precursors of Fascism.[55] From his earliest work, Gentile had been convinced that Mussolini's own ideas could not be written off as mere opportunism or propaganda, but were marked by a 'fascination' and seriousness of their own.[56] Similarly, Gentile denied that Fascism, in its first formation, could be easily seen as originating from Left or Right; rather, it had a specific and individual ideological humus. Fascism, he argued in one of his first books, might not have been an ideology of the masses; but it was one directed at them.[57]

As he studied the intellectual background of Fascism, Gentile became convinced of the influence and originality of the dissident intellectuals of pre-1914 Giolittian Italy. Mussolini's meeting with the editorial group who published *La Voce* was, Gentile declared, 'fundamental and decisive' for the

52 E. Gentile, *La via italiana al totalitarismo*, p. 148.
53 E.g. over the difference between 'Fascism movement' and 'Fascism regime', for which see Chapter 5.
54 See e.g. G. Mosse, *Nazi culture: intellectual, cultural and social life in the Third Reich*, London, 1966; *The nationalisation of the masses: political symbolism and mass movements from the Napoleonic wars through the Third Reich*, New York, 1975.
55 See e.g. E. Gentile, *Le origini dell' ideologia fascista (1918–1925)*, Bari, 1975; *Il mito dello stato nuovo dall'antigiolittismo al fascismo*, Bari, 1982.
56 E. Gentile, *Le origini dell'ideologia fascista*, p. vi.
57 E. Gentile, *Le origini dell'ideologia fascista*, pp. 141, 423.

future *Duce*.[58] In turn, these debts implied that Fascism was underpinned by a genuine intellectual base. In government, the regime could appeal to intellectuals who believed what they said, especially when they looked to the creation of some organic variety of nationalism which might assist in the modernising of Italy. Generally deploying De Felice's notion that Fascism had two faces, a largely conservative one which had been denominated 'Fascism regime' and a radical one called 'Fascism movement', Gentile stressed the novel nature of Fascism and agreed that, in its way, it amounted to a 'revolution'. By implication, it was a revolution which was as real as any communist, socialist or liberal democratic one.

In his focus on Fascist ideas and their modernity, Gentile moved naturally to an intellectual meeting with Mosse, an older generation historian who had both written about the fascist era and lived through it. Coming from a rich and distinguished German-Jewish publishing family, Mosse had fled Nazism, reaching eventual sanctuary in the USA. There, in 1966, with another emigré, the much more straightforwardedly liberal-conservative and anti-communist Walter Laqueur,[59] Mosse founded the *Journal of Contemporary History* and pioneered the scholarly study of fascism both in its German and other manifestations[60] (even if at first he may not have taken the Italian version too seriously).[61] Mosse's own memories included travel through Fascist Italy in 1936 and a conventional meeting with the Italians of the time whom he considered *brava gente*, recalcitrant to discipline and thus to 'genuine' fascism:

> If there really was a difference [between Fascism and Nazism] it was a difference of national character. Let me tell you a story which perhaps better illustrates it than any great historical analysis. I remember in 1936 riding in a train from Florence to Rome and every train had a carabiniere on it with a machine gun. The people in my compartment were telling anti-Mussolini jokes. The carabiniere of course walked up and down the train corridor and I, coming from a German ambience, was terrified. But what happened in the end was that the carabiniere came into the compartment, not to arrest us, but to tell other Mussolini jokes. . . . Such an episode could never have happened in Germany.[62]

58 E. Gentile, *Il mito dello stato nuovo dall'antigiolittismo al fascismo*, p. 103.
59 For something of an autobiography, see W. Laqueur, *Thursday's child has far to go: a memoir of the journeying years*, New York, 1992; cf. also his earlier essays, *Out of the ruins of Europe*, London, 1971.
60 See *Journal of Contemporary History*, 1, 1966.
61 The initial issue of the journal did contain a rather critical review by the anti-Fascist Stuart Woolf of the first volume of De Felice's biography of Mussolini. S. J. Woolf, 'Mussolini as revolutionary', *Journal of Contemporary History*, 1, 1966, pp. 187–96.
62 G. Mosse, *Nazism: a historical and comparative analysis of National Socialism*, New Brunswick, NJ, 1978, pp. 104–5.

These memories were actually first published in Italy in 1977, as part of the same series of discussions in which De Felice had participated.[63] Mosse, too, had been interviewed by Michael Ledeen.[64] An academic axis was plainly in formation. Academic politics apart, for Gentile the most important aspects of Mosse's work, and the ones best imported to Italy, were the emphasis on nationalism and its surrogates as a secular religion, and the resulting implication that Fascism needed to be explored through its myths and symbols, all of which had constituted what might be defined as a 'collective mentality'.[65] Somewhat ironically, Mosse could be seen as prefiguring the Foucaultian 'linguistic turn', with its thesis that words and 'culture' were decisive forces for humankind. Another implication derived from this 'culturalist' approach to Mussolini's regime was that Fascism was best comprehended in inter-class terms.[66] Fascist culture, fascism as a 'political religion',[67] squared the circle against traditional Marxist claims that fascism expressed a class reality and a class purpose, and that, in Horkheimer's celebrated words, 'whoever refuses to discuss capitalism should keep silent about fascism'.[68]

In the last decade this culturalist approach has probably become the dominant historiographical reading of the Italian Fascist era. Gentile has proceeded with his own research labours. In 1997, in a new book perhaps reflecting the internal debates among the De Feliceans, he argued the provocative and curiously nostalgic case that popular identification with the Italian nation reached its apogee in 1911 and that thereafter ideological division entailed a weakening civic sense; the centenary of Italian unification and subsequent decades, claimed Gentile, had seen the national 'myth' as 'incapable of sustaining in Italians genuinely shared ideals, sentiments and

63 The tenth anniversary issue of the journal had also carried a highly favourable account by Ledeen of De Felice's work in those years. See M. A. Ledeen, 'Renzo De Felice and the controversy over Italian Fascism', *Journal of Contemporary History*, 11, 1976, pp. 269–83.

64 G. Mosse, *Intervista sul nazismo*, Bari, 1977. Ledeen had earlier been supervised in his Ph.D. at Wisconsin by Mosse. His Italian contacts would presumably help in soon giving Mosse the somewhat odd task of composing a polite interview-introduction to the lengthy, some would say deliberately meaningless, speeches of Aldo Moro. See A. Moro, *L'intelligenza e gli avvenimenti: testi 1959–1978*, Milan, 1979. Then Mosse, perhaps uniting his own story with that of Moro, opined that the Christian Democrat was always searching for 'a balance between society and the parliamentary system' as it existed in Italy, and thus was pondering the great issue of how 'a man, gifted with reason and criticial capacities, could survive and even have some influence in this epoch of the masses' (pp. xxii, lxxv).

65 E. Gentile, 'Mosse e la storiografia del nazionalismo', *Mondo operaio*, August, 1982, pp. 137–9. This paper provides a very favourable review of Mosse's book of essays, *Masses and man: nationalist and Fascist perceptions of reality*, New York, 1980.

66 E. Gentile, 'Mosse e la storiografia del nazionalismo', p. 139.

67 See the article, made available both in Italian and in English, E. Gentile, 'Il fascismo come religione politica', *Storia contemporanea*, 21, 1990; 'Fascism as political religion', *Journal of Contemporary History*, 25, 1990; cf. also in much greater detail, E. Gentile, *Il culto del littorio: la sacralizzazione della politica nell'Italia fascista*, Bari, 1993; now available in English as E. Gentile, *The sacralization of politics in Fascist Italy*, Cambridge, Mass., 1996.

68 See e.g. as quoted by A. J. Mayer, *Why did the heavens not darken? the final solution in history*, New York, 1988, p. 94.

emotions and the evocation in them of memories, pains and hopes'.[69] Whatever their reaction to Gentile's latest line, a considerable number of Italianists, especially American ones, have come together in what probably should be defined as a 'culturalist', Mossean school.[70] Their views were expressed in the thirtieth anniversary edition of the *Journal of Contemporary History* in 1996 which carried eight papers examining Fascist art, architecture, museums and spectacle, most with the same culturalist method and the same implied conclusion. Fascism, the authors here assembled maintained, had a culture of its own; it was not based on mimicry or opportunism. It also penetrated deep into Italian society and may well have left a legacy which lasted far beyond 1945. Fascist culture deserved to be re-constituted through 'thick description'.

As has been noted, in his voluminous writings De Felice himself rarely displayed an interest in methodological questions – it is hard to imagine him reading Derrida or Baudrillard for fun or enlightenment. Instead, he was given to voicing such clichés as that the past can be better understood when it is furthest away in time from the present, or that the way best to interpret the past is to write its history.[71] Similarly, neither Gentile nor the usual publications of the *Journal of Contemporary History* have shown many signs of seeing historical research as anything other than a straightforward empirical activity.[72] It is therefore somewhat ironic that, in the late 1990s, culturalist readings of the Fascist past are intermeshing with what is presently the most modish of the many possible approaches to history – the 'ethnographic'. Owing some sort of debt to Princeton anthropologist Clifford Geertz,[73] ethnographic historians describe intricate 'webs of significance' in order to portray the past 'on its own terms'. As one of its leading practitioners defines it: 'ethnographic history . . . is an attempt to represent the past as it was actually experienced in such a way that we understand

69 E. Gentile, *La Grande Italia: ascesa e declino del mito della nazione nel ventesimo secolo*, Milan, 1997, p. 373.
70 The most productive of its American practitioners is Walter Adamson, whose research on pre-Fascist and Fascist intellectuals has very much seconded Gentile's work. See e.g. W. L. Adamson, 'Fascism and culture: avant-gardes and secular religion in the Italian case', *Journal of Contemporary History*, 24, 1989, pp. 411–35; 'Modernism and Fascism: the politics of culture in Italy, 1903–1922', *American Historical Review*, 95, 1990, pp. 359–90; 'The language of opposition in early twentieth-century Italy: rhetorical continuities between pre-war Florentine avant-gardism and Mussolini's Fascism', *Journal of Modern History*, 64, 1992, pp. 22–51; 'The culture of Italian Fascism and the Fascist crisis of modernity: the case of *Il Selvaggio*', *Journal of Contemporary History*, 30, 1995, pp. 555–76. For further evidence of the functioning of this academic alliance, see G. Mosse, 'Futurismo e culture politiche in Europa: una prospettive globale', in R. De Felice (ed.), *Futurismo, cultura e politica*, Turin, 1988, pp. 14–31.
71 See e.g. R. De Felice, *Fascism: an informal introduction*, pp. 36–7.
72 For a traditionalist example from one of the journal's new editors, see A. Marwick, 'Two approaches to historical study: the metaphysical (including "postmodernism") and the historical', *Journal of Contemporary History*, 30, 1995, pp. 5–35.
73 For his autobiography see C. Geertz, *After the fact: two countries, four decades, one anthropologist*, Cambridge, Mass., 1995.

both its ordered and its disordered natures'.[74] Here, then, in a curious and not always well-considered way, among Italianists Rankeanism mingles with postmodernism, and the most conservative of methodologies finds a way to enter into coalition with the most (self-consciously) radical elements in the discipline of history.

In the reading of Fascism with these techniques, it is the American cultural historian Jeffrey T. Schnapp who has gone furthest. One example of his work must suffice. In an article in the journal *Representations*, Schnapp reviewed '*18BL*', a theatrical event which was 'the featured end of the 1934 Littoriali della Cultura e dell'Arte', a sort of Fascist youth games, in Florence. The hero of the performance, *18BL*, was a truck (only belatedly does Schnapp reveal that it was a Fiat truck),[75] and this theatre 'of and for the masses'[76] played with the idea of the merging of man and machine. According to Schnapp, the new men who were very self-consciously involved in this staging demonstrated the Fascist regime's success in building a novel and 'modern' culture. Indeed, in Schnapp's understanding, everything to do with Fascism was in the mind. Fascism 'was little more than a complex of ethical principles, credos, and aversions, held together by a rhetorical-aesthetic glue'. Fascism entailed 'the wholesale theatricalisation of Italian life'. All in all, 'Fascism's interpellative success in post-World-War-I Italy . . . points less to the efficacy of certain violent tactics and policy initiatives or to the crisis of the liberal state than to the fact, well understood by Georges Bataille, that fascism elaborated a myth far more powerful and psychologically astute than that provided either by its liberal or socialist rivals.'[77] In this analysis, it seems, Fascism not only created a culture in its own right, but in many ways brought into being the best or the most alluring of modern cultures.

It does not take very long to see certain problems with Schnapp's interpretation. How many people actually viewed the staging?[78] – not many, and of those who did quite a few were irritated because they could not see the stage.[79] What, in any case, did so fleeting, mannered and self-consciously avant-garde an event have to do with the ordinary lives of those peasants

74 G. Dening, *Mr Bligh's bad language: passion, power and theatre on the Bounty*, Cambridge, 1992, p. 5.
75 J. T. Schnapp, '*18BL*: Fascist mass spectacle', *Representations*, 43, 1993, p. 106. Cf. also his book-length version, J. T. Schnapp, *Staging fascism: 18BL and the theater of masses for masses*, Stanford, 1996.
76 J. T. Schnapp, '*18BL*: Fascist mass spectacle', p. 109.
77 J. T. Schnapp, '*18BL*: Fascist mass spectacle', pp. 90, 92–3; in 1996, Schnapp provided a deferential Mossean introduction to that issue of the *Journal of Contemporary History* devoted to Italian Fascist culture. See J. T. Schnapp, 'Fascinating Fascism', *Journal of Contemporary History*, 31, 1996, pp. 235–44.
78 Like all Italian cities, Florence possesses a very special history and one that drastically separates it from Milan or Turin, not to mention Naples or Reggio Calabria. Schnapp's analysis entirely ignores this difference.
79 J. T. Schnapp, '*18BL*: Fascist mass spectacle', p. 111.

and workers who constituted the great majority of Italians? Could it be, too, that Giovanni Agnelli did not much mind young Fascist intellectuals seeking inspiration in one of his vehicles? Perhaps the silences, the omissions and the implications of the ceremony disclose more about Italian history than its organisers intended or than Schnapp discerned, and the most obvious message of the *18BL* 'event' is one of a division between state and society, a dialogue of the deaf between official or intellectual culture and popular culture, a yawning gap between what Fascism said mattered and what actually did matter. In sum, Schnapp's work is an extreme example of how, in their determination to be apolitical and to treat Fascism on its own terms, the culturalist historians often credulously report what Fascism said rather than critically exploring what it meant.[80]

If Schnapp demonstrates the limits of the culturalist approach to Fascism at a microcosmic level, there are problems with the macrocosmic approach as well. In its commitment to deal with Fascism on its own terms, the school around De Felice and Gentile has regularly ignored important comparisons between Italy and other states and societies. Another major plank in the De Felicean interpretation of Fascism is that Mussolini's regime was *sui generis*, its culture and policies clearly distinguishing it from Nazi Germany, for example. Asserting that Fascism bore no direct responsibility for Auschwitz and the other Nazi crimes,[81] De Felice has presented Italy and Germany as tactical rather than ideological allies. Indeed, in his volumes covering the Second World War, one of his major themes is a somewhat unhistorical regret that Hitler, doggedly committed to the Eastern front, could not bring himself to accept Mussolini's more accurate comprehension that the heart of the war lay in the Mediterranean.[82]

Here is parochialism of a quite remarkable stripe, but the failure to think comparatively extends further. One of Gentile's reiterated arguments is that Fascism earned its special position in national history because it was the first Italian regime 'to bring mythical thought to power'. As has been noted, this cloudy concept springs from Gentile's knowledge of pre-1914 theoreticians like Gustave Le Bon and Georges Sorel, who were read by the young Mussolini, and who argued that society in the age of the masses required an organising myth. The most obvious one was national identity, and Gentile is convinced that the Fascist regime was committed to the nationalisation of the Italian masses.

80 The great exception here is Ruth Ben-Ghiat who, in a number of fine papers, has read between the lines of the work of both Fascists and purported anti-Fascist intellectuals. See e.g. R. Ben-Ghiat, 'Fascism, writing, and memory: the realist aesthetic in Italy, 1930–1950', pp. 627–65; 'Italian Fascism and the aesthetics of the "third way"', *Journal of Contemporary History*, 31, 1996, pp. 293–316.
81 For the background, see R. J. B. Bosworth, *Explaining Auschwitz and Hiroshima*, pp. 138–9.
82 R. De Felice, *Mussolini l'alleato I. L'Italia in guerra 1940–3*, Turin, 1990, pp. 177–8, 246, 286, 363, 371–2, 390, 396, 406, 470–2, 566–9. See further Chapter 4.

It is not difficult, however, to perceive that nationality had a competitor in that twentieth-century world in which myths or realities were restructuring identities. Consumerism, especially American-style, capitalist, 'liberal-democratic' consumerism, not by any means always in open conflict with nationality, became the triumphant ideology of the twentieth century. It was consumerism which most obviously defeated communism in the 1980s. In Fascist Italy, too, the myth of the United States exercised its charm, both among young intellectuals attracted by Hollywood, jazz and other aspects of American 'popular culture', and among peasants whose traditional connections with the emigrant world had long encouraged the belief that the USA was the ultimate paradise. Fascist propaganda was all very well, and presumably won its quota of converts, but Madison Avenue had done it first and best and, given its triumphs, few from the 1920s, if not before, subscribed to the religion of Fascist nationality without the sneaking hope that they would, in happier times, be re-made as some sort of American.[83]

But the limits and ambiguities of a culturalist reading of the history of Fascism did not stop here. If consumerism tailored Italian lives in a way that Fascism neither willed nor necessarily wanted, other great ideologies also eddied through Italian life: Catholicism may have shared some Fascist ideals, but it rejected others.[84] Any serious totalitarian regime must surely have sought to eject the Vatican from its position of prominence in Italian life, both in a directly religious sense and in a more vague and muted cultural one, especially given the piety typically inculcated by female teachers in elementary schools. Yet both Mussolini and his regime remained equivocal in their relationship with the institutions and ideas of the Catholic Church and scarcely expunged Catholicism from the mind-set of Italians (consumerism, by contrast, offered a more radical challenge to the Church).

A very similar story can be told of another of the great institutions of the Italian peninsula, the 'Italian family'. To be sure the family needs its history to be composed carefully, with a sense of change and variation and with an awareness that the subject has been frequently mythologised. None the less, a totalitarian regime aspiring to reach into the heart of society and control commonsense ought to have sought more drastically to harness family life in its cause. No doubt, especially in the 1930s, Fascism was active as an educator and, as they grew up, enrolled Italian children as *balilla* or 'daughters of the she-wolf'. No doubt Fascism was troubled by demographic issues, and launched and sought to win the 'Battle of the Births'.[85] However, did Fascism really ensure that this enrolling and these

---

83 To be fair, Gentile has himself addressed the matter in one rather earnest article in which he delineates the unsurprising fact that the more true-believing of Fascist intellectuals and officials were at times hostile about the claims of the USA to embody modernity. See E. Gentile, 'Impending modernity: Fascism and the ambivalent image of the United States', *Journal of Contemporary History*, 28, 1993, pp. 7–29.

84 For more on the social history of Fascism, see further Chapter 6.

85 For a review of the issue, inclined to take Fascist achievement very seriously, see C. Ipsen, *Dictating demography: the problem of population in Fascist Italy*, Cambridge, 1996.

campaigns entailed a social and cultural revolution? Did it ever intrude very far into family networks? Again, the answer seems, in most cases, to be no.

What, then, is the record late in the 1990s of those historians who have followed the lead of Renzo De Felice and Emilio Gentile, especially of those who have sought to outline a unique Fascist culture? By now it should be apparent that, in my view, the commitment of De Felice and Gentile to a history detached from politics, however worthy in its initial motivation, has not worked, given the inevitable linkage between past, present and future. What their scholarship has instead inspired is the rise of an 'anti-anti-Fascist orthodoxy'. Anti-Fascism was once committed to a thesis of 'never again'; it was emphatic that the record of Fascism had been scoured by brutality, death and defeat; it urged that, from 1919 to 1945, too many rich and powerful Italians had at a minimum fellow-travelled with dictatorship and tyranny. Now, anti-anti-Fascism became a weapon in the hands of those in the 1990s who were anxious to blot out this interpretation, the better to assert the virtue of their wealth and the advantage of their power in present and future. Moreover, in a narrowly historiographical sense, the culturalist approach, despite some useful achievements, has not provided a sufficiently articulated account of the Fascist experience. To rediscover the variations in the lives of Italians of different classes, regions and genders, it is best to go beyond the De Felice school and examine other approaches to the history of Italian Fascism.

The review of one specific example may be a useful way to start such an examination. In 1992, the American historian Victoria De Grazia published a general study of how Fascism ruled Italian women.[86] The author of an earlier book on the organisation of leisure during the regime,[87] De Grazia wrote both as an anti-Fascist and a feminist. If De Felice were to be believed, De Grazia's political commitments should reduce her to the despised ranks of 'historical journalists'. In fact, however, De Grazia's work contrasts favourably with some De Felicean explorations of women's history, attempts which suffer from the school failing of reading the evidence too literally.[88]

De Grazia's account, by comparison, is full of nuance. True, she starts with condemnation: 'Mussolini's regime stood for returning women to home and hearth, restoring patriarchal authority, and confining female destiny to bearing babies.' 'The fascist state favoured men at the expense of women in the family structure, the labor market, the political system, and society at large.'[89] After that beginning, however, ironies abound. The

---

86 V. De Grazia, *How Fascism ruled women: Italy 1922–1945*, Berkeley, 1992.
87 V. De Grazia, *The culture of consent: mass organisation of leisure in Fascist Italy*, Cambridge, 1981.
88 For a typical English-language example, see M. Fraddosio, 'The Fallen Hero: the myth of Mussolini and Fascist women in the Italian Social Republic (1943–5)', *Journal of Contemporary History*, 31, 1996, pp. 99–124.
89 V. De Grazia, *How Fascism ruled women*, pp. 1, 5.

regime talked about nationalising even the female masses, but its economic policies, especially those through which Italy became 'the only industrialised country in which wages fell continuously from the start of the 1920s through the outbreak of World War II',[90] drove the family in on itself, often making survival its dominant ambition. In this sense, De Grazia argues, the family became 'more privatised' in the Fascist years than it had been before, despite the regime's intention to expand the influence of the state over domestic matters.

Notoriously, Mussolini also demanded demographic increase, urging a women's delegation: 'Go back home and tell the women I need births, many births,' while elsewhere pronouncing, 'He who is not a father is not a man.'[91] Here again, however, lurked much contradiction. Fascism did develop an array of welfare policies for women, notably over natal matters, and infant mortality rates duly fell (if remaining well above the level existing in France and Germany). The regime, however, did not alter regional imbalance – poorer and more agrarian regions continued to have a higher reproduction rate than did richer and more urban ones. Fascist words were refuted by deeds in a more general sense. As De Grazia puts it, Fascist 'policies . . . pressed people to have bigger families, whereas commonsense family strategies [influenced by the diminishing working-class pay packet] argued for smaller ones'.[92] Here, too, a battle raged which was certainly not exclusively defined by Fascism. Catholicism demanded many children (and the Church was rather more adamantine than the regime in its rejection of abortion). Consumerism (the great department store chains of post-war Italy, *UPIM*, *Standa* and *Rinascente*, opened their doors under Fascism), by contrast, even if for the great majority of the population it offered only the faint hope of the 'good life', counselled few children. All in all, concludes De Grazia, 'Fascism spoke of the family as the pillar of the state, but family survival strategies in the face of terrible economic want accentuated the antistatist tendencies of Italian civil society.'[93]

The theory of Fascist women's policies was negated in a still more general way by Fascist practice. The regime's patriarchal ideology required women to return to the kitchen and the bedroom. However, the regime was also, by its very nature, activist. Its parades enlisted women, too. Propaganda praised the 'new' woman, often for being a good and fertile mother, but not exclusively for that. On Fascist public occasions or while reading some Fascist literature, women might leave the confines of their home and their

90 V. De Grazia, *How Fascism ruled women*, p. 9.
91 V. De Grazia, *How Fascism ruled women*, pp. 41, 43. Ipsen reports nicely that, in 1937, the members of the Fascist Grand Council themselves only had a reproduction rate of some 1.9. Mussolini led the way with five children and two of his colleagues had four. But five leading Fascists (Acerbo, Angelini, Cianetti, De Bono and Solmi) were deplorably both married and childless. C. Ipsen, *Dictating demography: the problem of population in Fascist Italy*, p. 179.
92 V. De Grazia, *How Fascism ruled women*, p. 81.
93 V. De Grazia, *How Fascism ruled women*, p. 275.

family; at such times, they were given practical and imaginative space of their own and the promise of a certain sort of modernity. Thus, concludes De Grazia, Fascist women's policies were fundamentally bifurcated, with Mussolini's regime offering 'a disconcerting experience of new opportunities and new repressions'.[94] The existence of a 'totalitarian state' had certainly not eliminated the capacity of Italian women to take 'agency' for their own lives. Indeed, Fascism ruled women only to a certain extent; portions of Italian women's history are best understood as part of a specifically Fascist history, but much is more structural and moves with a rhythm by no means identical with that of any political ideology, Fascist or otherwise.

This point about difference is crucial for those who might best be defined as the social historians of the Fascist period, and whose work will be reviewed in greater detail later in this book. Suffice it for the moment to note that social history is itself a term lacking precision; it can span from researchers who examine places where state and society intersect to what have been called the 'barefoot historians' of 'everyday life'.[95] None the less, social historians of Nazi Germany and of the USSR have produced a pile of evidence which prompts doubt as to whether the totalitarian, 'top-down', state-centred model is an acceptable explanatory device for these regimes. Social histories have typically indicated that, in practice, even these tyrannies left room for individual initiative and will. The historiography of Fascist Italy is not as rigorous or sophisticated in its questioning of the relationship between state and society as is German historiography, nor is it as determined to uncover the exact decision-making process in the regime – the great majority of historians seem to assume that Mussolini could in no sense have been a 'weak dictator'. It is true that Luisa Passerini and others have provided some case studies of humdrum life in Fascist Italy.[96] The journals *Rivista di storia contemporanea*, *Passato e presente* and *Italia contemporanea*, each owing a commitment to anti-Fascism, and *Studi storici*, directly linked to the PCI, as well as *Quaderni storici*, something like the Italian equivalent of the *Annales*, have published widely in these areas. However, as yet there has been no attempt to write a full-scale social history of Italy during the dictatorship. Popular culture,[97] too, awaits its historian,

94 V. De Grazia, *How Fascism ruled women*, p. 1.
95 For the major example in this genre on Germany and as available in English, see D. J. K. Peukert, *The Weimar Republic: the crisis of classical modernity*, Harmondsworth, 1991; *Inside Nazi Germany: conformity, opposition and racism in everyday life*, Harmondsworth, 1989. Rather different in its approach, but with a similar exposition of the mentality of the ordinary subjects of the USSR, is S. Fitzpatrick, *Stalin's peasants: resistance and survival in the Russian village after collectivisation*, Oxford, 1994.
96 For those who wish to study the historian before they study the facts, see L. Passerini, *Autobiography of a generation: Italy 1968*, Hanover, 1996. Cf. Chapter 6.
97 Cf. S. Colarizi, *L'opinione degli italiani sotto il regime 1929–1943*, Bari, 1991. This work, from the De Felice school, disappointingly insists on 'the iron and total control by the regime on the whole nation' (p. 185), even though Colarizi's own evidence frequently seems to contradict this 'totalitarianist' interpretation.

while culturalist historians, somewhat ironically, keep their focus on how the regime purported to construct culture rather than on how it was received and, presumably, as De Grazia's book indicates in the case of women, manipulated and adapted by its recipients.

A great deal of social history has, however, been published. The most long-standing genre, and one not at all surprising in so regionally diverse a country as Italy, is the local study. Here there is a mammoth literature available in Italian – a pertinacious reader can find, for example, a rather acute study of the imposition and development of Fascism in San Marino[98] – and an extensive one in English. Typically, such accounts have investigated the rise to power of Fascisms which will not be quite the same in Ferrara or Bologna or Brescia (and their hinterlands)[99] as in Tuscany or Puglia or a Sicilian village.[100] Moreover, these works usually indicate that local Fascisms tended to possess both a radical and self-consciously 'revolutionary' side and a more conservative and respectable one, with considerable links to the pre-1914 ruling elite.[101]

What the regional studies are especially good at is reminding any student of the regime of the multiple currents of time which run through any society, including a 'totalitarian' one. The idea of a single homogeneous nation called Italy is, very plainly, a construct, and one evidently bearing only a partial explanatory power in regard to the history of 'Italians'. The claims by De Felice and Gentile that Fascism had its own individual characteristics which severed its history from that of Liberal Italy before 1922 and of Republican Italy after the Second World War, in other words the recent neo-Rankean revival of the 'parenthesis thesis', can only be false. In fact, a decade ago, before the 'fascination' of Fascist culture was quite as apparent as is presently asserted, the liberal historian Roberto Vivarelli argued that cultural time was not identical with political time, and concluded therefore that cultural practitioners under the regime should not simply be written off as 'Fascists'.[102]

If this plea can be made for culture, it can more easily be maintained for many aspects of social life and even for quite a lot of politics. Perhaps a better definition of social histories would be a structural one, since they

---

98 A. L. Carlotti, *Storia del partito fascista sammarinese*, Milan, 1973.
99 See e.g. P. Corner, *Fascism in Ferrara 1915–1925*, Oxford, 1975; A. L. Cardoza, *Agrarian elites and Italian Fascism: the province of Bologna 1901–1926*, Princeton, 1982; A. A. Kelikian, *Town and country under Fascism: the transformation of Brescia 1915–26*, Oxford, 1986.
100 See e.g. F. M. Snowden, *Violence and great estates in the south of Italy: Apulia, 1900–1922*, Cambridge, 1986; and his *The Fascist revolution in Tuscany 1919–1922*, Cambridge, 1989; C. G. Chapman, *Milocca: a Sicilian village*, London, 1973 and see further Chapter 6.
101 For just one example, see L. Ponziani, *Notabili, combattenti e nazionalisti. L'Abruzzo verso il Fascismo*, Milan, 1988, exploring the career of the Fascist minister Giacomo Acerbo.
102 R. Vivarelli in B. Vigezzi (ed.), *Federico Chabod e la 'Nuova Storiografia' italiana dal primo al secondo dopoguerra (1919–1950)*, Milan, 1984, pp. 489–90.

examine factors which lie behind the political stage and which often last longer than this regime or that. For most structural historians, Fascism is best understood by examining the whole fabric of Italian life from 1922 to 1945. When examination demonstrates how, say, landowners could manipulate national or international political ideologies to their own ends, the resultant evidence implicates local elites in the national tyranny. Indeed, sometimes those who exercised local power did so more ruthlessly, and with more immediate casualties, than did the government in Rome. The other 'naturally' anti-Fascist implication of structural accounts of twentieth-century Italy is that a whole series of social problems were not resolved by the fall of Fascism but rather ran on into the Republic, the 'Southern question' being the most flagrant. Injustices present in 1922 (and rarely much reformed by the regime) remained injustices after 1945. These continuities in time and extent may limit the meaning of Fascism – perhaps Mussolini and the other Fascist chiefs only thought they possessed power as they orated in Rome; perhaps Fascism was 'mere politics' and should be downplayed as such? More generally, however, structural historians, aware of the inevitable connections between politics and society, have concluded that Fascism should be regarded as something more than the formal institutions and legislation of the regime. Rather it must be appraised as bearing responsibility for, if not necessarily having complete control over, all of Italian life until the end of the Second World War.

Such appraisal is likely to reinforce a commitment to anti-Fascism. None the less, structural accounts do not automatically result in a single, simple and uniform leftist reading of history. To give two English-language examples, one microcosmic, the other more general: Jonathan Morris, scrutinising a segment of the population of Milan, has rescued the small shopkeepers of that city from the enormous condescension of vulgar Marxist accounts which declared that members of the petite bourgeoisie were automatically Fascists. Morris, by contrast, arguing that those shopkeepers who from 1888 had organised themselves into a *Federazione degli Esercenti*, had developed their own commercial identity and sought autonomy for themselves in the civil and economic life of their city, concludes: 'The *esercenti* movement dealt with the Fascists as it did with other political parties, applauding actions of which it approved and decrying those of which it did not, and continued to do so within the increasing constraints imposed after 1922.'[103]

Douglas Forsyth, by contrast, has returned from periphery to centre, with some questions presumably prompted by current financial preoccupations. In his view, as long as Liberal Italy was characterised by its original sin, namely that large sections of its elite were determined that Italy should both be a Great Power and obtain a 'strategic industrial base', no

103 J. Morris, *The political economy of shopkeeping in Milan 1886–1922*, Cambridge, 1993, p. 284.

conceivable government having fought the First World War could stabilise the economy domestically and internationally and long retain any sort of popularity. Italian institutions fell into crisis, according to Forsyth, because it was 'difficult to see how liberal leaders could have won the allegiance of the mass political parties, while pursuing orthodox monetary and financial policies, however necessary they felt the latter to have been'.[104]

English-language historians, then, still debate the question of the rise of Fascism. With the notable if curious exception of Roberto Vivarelli,[105] current Italian historiography is more likely to concentrate on the regime itself or, frequently, on the Second World War and the Resistance, that period which De Felice's biography of Mussolini had begun to reach by 1990. Here again a key study requires review. It is Claudio Pavone's *Una guerra civile*, a book which, despite its title, does not spring from the De Felicean school but, rather, was written by a distinguished anti-Fascist, one guided by his own memories of the Resistance.[106] Pavone's work, read alongside those of De Felice and Gentile, provides the basic introduction to the current Italian understanding of Fascism and anti-Fascism.

It should be noted at once that Pavone has little to say about Fascism. He does argue that historians, even while agreeing that 'the Italian Social Republic could not have lasted for a single day without German support', should investigate that complex of ideals and accidents which could lead an individual to favour the Salò regime. Some of these ideals, he admits, could carry a certain sort of 'leftist' idealism and a hope for a more equal and just society.[107] These commonsense comments apart, however, what interests Pavone is anti-Fascism. He aims to uncover the character of the 'Armed Resistance' during the period from 1943 to 1945. Although he remains fundamentally committed to anti-Fascism, recalling with favour Vittorio Foa's remark: 'During the Resistance and, for a brief moment, on liberation, everything seemed possible',[108] he is anxious to review the national understanding of this period of Italy's past. There are also quite a few hints in his work that this review has become more urgent, given the political crisis enveloping the First Republic as he wrote.

Pavone is insistent that the 'Armed Resistance' consisted of three conflicts rolled into one: 'a patriotic war, a civil war and a class war'.[109] The phrase 'civil war', he recalls somewhat defensively, was used at the time by so

104 D. J. Forsyth, *The crisis of Liberal Italy: monetary and financial policy, 1914–1922*, Cambridge, 1993, pp. 3, 289.
105 See Chapter 5.
106 C. Pavone, *Una guerra civile: saggio storico sulla moralità nella Resistenza*, Turin, 1991. In his preface, Pavone says that one of his purposes in writing the book had been to pass on a sense of his own youth to the newest generation (pp. xi–xii). In his interview with Chessa, De Felice did admit that Pavone's work had an able side, despite its leftism. R. De Felice, *Rosso e nero*, p. 11.
107 C. Pavone, *Una guerra civile*, pp. 231–2.
108 C. Pavone, *Una guerra civile*, p. 3.
109 C. Pavone, *Una guerra civile*, p. xi.

solidly communist a historian as Emilio Sereni,[110] while, he adds, the democratic anti-Fascist historian Franco Venturi declared that civil wars were the only ones worth fighting.[111] The issues raised by this nomenclature were something of a distraction, however, and Pavone's main intention seems to have been to add nuance to existing anti-Fascist accounts of the Resistance. In his version, some who joined the (communist) Garibaldi brigades or became Nazi-fascist *repubblichini* did so as much by accident as through ideological commitment. Some who endured bombing cursed the Anglo-Americans and hoped for revenge (even while they could be appeased by the thought that the Germans were suffering more); some in the Resistance could fraternise with those who still gave allegiance to Mussolini; some partisans were guilty of extortion, violence and murder;[112] some, too, thought of themselves as southerners rather than Italians, or as workers rather than peasants.[113]

Most of these conclusions are sensible and just (and second the conclusions being reached at much the same time in the English-language literature by Roger Absalom). None the less, in the political circumstances of 1990s Italy (and illustrating yet again how inevitably history is imbricated with present and future), Pavone's book sparked very considerable controversy. Critics on the Left thought that his emphasis on the complexity of the human experience clouded issues which needed to remain clear – 'in reality,' one reviewer remarked severely, 'the Resistance should not be dismembered into three wars', since it was, rather, a conflict fought on a number of fronts.[114] Some on the Right, by contrast, including, mutedly, De Felice,[115] hailed Pavone's work for its dissipation of the myth of the Resistance. Pavone himself, however, continued to argue that anti-Fascism had not surrendered its historical virtue, and he implicitly condemned De Felice when he asserted that 'it is indeed a weird reversal both of politics and of ideology to allege that 8 September and then the Resistance destroyed Italian national identity and prevented its reconstruction. [Were this line to be accepted,] should we perhaps reach a situation where we regret that Fascist Italy did not win the war?' In any case, Pavone concluded, a serious debate about the Resistance was a healthy 'sign of cultural sanity'.[116]

110 For his classic work, see E. Sereni, *Il capitalismo nelle campagne (1860–1900)*, rev. ed. Turin, 1968; first publ. 1947).
111 C. Pavone, *Una guerra civile*, pp. 221–5, 250–1.
112 Pavone concludes that 44 720 died as partisans and 9980 in reprisals while 21 168 were severely wounded. These needed to be compared with the about 200 000 Italian soldiers lost before 1943 and the 12 000 to 15 000 Fascists killed with liberation. C. Pavone, *Una guerra civile*, pp. 413, 511–12.
113 See e.g. C. Pavone, *Una guerra civile*, pp. 35–8, 140, 151–5, 200–1, 210, 277–8, 347, 381, 413–16, 450–1, 468–70.
114 S. Cotta in *Passato e presente della Resistenza e della Guerra di Liberazione*, Rome, [1994], p. 36. This book was published under the imprint of the Italian Prime Minister's office, and consisted of papers and comments presented to a conference under the auspices of a coalition of Anti-Fascist organisations and with the ultimate patronage of President Scalfaro.
115 See e.g. R. De Felice, *Rosso e nero*, p. 11.
116 *Passato e presente della Resistenza e della Guerra di Liberazione*, p. 111.

If the history trade is taken in isolation, it is easy to applaud Pavone's words. And yet his book and the debate which resulted from it did not occur in a political and cultural vacuum, but rather at a time in which the lessons of the past and their meaning for the present and future seemed particularly obscure. In the 1990s Italy certainly needs textured and subtle accounts of its experience of Fascism and anti-Fascism. It remains to be seen, however, in what way academic works, whether composed by a Pavone or a Gentile, will be read by the populace at large and, perhaps more importantly, how accurately and critically the transmission of complex ideas to that populace will take place in the new world order of virtual politics and of a largely unchallenged hegemony of economic rationalism. In this context, a pessimist might say that Italy has lost a past which, since 1945, helped it to advance towards democracy, and may be acquiring instead a confused but vaguely patriotic heritage, designed to entertain rather than to instruct, to lull and, above all, to discourage commitment of any kind.[117] As a reading is made of many histories of Fascism in the succeeding chapters of this book, it will often be necessary to wonder whether a history with the morality or moralising left out is a useful or possible project, and to ask again whether our ideological and political uncertainties in the 1990s are not being prompted by, and prompting a past which has lost its certainly (and even its uncertainty).

117 Here cf. D. Lowenthal, *Possessed by the past: the heritage crusade and the spoils of history*, New York, 1996, for a context beyond Italy, even though Lowenthal himself could have a stronger sense of historical change, exaggerates the distinction between academic history and popular heritage, and fails to ask rigorously enough who is constructing each and to what end.

2

Italian Fascism: Early Understandings, 1919–1959

Fascism is a word which has launched a thousand philippics. Especially in the 1960s and 1970s, when a kind of radicalism was in vogue, it was utilised to describe many a regime or individual, always with an avowedly negative connotation. Somewhat oddly, given the relative power and influence of Mussolini's Italy and Hitler's Germany,[1] the term 'fascism' eclipsed Nazism as the most common disapprobation of right-wing political ideas and actions. This extensive, if somewhat vague meaning is not inappropriate for a word which has moved into virtually all languages from Italian but which, in its Italian origin, was of imprecise and generalised meaning.

During Mussolini's regime the words *fascismo*, *fascista* and *fascio* were increasingly understood as proving the 'Roman' inheritance of Fascism. The *fasces*, that bundle of rods and axes carried by a lictor in classical times since it was he who embodied the law, came to symbolise the public meaning of a regime. Fascism, it was claimed, was creating a society in which the people were bound together infrangibly and in which law and order prevailed. The *fasces* became a special token of the Fascist 'Corporate State'; each stick in the bundle represented a single corporation, whether of heavy industry, or agriculture, or education, or even tourism and leisure, and, together, the sticks composed the nation. Each Italian citizen was simultaneously loyal to both the corporation and to Italy, as well as to the Fascist regime which had fostered such a happy marriage of economic and political interests. Fascism, then, drew its meaning from the alleged fact that it had created a vertically organised society, arranged to deny absolutely the 'horizontal' paradigm of Marxism, in which one class was destined to war against another and in which the nation had to face external enemies while itself in disarray.

---

1 For further comment on the relative images of Hitler and Mussolini, in which the effect of the nomenclature was reversed and Hitler was viewed as the 'real' fascist and Mussolini as more the mimic, or the fascist without the real courage of his evil convictions, see Chapter 9.

The Fascist claim to ownership of the 'myth of Rome' was, of course, false; there were plenty of Liberal predecessors who had summoned the ghosts of classical Rome to the aid of the 'Third Italy'[2] well before the Fascists constructed Roman history as their own. And if the so-called *romanità* of Fascism was not original, nor was the title of the regime entirely new. In the 1890s Sicilian peasants, disgruntled through decades of malign neglect from the Liberal government in Rome, banded together in a *fascio*, or united group, in the cause of what, with a hopeful vagueness, they called 'socialism'.[3] As first utilised in modern Italian political discourse, the term *fasci* had a leftist connotation. None the less, it did not establish itself as belonging to the left as the governments of the period, especially those headed by the Sicilian revolutionary turned reactionary nationalist Francesco Crispi, put down the peasants with a predictably condign rigour and relegated the Sicilian *fasci* to the realm of hidden memory.

During the First World War the word's placement on a left–right spectrum grew more uncertain. In 1915, a *Fascio d'azione interventista* brought some unity to syndicalists and other dissident leftists who had decided to favour the war in order to further the revolution. In December 1917, by contrast, a large number of deputies and Senators, including the arch-conservative Antonio Salandra, the ex-Prime Minister who, in May 1915, had taken Italy into the First World War, created a so-called *Fascio parlamentare di difesa nazionale* (Parliamentary Union for National Defence), pledged to pursue the war effort to the utmost.[4] This rightist *fascio* was still in existence when the war ended and, at least in the eyes of its members, had contributed crucially to national unity and national victory.

At that time the ex-socialist turned radical patriot Benito Mussolini was neither an enemy of the nationalist politicians nor yet their adamantine friend. It was true that, as early as February 1915, he had talked about *noi, interventisti e fascisti* (we, interventionists and fascists),[5] but the word as yet had no special meaning. Still, two years later, Mussolini preferred to call himself the leader of the *trincerocrazia*[6] (from *trincea* or trench, meaning those who had been through the full war experience and who, thus tempered, deserved to become the new ruling class). He favoured the social advance of people like himself, ex-soldiers and what he called the 'productive elements' in society. Thus, when on 23 March 1919, in a room overlooking the Piazza San Sepolcro in Milan, Mussolini assembled a score or so of like-minded acquaintances, generally from a background in 'left

---

2 For some examples, see R. J. B. Bosworth, *Italy the least of the Great Powers: Italian foreign policy before the First World War*, Cambridge, 1979, esp. pp. 5–9.
3 For a basic account of their activities, see F. Renda, *I fasci siciliani 1892–94*, Turin, 1977.
4 R. De Felice, *Mussolini il rivoluzionario 1883–1920*, Turin, 1965, pp. 370–3.
5 B. Mussolini, *Scritti e discorsi adriatici* (ed. E. Susmel), Milan, 1942, i, p. 29.
6 R. De Felice, *Mussolini il rivoluzionario*, p. 403.

interventionism',[7] and launched the *Fasci di combattimento*, the title meant little more than league of returned soldiers who lacked a political base elsewhere.[8] *Fascio*, *fascismo* and *fascista* would express their reality[9] in the doing and the making. The name came first, the meaning after.

What, then, at the moment of their foundation, did Fascists think that they were offering Italy, both in the period leading up to their entry into coalition government after the 'March on Rome' in October 1922, and subsequent to the declaration of the dictatorship in January 1925 and the creation of what was called a 'totalitarian' state? What was the fundamental Fascist explanation of Fascism?

It is notorious that this question has no simple answer. In 1919 Fascists belonged to a 'movement', not a party. Some enthusiasts, then and later, would prefer to define themselves as members of a 'militia',[10] a crusading force sworn to put the nation right and to eschew the sort of ideological hair-splitting favoured by intellectuals (and historians). Less than a month before he became Prime Minister, Mussolini provided a straightforward but somewhat unsubtle explanation of Fascism: 'The democrats of *Il Mondo* want to know our programme? It is to break the bones of the democrats of *Il Mondo*. And the sooner the better.'[11] Other early Fascists did not demur. As one stated in 1920: 'The fist is the synthesis of our theory.'[12] Another young Fascist saluted the Browning pistol as the summit of Fascist faith and a responsive object of 'almost carnal love', more faithful than any woman.[13] As late as the 1970s, neo-Fascists were still cheerfully invoking the virtue of the *santo manganello* (holy club).[14] Here, then, was a political movement standing for the triumph of the will, and frequently proclaiming that it needed no other justification than that it intended to seize the state and to manage it in a new way.

None the less, political participation of whatever kind did inevitably entail the development of a rather more complex programme. In addition, time and detail also brought complication. At Piazza San Sepolcro

---

7 See R. De Felice, *Mussolini il rivoluzionario*, pp. 473–81.

8 The standard account of the fluctuating relationship between the Fascists and the main ex-combatant organisation, the *Associazione Nazionale dei Combattenti* (ANC), is G. Sabbatucci, *I combattenti nel primo dopoguerra*, Bari, 1974.

9 Another area of uncertainty about Fascism was its pronunciation. In many circles during the inter-war period it was pronounced 'fassist', as though the word derived from French rather than Italian. It is said that Mussolini, aspirant intellectual and sometime teacher of primary-school-level French, also long used that pronunciation. See O. Mosca, *Nessuno volle i miei dollari d'oro*, Naples, 1958, p. 199.

10 The major recent advocate of this interpretation is E. Gentile, *Storia del partito fascista 1919–1922: movimento e milizia*, Bari, 1989.

11 Mussolini in *Il Popolo d'Italia*, 4 October 1922, as cited by E. Weber, 'Introduction' to H. Rogger and E. Weber (eds), *The European Right: a historical profile*, London, 1965, p. 16. For the background to *Il Mondo*, see S. Colarizi, *I democratici all'opposizione: Giovanni Amendola e L'Unione nazionale (1922–1926)*, Bologna, 1973.

12 E. Gentile, *Storia del partito fascista 1919–1922*, p. 497.

13 Cited by E. Gentile, *Storia del partito fascista 1919–1922*, p. 498.

14 Thus the naming of the Fascist killer in *The Conformist* as 'Manganiello' (see Chapter 7).

Mussolini had advocated to the *Fasci di combattimento* a series of decidedly radical policies which, in June 1919, were marketed as constituting an 'antidogmatic and antidemagogic' 'revolution', while remaining 'soundly Italian' (that is, determined to uphold the merit of the war).[15] However, the colour of this revolution became more motley as time passed and the Fascist movement broadened to attract social groups who were not present in the initial stages. By 1920 'border nationalists', enthusiasts for what today might be called ethnic cleansing in Trieste[16] or the Alto Adige, were bringing their special imprint to Fascism. The next year saw the arrival into party ranks of considerable numbers of anti-socialists from Northern and relatively modernised agricultural Italy, notably in the Emilia-Romagna and Tuscany. What had seemed set policies went into reverse. A republican movement accepted the monarchy; anti-clerical pronouncements were succeeded by polite and astute dealings with the Vatican; economically interventionist plans were replaced by a preference for the free market (at least for a while);[17] and the definition of Fascist syndicalism grew more opaque and contradictory.[18] As Italo Balbo, the *ras* or boss of Ferrara, noted blithely in April 1922: 'Our movement has the good fortune to be both idealistic and realistic.'[19] In the fine print, what he meant was that Fascism was proud to be incoherent and had no intention of becoming the reverse.

Even Mussolini's position could be contested. Fascists talked, then and later, about their commitment to both 'democracy' (in the sense of an openness to the masses) and hierarchy, but a *Führerprinzip* still seemed an alien idea. Throughout the summer of 1921 Mussolini's leadership fell into deep crisis, and the *Duce* for a time resigned his office, regaining his position only after changing some of his policies and abandoning some of his nearest allies, notably the ex-syndicalist Umberto Pasella.[20] This conflict between

---

15 There is a very useful English-language documentary collection on Fascism: C. Delzell (ed.), *Mediterranean Fascism 1919–1945*, New York, 1970; pp. 1–44 cover the rise to power. The fundamental account of this rise is R. De Felice, *Mussolini il fascista I. La conquista del potere 1921–1925*, Turin, 1969; cf. also the latter section of the preceding volume of the biography, R. De Felice, *Mussolini il rivoluzionario*, Turin, 1965. In English the fullest history is A. Lyttelton, *The seizure of power: Fascism in Italy 1919–1929*, London, 1973.

16 For a still-useful detailed English-language account, see D. L. Rusinow, *Italy's Austrian heritage 1919–1946*, Oxford, 1969. It is in these regions that Italy is best read as just another part of the ethnic and socio-political inter-war crisis of Central and Eastern Europe. For some acute commentary on post-1945 historicisation, see G. Sluga, 'Trieste: ethnicity and the Cold War, 1945–1954', *Journal of Contemporary History*, 29, 1994, pp. 285–303.

17 See further Chapter 5.

18 For an English-language account, see D. D. Roberts, *The syndicalist tradition and Italian Fascism*, Manchester, 1979.

19 I. Balbo, *Diario 1922*, Milan, 1932, p. 42.

20 Pasella is now thought to have been the first key organiser of the Fascist movement, being all the more significant in Gentile's eyes as one who carried syndicalist beliefs into early Fascism. E. Gentile, *Storia del partito fascista 1919–1922*, pp. 37–9. (For Pasella's fall, see p. 313.)

the leader and his party remained a running theme of Fascist history until well after the construction of the 'totalitarian' state.

The actual circumstances of the 'March on Rome' did little to clarify what was the bedrock of Fascism. In the smaller cities of northern Italy, in Trieste, Ferrara, Bologna, Florence, Empoli and the rest, a partial 'revolution' had occurred well before October 1922. In such places Fascists had imposed the rule of themselves or their friends, often violently, by the 'seizing' of local power. To be sure, a degree of ambiguity lingered after such events since, frequently enough, Fascists, in their anti-socialism, could expect at the very least the sympathy of the Army, the prefects and the police, that is, those agents of the Liberal state with the most direct access to armed force. Nor, once the Fascists had marched on a certain city and expelled its socialist or otherwise anti-Fascist council, was it very clear what would come next. As Giovanni Giolitti, in some eyes the sage of liberal politics, had remarked in 1921: 'You will see. The Fascist candidates [with whom he had allied electorally] will be like fireworks. They will make a lot of noise but will leave nothing behind except smoke.'[21]

This confusion worsened in 1922 because of the difficulty of deciding exactly how the Fascists had earned a place in the coalition government headed, from 30 October, by Mussolini in Rome. Had there been a *coup d'état*? Perhaps there had. After all, the Fascist movement had held its congress at Naples which concluded on 24 October with agreement that an armed act should take place and, from 27 October, Fascist squads, however bedraggled by autumnal rain and heterodox in their political intent, had duly assembled and marched towards the capital. Mussolini had not accompanied them. He had remained in his office in Milan, negotiating by phone in the classic manner of a 'transformist' Italian politician, the nearness of a Swiss sanctuary a reassuring thought should the coup be seen as treason, and should it fail. Eventually King Victor Emmanuel III had invited the *Duce* to form a government and the invitation had been applauded by the vast majority of that segment of the national political world which possessed wealth, status and power. Old liberals, leading figures in the armed services, in the Catholic Church, in the business world and in the Nationalist movement, all accepted cabinet places in the new administration. A precedent for Mussolini's promotion existed. In 1898, a social and economic crisis had prompted the monarch, then Umberto I, to bypass parliament and to summon a general, Luigi Pelloux, to the Prime Ministership with the promise of firm policies. Similarly, the Salandra-Sonnino government which had presided over the crisis of 1914–15 and taken Italy into the war had, like the Fascists, lacked a genuine parliamentary majority and hardly claimed to reflect the will of the Italian people. Was Fascism just another example of the fragility of the parliamentary order in Italy? Was there yet anything really novel about

21 C. Sforza, *L'Italia dal 1914 al 1944 quale io la vidi*, Milan, 1944, p. 97.

Fascism, apart from a certain kind of rhetoric, explicable in the aftermath of
the war and reflecting that terrible conflict's values? Even as Mussolini took
office, the meaning of Fascism was unclear. As Guido Dorso, a liberal
democrat with expertise on the Southern question, would remark, Fascism
in 1922 was 'an uneasy amalgam of discordant and contradictory forces'.[22]

Power inevitably brought complications of its own, and any account of
the history of Fascism must acknowledge the twisted road which
Mussolini's regime pursued, certainly in the 1920s and arguably throughout
its history. None the less, the drama of its rise, and Mussolini's youth and
flamboyance in word and deed, did now persuade commentators to reflect
in greater detail and depth on the Fascist movement. What, they began to
ask, did it stand for? Who constituted its social base? What would it do to
Italy? How did it relate to other better-known ideologies, to liberalism,
socialism, communism, Nationalism and syndicalism? How, after all, was
Fascism to be defined?

The Fascists gradually built up their own answers to these questions. The
Mussolini government, they said, had brought a revolution to Italy, but one
that was distinct from the socialist or Bolshevik version – it was 'an Italian
and not a muscovite revolution'.[23] Fascism stood for social unity, for
'corporatism'. It would make a 'Corporate State' in which different classes
would be bonded together in service of the nation. Party, officialdom and
nation would in any case merge into what began to be called a 'totalitarian'
state. This social unity would foster national grandeur abroad[24] and greater
productivity at home. Without being definitively assigned to the right, the
left or the centre, Fascism would be modern in a new and better sense,
reversing that tide of moral anarchy and decay originating in the French
revolution.[25] It would complete the process begun but not finished in the
Risorgimento, and only revived in the Great War;[26] it would give meaning
to Italian history. Fascism was 'not for export' and yet it might prove to be
the ideology of the twentieth century. It would bury old-style corrupt
parliamentary democracy and replace it with a 'new, efficient, real
democracy'.[27] It would express the spirit of youth and, in doing so, be

22 G. Dorso, *La rivoluzione meridionale*, Turin, 1972, p. 88 (the book was first published in
   1925).
23 See e.g. Fascist historian G. Volpe in B. Mussolini, *La dottrina del fascismo: con una storia
   del movimento fascista di Gioacchino Volpe*, Rome, 1932, p. 46.
24 One of the first Fascist accounts to be spread abroad was P. Gorgolini, *The Fascist
   movement in Italian life*, London, 1923. Gorgolini emphasised the fundamental anti-
   communism of the movement and its opposition to state ownership, while also urging that
   it expressed 'the ideal of youth . . . [voicing] a rebellion of the spirit against a suffocating
   materialism' (pp. 22–3, 56, 84).
25 For this thesis, see e.g. D. Cantimori, 'Destra', in PNF (ed.), *Dizionario di politica*, Rome,
   1940, p. 780.
26 See e.g. G. Volpe in B. Mussolini, *La dottrina del fascismo*, p. 40.
27 For this last, see C. Curcio, 'Democrazia', in PNF (ed.), *Dizionario di politica*, p. 764; cf.
   also Dino Grandi's early declaration that Fascism intended to introduce a 'new national
   democracy'. D. Grandi, *Le origini e la missione del fascismo*, Bologna, 1922.

'transcendent', making youthful the nation as a whole.[28] Mussolini himself was the special incarnation of the revolution, 'a super-genial assimilator and improvisor, and as such the perfect Italian, full of colour, passion, and a man of complete mental balance and the ideal physical type'.[29] His was the gift of inscribing into his people 'a new concept of Man'.[30] Fascism, as the *Duce* remarked in the article which, with the help of philosopher Giovanni Gentile, he wrote in 1932 in an attempt to give a formal definition of the regime on its tenth anniversary in office, was therefore 'not only a system of government but also and above all a system of thought'.[31]

Of course, Fascist philosophy was shot through with contradictions and banalities. A pinch of Social Darwinism here and of 'Victorian values' there (historian Gioacchino Volpe typically claimed that much about Fascism was summed up in the Latin tag *mens sana in corpore sano*);[32] an uneasy mixture of populism and productivism; a servility to a leader who was in turn anxious to cut an intellectual dash but who lacked constancy or profundity – there was a multitude of issues which Fascism had not thought through. The movement's pretensions to a clear definition of itself remained contestable. It is thus no surprise to find that, from the very first days, anti-Fascists were rather more skilful at decoding the movement than were the Fascists themselves.

Two important early commentators were Mario Missiroli and Luigi Salvatorelli. Each held an allegiance to liberalism, though Missiroli was the more attracted by nationalism[33] and Salvatorelli the more committed to some form of democracy. Writing before the March on Rome, Missiroli asserted that Fascism represented something beyond the eclectic spirituality claimed by its proponents or the simple instrumentality 'exposed' by its socialist opponents. It did not merely constitute a 'white guard'. Partly, Missiroli went on, Fascism genuinely reflected the war experience. It was 'victory's claim for attention' mounted by the 'people', or at least by those

28 See e.g. G. Volpe in B. Mussolini, *La dottrina del fascismo*, p. 61. For some English-language translations of Mussolini's own doctrinal statements, see B. Mussolini, 'The political and social doctrine of Fascism', *Political Quarterly*, 4, 1933, pp. 341–56; B. Mussolini, *Fascism: doctrine and institutions*, Rome, 1935; B. Mussolini, *The Corporate State*, New York, 1975. See also C. Delzell (ed.), *Mediterranean Fascism 1919–1945*, pp. 90–106.

29 G. Volpe in B. Mussolini, *La dottrina del fascismo*, p. 103.

30 G. Volpe in B. Mussolini, *La dottrina del fascismo*, p. 129.

31 C.F. Delzell (ed.), *Mediterranean Fascism 1919–1945*, p. 93.

32 G. Volpe in B. Mussolini, *La dottrina del fascismo*, p. 129. For Volpe's emphasis to his schoolchildren readers that Fascism embodied a 'national revolution', connected with the positive side of the Risorgimento, see A. Scotto di Luzio, *L'appropriazione imperfetta: editori, biblioteche e libri per ragazzi durante il fascismo*, Bologna, 1996, pp. 172–6. Perhaps the drollest piece of Fascist Victoriana is S. Smiles, *Passi scelti del Character con note tolte dai discorsi e dagli scritti del Duce*, ed. C. Cucchi, Milan, 1938.

33 For some of his ambiguities and, notably, his deepening conviction that the Fascist regime did constitute a 'national' revolution, see e.g. M. Missiroli, *L'Italia di oggi* rev. ed., Bologna, 1943. Missiroli can even be found endorsing the view that Fascist Italy needed *spazio vitale* (Lebensraum) (p. 221).

who had devoted themselves to the war. It attracted young men who felt betrayed by socialism and abandoned by the upper middle classes and the 'official culture' of liberalism. It was favoured by those middling classes who had themselves emerged on the political and economic scene as a result of the war. It appealed to an urban group who, at least in Missiroli's eyes, were justified in resenting the peasant effort to 'starve the cities'. Fascism would bring to the nation the good of socialism but eschew maximalist class conflict and lack of patriotism. In sum, Fascism offered to Italy at least the promise of a 'new democracy',[34] and might yet turn out to be 'revolutionary conservatism'.[35]

Luigi Salvatorelli (died 1974) was a distinguished historian[36] who eventually participated directly in the Resistance as a supporter of the democratic *Partito d'Azione*. He had admired the calm astuteness and efficiency of Giolitti and, while remaining in Italy between the wars, defined himself as 'a rationalist [man] in an age of spreading irrationalism'.[37] During the Fascist rise to power, Salvatorelli wrote a series of essays on Fascism for the Turin establishment paper *La Stampa*. These were collected and published in 1923 under the title *Nazionalfascismo*.[38] Salvatorelli agreed that the movement contained plenty of internal contradictions and that it often worked to the benefit of the existing order. The Fascist view of itself was, he argued, particularly unhelpful. Rather, the essence of Fascism lay in its expression of petit bourgeois revolt: 'Fascism, thus, represents the "class struggle" of the lower middle class, crushed between capitalism and the proletariat, as a third force between two disputants.'[39] Moreover, the war had ensured that this class could use the 'myth of the nation' as 'the standard of their revolt'.[40] Since capitalists had never been wholly committed to the nation, a full triumph of Fascism would entail the overthrow of 'capitalist civilization'. Though fundamentally anti-socialist,

34 M. Missiroli, *Il fascismo e la crisi italiana*, Bologna, 1921, as anthologised in R. De Felice (ed.), *Antologia sul Fascismo: il giudizio politico*, Bari, 1976, pp. 23–35. Cf. R. De Felice, *Le interpretazioni del fascismo*, Bari, 1971, pp. 181–3. Missiroli's line may be assumed to have had a major influence on the De Felicean interpretation of Fascism as the embodiment of the 'emerging middle classes' (see further Chapter 5).

35 This last term was endorsed by the early liberal American commentators H. W. Schneider and S. B. Clough (the latter the eventual author of an important post-war economic history of Italy). See H. W. Schneider and S. B. Clough, *Making Fascists*, Chicago, 1929, p. 199; cf. H. W. Schneider, *Making the Fascist state*, New York, 1928 and S. B. Clough, *The economic history of modern Italy*, New York, 1964.

36 In English, see e.g. L. Salvatorelli, *The Risorgimento: thought and action*, New York, 1970.

37 C. F. Delzell, introduction to Salvatorelli, *The Risorgimento*, p. xv.

38 L. Salvatorelli, *Nazionalfascismo*, Turin, 1977. This republished version came with an introduction from the PCI leader, Giorgio Amendola. (He was the son of the liberal democrat anti-Fascist, Minister, Giovanni Amendola, a 'martyr' to Fascism).

39 L. Salvatorelli, *Nazionalfascismo*, p. 12; cf. also the somewhat similar views of the social democrat Ivanoe Bonomi, twice a weak Prime Minister, 1921–2, 1944–5: I. Bonomi, *From Socialism to Fascism: a study of contemporary Italy*, London, 1924. Bonomi's own compromises during the rise of Fascism may be traced in M. Vaini, *Le origini del fascismo a Mantova (1914–1922)*, Rome, 1961.

40 L. Salvatorelli, *Nazionalfascismo*, p. 13.

Fascism borrowed much of its rhetoric and practice from the maximalist variant of socialism. Fascism's obsession with the nation was, in turn, testimony to Italian backwardness. In power, it had frequently accepted the ideas of the Nationalist Association and, indeed, had turned into 'national fascism'. Its most convinced and basic enemy remained those whose credo retained the good sense, tolerance and justice of liberalism.[41]

The most celebrated of all liberal analysts of Fascism was the great philosopher and historian Benedetto Croce, who, like Salvatorelli, stayed in Italy during the dictatorship but, from his palace in Naples, made courteously obvious his dissent from the regime.[42] Croce was a leading signatory of the 'Manifesto of anti-Fascist intellectuals', published in May 1925.[43] In the succeeding years he used his histories to highlight the virtues of liberalism, especially as it had existed in Italy from the Risorgimento until the First World War.[44] Croce's comprehension of the non-Fascist past was duly contested by the Fascist historian Gioacchino Volpe who, in his histories of the same period, urged instead that the dictatorship was fortified by the best aspects of the Risorgimento legacy.[45] Both in what he said, and, even more, in what Fascists said about him, Croce evinced a scorn for Fascism, a pronouncement which would not be hushed that Mussolini presided over a shallow and brittle regime.

As was noted in the introduction, it was in the immediate aftermath of Fascism that Croce joined other liberals, anxious to slough off any responsibility their ideology and class might have had for 'Auschwitz', in seeking a usable account of the Fascist era; and it was only then that he made fully plain his conclusions about the nature of the regime. Croce now explained that Fascism was a European and not a specifically Italian (or German) issue. The dictatorships, which had so vexed the history of inter-war Europe, had been the symptoms of a general 'moral sickness', which itself had been the result of the wrenching violence of the First World War. Chronologically, Fascism was thus a highly specific event. A 'parenthesis' separated it from the liberal past and, by implication, from a restored liberal

41 L. Salvatorelli, *Nazionalfascismo*, pp. 32, 41, 66–70. After 1945, Salvatorelli would join a younger anti-Fascist colleague in producing the first serious narrative history of the regime. See L. Salvatorelli and G. Mira, *Storia d'Italia nel periodo fascista* (2 vols.), Turin, 1964.

42 For a more sceptical view than is usual of the effect of this opposition, see D. Mack Smith, 'Benedetto Croce: history and politics', *Journal of Contemporary History*, 8, 1973, pp. 41–61.

43 For the background see R. De Felice, *Mussolini il fascista II. L'organizzazione dello Stato fascista 1925–1929*, Turin, 1968, p. 118.

44 The classic text is B. Croce, *Storia d'Italia dal 1871 al 1915*, Bari, 1967 (first published 1928). It rapidly appeared in English translation as B. Croce, *A History of Italy 1871–1915*, Oxford, 1929. Cf. also his *History as the story of liberty*, London, 1941 (first published in Italian 1938).

45 See e.g. G. Volpe, *L'Italia in cammino: l'ultimo cinquantennio*, Milan, 1927; *Italia moderna 1815–1914*, Florence, 1973 (first published 1943–5). In English, cf. G. Volpe, *History of the Fascist movement*, Rome, 1936.

future.[46] Socially, by contrast, Mussolini's regime was not at all specific. Fascism had not appealed to any single segment of the Italian populace, but rather could only be understood as an 'interclass' movement.[47] The moral, political and methodological implications were clear. Fascism should be condemned as tyrannous and destructive, but there was no need to be too obsessed with the condemnation, since the Fascist moment in human history had been brief and would not return. Clearing a path for such liberal successors as Renzo De Felice and Emilio Gentile, who would seek to describe Fascism 'on its own account', Croce implied haughtily that there was no reason not to write the history of Fascism on its own terms, since there were no others.

Other commentators differed. More radical elements than Croce were anxious to charge Mussolini's liberal predecessors with some responsibility for the Fascist regime. The historian Gaetano Salvemini was emphatic and untiring in his argument that Fascism was corrupt and corrupting, reflecting all that was worst in Italy.[48] Emilio Lussu, a Sardinian[49] democratic interventionist[50] who ranked the value of democracy above that of nationalism, was only one[51] to state that Fascism expressed Italy's secular ills. Fascism, he would write in 1943, 'has been the natural product of Italian political civilization, a sickness of the Italian people, born in its body and its blood'.[52] The Fascist movement may not always have been confined to a class struggle on behalf of reaction and yet, in office and to consolidate their power, the Fascists did work in the interests of the old order.[53]

Another of the very public opponents of Fascism was the socialist Pietro Nenni.[54] He had been a close friend of Mussolini in the latter's socialist days

46 Croce was even unwilling fully to denounce Italian imperialism, and used the resonant term *Diktat* to describe the peace treaty of 1947. For background, see R. J. B. Bosworth, *Italy and the wider world 1860–1960*, London, 1996, pp. 54–6; R. De Felice, *Le interpretazioni del fascismo*, pp. 29–30.

47 For further details, see B. Croce, *Scritti e discorsi politici (1943–1947)*, Bari, 1963.

48 G. Salvemini, *The Fascist dictatorship in Italy*, New York, 1927.

49 For a useful study of Sardinia in the *dopoguerra*, see S. Sechi, *Dopoguerra e fascismo in Sardegna: il movimento autonomistico nella crisi dello Stato liberale (1918–1926)*, Turin, 1969.

50 Lussu was the author of the Italian equivalent of the anti-First-World-War book of the style of *All Quiet on the Western Front* or *Goodbye to All That*. See E. Lussu, *Sardinian brigade*, New York, 1967; cf. also his witty account of the rise of Fascism, the regime which would imprison him, E. Lussu, *Enter Mussolini*, London, 1936.

51 The arch-conservative Giustino Fortunato, a Southern reformer perpetually terrified by peasant backwardness gathering ominously outside the gates of his family estate, was another convinced that Fascism did not 'come from the skies'. For an analysis see G. Amendola, *Fascismo e movimento operaio*, Rome, 1975, p. 78.

52 E. Lussu, *Essere a sinistra: democrazia, autonomia e socialismo in cinquant'anni di lotta*, Milan, 1976, p. 123.

53 M. Brigaglia, *Emilio Lussu e 'Giustizia e Libertà'*, Cagliari, 1976, p. 58.

54 For some English-language reckoning of his career, see G. Tamburrano, 'Survival in defeat: Pietro Nenni' and B. Painter, 'Historicizing Nenni', in S. M. Di Scala (ed.), *Italian socialism between politics and history*, Amherst, Mass., 1996, pp. 59–79. The depressing atmosphere of *Tangentopoli* and of the collapse of organised socialism in Italy hangs heavily over this book.

in the Romagna – Nenni recalled a meeting in gaol when the future *Duce* regretted only the absence of his violin and of his little daughter, Edda.[55] Under the Fascist regime, Nenni duly went into exile and, from a base in Paris, he, too, contemplated the meaning of Fascism.[56] Though a Marxist, he was convinced that Fascism was not simply a reactionary movement and that it had very much sprung from the world war. The real key to the movement, he argued, lay in an exasperated nationalism.[57] The special Italian sense of inferiority, in existence before 1914 and, indeed, before the Risorgimento, had deepened at Versailles, and events during that conference drove the middle class to place national grandeur above all other ambitions.[58] Thereafter, Fascism may have become 'hydra-headed' and frequently assisted the reactionary cause, but Mussolini, for one, was hard to pin down: 'In his private conversations, he endeavours to convince his former [socialist] comrades that he is quite unchanged.'[59]

Yet another political exile from Fascist Italy was the Sicilian priest and former leader of the Catholic *Partito Popolare*, Luigi Sturzo. Anxious to defend national history, Sturzo believed that the origins of inter-war tyrannies should not be sought too far back in time, even if Giolitti, he thought, had presided over a 'disguised dictatorship'.[60] Rather, Italy's worst problems sprang from the war, and, more specifically, from the dislocating effect of the Russian Revolution. Mussolini was a chameleon whose regime achieved the opposite from that which the *Duce* had first laid down for it.[61] By the onset of the Second World War, Sturzo believed that he had diagnosed a general strain of evil. The Stalin, Hitler and Mussolini regimes had a lot in common: they 'were phases of nationalistic, anti-social and totalitarian revolution that developed in Europe, after [1917]. . . . Thus it was justly said that Bolshevism was a Fascism of the Left and Fascism was a Bolshevism of the Right.'[62]

The fullest and most subtle analyses of Fascism during the inter-war period, however, were those produced by the successive leaders of the PCI, Antonio Gramsci and Palmiro Togliatti, and by the ex-Communist Angelo Tasca (he was expelled from the Party in 1929). As Fascism rose to power and consolidated itself in office, Gramsci, mixing journalism with political

55 P. Nenni, *Ten years of tyranny in Italy*, London, 1932, p. 24.
56 See P. Nenni, *Storia di quattro anni (1919–1922)* rev. ed., Turin, 1946 (first published 1926).
57 Fascists, he noted in words to be repeated by Palmiro Togliatti, regularly took over ideas from the ANI. See P. Nenni, *La battaglia socialista contro il Fascismo 1922–1944* (ed. D. Zucàro), Milan, 1977, p. 13.
58 R. De Felice, *Le interpretazioni del fascismo*, pp. 203–4.
59 P. Nenni, *Ten years of tyranny in Italy*, p. 140. Cf. also G. Matteotti, *The Fascisti exposed: a year of Fascist domination*, New York, 1969 (first published 1924), with its emphasis that the real nature of the dictatorship was displayed in its 'corruption' and in the accompanying benefits which it brought to 'the speculators and the capitalists' (p. 1).
60 L. Sturzo, *Italy and Fascismo*, London, 1926, p. 65.
61 L. Sturzo, *Italy and Fascismo*, p. 100.
62 L. Sturzo, *Italy and the new world order*, London, 1944, p. 44.

leadership, puzzled over the meaning of history as it unfolded before him. At first he, like other Marxists, saw in Fascism no more than a variety of white guard. Its proponents, he wrote scathingly, were like Kipling's 'Monkey People', a petite bourgeoisie in decline: 'After having corrupted and ruined the institution of Parliament, the petty bourgeoisie is now corrupting and ruining the other institutions as well, the pillars of the State: the army, the police, the magistrature [*sic*].'[63] These members of the lower middle class would, of course, love to build their own state, but they lacked the necessary political and intellectual rigour to achieve that end. Partly, the explanation for the outbreak of Fascist violence lay in national traditions: 'Italy is the country where mothers educate their infant children by hitting them on the head with clogs.'[64] But mostly Fascism was simply an organisation designed to repress the poor and defend the powerful. Perhaps, Gramsci began to muse, there were 'two fascisms',[65] but the more urban, petit bourgeois and radical sort was destined to lose out to the more clear-sighted, bourgeois, cynical and brutal reactionaries. In August 1921 the party power base had moved from Milan to Bologna, that is, away 'from elements like Mussolini – always uncertain, always hesitating as a result of their taste for intellectualist adventures and their irrepressible need for general ideologies', towards 'the agrarian bourgeoisie, without ideological weaknesses or uncertainties in action'.[66]

Even after Mussolini became Prime Minister, Gramsci continued to argue that Fascism was in part the servant of some version of the old order. In a moment of optimism during the Matteotti crisis, he used a Leninist metaphor to predict that Fascism was dying through its failure to deliver any rewards to the petite bourgeoisie. The PNF, Gramsci wrote, 'is still sustained by its so-called fellow-travelling forces, but it is sustained in the way that the rope supports the hanged man'.[67] However, as he worked to persuade communists to face up to the magnitude of their defeat and to refine the tactics which would ensure the eventual overthrow of the dictatorship, Gramsci, growing more pessimistic about the probable longevity of the regime, postulated that Fascism did amount to 'a mass organisation of the petty bourgeoisie'.[68] He continued to prophesy Fascism's fall, but now admitted that, a prey to the Fascist assault, the 'working class has lost all form and all organicity; it has been reduced to a disconnected, fragmented, scattered mass'.[69] The leader as well as his party remained an object of Gramsci's fascination. In 1925, he advised that the *Duce* was

63 A. Gramsci, *Selections from political writings (1910–1920)*, London, 1977, pp. 372–4.
64 A. Gramsci, *Selections from political writings (1921–1926)*, London, 1978, p. 39.
65 A. Gramsci, *Selections from political writings (1921–1926)*, pp. 63–5.
66 A. Gramsci, *Selections from political writings (1921–1926)*, p. 61.
67 A. Gramsci, *Selections from political writings (1921–1926)*, p. 258.
68 A. Gramsci, *Selections from political writings (1921–1926)*, p. 260 and cf. J. Joll, *Gramsci*, Glasgow, 1977, p. 57.
69 A. Gramsci, *Selections from political writings (1921–1926)*, p. 269.

seeking 'a Mussolinian rather than a Fascist' platform, adding that the dictator was manufacturing a 'conservative party' to prolong his tenure of power.[70]

But it was in the 'Lyons thesis' of January 1926 that Gramsci drew his ideas together. In association with Togliatti, he now urged that Fascism embodied both the old and the new. It 'fitted into the framework of traditional Italian ruling-class policies, and into capitalism's struggle against the working class', and, thus, it 'would be absurd to call this a revolution'. None the less, Fascism possessed a genuine social base – 'in the urban petty bourgeoisie, and in a new rural bourgeoisie thrown up by the transformation of rural property in certain regions (phenomena of agrarian capitalism in Emilia)'. Moreover, in its way, Fascism had seized power in 'a conquest of the State, [directed] against the old ruling strata'. It had amended the practices of Italian political life. From a system of 'agreements and compromises', it had moved to 'the project of achieving an organic unity of all the bourgeoisie's forces in a political organization under the control of a single centre, which would simultaneously direct the party, the government and the State'.[71]

Later that year Gramsci was arrested by Fascist police; he would not emerge from prison until his death was imminent in 1937. His intellect, however, was never suppressed and, recording his thoughts in his celebrated *Prison notebooks*, he engaged in a more thorough and wide-ranging analysis of Italian history than had been possible while he was still a political activist. Now he examined such long-term structural issues as the Southern question, the nature of the Risorgimento as a *rivoluzione mancata* and the creation of 'hegemony', that insidious control of commonsense which intellectuals of the regime shored up and which 'organic' and revolutionary intellectuals must seek to undermine.[72]

Even in prison and while dissenting in some degree from the Stalinist course of international communism,[73] Gramsci's mind turned to the problem of how his party could gain power in Italy. He thus remained alert to any hint that a crisis might be coming to the Fascist regime. However, such a happy moment did not eventuate and, by the 1930s, the destiny of the PCI no longer lay in Gramsci's hands, even if, after his death, his myth would prove to be of great durability and enormous saleability as far as the party was concerned.[74] Instead, it was the new Communist leader, Palmiro

70 A. Gramsci, *Selections from political writings (1921–1926)*, pp. 277–8.
71 A. Gramsci, *Selections from political writings (1921–1926)*, pp. 349–50.
72 Fascism, he thought, was a typical example of a regime which had managed to dominate commonsense. See A. Gramsci, *Selections from the Prison Notebooks*, London, 1971, p. 203.
73 For a translated account, see P. Spriano, *Antonio Gramsci and the party: the prison years*, London, 1979. Cf. P. Spriano, *I comunisti europei e Stalin*, Turin, 1983.
74 For a detailed examination of the shifts in the reading of his life and ideas, see G. Liguori, *Gramsci conteso: storia di un dibattito 1922–1996*, Rome, 1996.

Togliatti – *il professore italiano*, as Stalin called him with a hint of menace[75]
– who now sought to comprehend the ideology of the regime which ruled
Italy, and to see if he could detect when and how that regime might fall. In
Moscow in 1935, Togliatti, prompted by the onset of the Ethiopian war but
shutting his eyes to the troubles which swirled about the USSR, behaved
indeed like a good professor, offering to party cadres who had escaped from
Fascist Italy his 'lectures on Fascism',[76] disquisitions of considerable subtlety
and acuity which are still worth reading.

Togliatti began by noting that he approached the Fascists as 'adversaries'
and with the intention of improving communist tactics against them: 'Every
time the Communist Party is able to find a crack, a fissure in fascism, it must
drive a wedge into it, in order to render the situation mobile again and thus
reopen the possibilities of struggle.'[77] He also began with a definition, that
on which the Comintern had agreed: 'The most complete definition of
fascism was given by the thirteenth meeting of the Enlarged Executive of the
Communist International and is as follows: "Fascism is the open terrorist
dictatorship of the most reactionary, most chauvinistic, most imperialist
elements of finance capital" '.[78] Having so effusively endorsed the party line,
Togliatti spent much of his lectures demonstrating that it was inadequate
and simplistic. One of the problems confronting communists as they sought
best to resist Fascism, he explained, was precisely the eclectic and
'chameleon' nature of Mussolini's regime. Rather than being the creature of
the banks and stock market, it should be understood as a soldering together
of diverse and potentially opposed factions, and especially of the wealthy
bourgeoisie and the lower middle class.[79] Similarly, it was a mistake to see
the regime's history as too predestined. What actually happened could
scarcely have been predicted when Fascism was first formed.[80] Indeed, at
Fascism's foundation it had not been at all clear with which social and
economic forces it would work. In practice, after 1922, it was the
Nationalists of the ex-ANI who became the crucial influence in Italy's
domestic and international behaviour: 'In every stage [since 1919], a
struggle has been waged between Fascists and Nationalists to solve the
fundamental problems of the state and of the party. The substance of the
solution to these problems has always come from the Nationalist party.'[81] In
office, Fascism had seen most of its radical edge blunted so that, by the

---

75 G. Cerreti, *Con Togliatti e Thorez: quarant'anni di lotte politiche*, Milan, 1973, p. 36.
76 P. Togliatti, *Lectures on Fascism*, London, 1976. These lectures were republished in Italy,
    under the editorship of Ernesto Ragionieri in 1969. For a later analysis of the Togliatti line,
    see R. De Felice, *Le interpretazioni del fascismo*, pp. 212–17. De Felice hails Togliatti's
    relative 'realism and lack of prejudice' (p. 215).
77 P. Togliatti, *Lectures on Fascism*, pp. 4, 20.
78 P. Togliatti, *Lectures on Fascism*, p. 1.
79 P. Togliatti, *Lectures on Fascism*, pp. 9–10.
80 P. Togliatti, *Lectures on Fascism*, p. 14.
81 P. Togliatti, *Lectures on Fascism*, p. 36.

1930s, German fascism seemed to possess a more openly 'rebellious' and activist character than did the Italian version.[82]

For all his emphasis on the manipulative side of Fascism – in one lecture he defined it as a sort of replacement for Freemasonry which, in Liberal Italy, had once acted as the 'united political organisation' of the bourgeoisie[83] – Togliatti also implied that, by the mid-1930s, it retained some sort of mass base. Fascist trade unions, he argued, should not be written off as a mere bosses' conspiracy. Rather, they offered opportunity for an alert party cadre to convert the confused democracy of Fascism into the more genuine democracy of communism. The same could be said of the *dopolavoro* and other mass leisure organisations.[84] In Togliatti's not altogether unpredictable analysis, Fascism might yet be inching Italy towards a real, and thus communist, revolution.

Rather different were the views of Angelo Tasca, who in 1938, under the pseudonym of A. Rossi, published in French an account of the Fascist acquisition of power. It was rapidly translated into English as *The Rise of Italian Fascism*[85] and has remained one of the key accounts of the Fascist phenomenon, if only because Tasca's comment that before Fascism could be understood its history must be written was taken up by Renzo De Felice, right at the beginning of his career, to provide the most basic justification of his neo-Rankeanism.[86] Indeed, according to De Felice, Tasca's book represented the moment at which the study of Fascism, previously riding on a sea of ideological bias and confusion, reached 'the shore-line of real history'.[87] What, then, did Tasca have to say?

Being a dissident of the Left,[88] Tasca devoted quite a lot of his attention to recounting the mistakes of his ex-comrades in dealing with the rise of Fascism. As De Felice was not unnaturally swift to discern, Tasca argued that any model of Fascism lacked conviction unless it took into account the

---

82 P. Togliatti, *Lectures on Fascism*, pp. 56–7.
83 P. Togliatti, *Lectures on Fascism*, p. 31.
84 P. Togliatti, *Lectures on Fascism*, pp. 59–64, 75. Togliatti joked that the *dopolavoro* of Trieste had organised for itself a visit to Odessa, Eisensteinian cradle of the revolution, even if the returning Fascists were gaoled once they got back to Italy (p. 85). Cf. the moving autobiography of a young and very upper-class communist who did well as a boxer in Fascist youth clubs: G. Amendola, *Una scelta di vita*, Milan, 1976, and his more theoretical account, G. Amendola, *Fascismo e movimento operaio*, p. 90.
85 A. Tasca, *The rise of Italian Fascism 1918–1922*, New York, 1966. In Italian, the book appeared after the fall of Fascism as A. Tasca, *Nascita e avvento del fascismo* (2 vols.), Bari, 1965 (first published in Florence, 1950). The 1965 edition has a preface by R. De Felice, the English-language edition one from S. H. Finer, himself the author of *Mussolini's Italy*, London, 1935, a critical account of the regime on its invasion of Ethiopia, which appeared with the Left Book Club.
86 R. De Felice, *Mussolini il rivoluzionario*, Turin, 1965, p. xxii. He repeated the phrase more knowingly in R. De Felice, *Le interpretazioni del fascismo*, p. 220.
87 R. De Felice, *Le interpretazioni del fascismo*, p. 219.
88 In 1940 Tasca, a French citizen, made his position more troubling by working for the Vichy press office. This dereliction was not forgotten by loyal members of the PCI. See P. Spriano, *Storia del Partito comunista italiano IV. La fine del Fascismo. Dalla riscossa operaia alla lotta armata*, Turin, 1973, p. 33.

influence on national history of the failings, divisions and delusions of the socialist movement.[89] Mussolini, Tasca believed, was still a kind of revolutionary in 1919–20.[90] Even in Ferrara, Fascism, for all its backing by the wealthy and by urban dwellers, drew popular sympathy and favour with its slogan: 'The land for those who work it.'[91] Moreover, as late as August 1922, the victory of Fascism was not certain and the movement not united; at that time, although its membership was certainly growing, Fascism still constituted little more than a fluid 'army of occupation' of certain parts of the peninsula.[92] Mussolini, too, was a key influence, though opportunism and adroit tactics were his greatest skills.[93] Fascism could scarcely be understood without him. Tasca agreed with more orthodox Marxist accounts that, in office, Fascism turned reactionary,[94] but that result was neither automatic nor necessary, and the multiple currents which had flown into early Fascism were never eliminated from Mussolini's regime.

At the moment of its fall, then, explanations of Fascism seemed to cluster around two major poles. Marxists, with varying degrees of subtlety, urged that, in the final analysis, it was a reactionary movement which 'saved' the bourgeoisie from social democracy. None the less, such commentators frequently admitted, Fascism did possess some sort of mass base, notably among the petite bourgeoisie of both city and countryside, enhanced in number and ideologically stiffened by those who had recently experienced war. In many ways, too, Fascism reflected the survival of long-standing national domestic and international problems, summed up in Gramsci's phrase about the Risorgimento as *rivoluzione mancata*. Mussolini's regime was thus to a considerable degree the 'revelation' of Italian history. In turn this connection with the underlying structures of national life implied that, though defeated in war by 1945, Fascism had not necessarily been excised from the Italian soul. Some version of it might return if, for example, the bourgeoisie again felt as threatened socially and economically[95] as they had been in 1919–21. In that sense Fascism could be imagined without Mussolini.

Liberals disagreed with this interpretation on many points. In their eyes, there was nothing wrong with Liberal Italy; it was a 'democracy in the

89 See e.g. P. Spriano, *Storia del Partito comunista italiano IV*, p. 220 and cf. A. Tasca, *The rise of Italian Fascism 1918–1922*, pp. 16–17. Similarly emphatic about the inadequacies of the Italian socialist movement was the liberal Federico Chabod, better known for his work on foreign policy (see Chapter 4), but also the author of a translated history of Fascism. See F. Chabod, *A history of Italian Fascism*, London, 1963, p. 32.
90 A. Tasca, *The rise of Italian Fascism 1918–1922*, pp. 31, 40–1.
91 A. Tasca, *The rise of Italian Fascism 1918–1922*, pp. 101–2.
92 A. Tasca, *The rise of Italian Fascism 1918–1922*, pp. 245–7.
93 Again Chabod agreed. See F. Chabod, *A history of Italian Fascism*, p. 48. He also argued that, even while being dependent on violence, the regime did win considerable 'consent', at least until the onset of the Second World War (p. 70).
94 F. Chabod, *A history of Italian Fascism*, pp. 342–3.
95 See e.g. the early post-war account of the alleged relationship between industry and Fascism, E. Rossi, *Padroni del vapore e fascismo*, Bari, 1966 (first published 1955).

making',[96] and the Risorgimento had been, on balance, a positive event. Fascism was not deeply rooted, but was occasioned by the First World War and by the series of rather unexpected events which followed that terrible conflict, quite a lot of them occasioned by the foolish 'revolutionism' of maximalist socialists and other deluded admirers of the Russian Revolution. The Fascist support base could not be differentiated by class, though the movement did appeal to youth and to those who had learned their violence in war. Mussolini was a central if ambiguous figure, since his rallying to the old order also seemed to have had much that was contingent about it and to have been regularly contradicted by a lingering Fascist enthusiasm, which the *Duce* himself never overcame, for some sort of revolution.

It was soon plain, however, that these two interpretations did not exhaust the subject. The occasional post-war Fascist still wrote in defence of the regime, usually with the arguments that it stood for a revolution and a third way between liberal capitalism and Soviet socialism, and that it had strenuously defended the national cause in a Social-Darwinian world.[97] In Italy itself, members of the MSI and its flanking and generally more revolutionary youth groups still talked as though Fascism had indeed offered one of the ideologies of the twentieth century. However, they made few converts outside the extreme right. The most powerful interpretation of Fascism, given extra force in a world subject to the Cold War, was located in the so-called model of totalitarianism.[98]

The word 'totalitarian' has a history which is not at all dissimilar to that of fascism. It was coined in Italy, initially by the Left as a complaint about Mussolini's tyranny, only to be swiftly taken up by the regime as a boast. The Fascist 'totalitarian state', it was said, was more powerful, more 'modern', more 'totally total', than any of its predecessors.[99] The grand sound of the term 'totalitarian' and its somewhat opaque meaning gave it a complex history in the 1930s, when its usage ranged widely indeed. General

---

96 See the liberal-democrat, Italo-American account (with a preface by Gaetano Salvemini), A. W. Salomone, *Italy in the Giolittian era: Italian democracy in the making, 1900–1914*, Philadelphia, 1945 and cf. A. W. Salomone, *Italy from the Risorgimento to Fascism: an inquiry into the origins of the totalitarian state*, New York, 1970. For a more recent example of Italo-American piety about the post-Risorgimento state, see R. S. Cunsolo, *Italian nationalism from its origins to World War II*, Malabar, Fla., 1990.

97 In English the only available example is L. Villari, *The liberation of Italy 1943–1947*, Appleton, Wisc., 1959 which has special focus on the limitations of the Resistance and the virtue of the Salò Republic. Villari was a regular propagandist for the regime from a background in Nationalism. See e.g. L. Villari, *The Fascist experiment*, London, 1926. In Italian Pino Rauti remained the most determined to defend and adapt Fascism as a revolutionary ideology allegedly able to grant continuing insights into society. For the development of his ideas see G. Rauti, *Le idee che mossero il mondo*, Rome, 1965; *L'immane conflitto: Mussolini, Roosevelt, Stalin, Churchill, Hitler*, Rome, 1966; P. Rauti and R. Sermonti, *Storia del fascismo* (5 vols.), Rome, 1976–7.

98 For further discussion see Chapter 9.

99 For an account see especially A. Aquarone, *L'organizzazione dello stato totalitario*, Turin, 1965. Some sense of his work can be gained in English from A. Aquarone, 'Italy: the crisis and the corporative economy', *Journal of Contemporary History*, 4, 1969, pp. 37–58.

Ioannis Metaxas, who became a kind of dictator of Greece in 1936, thought
that the claim that he was building a totalitarian regime gave him cachet.[100]
The Nazis in Germany, by contrast, did not adopt the word to describe
themselves. Indeed, the term was most frequently deployed by critics of the
politics of the period, especially those who wished to separate themselves
simultaneously from Stalin's USSR and from fascism – in other words, by an
array of social democrats, liberals and conservatives, and even by anarchists
and dissident communists.[101] Matters were further complicated by a
substratum of Italian Fascists who thought that Stalin might indeed be
pursuing policies which were akin to Mussolini's, this alleged association, of
course, being viewed as a positive.[102] By the end of the 1930s, especially for
those to whom the Ribbentrop–Molotov Pact seemed more than a piece of
Realpolitik, the word was reinforced in meaning and became a crucial
factor in the semantic armoury of those conservatives who, with whatever
doubt and delay, had finally rejected Nazism and decided to oppose it.[103]

With the onset of the Cold War this drift was confirmed. Now,
totalitarianism became the key explanatory and justificatory device of the
American or 'Western' side in the conflict with the USSR. In the Second
World War, all good men and women had come to the aid of the anti-fascist
cause; communists, liberals, social democrats and conservatives had striven
shoulder to shoulder as friends, allies and victors against the Nazi–fascist
evil, and the virtue of this cause was confirmed by the revelations about
genocide. Wartime unanimity evaporated, however, at or before victory. The
new conflict, the 'Cold War', could be converted into another just war if a
device could be found to link the present enemy, communism, with that of
the recent past, Nazi–fascism. And that was precisely what the word
'totalitarianism' did. In 1956, the year of the twentieth Soviet party congress
and the invasion of Hungary, two emigré American political scientists, Carl

100 S. G. Payne, *A history of fascism, 1914–1945*, Madison, Wisc., 1995, p. 319. Metaxas
    also adopted the 'Roman salute', but insisted that it was 'Greek'. M. Cervi, *The hollow
    legions: Mussolini's blunder in Greece*, New York, 1971, p. 1.
101 For some examples, see the word's usage by historian I. Deutscher, who defined himself as
    'one whom Stalin cruelly defeated'. For the background, see R. J. B. Bosworth, *Explaining
    Auschwitz and Hiroshima: history writing and the Second World War 1945–1990*
    London, 1993, pp. 155–8.
102 In English the only relevant study is the simplistic J. C. Clarke III, *Russia and Italy against
    Hitler: the Bolshevik–Fascist rapprochement of the 1930s*, Westport, Conn., 1991. In
    Italian, see e.g. the ISPI publication, L. Cappuccio, *U.R.S.S.: precedenti storici,
    organizzazione interna, politica estera*, Milan, 1940. Mussolini himself also wondered
    whether or not Stalin, despite his 'semi-barbarous' Georgian background, might have
    fascist tendencies and, for a while, imagined the same was possible of F. D. Roosevelt. See
    B. Mussolini, *Opera omnia* (ed. E. and D. Susmel), Florence, 1958–9, xxvi, p. 10 (article
    in *Il Popolo d'Italia*, 28 June 1933, on FDR); xxix, pp. 61–4 (article in *Il Popolo d'Italia*,
    6 March 1938, on Stalin and the purges). For more recent commentary, see R.
    Quartararo, 'Roma e Mosca: l'immagine dell'Urss nella stampa fascista (1925–1939)',
    Storia contemporanea, 27, 1996, pp. 447–72.
103 A classic example is the Danzig conservative Hermann Rauschning: see his evocatively
    entitled *The beast from the abyss*, London, 1941.

Friedrich and Zbigniew Brzezinski, picking up the rather m‹ earlier work of Hannah Arendt and Jacob Talmon, crafted totalitarianism which, even today, continues to win acceptance.[104]

In their analysis, and that of others, Italy was generally assigned a minor role. Hannah Arendt, for example, had concluded, not altogether convincingly, that 'Mussolini's Fascism . . . up to 1938 was not totalitarian but just an ordinary nationalist dictatorship developed logically from a multi-party democracy.'[105] By contrast, Jacob Talmon, in his efforts to trace the sinfulness of humankind back to the French Revolution and the Enlightenment – ironically, his thesis bore some comparison with the ideas of Mussolini and Giovanni Gentile about the need to overcome the legacy of 1789 – made frequent reference to Italy. Italian Jacobins like Filippo Buonarroti joined Rousseau and Robespierre as the arch-sinners of the revolutionary era.[106] According to Talmon, later in the nineteenth century Mazzini was a special carrier of the ills of 'political messianism'.[107] Mazzini's malevolent legacy was passed on to Mussolini who, learning as well from Le Bon, Pareto and other new intellectuals of the *belle époque*, journeyed from a socialism of violence to Fascism, and thus from 'social messianism to imperialism'.[108] However, Talmon had progressed slowly in his totalitarianist history of European ideas and, by the time his writing reached Mussolini, the argument was neither fresh nor original.

Back in the 1950s, Friedrich and Brzezinski had made only scattered reference to Fascist Italy; the character of that regime was not nearly so influential in their model as was that which they thought they saw in Nazi Germany and the Soviet Union. At a visceral level, Nazism and Soviet communism had seemed to them to embody evil. Fascism, by contrast, was only a bit-player in the story of human wickedness. In their account, Italy thus usually turned up as a sort of aside. They did, for example, contend that the Italian regime, like its totalitarian fellows, maintained 'a conscious stress on myth', but they were scarcely convincing when they tried to illuminate Fascist foreign policy with the comment: 'The love all Italians feel so passionately for their country was projected in terms of conquest and imperial violence, which were sanctified by the memories of a historical past.'[109]

In footnotes, the two authors made plain their debt to a young Italo-American Harvard Ph.D. student, Dante Germino, on whose knowledge of

---

104 C. J. Friedrich and Z. K. Brzezinski, *Totalitarian dictatorship and autocracy*, Cambridge, Mass., 1956. For further comment see R. J. B. Bosworth, *Explaining Auschwitz and Hiroshima*, pp. 21–5 and cf. Chapter 9 below.
105 H. Arendt, *The origins of totalitarianism*, Cleveland, OH, 1958, p. 257.
106 J. L. Talmon, *The origins of totalitarian democracy*, London, 1952.
107 J. L. Talmon, *Political messianism: the romantic phase*, London, 1960.
108 J. L. Talmon, *The myth of the nation and the vision of revolution*, London, 1980, p. 493. This third in Talmon's trilogy was published posthumously.
109 C. J. Friedrich and Z. K. Brzezinski, *Totalitarian dictatorship and autocracy*, p. 101.

Mussolini's regime they frequently drew.[110] Three years later Germino published his own account of 'totalitarian rule' in Italy.[111] A decade afterwards, however, Germino's work had been largely discounted, especially when, during the thaw of the 1960s, the model of totalitarianism lost academic ground on most fronts. None the less, Germino's theories have recently been revived by Emilio Gentile, who views them as a significant early reading of the nature of the Fascist regime.[112]

Germino wrote as a junior political scientist, politely anxious to celebrate the work of his mentors, Friedrich and Brzezinski. His methodology, in essence, was to take their seven-part totalitarian model (charismatic leader, single party, all-embracing ideology, control over communications and weapons, terror, anti-capitalism and foreign aggression) and apply it to Italy. In Germino's explanation, Mussolini's regime was new, though the real novelty had commenced in Petrograd in 1917.[113] Mussolini, 'an unscrupulous fanatic with a flair for propaganda, organization, political strategy, and mass agitation', was 'content with nothing less than the perpetual expansion of his own system of political faith'.[114] He was aided by 'the indispensable party',[115] which, with the police, aimed 'to create conditions under which revolt would not even be thought of'.[116] The *dopolavoro* and other such structures assisted the regime to control the personal life of the populace and to build 'a new ethic, a Mussolinian and Fascist ethic', especially among the young.[117] The regime was aggressive in its foreign policy, and Mussolini's 'totalitarian temperament' was exhibited in his decision to join the Nazis in war.[118] All in all,

> Italian Fascism was neither a comic opera nor a South American palace revolution. It was a political religion, equipped with the machinery necessary to realize its program. During its twenty-odd years of existence the Italian Fascist dictatorship developed relentlessly toward the totalitarian pattern. The twilight shadows of late Italian Fascism were inexorably deepening into totalitarian night.[119]

Germino thus concluded with a two-way bet. Fascism, he admitted, did present some inconsistencies if read as a fully blown totalitarian society, but such problems could be set aside since, he was sure, Fascism by 1936 was on

---

110 C. J. Friedrich and Z. K. Brzezinski, *Totalitarian dictatorship and autocracy*, p. 320.
111 D. L. Germino, *The Italian Fascist party in power: a study in totalitarian rule*, New York, 1971 (first published Minneapolis, 1959).
112 E. Gentile, *La via italiana al totalitarismo: il partito e lo stato nel regime fascista*, Rome, 1995, pp. 65–9.
113 D. L. Germino, *The Italian Fascist party in power*, p. 6.
114 D. L. Germino, *The Italian Fascist party in power*, pp. 5–7.
115 D. L. Germino, *The Italian Fascist party in power*, pp. 18–31.
116 D. L. Germino, *The Italian Fascist party in power*, p. 20.
117 D. L. Germino, *The Italian Fascist party in power*, pp. 41–2, 70.
118 D. L. Germino, *The Italian Fascist party in power*, pp. 30–1.
119 D. L. Germino, *The Italian Fascist party in power*, p. 144.

a track which led to complete totalitarianism and the German or Soviet model. If 'Hitler' had not lost the Second World War, totally total totalitarianism, it seemed, might eventually have arrived in Rome, too.

Such a willingness to predict a future which did not happen was a little rash on Germino's part, and it is hard not to conclude that his book, despite its occasional moments of insight, is both shallow and implausible. As he is not a historian, it is no surprise to find that his model is scarcely backed by a mass of historical detail. In any event, the end of the 1950s would signal the passing of what might be called the pre-historiography of Italian Fascism. From the 1960s, the opening of archives and a changed political and social atmosphere would stimulate a vast amount of professional 'academic' history writing about the Fascist era. Italy was not unique in this timing. Indeed, the new decade would commence with a whole series of books (A. J. P. Taylor's *The Origins of the Second World War*, Fritz Fischer's *Griff nach der Weltmacht*, E. H. Carr's *What is History?* to name but three) and events (the election of President John Kennedy, the trial of Adolf Eichmann, the holding of the Second Vatican Council, the defeat of Tambroni and the commencement of the 'Opening to the Left' in Italy) which seemed to presage a new present, a new future and a new past. The silence, or, to be more accurate, the populist and conservative readings of the horrors of 'Auschwitz' now seemed to have been overborne by a renewed desire to obtain a more profound and detailed appraisal of the meaning of the 'long' Second World War, and a deeper judgement about responsibility for it. In the pages that follow I shall explore the extent to which a satisfactory historical reckoning with that war and its explanation was reached in Italy but, before I do, it is necessary to pick up two of the major themes of the model of totalitarianism and review them in detail in their Italian setting. Was Mussolini indeed a charismatic dictator, and how has his charisma been successively understood? What, too, of his foreign policy? Was his Fascist regime hell-bent on war? Or did it, in this and in other policy areas, remain as much an Italian dictatorship as a Fascist, let alone a 'totalitarian', one?

|3|

Mussolini the Duce: Sawdust Caesar, Roman Statesman or Dictator Minor?

A Chief is everything in the life of a man: beginning and end, justification and scope, starting point and finishing line. If the Chief falls, then it creates a terrible solitude inside a man. I want to re-find my Chief, to put him back at the centre of my world, to re-order this my world around him. But I am afraid, terribly afraid, that I shan't succeed in doing this again.[1]

So a supposedly intelligent and independent[2] Fascist minister, Giuseppe Bottai, confessed to his diary in January 1941, when the inadequacies of Fascism became impossible for him to deny. Despite his experience of 19 years in power, and his realisation that the regime was wearing down and displaying more and more frequently a gap between its theory and its practice, Bottai clung to a religious awe in approaching his *Duce*. In his eyes at least, Mussolini had a lustre not possessed by other men.

Understanding charisma, and at the same time being able to appraise it critically, is not an easy task for a present-day historian. In most fields covered by our discipline, the 'Great Man' approach to history is well out of favour, and sentiments like those of Bottai are dismissed with cynicism and

---

1 G. Bottai, *Diario 1935–1944*, ed. G.B. Guerri, Milan, 1982, p. 247.
2 It is the De Felice school of historians who are particularly inclined to take Bottai seriously as a political figure and to overlook such troubling matters as his involvement in the racial campaign after 1938. De Felice himself, for example, maintained that Bottai, a figure of 'totalitarian intransigence', expressed, after Mussolini, 'intrinsically and genuinely the substance of real Fascism'. See R. De Felice, *Mussolini il duce II. Lo stato totalitario 1936–1940*, Turin, 1981, p. 145. A reading of Bottai's jejune diary as a post-war member of the French Foreign Legion, however, might suggest that his mind lacked intellectual and ethical originality and profundity. See G. Bottai, *Quaderno affricano*, Florence, 1995; cf. also G. Bottai, *Diario 1944–1948*, ed. G.B. Guerri, Milan, 1988 and G. Bottai and G. De Luca, *Carteggio 1940–1957*, ed. R. De Felice and R. Moro, Rome, 1989. The distinction of Bottai's son Bruno, who rose to become Secretary General of the Italian Ministry of Foreign Affairs (1987–1994), may also have helped to revive Giuseppe Bottai's reputation. See further the very filial B. Bottai, *Fascismo familiare*, Casale Monferrato, 1997.

incredulity. To some extent, however, the history of Fascism and, more generally, that of twentieth-century European politics, is an exception to the above rule. Here, Great Men in their pomp frequently survive. As has been noted in earlier chapters, 'intentionalism' is a powerful, arguably the most powerful and certainly the most pervasive, current interpretation of 'Hitler's Germany' and 'Stalin's Russia'. Similarly, the phrase 'Mussolini's Italy' still signals, in many minds, the best, almost the automatic, way to approach the history of Fascism. As with love and marriage in the old song, dictator and his dictatorship seem to go together like a horse and carriage, and it is pointless and even silly to try to separate them.

The words 'Mussolini's Italy', none the less, have different resonances from those which sum up the German and Soviet tyrannies. 'Mussolini', certainly in the popular mind outside Italy, conjures up the image of a failed dictator, at least in contrast with Hitler and Stalin. They ruled by terror and their careers are still contemplated with an almost salacious fear; they were the worst and the most dread that human history can record.[3] Mussolini's image is instead the more traditional one of the dictator with limited ability to dictate, of a politician devoted as much to speechifying as to conquest, and thus of a man whose self-importance outweighed his actual importance: a latter-day Caesar, impressive for a time perhaps, but whose empire was composed more of sawdust[4] than of marble. In this conventional reading, the *Duce* is reduced to a personage who embodied the truism that Italian history is best typified as a chronicle of the least of the Great Powers, a topic about which to laugh rather than to cry (or to salivate).[5]

In the rest of this chapter I shall try to separate these interpretations of Mussolini as a Roman statesman, as the least of the dictators, and as just a

3 Worthy of exploration in this regard is the comic strip image of the SS as a sado-masochistic organisation, populated by semi-naked blondes, men and women with whips, thigh-high leather boots and nothing else. Just occasionally such an image is transferred also to communism, even if usually in a decidedly muted form (see e.g. early James Bond movies). Hardly anyone outside Italy has thought of Fascism as a serious competitor in deviant sexual allure. For further comment in relation to film representation in this regard, see below in Chapter 7.
4 For the origins of this image see the very successful book by the radical American journalist George Seldes, which came out during the Ethiopian war (it was reprinted four times between January and April 1936, and a further three times in 1937–8 in a cheap edition). G. Seldes, *Sawdust Caesar: the untold history of Mussolini and Fascism*, London, 1936. Seldes had been expelled from Italy in 1925 for allegedly tendentious reporting of the Matteotti murder. He had then begun writing *Sawdust Caesar*, but was unable to get a publisher either in the US or the UK until Mussolini became a *cause célèbre* during the Ethiopian war. See J. P. Diggins, *Mussolini and Fascism: the view from America*, Princeton, 1972, pp. 53–5.
5 For my own exploration of some of these 'unspoken assumptions', see R. J. B. Bosworth, 'Mito e linguaggio nella politica estera italiana' in R. J. B. Bosworth and S. Romano (eds), *La politica estera italiana 1860–1985*, Bologna, 1991. It is perhaps characteristic that a (British) crime writer has introduced the character 'Benito Mussolini' into one of his stories set in Italy (the plot involves a sort of *Lega Jesolo*, bent on independence for their community). This Mussolini is a photographer, blackmailer and murder victim, who owns a monkey which is smarter than he is. See T. Holme, *The devil and the dolce vita*, New York, 1982.

hollow tyrant. I shall do so both in regard to Italy and to the world outside, especially the English-speaking one. My major focus will be on the *Duce*'s image during his regime, but the chapter will conclude with some comments on biographical work since 1945.

With regard to the Mussolini imagined until the onset of the Second World War, my path has been charted by a fine book, Luisa Passerini's *Mussolini immaginario*, which, as her subtitle explains, is the 'history of a biography'.[6] The first such account of the later dictator, Passerini explains, was that written in 1915 by Torquato Nanni, a fellow Romagnole, interventionist socialist and old friend.[7] Nanni's version presented Mussolini in romantic vein, as a domineering force of nature:

> Thirty-two years. A soul of steel serving a formidable will.
> Here is Benito Mussolini. . . .
>
> Benito Mussolini has a physical horror of easy options. He never lounges about, savouring and digesting a long lunch.[8]

The meaning of these words, the sentence structure, the paragraphing, all urged that Mussolini was a *Duce*, a leader; they fashioned a man who had sprung from the people and who incarnated its *virtù*. This superman of steel was also quintessentially modern. He embodied a new Italy being forged in the cauldron of the Great War – Mussolini, in his own first autobiographical writings as a soldier wounded in the epic conflict, similarly celebrated the nationalisation of his own self and of the masses. His diary entry of 18 April 1916, Passerini tells us, celebrated the way in which 'this war is the great crucible in which all Italians are mixed and fused. Regionalism is no more.'[9] In sum, well before Fascism was invented the young Mussolini was already constructing himself, and being constructed by others, as a chief, or *Duce*, and as a new and dynamic type of leader through whom, somehow, the spirit of the masses throbbed.

It is a pity that the spotlight of such research so strictly plays on Mussolini himself. How many other mute, forgotten *duci*, it might be wondered, were engaged in similar exercises in image manufacture?[10] What, too, of those rival segments of Italian society anxious to mythologise themselves and their chiefs? After all, Italy remained the home of the Vatican, to many the quintessence of pomp and circumstance. Before having

---

6 L. Passerini, *Mussolini immaginario: storia di una biografia, 1915–1939*, Bari, 1991.
7 In regard to Nanni's early contact with Mussolini, see R. De Felice, *Mussolini il rivoluzionario 1883–1920*, Turin, 1965, pp. 62–4, 81–3.
8 Quoted by L. Passerini, *Mussolini immaginario*, p. 33.
9 Quoted by L. Passerini, *Mussolini immaginario*, p. 24.
10 In his wonderfully funny post-1945 novel Vitaliano Brancati implied that *gallismo* (cockism) made every boy a (fake) *duce*, and Carlo Emilio Gadda argued much the same in his extraordinary study of Eros and Priapus. V. Brancati, *Bell'Antonio*, London, 1993 (first published in Italian, 1949); C. E. Gadda, *Eros e Priapo (da furore a cenere)*, Milan, 1967. For a fuller discussion, see Chapter 7.

a full appraisal of the imagined Mussolini, do we not need to know more about twentieth-century techniques of marketing the Papacy, and of inventing traditions which might be needed to justify contemporary change in that institution and its social and religious role? At the same time, should we not seek better to understand how the myth of the Papacy in all its intricacy was translated and absorbed by the popular mind?

What, too, of the monarchy?[11] Doubtless the Savoy dynasty was a poor thing and arguably not Italy's own, but attempts were made to fasten charisma even to such unlikely princelings as members of that royal house, to insinuate King Victor Emmanuel III, Queen Elena, Crown-Prince Umberto and the rest into Italian hearts, and we need to understand more about that process and its presumed limitations. More successful dynasties, such as the British, were early in the field in adapting their image to the new era. How was this adaptation done? Was there a major distinction between the making of the imagined Prince of Wales in the 1920s, for example, and the construction of the image of a dictator? Or were both, already as it were, *flaneurs* on Madison Avenue, borrowing for their own little politics the much more powerful and pervasive skills and techniques of capitalist consumerism?

Sports stars, film stars, the other icons of twentieth-century 'popular' culture, similarly deserve analysis. In her account of the imagined Mussolini, Passerini seems near to accepting the view of Emilio Gentile that Fascism brought mythical thought to power. But Gentile does not recognise that 'mythical thought' was coming to power and influence all over the place in the twentieth century and not only in Fascist Italy. The advertising industry would find it easier to conquer the world than would those self-consciously 'new intellectuals', anxious to find a rewarded place in their nationalised societies, whose phrases recent historians treat with such reverence.

None the less, the tracing of the varieties of imagined Mussolinis remains an instructive task. It was predictable that the move of the Fascists into government in Rome should touch off a rash of fresh accounts of the life of the new Prime Minister. These biographies of the early 1920s – the bestseller, especially in translation abroad, was that written by Mussolini's Jewish sometime mistress[12] Margherita Sarfatti[13] – tended to inscribe the

---

11 In this regard the study by Denis Mack Smith of the successive Italian kings is particularly disappointing. D. Mack Smith, *Italy and its monarchy*, New Haven, 1989. Mack Smith's failure to approach the issue of the marketing of monarchs perhaps reflects a certain monarchism on his own part which led him, at least in the Italian press, to defend the cause of Princess Diana, even while he was being decidedly critical of the Savoys. See e.g. P. Filo Della Torre, 'Dio salvi il re anche divorziato', *L'Espresso*, 38, 29 November 1992.

12 The English version is M. Sarfatti, *The life of Benito Mussolini* (with a preface by Benito Mussolini), London, 1925.

13 An English-language biography of her is now available (though a sceptical reader might think that it is naïve in its estimation of Sarfatti's character and of her influence in Fascist Italy). See P. V. Cannistraro and B. R. Sullivan, *Il Duce's other woman*, New York, 1993.

dictator as the greatest of the great in Italy[14] or the world. They also moderated some aspects of his earlier image. Mussolini still stood for the masses, and thus for equality, liberty and individuality; but, in what now became the most common interpretation, he, the medium of the mass age, had mysteriously harnessed these aspects of the times, and his harnessing implied that democratic or mass forces were under control in so far as the nation of Italy (or its ruling elites) were concerned. In other words, Mussolini was now depicted at one and the same time as the 'new man and as a man alone'.[15]

In somewhat different key, Passerini notes in the biographies published after 1922 a rise in the significance of Rosa Maltoni, the *Duce*'s elementary-schoolteaching and conventionally pious mother. For all his flaunted virility, Passerini says, Mussolini was being written as a male leader who mysteriously carried within himself the best of Italian woman.[16] Just as he acted as a conducting rod for the masses yet warded off real democracy, so, embodying the hopes of women, he could avert any need to amend the national gender order.

The growing emphasis on the *Duce*'s uniqueness also caused the new biographies to exaggerate the poverty of Mussolini's background. As the young *Duce* grew to manhood in the foothills of the Romagnole Apennines, so Sarfatti for one assured her readers, father instructed son. Such instruction was necessary, since life there 'was apt to be a hard and pitiless master'.[17] In fact, there are many reasons to question this sentimental picture. Alessandro, Mussolini's socialist father, may have been a radical,[18] but he also came from a family of small landholders, and on occasion seems to have been addressed by the local peasantry as *signor padrone*. His wife employed some domestic help, especially after she received a legacy from a relative.[19] Mussolini may have been a provincial, and ill at ease for a time in

14 It would take a few years before the word *Duce* would oust *Presidente* as the customary form of address and reference to the leader of the Fascist state, and such old companions as Italo Balbo, advising Mussolini of their seniority and hinting at their lingering independence, would never adopt the newer term. G. B. Guerri, *Italo Balbo*, Milan, 1984, p. 95. This usage did, however, occur elsewhere, for example within the Mussolini household or among journalist 'colleagues'. See e.g. G. Pini, *Filo diretto con Palazzo Venezia*, Milan, 1967, p. 10; R. Zangrandi, *Il lungo viaggio attraverso il fascismo*, Milan, 1964, p. 19. According to one source, bureaucrats were accustomed to call Mussolini 'Eccellenza' in the same way that they had pre-Fascist politicians. See Q. Navarra, *Memorie del cameriere di Mussolini*, Milan, 1946, p. 53. Perhaps the best story about finding the right address for Mussolini is that which says that his wife, Rachele, called him *'professore'* (a title earned through his qualifications to teach primary-school French) until after the birth of their fourth child. See R. Mussolini, *The real Mussolini*, Farnborough, 1973, p. 66.
15 L. Passerini, *Mussolini immaginario*, p. 56.
16 L. Passerini, *Mussolini immaginario*, pp. 48–50.
17 M. Sarfatti, *Life of Benito Mussolini*, p. 32.
18 Mussolini was born on 29 July 1883 at Dovia near Predappio in the Romagna. He was named Benito Amilcare Andrea in homage to Juarez, Cipriani and Costa. For more detail, see R. De Felice, *Mussolini il rivoluzionario*, pp. 3–9.
19 D. Mack Smith, *Mussolini*, London, 1981, pp. 11–12; E. Mussolini, *Mio fratello Benito: memorie raccolte e trascritte da Rosetta Ricci Crisolini*, Florence, 1957, p. 16.

the great worlds of Milan and Rome; but, certainly compared with Stalin[20] and perhaps with Hitler,[21] by contemporary local standards he was relatively well off. Of perhaps greater importance psychologically, the Mussolinis claimed a relatively distinguished past in the social fabric of the region around Predappio. In this family history, Benito became the figure who would restore a lost eminence, and who possessed the self-confidence to make that possible.

By the second half of the 1920s, with the Fascist or Mussolinian regime secure in office, other aspects of Mussolini's character acquired space in his story. The unashamed recourse to dictatorship from 3 January 1925, the creation of the 'totalitarian state' in 1926–7, the 'historic' accord with the Vatican in the Lateran Pacts of 11 February 1929, all these exalted the *Duce* above his already giddy heights. There may be some profundity in exiled liberal Carlo Sforza's remark late in the 1930s that, even then, Mussolini only esteemed himself as a genius, but Hitler knew that he was a god.[22] However, something resembling a deification was inflating Mussolini's image, especially as promulgated in its most popular forms. A Catholic education may have assisted the Fascist journalist, Edgardo Sulis, in his 1933 study, *Imitazione di Mussolini*, to recall: 'Alessandro Mussolini and Rosa Maltoni were no more than Josephs in regard to Christ. They were instruments of God and history given the task of looking after one of the greatest national Messiahs. Indeed, without question, the greatest [Messiah].'[23] In the full Fascist piety of such accounts the radicalism of Mussolini's own early days was obscured, to be replaced by a more conventionally respectable image of boyhood discipline, effort and success. Having moved his office in September 1929 from that of earlier Prime Ministers in the Palazzo Chigi to the grandiose surrounds of the Sala del Mappamondo in the Palazzo Venezia, the *Duce* steadily became a more distant figure, directing the masses, rather than just emanating from them, risen now to be the ultimate master of history itself.[24]

Though she does not altogether answer the question, Passerini asks importantly whether this change was being pushed from above or below.[25]

20 For what remains the finest evocation of his character and background, see I. Deutscher, *Stalin: a political biography*, Harmondsworth, 1966, p. 44. There the biographer notes with great psychological acuity that, for the young Stalin, son of a drunken cobbler and ex-serf, from the periphery of the Russian empire, 'class hatred was not his second nature – it was his first'.

21 Hitler was certainly nearer to Mussolini in class background. He had the social advantage of growing up in bigger centres than Predappio, while his bureaucrat father naturally could claim a certain social status. An aura of failure and of a lack of intellectual interest none the less existed in Hitler's family which does not seem to be true among the more self-confident Mussolinis.

22 C. Sforza, *Panorama europeo: apparenze politiche e realtà psicologica*, Rome, 1945, p. 112. This book was first published in French in 1937.

23 Cited by L. Passerini, *Mussolini immaginario*, p. 90.

24 L. Passerini, *Mussolini immaginario*, pp. 116, 144.

25 L. Passerini, *Mussolini immaginario*, p. 79.

Was there a conscious manufacture of an image either by Mussolini himself or by other architects of the regime, or was there a sense in which the Italian masses were constructing their own version of their dictator? To what extent were fans of the *Duce* framing the object which they were venerating?

Research on the popular imaginary of politicians is still at an early stage and, in the case of Mussolini, existing studies have provided more hints and suppositions than hard evidence or scrupulously scholarly analyses. None the less, some comment can be made. With Bottai's remarks quoted at the beginning of this chapter in mind, we might consider also for a moment the words of another Fascist hierarch, Carlo Scorza. This apparently hard-bitten politician wrote in 1933, 'We Fascists must look to the *Duce* with the same spirit that we had as children when we regarded the image of our local Saint, listening to the marvellous tale of his miracles. This is why, when we come before Him [*sic*], we are trembling with emotion.'[26] No doubt self-interest tinctured such remarks. A dictatorship with a secret police always produces a society in which it is best to conceal doubts, while the flaunting of a craven honesty, even in the privacy of a diary entry, may encourage at least the hope of reward. Yet it would be a mistake to impugn altogether the sincerity of Scorza, Bottai and their like. Rather, it is worth being alert to the semiotics of their comments on the *Duce*. Reverence towards the dictator regularly recapitulated the more traditional discourse of the Church. Was this, as a Mosse or a Gentile might like to claim, because Fascism, acting as lay religion, had won its converts? Or was it rather that the lingering presence of religious imagery reflected the survival of Catholic ideas and vocabulary even in those who were self-conscious in their modernity, anti-clericalism or atheism? Similarly, to what degree did evocations of a godlike Mussolini carry a certain unspoken uneasiness that, in modern times, this god, too, might be dead?

What of the populace at large? How did they translate their *Duce* into their minds? Passerini has reviewed at some length the image of the dictator in the children's literature of the regime, reporting how insistent Fascism had become about such matters by the 1930s and how cloying were some of its accounts of the leader.[27] She remarks, too, on the process through which Mussolini had earned a presence even in Italian dreams.[28] In regard to this formation of a *Duce* as a sort of household god, other historians have examined the letters which poured in from the people to their leader. This correspondence was a curious mixture. There were the worshipful writers who indeed accepted that 'Mussolini is always right' (*Mussolini ha sempre ragione* – one of the most pervasive and insouciant of the regime's propaganda slogans); in the phrases they inscribed, Mussolini was both a

26 Cited by L. Passerini, *Mussolini immaginario*, p. 104.
27 L. Passerini, *Mussolini immaginario*, pp. 153–234.
28 L. Passerini, *Mussolini immaginario*, p. 203.

father and an Eternal Father, *padre, padrone, padreterno.*[29] None the less, worship was frequently accompanied by a certain worldliness, and apparent humility by a search for personal advantage. Correspondents did not just hymn the *Duce*, they also expected, or at least presumed to hope for, an immediate return on their prayerful investment. Take the case of the woman who, in June 1938, announced the birth (after 19 hours of labour) of her twenty-fifth child, patriotically and Fascistically to be named Vittoria Romana. Apart from providing such birth details, this loyal subject of the *Duce* took the opportunity to point out that she owned neither sheets nor mattress nor furnishings, that the new daughter, despite her majestic name, had no clothes for her back, and that she and her brothers and sisters lived in 'terrifying poverty'.[30] Plainly this mother was punting optimistically that a small Roman victory would come her way, too, ideally in the form of a cash payment by return post.

What is to be made of such glimpses of the *Duce*'s social role and image? Did such letters, and the sentiments which they expressed, prove that the totalitarian state had affixed the myth of Mussolini deep in every Italian soul? Or did they rather indicate that the poor are always given to some sort of (self-deluding) hope, and will rest it on their nearest prospect in their permanent time of trouble, and invest him or her with 'charisma'? Do not all monarchs, popes, pop stars, lottery winners, and many politicians get similar mail to that which was delivered to the *Duce* of Fascism (and with a similar lack of effect so far as altering social hierarchies is concerned)?

Figures blessed or afflicted by charisma may, of course, be hated as well as loved. Prayers to the good Mussolini were matched by anathemas to the evil one. In a study undertaken prior to the publication of her book on Mussolini's image, Passerini utilised evidence from secret police files to demonstrate that, at least in Turin, toilet walls and other relatively private places might be sometimes scrawled with denunciations of the *Duce*.[31] In 1938, for example, there were at least two inscriptions of this acrostic:

Morirai	(You will die
Ucciso	at an assassin's hand
Seconda	in the second
Settimana	week
Ottobre	of October
Liberando	thus liberating
Intera	the whole
Nazione	nation
Italiana[32]	of Italy)

29 For a splendid example, see T. M. Mazzatosta and C. Volpi, *L'Italietta fascista (lettere al potere 1936–1943)*, Bologna, 1980, p. 109.
30 T. M. Mazzatosta and C. Volpi, *L'Italietta fascista*, p. 141.
31 L. Passerini, *Fascism in popular memory: the cultural experience of the Turin working class*, Cambridge, 1987, pp. 78–9, 94–5.
32 L. Passerini, *Fascism in popular memory*, p. 94.

Again the full meaning of such 'mock fortune-telling' is hard to plumb. Were these scribbles 'resistance' of some kind, at the very least 'passive dissent'? Or, by contrast, were such graffiti evidence of a successful totalitarianism which ensured that Mussolini was the man in all minds, even mentally disturbed ones? Or, in different genre still, did the image of Mussolini act in Turin as a useful figure, off-stage in thievish and distant Rome, who could be relied on to divert popular criticism and hostility from Giovanni Agnelli and the other employers and rich of the city? In the special surrounds of Turin, was the mythologised Mussolini ironically playing the part of the errant minister, to be blamed by those who would not or could not face up to the actual authority of King Fiat?

Another social group which seems to have constructed an image of Mussolini for its own purpose was Italy's emigrants, more than 10 million of them scattered across the world, with major groupings in North and South America.[33] A full-scale study of the political culture of these shards of the Italies has not been attempted, and yet evidence does exist that Fascism itself, usually best understood through the dominant figure of Mussolini, however vaguely drawn, did frequently give comfort to Italians outside Italy. The *Duce* could, for example, be invoked as a hero when immigrant Italians confronted negative racial stereotypes in the pubs and clubs of their new societies.[34] It is likely, too, that a positive memory of Mussolini often survived in such circles after 1945, and then was deployed against a new wave of immigrants to bolster the authority of existing 'pioneers'.[35] Having missed the actual experience of the Second World War in Italy, these old immigrants claimed a history of Fascism as their special usable past.

None the less, as one international crisis succeeded another in the 1930s, even among the emigrants popular thoughts about the *Duce* were confronting deepening complications. It is notorious that, in the aftermath of the Munich conference, Mussolini, to his own public irritation, was hailed by his less-than-warmongering populace as the 'Saviour of Peace'. Whatever his own understanding, secret police reports told him that the Axis with Nazism was viewed by many of his subjects as a problematic arrangement, justified half-heartedly as an act of Mussolinian cunning which would keep Germany in check, or accepted as a policy designed to bring immediate and large rewards to the Italian people.[36]

---

33 For an English-language introduction to their history, see R. J. B. Bosworth, *Italy and the wider world 1860–1960*, London, 1996, pp. 114–58.
34 For a small example, see R. and M. Bosworth, *Fremantle's Italy*, Rome, 1993, pp. 80–91.
35 Emigrant 'Italians', of course, did not directly experience the Second World War in the way that inhabitants of the peninsula did. A rash historiographer might wonder whether what often seems the less critical interpretation of modern Italian history by historians who work in the US, compared with those who work in the UK, reflects, however indirectly, some impact from the cultural, social and political past, present and future of Italo-America.
36 For a description of these views, see A. M. Imbriani, *Gli italiani e il Duce: il mito e l'immagine di Mussolini negli ultimi anni del fascismo (1938–1943)*, Naples, 1992. Imbriani very sensibly makes the point that there was not a single myth of the *Duce*, but he underestimates the possibility that multiple *Duces* could exist in the mind of a single citizen of Fascist Italy.

The actual Italian entry into the war in June 1940 was greeted with considerable short-term enthusiasm, and is best understood as a moment in which the great majority of Italians closed their eyes and walked behind a *Duce* who, they said with a certain desperate confidence, had mastered destiny. This acceptance of the war, however, came with clear reservations – it must be 'short, easy and victorious' (and must bring rich booty to every man and every woman).[37] If the conflict turned out to be long, arduous and full of defeats, then belief in the leader's charisma would rapidly fade, as though an implicit contract, a 'moral economy', was being broken. The military catastrophe in Greece in October 1940 and increasing evidence of troubles on the home front soon, indeed, induced this fading. The sense that Mussolini had betrayed his relationship with the Italian people was established well before they could celebrate his overthrow.

What, then, can be made of this array of images of Mussolini in Fascist Italy? A more thorough response to these and earlier questions must await full-scale research into the popular culture of Fascist Italy. However, some interim conclusions can be essayed. Various notions of the *Duce* did eddy around Italian society during his regime (and it is very likely that the influence of such currents did not quickly disappear in 1943–5).[38] In this sense, the myth of Mussolini was a powerful and pervasive part of twentieth-century Italian imagining, both conscious and unconscious. Mussolini was, indeed, the stuff of Italian dreams. However, much of the wording and the figuring of these dreams and imaginings was unoriginal, and did not necessarily imply that the Fascist regime had bent Italian minds in its own singular cause. Rather, part of the Mussolini myth among the Italian populace might be viewed as merely reflecting the fact that images and words are always waiting to attach themselves to any politician (and it is certainly striking how durable quasi-religious, 'pre-modern' imagery turns out to have been in allegedly 'modernising' Italian minds). Any Bearer of Success was a potential vehicle of charisma. In short, there was always something fragile about the imprinting of a myth of the *Duce* onto his subjects. As Passerini herself concludes: 'When, in 1938, the Ministry of Popular Culture banned foreign comics from appearing in Italian papers because it feared the competition of such paper personages and because the Fascists were not altogether sure that their chiefs could measure up against comic book heroes', the regime was indeed doubting the value and strength in any free market of its synthetic images.[39] Fascism was indicating to any who cared to look that its charms, its novelties and its power could scarcely match those of consumer capitalism. Should the truth be known, the *Duce*, in many an Italian mind confronting a Fascist military campaign, still came

37 A. M. Imbriani, *Gli italiani e il Duce*, p. 99. Imbriani shows that women were very early in expressing their doubts about the real demands to be made by the war (p. 107).
38 See the comments of L. Passerini, *Mussolini immaginario*, p. 5, noting that, in her early oral research, she had often run into surprisingly positive memories of the *Duce*.
39 L. Passerini, *Mussolini immaginario*, p. 230.

second in appeal behind Mary Pickford or Mickey Mouse,[40] and Mussolini's declaration of war 18 months later on that consumer bastion, the USA, would not be welcomed by the populace at large.[41]

If the image of Mussolini at home in Italy remains an object of vivid debate, the same is true of the way in which he was comprehended outside the borders of his state. De Felice and his school[42] have argued for a maximum thesis, that is, that the myth of Mussolini carried weight abroad as well as in Italian hearts. According to De Felice, Hitler for one remained 'fascinated' by his Italian predecessor.[43] Moreover, early in the 1930s Lloyd George allegedly told ambassador Dino Grandi,[44] 'Either the world decides to follow Mussolini or the world is lost';[45] while in 1935 there were suggestions from distinguished academic circles in Hungary that the *Duce* should be nominated for the Nobel Peace Prize.[46]

Other historians have seen these comments as an instance of the frequent tendency of De Felice to read texts without a proper consideration of their context. Citing Lloyd George is all very well, but Lloyd George's desperation at the depth of the Depression and at his own, by then long-standing, political irrelevance, as well as his desire to ingratiate himself with Grandi, need to be taken into account. It is, of course, quite easy to find British praise for Mussolini at one time or another. One of my favourite examples comes from Frank Fox, an imperialist and anti-communist journalist, who, like so many in his trade, was granted an interview with the *Duce*. Fresh from this meeting in 1927, Fox reviewed 'Italy today' in order, he wrote, to

> give a general impression of a nation which is being governed . . . on lines curiously suggestive of those ruling an English Public School, with the same worship of the community spirit and of the community type, with some of the same petty tyrannies as to 'form' and behaviour, and with the same high spirit of emulation and endeavour for 'the

40 In many ways, this is the fundamental message of Italy's greatest post-war film-maker, Federico Fellini. See further Chapter 7.
41 A. M. Imbriani, *Gli italiani e il Duce*, p. 154.
42 See, at greatest length and most controversially, R. De Felice, *Mussolini il Duce I. Gli anni del consenso, 1929–1936*, Turin, 1974, pp. 534–96; cf. also R. Quartararo, *Roma tra Londra e Berlino: la politica estera fascista dal 1931 al 1940*, Rome, 1980, p. 16, who asserts, incredibly, that in 1933 'on the quality of Mussolini as a statesman, no-one in England nourished any doubts'.
43 R. De Felice, *Mussolini il Duce I*, pp. 420–1.
44 Grandi is himself a figure who has occasioned major historiographical controversy between commentators who believe what he said and commentators who aver that he generally said what his collocutors, and especially Mussolini, wanted to hear. For his own account, see D. Grandi, *Il mio paese: ricordi autobiografici*, ed. R. De Felice, Bologna, 1985.
45 R. De Felice, *Mussolini il Duce I*, p. 543, n. 1. During the Spanish Civil War, by contrast, Lloyd George would memorably describe the Fascist defeat at Guadalajara as 'the Italian skedaddle'. See R. J. B. Bosworth, *Italy and the wider world 1860–1960*, p. 51.
46 R. De Felice, *Mussolini il Duce I*, p. 554.

good of the school' . . . [and] to give also some impression of the remarkable personality who is at once Head Master and Head Boy.[47]

This sort of praise, however, was almost always qualified by spoken or unspoken political and racial assumptions about the inferiority of Italians, and about the inadequacies of those liberal institutions which had existed in Italy before Fascism. Such ambivalent approbation usually carried 'Good-King'-style clichés about the possible virtue of Mussolini himself and about the vice of squadrist Fascism, especially when it showed signs of engaging in 'foreign adventures' (as they would typically be deemed). Even Fox qualified his encomium of Fascism by his complacent assumption that the British Empire already rejoiced in the 'results of cultivation', whereas Italy limped behind at the stage of learning the 'methods of cultivation'.[48]

Another highly characteristic commentator on Mussolini and his regime was G. M. Trevelyan, the epitome of an 'Italy-lover', a liberal historian, author of four 'wromantic' and rousing volumes on the Risorgimento, and, in the First World War, a volunteer for Red Cross service on the Italian front.[49] In 1923, Trevelyan produced a first account of Fascism which compared the task confronting its leader with that of King Henry VII of England at the end of the Wars of the Roses. To speed the country on its way towards something near modernity, Trevelyan penned in his inimitable prose a sort of Collect for Italian Fascism:

> Let us not be impatient with Italy if she is for the moment swerving from the path of liberty in the course of a very earnest attempt to set her house in order and to cope with the evils which the friends of liberty have allowed to grow up. . . . Signor Mussolini is a great man and, according to his lights, a very sincere patriot. Let our prayer for him be, not that he victoriously destroy free institutions in Italy, but that he may be remembered as a man who gave his country order and discipline when she most needed them, and so enabled those free institutions to be restored in an era happier than that in which it is our present destiny to live.[50]

47 F. Fox, *Italy today*, London, 1927, pp. v–vi. Before the war Fox, a British race patriot then resident in Australia, had been the pseudonymous author of a local 'war-scare' novel so typical of the time, in which Japanese immigrants took over the continent osmotically. See 'C. H. Kirmess', *The Australian crisis*, London, 1909.

48 F. Fox, *Italy today*, p. 48.

49 For his account of this war see G. M. Trevelyan, *Scenes from Italy's war*, London, 1919. It retained a certain patronising air: unlike Germans, Trevelyan remarked, 'above all, the Italian is fond of children. His family affections are very strong; his children are never beaten, and the mistake is another that they are too often petted and spoilt. The kind of neglect from which they often suffer is thoughtless neglect, combined with much affection.' (p. 10)

50 G. M. Trevelyan, *The historical causes of the present state of affairs in Italy*, Oxford, 1923, p. 20.

Other British accounts of Fascist Italy reflected the effortless sense of superiority so evident in Trevelyan's prose. One remarkable example is a book on ordinary Italian life by Colin Coote, a conservative journalist and sometime scholar of Balliol College, Oxford. For Coote, Italy was a place of colour and delight, but, to his mind, such pleasures confirmed that the native inhabitants of the peninsula were a 'race of children. . . . For young as is the nation [of Italy], its heart is yet younger, full of unbridled enthusiasms, vague passions and noble sentiments; capable of the greatest heights and also of the greatest depths', a mélange well typified in the character of Mussolini, but even better epitomised in the personality of Gabriele D'Annunzio.[51] The killing in June 1924 of the socialist deputy Giacomo Matteotti demonstrated to Coote a truth which he had always known: Fascist Italians were still Italians – 'The Fascists have behaved like arrant cads, and it is hard to credit them with what they have done in the face of one's disgust at what they are.'[52]

Such sentiments were common in British assessments of Italy. When it reported the details of the Matteotti murder, the London *Times* was magisterial in its assessment of the Italian regime. The crime had happened and was deplorable. And yet it could be forgiven, since, an editorial pronounced, 'murder is more common [in Italy] than in most of the civilised states'.[53] Nor were the British alone in manifesting a sense of superiority. The French fascist Robert Brasillach was untroubled by the Matteotti killing, still deeming Italy 'a land of painters and [of] "connoisseurs of matters pertaining to the soul"' (if not the regular guys he would eventually admire in Berlin).[54]

The proviso that any enthusiasm expressed for Mussolini himself outside Italy was usually conditioned by patronising assumptions both about Italy and about any ideology which might arise there is sometimes countered with the view that, in the early 1930s, Italy was seen in quite a number of places as having survived the economic, political and social storms of the Great Depression with relative ease.[55] It is true that, both in Britain[56] and in

---

51 C. R. Coote, *Italian town and country life*, London, 1925, p. 11.
52 C. R. Coote, *Italian town and country life*, p. 238.
53 *The Times*, 21 June 1924. For more background, see R. J. B. Bosworth, 'The British press, the conservatives and Mussolini, 1920–1934', *Journal of Contemporary History*, 5, 1970, pp. 163–82.
54 W. R. Tucker, *The Fascist ego: a political biography of Robert Brasillach*, Berkeley, 1975, p. 68.
55 R. De Felice, *Mussolini il Duce I*, pp. 544–5.
56 See e.g. P. Einzig, *The economic foundations of Fascism*, London, 1933, which both portrays Fascism in Italy as a triumph of 'planning' and separates it from Nazism (see e.g. pp. vii–viii). Cf. also his 'Signor Mussolini's dilemma' in his book *Bankers, Statesmen and Economists*, London, 1935, pp. 99–120, which, while expressing some doubts, recalls with pleasure a meeting between its author and Mussolini, in which the *Duce* allegedly displayed considerable familiarity with contemporary economic thought about deflation (p. 110).

the United States,[57] some economists and political scientists did then express great admiration for Fascism, and did wonder whether the Corporate State might not be a model which could be imitated, at least to some degree, in the liberal democracies. During the early 1930s it was also virtually a cliché for foreign commentators to hail Mussolini as a 'man of genius', though, naturally, the cliché was used of others, too.

Such apparently golden opinions were duly reinforced by the accessibility of the *Duce* to foreign visitors, some of decidedly moderate importance. Indeed, these interviews became one of the features of the Fascist government; and since everyone loves to feel that they are distinguished, they probably represented the most effective technique used by the regime to massage foreign opinion. Those who called on Mussolini, and were greeted with warmth, *politesse* and what often seemed sincere interest, frequently responded with commendation of the *Duce* thereafter.

They constituted a mixed group. Among them, for example, was the Sydney doctor, Catholic and rugby player Herbert Moran. At the *Duce*'s first meeting with Moran, Mussolini was sufficiently well-briefed to talk in a 'cool, calm and courteous' way about cancer cures, and to hail the initiation of the teaching of Italian at the University of Sydney. Charmed and impressed, Moran, for the next few years, became a stalwart advocate of Fascist policies, both at home and in Ethiopia (and was admitted to the *Duce*'s presence on a number of other occasions).[58]

Another of Mussolini's visitors was the somewhat unlikely figure of Mahatma Gandhi, who during a trip to Rome in December 1931 was granted a 10-minute interview. Accounts of the meeting vary: Mussolini's mastery of English was enough to impress Gandhi's secretary, Miss Slade, but the *Duce*, this time perhaps too well-briefed, barked out 44 questions in a row, a fusillade which succeeded only in bemusing his Indian guest.[59] Thereafter a legend spread that Gandhi had saluted Mussolini as 'the saviour of the new Italy'. The Mahatma seems rather to have carried away a mixed impression from his visit; he was positive about Fascist rural policies and land reclamation schemes, but dismayed by the violence he sensed in this as in other regimes, an impression which may have been reinforced by the peremptoriness and extent of the *Duce*'s questioning. Later in the 1930s Gandhi's estimation of Mussolini fell further, especially when Romain Rolland sent him Gaetano Salvemini's *Under the Axe of Fascism* to read in his British prison.[60]

57 See e.g. the two classic studies, H. W. Schneider, *Making the Fascist state*, New York, 1928; and H. W. Schneider and S. B. Clough, *Making Fascists*, Chicago, 1929. Influenced by Giuseppe Prezzolini, they depicted Fascism as a unique experiment in 'revolutionary conservatism'.
58 See H. M. Moran, *In my fashion: an autobiography of the last ten years*, London, 1946, pp. 3–4, 9. Cf. also H. M. Moran, *Letters from Rome: an Australian's views of the Italo-Abyssinian question*, Sydney, 1935.
59 G. Sofri, *Gandhi in Italia*, Bologna, 1988, pp. 55, 61.
60 G. Sofri, *Gandhi in Italia*, pp. 87–91.

Far less sceptical was the Hungarian diplomat Lajos Kemechey. It may be that his English translator rendered his prose a little breathless, but Kemechey's admiration for the *Duce* seemed at first glance unbounded. Mussolini, Kemechey wrote, indeed embodied 'the New Man', fearing nothing and humming with the dynamism of the twentieth century: 'dazzlingly many-sided, a regular hero of fiction. He rides like a Centaur, he drives a motor-car so well that he might race at Monza, and not long ago, after falling in his aeroplane and being laid up for some weeks, he went flying again. He fences like an expert fencing-master, and plays the violin as marvellously as a finished artist.'[61] For all the cries of wonder echoing through Kemechey's prose, another, contradictory understanding found its place there. Like Frank Fox, Kemechey could not eliminate from his mind the knowledge that Mussolini was an Italian. The *Duce* bore the stamp of his people:

> the swift lightnings of joy and the pale eruptions of fury which mark the Italian temperament. . . . Misery is strangling him by the throat, and yet he stops before the hotel Beau Rivage, because he has caught the sound of music. That is the Italian nature as it really is. That is the Italian revolutionist who throws bombs into the royal carriage, but admires the antique statues of the gods. That is the Italian nation which, with its ardent and intensive soul, assails heights and depths, like a boiling volcano, but stops delighted before the eternal enchantment of song and melody.[62]

In their different ways, Moran, Gandhi and Kemechey had certain reservations about Mussolini, even when their praise was at its most effusive. Moran was committed to the British Empire and would reject the Fascist regime when it went to war. Gandhi could have his momentary interest in the *Duce* readily deflected by the 'facts' retailed by anti-Fascists. Kemechey was full, even over-full, with love for Italy and delight in its leader, and yet, it must be assumed, pushed into a tight corner and when romance had to be set aside, his Hungary would have preferred, say, a German alliance to an Italian one.

The most celebrated visitor to Mussolini's office in the early 1930s, however, was the German-Jewish journalist 'Emil Ludwig' (his real name was Emil Cohn). Over almost a fortnight between late March and early April 1932, Ludwig went frequently to the Palazzo Venezia to talk to the *Duce*. He recorded their conversations, which were soon thereafter published in German – Mussolini allegedly checked the veracity of this text[63] – and other languages. Ludwig's book, its English title was *Talks with Mussolini*, sold well and, at least according to De Felice,[64] gives crucial

---

61 L. Kemechey, *'Il Duce': the life and work of Benito Mussolini*, London, 1930, pp. 75, 152. Kemechey added that Mussolini's 'dazzling success' was of a type which 'the long Calmuc face' of Lenin could not comprehend (p. 273).
62 L. Kemechey, *'Il Duce'*, p. 39.
63 E. Ludwig, *Talks with Mussolini*, London, 1932, p. 11.
64 R. De Felice, *Mussolini il Duce I*, pp. 45–7.

insight into Mussolini's mind, even if the *Duce* himself soon regretted the frankness of some of his comments.

The image of the dictator which Ludwig sketched was in large part favourable.[65] Though himself a liberal democrat, the journalist considered that, in 1932, 'the foundations of "democracy" and "parliamentarism" [were] crumbling'. Mussolini embodied the Nietzschean superman, and any observer had to acknowledge that 'the Fascist movement has done great things for Italy', though, Ludwig added quickly, 'transplanted to Germany', it would prove 'disastrous'.[66] Mussolini, Ludwig found, was a good-humoured and open interviewee and, on reflection, 'I have no hesitation in describing him as a great statesman'.[67] The *Duce* had to be accounted a 'real revolutionist' – current-day culturalist historians of Fascism are doubtless glad to learn that Mussolini told Ludwig that 'every revolution creates new forms, new myths, and new rites'.[68] Naturally enough, Mussolini spoke of the great future of the Italian nation, but he was sardonic when asked about race, declaring roundly: 'Nothing will ever make me believe that biologically pure races can be shown to exist today', even while he endorsed the idea of 'racial feeling'. 'National pride,' he concluded, 'has no need of the delirium of race.'[69] Indeed, the book ends with Mussolini's highly judicious advice that 'a ruler . . . needs ninety-nine per cent of kindliness and only one per cent of contempt' toward the ruled.[70]

Although Ludwig himself complained that, for all the civility of their discourse, he was aware of never having broken through to the private Mussolini,[71] it may well be that these interviews provided a more candid account of the *Duce* than many another (the dictator did confess that he felt himself always 'alone' and thus a sort of 'prisoner' of his 'power').[72] What they do not indicate, however, is some sort of widespread German admiration for Mussolini's Italy. A certain sympathy for Mussolini himself may have existed in a variety of German minds, but it was almost always accompanied by the knowledge that Mussolini was 'only' an Italian and that, in the First World War, the Italians had duly confirmed their longstanding 'historical' predilection for treachery and levity. More research on the subject is needed, but there are indications that the majority of Germans, then and at any time, agreed with Joseph Goebbels' eventual wartime assessment that 'the Italian people is not worth a row of beans'.[73]

65 Cf . also E. Ludwig, 'The Italian Autocrat', in his *Leaders of Europe*, London, 1933, pp. 313–45, which is still decidedly favourable in its reading of a constructive statesman.
66 E. Ludwig, *Talks with Mussolini*, pp. 12–14.
67 E. Ludwig, *Talks with Mussolini*, pp. 32, 37.
68 E. Ludwig, *Talks with Mussolini*, p. 70.
69 E. Ludwig, *Talks with Mussolini*, pp. 73–4.
70 E. Ludwig, *Talks with Mussolini*, p. 220.
71 E. Ludwig, *Talks with Mussolini*, p. 115.
72 E. Ludwig, *Talks with Mussolini*, p. 217.
73 J. Goebbels, *Final entries 1945: Diaries*, ed. H. Trevor-Roper, New York, 1978, p. 78.

It was not so much the originality or otherwise of German attitudes to Italy and Fascism which coloured Mussolini's image abroad after 1933 as the comparison between the *Duce*'s regime and Hitler's. Mussolini himself may well have been decidely lukewarm towards Nazism, about which, in the 1920s, he had been sporadically informed, and to which he gave some subsidies.[74] He may have greeted the Nazi acquisition of power in January 1933 in an ambivalent fashion, pleased by Hitler's own expressions of gratitude toward the senior dictator[75] but doubtful about Nazi ideology and the prospect of Nazi aggression. Indeed, after the Dollfuss murder in July 1934, Mussolini, true to what has been defined as his policy of 'open conflicts, openly arrived at',[76] was readier than any other European leader to go to war in order to prevent a Nazi *Anschluss*.[77] Yet such detail of Italo–German relations had minor relevance to the state of external opinion after 1933. Once Hitler was in power and had become such an evidently disruptive element on the international stage, Mussolini almost inevitably was relegated to the rank of dictator minor. As an American diplomat has recalled, the US State Department regarded the *Duce*'s actions 'as a detail and felt that Germany remained the key to the whole European situation'.[78] Experts could argue about the morality or good sense of Mussolini's acts as a statesman; politicians could speculate about whether they should seek to win Italy to an anti-German bloc or concentrate their appeasement on Hitler; but, from 30 January 1933, the leader of Fascist Italy became no more than the leader of the least of the Great (European) Powers. The statesmanlike qualities which Ludwig and others had once perceived in Mussolini had lost a degree of credibility. By 1933 and henceforth, the *Duce*'s ideology and personality would rarely be viewed as the driving force of world politics. The myth of Fascism had already suffered a massive defeat at the hands of the myth of Nazism.

The apparent triumph of Nazism brought opportunity on other fronts for Fascism's opponents. As has been noted above, over the past decade the historiography, and especially that of the De Feliceans, has frequently redimensioned proud assertions about the role of anti-Fascism in rejecting Mussolini's regime. I shall discuss further below some of the issues involved,[79] but, for the present, it should be noted that after 1933, whatever their failings at home, anti-Fascists abroad came into their own.

74 R. J. B. Bosworth, *Italy and the wider world 1860–1960*, pp. 36–54 provides a background to Fascist Italy's international dealings. For further detail, see R. De Felice, *Mussolini il Duce I*, pp. 418–37.
75 As early as 31 January, Hitler took time to express such views to Mussolini's private informant in Berlin, Giuseppe Renzetti, for transmission to Rome. See R. De Felice, *Mussolini il Duce I*, p. 436.
76 R. J. B. Bosworth, *Italy and the wider world 1860–1960*, p. 45.
77 R. De Felice, *Mussolini il Duce I*, pp. 467–506.
78 W. Phillips, *Ventures in diplomacy*, London, 1955, p. 80.
79 See esp. Chapters 5 and 8.

In the first few years following its acquisition of power, the Fascist regime had harried a number of its eminent political opponents into exile. They included a former Prime Minister (1919–20), F. S. Nitti,[80] and an ex-Foreign Minister (1920–1), Carlo Sforza.[81] Each continued his public criticism of Mussolini. However, undoubtedly the most pertinacious and prolific[82] critic of Fascism, at least in the Western world,[83] was the historian and political commentator Gaetano Salvemini who, in 1934, was appointed lecturer in the 'History of Italian civilisation' at Harvard University.[84] Secure from that base, Salvemini produced for the Left Book Club, an imprint which ensured a wide circulation, a classic anti-Fascist account of Mussolini's regime entitled *Under the Axe of Fascism.*

In this book Salvemini enlarged on his previous denunciation of Fascist state and society with the aim of displaying the hollowness of the corporate system. To Salvemini, Mussolini was a demagogue, and a propagandist interested chiefly in shoring up his own power, while currying favour with the already rich and influential and offering nothing concrete to the poor. Ascribing a serious or genuine ideology to the *Duce* or his regime, Salvemini wrote, amounted to 'looking in a dark room for a black cat which is not there'.[85]

In his negative assessment of Fascism, Salvemini, by 1936, was offering only one account among many. De Felice has demonstrated how, in Italy, the Ethiopian campaign of 1935–6 rallied what was left of anti-Fascist opinion to the regime and produced a 'consensus' to an extent unparalleled certainly by any previous and perhaps by any successive government.[86] Even if this

80 It was his nephew Francesco Fausto Nitti who was the most active family resister and who wrote an English-language account of his prison breakout. See F. F. Nitti, *Escape*, New York, 1930. F. S. Nitti provided a preface to this work in which he noted in words which he must have thought that his audience would understand (p. ix): 'The order reigning in Italy is not any different from that of Sing-Sing. It is not spontaneous order but a crystallised disorder'.

81 For some of Sforza's writing, see C. Sforza, *Diplomatic Europe since the Treaty of Versailles*, New Haven, 1928; *European dictatorships*, New York, 1931; *Europe and the Europeans: a study in historical psychology and international politics*, London, 1936. Sforza eventually returned as Foreign Minister, after the war and despite several British attempts to veto him.

82 Salvemini's 'minder' was the Fascist publicist Luigi Villari. Throughout the inter-war period the two regularly fired salvoes at each other in the press of Britain, the United States and elsewhere. Villari also published a series of English-language eulogies of Fascism. See e.g. L. Villari, *The Fascist experiment*, London, 1926; *The expansion of Italy*, London, 1930; 'The economics of Fascism', in G. S. Counts (ed.), *Bolshevism, Fascism and Capitalism: an account of three economic systems*, New Haven, 1932; *On the roads from Rome*, London, 1932; *The war on the Italian front*, London, 1932; 'Italian foreign policy', *International Affairs*, 45, 1935, pp. 320–45.

83 For his earlier account of what he regarded as a murderous tyranny, see G. Salvemini, *The Fascist dictatorship in Italy*, New York, 1927.

84 For a sympathetic biography, see M. Salvadori, *Gaetano Salvemini*, Turin, 1963.

85 G. Salvemini, *Under the Axe of Fascism*, London, 1936, p. 114.

86 R. De Felice, *Mussolini il Duce I*, p. 758. For a further discussion of De Felice's decidedly controversial views, see Chapters 5 and 8.

consensus at home can be seen as to some degree justifying De Felice's controversial conclusion that the victorious campaign in Ethiopia and the resulting proclamation of the Fascist Empire represented 'Mussolini's political masterpiece',[87] it is hard to deny that the war brought serious harm to the international reputations of both Mussolini and his regime. The East African conflict was fought under greater press scrutiny than any earlier war, and the flaunted brutality of Fascist warmaking, itself in part with propaganda intent, was described and deplored[88] around the world. Now a respectable journalist who narrated the bombing of a Red Cross unit would almost automatically suggest that the pilot was the *Duce*'s eldest son, Vittorio, that his act was both cruel and cowardly, that he lied about it subsequently, and that the entire event proved that 'a criminal strain must run in the [Mussolini] family'.[89] Now the London *Times*, at least in its own eyes the most authoritative of newspapers, could inveigh against Mussolini's barbarism: 'If there are degrees in turpitude in the wilful destruction of agreements, zero in the scale has been reached when a Power claiming the characteristics of civilisation takes to the indiscriminate employment of gas against a primitive people who neither possess nor can acquire the means of defence against it.'[90] Now long-term ideological opponents of Fascism could get a hearing when they described Mussolini as puffed up with pride, power and a lust to kill, an 'Aesopian bull-frog'.[91] Now, too, George Seldes, in his recounting of the life of the 'Sawdust Caesar', could dismiss the *Duce* as an 'egotist', a 'coward' and a 'traitor'.[92]

If the glare of publicity which swept over Mussolini during the Ethiopian campaign made him seem in many foreign eyes the crudest and most irresponsible of international aggressors, this reputation was little amended in the next years. The Spanish Civil War commenced as soon as the Ethiopian conflict ended, and Franco's nationalist, Catholic and reactionary (some would say fascist) cause was swiftly seconded by great numbers of Italian Fascist 'volunteers'.[93] The blatant nature of this intervention simply

---

87 R. De Felice, *Mussolini il Duce I*, p. 642. The full sentence reads, 'The Ethiopian war was Mussolini's political masterpiece and his greatest success because he probably believed in it more profoundly than in any of his other political initiatives.' De Felice's full acount of the war continues through pp. 597–757, these 160 pages constituting, typically, a single chapter of his book. For a summary of the debate unleashed by the definition of the imperial triumph as a 'masterpiece', see P. Meldini (ed.), *Un monumento al Duce? Contributo al dibattito sul fascismo*, Florence, 1976.
88 It was now that Cole Porter dropped from his song the line 'you're the tops, you're Mussolini'. J. P. Diggins, *Mussolini and Fascism*, p. 287. For further on the impact in Africa of the war, see S. K. B. Asante, *Pan-African protest: West Africa and the Italo-Ethiopian crisis, 1934–1941*, London, 1977.
89 G. L. Steer, *Caesar in Abyssinia*, London, 1936, p. 279.
90 *The Times*, 8 April 1936. It repeated its condemnation on both 9 and 11 April.
91 A. Borghi, *Mussolini red and black*, London, 1935, p. 10.
92 G. Seldes, *Sawdust Caesar*, p. 375.
93 For the basic narration, see J. F. Coverdale, *Italian intervention in the Spanish Civil War*, Princeton, 1975.

confirmed the now-established view, certainly on the Left but also among many liberal democrats, that Mussolini was an international outlaw,[94] a sort of diplomatic Al Capone, who embodied the worst features both of dictators and of what was widely thought to be the Italian national character, the *mafioso* whose unwanted presence disrupted the global concert.

The Second World War itself did little to challenge these assumptions. The character of Italian intervention against France (typically defined as a 'jackal' act, a 'stab in the back'), the calamitous Greek campaign, and the feeble nature of the Italian war effort, all reinforced existing stereotypes about Mussolini, his people and his regime. Winston Churchill duly declared that 'one man alone'[95] was responsible for Italy's ills, and demanded his overthrow and punishment. At the same time, however, racial assumptions about the general inferiority and military incompetence of Italians frequently surfaced in both British and American minds.[96] In this sense, the war seemed to confirm that Mussolini was an Italian, that the Italians at least half-deserved Mussolini, and that neither the dictator nor his people possessed what was still readily called 'historical greatness'.

As the conservative historian Sir Lewis Namier explained in a much-cited review first published just after the war was won:

> Recurrent situations in history reproduce analogous forms; there is a morphology of politics. But to the basic repetition and the individual variations of organic growth an element is added peculiar to man: imitation engendered by historical memory. The modern dictatorship arises amid the ruins of an inherited social and political structure, in the desolation of shattered loyalties – it is the desperate shift of communities broken from their moorings. . . . It is the monolatry of the political desert. The more pathological the situation the less important is the intrinsic worth of the idol. His feet may be of clay and his face may be a blank: it is the frenzy of the worshippers which imparts to him meaning and power.

Napoleon III, Namier argued, was the 'first mountebank dictator'. Mussolini and Hitler were his mimics in the methods of 'plebiscitarian Caesarism',

> with its direct appeal to the masses: demagogical slogans; disregard of legality in spite of a professed guardianship of law and order;

---

94 See e.g. G. T. Garratt, *Mussolini's Roman Empire*, Harmondsworth, 1938, a widely circulated 'Penguin special'.
95 Churchill used the phrase in a broadcast to the Italian people of 23 December 1940. It was picked up by the journalist M. H. H. Macartney, *One man alone: a history of Mussolini and the Axis*, London, 1944, in his wartime assessment of Fascist foreign policy.
96 For some examples, see R. J. B. Bosworth, *Italy and the wider world 1860–1960*, pp. 52–3, 136. The classic statement is probably that in an offical British memo of July 1943. See P. Sebastian, *I servizi segreti speciali britannici e l'Italia (1940–1945)*, Rome, 1986, p. 30.

contempt of political parties and the parliamentary system, of the educated classes and their values; blandishments and vague, contradictory promises for all and sundry; militarism; gigantic, blatant displays and shady corruption. *Panem et circenses* once more – and at the end of the road, disaster.[97]

In the decades which followed 1945 Namier's words, with their own florid political colouring, seemed an inadequate summary of the nature of Nazi Germany. The idea that Mussolini was just another 'mountebank dictator', however, has carried an enduring weight, and to a considerable extent remains the standard interpretation of the *Duce*. Perhaps this degree of consensus helps to explain why Mussolini has not become an object of great biographical focus of an intimate rather than a simply political kind. The careers of both Hitler[98] and Stalin[99] have, for example, stimulated psycho-historians to examine their cases, but Mussolini's has not. Some journalists have provided narrations of the *Duce*'s life – probably the most widely circulated is Christopher Hibbert's rollicking account.[100] Rather more sensational was a later study by Richard Collier.[101] Neither of these authors, however, brought much in the way of interpretation to their works.[102] They told a good story, and if in the telling (especially by Collier) Mussolini acquired a certain glamour, that is a common effect of the biographer's art. But such accounts scarcely elevated the historical Mussolini to the status of a rival, either in interest or sales appeal, to the other great twentieth-century dictators.[103]

In Italian the standard descriptive biography of the *Duce* was the openly sympathetic four-volume work by two ex-Fascist journalists, Giorgio Pini and Duilio Susmel.[104] This study would not be superseded until De Felice

97 L. Namier, *Vanished supremacies: essays on European history 1812–1918*, New York, 1958, pp. 54–5.
98 The most scholarly, if still highly dubious, effort is that by R. G. L. Waite, *The psychopathic God: Adolf Hitler*, New York, 1977.
99 The most respectable is R. C. Tucker. See his *Stalin as revolutionary 1879–1929*, London, 1974; *Stalin in power: the revolution from above, 1928–1941*, New York, 1992.
100 C. Hibbert, *Benito Mussolini: the rise and fall of Il Duce*, Harmondsworth, 1965 (first published in hardback in 1962). Less lively was the biography by the ex-diplomat Ivone Kirkpatrick. It presented an opportunist Mussolini, but one who went most wrong once he abandoned friendship with Great Britain. See I. Kirkpatrick, *Mussolini: study of a demagogue*, London, 1964.
101 R. Collier, *Duce! The rise and fall of Benito Mussolini*, London, 1971. The most recent works in this genre are E. P. Hoyt, *Mussolini's Empire: the rise and fall of the Fascist vision*, New York, 1994 (Hoyt is not so racy a writer as Collier, and presents a somewhat unlucky Mussolini, ruined by the German alliance), and the more stylish J. Ridley, *Mussolini*, London, 1997.
102 Each showed the influence of P. Monelli, *Mussolini: an intimate life*, London, 1953, a book which was an early Italian venture into the art of journalistic description. It was first published in Italian as *Mussolini, piccolo borghese*, Milan, 1950.
103 Other notable biographies were those written by Laura Fermi, *Mussolini*, Chicago, 1961; and M. Gallo, *Mussolini's Italy: twenty years of the Fascist era*, London, 1974. Of these, Fermi was the more determinedly anti-Fascist. Gallo had more verve.
104 G. Pini and D. Susmel, *Mussolini: l'uomo e l'opera* (4 vols.), Florence, 1953.

began to publish his lengthy account. It should, however, be noted that, by the 1970s,[105] one scholar from the Anglo-Saxon world had gone further than De Felice in averring that Mussolini was indeed a Great Man. A. James Gregor was an anti-Communist[106] political scientist, and also a believer in 'developmental dictatorship', in which category he placed Fascism – 'one of the most consistent ideologies of our time', 'as coherent and persuasive as any other'.[107] By Gregor's reckoning Mussolini was a genuine revolutionary, rightly defined as a 'Marxist heretic' in recognition of his perpetual striving for a real revolution and his rallying of the populace behind his ideas.[108] When his life was studied in the appropriate manner, concluded Gregor, Mussolini could be applauded as one of the most original and influential thinkers of the twentieth century. By 1937 he had modernised the country, founded an empire, justified Italy's rank as a Great Power and achieved a 'national, syndicalist and corporative revolution'. Only the 'tragedy' of the Second World War had obscured this success,[109] and even in the Salò Republic, Gregor contended, Mussolini was trying to assemble a serious political legacy which could outlive the war.[110]

In his rehabilitation of the *Duce*, however, Gregor outran most of his readers. Until the conservative turn of the 1990s and outside some elements of the American Right, he remained an isolated and even eccentric figure. Rather, the majority position in the scholarly literature was reflected by the liberal English historian and well-publicised rival to De Felice, Denis Mack Smith. Back in the 1950s Mack Smith had swiftly established a reputation as the major English-language historian of the Risorgimento.[111] His

---

105 For his intervention in the De Felice debates of the time, see A. J. Gregor, 'Professor Renzo De Felice and the fascist phenomenon', *World Politics*, 30, 1978, pp. 443–9.

106 See e.g. A. J. Gregor, *A survey of Marxism: problems in the philosophy and the theory of history*, New York, 1965.

107 A. J. Gregor, *Italian Fascism and developmental dictatorship*, Princeton, 1979, p. 256; *Sergio Panunzio: il sindacalismo e il fondamento nazionale del fascismo*, Rome, 1978, p. 8. This latter work was published by Giovanni Volpe Editore, the publishing house of the son of Gioacchino Volpe. Gregor had earlier published his *Il fascismo. Interpretazioni e giudizi*, Rome, 1976, with the same firm. It was perhaps appropriate that Gregor should dedicate one of his main books to 'the memory of [the Fascist historian] Gioacchino Volpe and those he loved'. A. J. Gregor, *Italian Fascism and developmental dictatorship*, p. v. For more on Volpe, see Chapters 2 and 4.

108 A. J. Gregor, *Young Mussolini and the intellectual origins of Fascism*, Berkeley, 1979, pp. 251–3; cf. his *Interpretations of fascism*, Morristown, NJ, 1974.

109 A. J. Gregor, *Sergio Panunzio: il sindacalismo e il fondamento nazionale del fascismo*, p. 66.

110 A. J. Gregor, *The ideology of Fascism: the rationale of totalitarianism*, New York, 1969, pp. 292–3. The Italian translation of this work, *L'ideologia del fascismo*, Milan, 1974, was published by Edizioni del Borghese, a firm linked to the strident neo-Fascist weekly *Il Borghese*.

111 His chief Italian rival in interpreting the Risorgimento was Rosario Romeo who, by the 1970s and 1980s, had become a close friend and political colleague of De Felice. Throughout these decades Romeo kept up a running attack on what he regarded as Mack Smith's levity. For background, see R. J. B. Bosworth, *Italy and the wider world 1860–1960*, p. 11.

sparkling prose, and the apparent compatibility of his views with those of Gramsci which were contemporaneously being circulated by pro-PCI historians, made him a special hero on the Left and among all those who had critical views of the history of United Italy or who still thought of themselves as anti-Fascists.

In 1959, Mack Smith moved beyond his previous concentration on the Risorgimento to publish a general history of Italy which, at least implicitly, endorsed a continuity thesis and explained Fascism as 'the autobiography of a nation' and the 'revelation' of the inadequacies of the unification process. Mack Smith's Italy pursued a negative *Sonderweg*, one that seemed very much its own but would turn out to be not so different from that which critical historians would soon be discerning in Imperial, Weimar and Nazi Germany. When Mussolini appeared in this account he was described as an exponent of 'pure opportunism', a shallow politician given to 'posturing' and 'megalomania'.[112] It was not so much in the general history as in a semi-scholarly essay, however, that Mack Smith arrived at his most long-standing comprehension of Mussolini. The *Duce*, Mack Smith declared, was 'an artist in propaganda', the eternal superficial journalist turning a line. Indeed, so compelling was Mussolini's propaganda that, according to Mack Smith, he ended up believing it himself. Though he was sold as a Superman, the *Duce* was really a somewhat timid opportunist, and he presided over a regime which was in the final analysis as superficial and hollow as he was himself.[113]

This view scarcely marked a radical departure from Namier's or from that of other non-Italian biographers of Mussolini. In the next decade Mack Smith remained best known for his books on the Risorgimento, which continued to be published in a steady stream, only occasionally commenting on Fascist Italy, usually with wry evidence about its meretriciousness.[114] However, in the mid-1970s he was drawn into the controversy which raged within and outside Italy after the publication of another volume of De Felice's biography. Mack Smith now wrote two books on Fascism, the first a study of Fascist foreign policy;[115] the second was his own biography of the *Duce*.

In these two new books there was the occasional grudging admission of apparent Mussolinian achievements but, as Mack Smith at once made plain, in any hard analysis Mussolini must be assessed a failure, a victim of 'flattery', unable to do what he said, the chief of 'a movement that could be dressed up to look plausible' but which, in reality, left a legacy of 'dust and ashes'. 'Italian fascism,' concluded Mack Smith, 'was more than just

---

112 D. Mack Smith, *Italy: a modern history*, Ann Arbor, 1969, pp. 324–5.
113 D. Mack Smith, 'Mussolini, artist in propaganda', *History Today*, 9, 1959, pp. 223–31.
114 See e.g. D. Mack Smith, 'Anti-British propaganda in Fascist Italy', in *Inghilterra e Italia nel 1900: atti del convegno di Bagni di Lucca ottobre 1972*, Florence, 1973.
115 D. Mack Smith, *Mussolini's Roman Empire*, London, 1976.

Mussolini. But the quirks of character in this one man were a crucial factor in both its successes and failures.' In truth, Mussolini was little more than 'a gifted actor; his one superlative ability was as a propagandist'.[116] As a consequence, it was no surprise that the *Duce* would finish 'strung up by the heels in the Piazzale Loreto at Milan, mocked and vilified by the mob'.[117]

As these last words of Mack Smith's book indicate, in the early 1980s ideas about a sawdust Caesar had not perished, at least in the non-Italian world. It is doubtful if the situation has changed much since then (even if Italian 'post-fascists' cleave to the line that Mussolini was 'the greatest statesman of the twentieth century'). Rather, the present image of Mussolini is a highly paradoxical one. The dominating 'intentionalists' regularly underline the fact that the *Duce* ran a major European country for a generation, but then usually go on to point up the many hypocrisies, inconsistencies and failures of the Fascist regime, and ascribe such limitations to Mussolini's personal inadequacies. Structuralist historians, by contrast, tend just to ignore the *Duce* as they examine features of Italian life in the *longue durée*. A convincing study of the decision-making process in Italy from 1922 to 1945 has not yet been written and, until it is, no full appraisal of Mussolini can be made, for all my own suspicion that the chief of an 'Italian dictatorship' must have been something like the least of the dictators, a leader who deceived himself when he proclaimed that, as a Roman statesman, he was bending foreign and domestic history to his will.

116 D. Mack Smith, *Mussolini*, London, 1981, pp. xiii–xiv.
117 D. Mack Smith, *Mussolini*, p. 320.

4

Fascist Foreign and Racial Policies: 'One Man Alone'?

In one of those throwaway 'goaks' which so enliven his prose and so enrage the more dull-witted of his critics, A. J. P. Taylor, more than 30 years ago wrote himself off as just a hack, old-fashioned, diplomatic historian.[1] In so doing Taylor was already alert to the decline of international relations as a topic within the discipline of history. Rather as with Great Men, issues of foreign policy have steadily lost ground as the object of research, given the rise first of social history, and latterly both of postmodernist approaches to the past and of cultural history. In the absolute relativism of the more extreme postmodernists, diplomatic historians have been categorised as scholars who enter archives proclaiming their empiricism, while their real intention is just to lie for their country.[2] Though issues of peace and war continue to beset the world, even under the current largely uncontested hegemony of the USA, historians who aspire to reach the cutting edge of the discipline these days rarely occupy themselves with narrating the official version of international relations. A number of diplomatic historians continue to research and write; some journals still publish their works. Outside their own immediate circles, however, these scholars attract little attention or respect from the rest of the profession.

In Italy the matter is further complicated by the local structure of university teaching. Quite a few diplomatic historians survive, but they generally do so through an overt relationship to the Italian state. They are quite openly in state service. Thus, one of Italy's most distinguished, productive and moderate diplomatic historians of the last generation has

---

1 For the background, see R. J. B. Bosworth, *Explaining Auschwitz and Hiroshima: history writing and the Second World War 1945–1990*, London, 1993, pp. 41–5.
2 See, in English at its most summary, K. Jenkins, *Re-thinking history*, London, 1991 and, less convincingly, his follow-up book, *On 'What is History' from Carr and Elton to Rorty and White*, London, 1995.

been Enrico Serra.[3] Before his retirement it was natural that he should both preside over the archives of the Italian Ministry of Foreign Affairs and hold a chair in the 'history of treaties and international relations' at the University of Bologna. It was similarly normal for him to publish a stream of learned papers and books on Italian diplomacy, studies which originated in the research that he was able to complete in the archives he ran. At the same time, a considerable proportion of his teaching[4] was consumed by those who each year sought or won entry into the national diplomatic service; courses on the history of treaties and international relations were typically directed at that market.

Serra is not alone.[5] The mainstream of researchers into the history of Italian foreign policy frequently retain a direct tie to the present practice of Italian diplomacy. Though, inevitably, the quality and character of their work varies, they are unlikely to launch too many radical[6] attacks against Italy's behaviour on the international stage.[7] As has been noted above, one of the clichés of contemporary Italian intellectual and political history is that, in the 1970s, Marxism achieved almost unchallenged dominance in national culture. This cliché is untrue for diplomatic historians. Moreover, their backgrounds and the nature of their work make it unusual for them to have much sympathy for, or connection with, historians who research in other fields of national history, or who pursue methodologies beyond the

3 For his evocative memoirs of his career first as a Fascist tank-commander and then as an anti-Fascist, close to Ferruccio Parri and aware of his own leadership qualities while doubtful of the 'readiness' of the Italian people, see E. Serra, *Tempi duri: guerra e resistenza*, Bologna, 1996.

4 See e.g. his text book for such courses, E. Serra, *La diplomazia in Italia*, Milan, 1984. Serra's son Maurizio entered the Italian diplomatic service in 1978, and since then has found time to be a historian of modern culture, with methodological and political assumptions near to the De Feliceans. See e.g. M. Serra, *Una cultura dell' autorità: la Francia di Vichy*, Bari, 1980; *La ferita della modernità: intellettuali, totalitarismo e immagine del nemico*, Bologna, 1992.

5 For another emblematic case, see the work of Mario Toscano, a predecessor of Serra at the Ministry of Foreign Affairs. Toscano was both extremely patriotic and Jewish. The patriotism is easily found in his work both before 1938 and after 1945. See, among his voluminous publications, e.g. M. Toscano, *Il patto di Londra: storia diplomatica dell'intervento italiano 1914–1915*, Bologna, 1934; *Storia diplomatica della questione dell'Alto Adige*, Bari, 1967; his *The origins of the Pact of Steel*, Baltimore, 1967 is the major work available in translation. Toscano, Serra, Pastorelli and the rest, continuing to combine scholarship and service to the state, were also typically editing numbers in the still unfinished and highly professional series of *Documenti diplomatici italiani*.

6 See e.g. the collection of essays by R. J. B. Bosworth and S. Romano (eds), *La politica estera italiana 1860–1985*, Bologna, 1991 and contrast the tone, say, of my own chapter with those of the five distinguished Italian contributors.

7 Serra's successor in charge of the archives is the much more overtly conservative and nationalist Piero Pastorelli who teaches 'the history of treaties and international relations' at the University of Rome. For his work and attitudes, see e.g. P. Pastorelli, *La politica estera italiana del dopoguerra*, Bologna, 1987; 'Il principio di nazionalità nella politica estera italiana', in G. Spadolini (ed.), *Nazione e nazionalità in Italia: dall'alba del secolo ai nostri giorni*, Bari, 1994, pp. 185–208. In this latter paper Pastorelli argues, remarkably, that the key to all Italian diplomacy was the desire to complete the nation.

simple Rankean one of reading what one clerk said to another. The diplomatic historians of modern Italy very much constitute a caste of their own, writing, to a considerable extent, about themselves and for themselves.[8]

Diplomatic historians may preside over or be confined to their special arena, and be ignored or discounted by the rest of the profession. However, as with Great Men, one exception to this rule lies in the history of the origins of the Second World War, as well as of the Cold War which succeeded it. Another appears in assessments of those racial policies, certainly of Nazi Germany and perhaps of the other fascist regimes, which drove the world into the abyss of the Holocaust and 'Auschwitz'. In the debates which still circle around the Second World War it remains mandatory to discuss issues of foreign policy and to define them as expansively as possible. Historians of Fascism can scarcely avoid diplomatic history, but it is best for them to approach the existing literature in critical vein.

What, then, are the fundamental questions about the relationship between Mussolini's regime and the world outside Italy? Did Fascism mean war? Was Italy's Second World War the inevitable result of the installation in power in Rome of a dynamically nationalist ideology, both militarist and militant? When the egregious Achille Starace, Fascist Party Secretary from December 1931 to October 1939, remarked that making war was, to him, as natural and trifling a matter as eating a plate of macaroni,[9] was he expressing a Fascist drive to armed conflict or just being a fool? Similarly, was Fascism by its very definition racist? Did its commitment to national grandeur and expansion inevitably entail a blithe eventual acceptance of genocide? Or were Italians, in spite of Fascism, a people who well exemplify the 'banality of good' and were never, therefore, 'Hitler's willing executioners'? These are the issues which still preoccupy all attempts to define and comprehend Fascism. What conclusions have currently been reached in the debates over such matters, and how do present views relate both to the previous historiography and the contemporary context inside and outside Italy?

Here one starting-point might be Taylor's finely honed prose in his *Origins of the Second World War*, the seminal book which gave short shrift to Fascist foreign (and, indeed, domestic) policy. For Taylor,

Fascism never possessed the ruthless drive, let alone the material strength, of National Socialism. Morally it was just as corrupting – or perhaps more so from its very dishonesty. Everything about Fascism was a fraud. The social peril from which it saved Italy was a fraud; the revolution by which it seized power was a fraud; the ability and policy

8 This situation may be exaggerated in the Italian case, but is not unknown in other countries.
9 C. Senise, *Quando ero Capo della polizia, 1940–1943*, Rome, 1946, p. 35.

of Mussolini were fraudulent. Fascist rule was corrupt, incompetent, empty; Mussolini himself a vain, blundering boaster without either ideas or aims.[10]

Taylor's words were doubtless crafted with greater panache than those of many another commentator. As has been indicated in the previous chapter, however, they were scarcely original. Rather, they replicated the standard line, held especially outside Italy, that Mussolini was a mountebank dictator[11] and a sawdust Caesar, and that his regime could in no way match 'the horror, the horror' of the Nazi or Stalinist hearts of darkness.

In the immediate post-war period this interpretation of Mussolini as an international aggressor, but one with decidedly limited achievements, had been given weight in a detailed study of the regime's foreign policy,[12] published by the liberal-democrat anti-Fascist historian Gaetano Salvemini. Returning from Harvard to the University of Florence in 1949, Salvemini used the occasion to amplify his earlier accounts of the Fascist regime[13] with a scholarly reckoning of Fascist foreign policy. Mussolini, his fellow travellers at home and those who tried to appease both Hitler and him abroad very much deserved responsibility for the 'Prelude to World War II', as Salvemini's book was entitled.[14] Each of these 'guilty men' none the less behaved in his own distinctive way. Mussolini, for example, Salvemini argued, 'was never the great statesman many believed him to be'. He was, rather, 'always an irresponsible improviser, half madman, half criminal, gifted only – but to the highest degree – in the arts of "propaganda" and mystification'.[15] By some ultimate standard of evil, then, Hitler was still the 'arch-criminal', but Mussolini had not foregone that status for want of trying. The Italian dictator, concluded Salvemini, 'did his wicked utmost to follow Hitler's footsteps, his evil-doing being limited solely by his inability to do worse'.[16] In Salvemini's view, Mussolinian Italy meant war, but it also meant chaotic, poorly organised and managed, unsuccessful and unpopular war.

Recognising that his views were after all his own, Salvemini, in his preface, had some surprisingly sharp words for historians who held a simple empiricist understanding of their activities: 'There are certain historians . . . sincerely convinced that they are unbiased, impartial, "scientific", who

10 A. J. P. Taylor, *The Origins of the Second World War*, Harmondsworth, 1964, pp. 84–5.
11 It is intriguing to see the term reappear in an otherwise rather pedestrian account of Fascist foreign policy. H. J. Burgwyn, *Italian foreign policy in the interwar period 1918–1940*, Westport, Conn., 1997, p. 222.
12 Less noticed abroad were two ex-Fascist accounts of the era which sought to reclaim virtue, at least for nationalist aims. See A. Tamaro, *La condanna dell'Italia nel trattato di pace*, Rocca San Casciano, 1952 (and cf. his more general A. Tamaro, *Venti anni di storia 1922–1943*, Rome, 1953); L. Villari, *Affari esteri, 1943–1945*, Rome, 1948.
13 See Chapter 3.
14 G. Salvemini, *Prelude to World War II*, London, 1953.
15 G. Salvemini, *Prelude*, p. 10.
16 G. Salvemini, *Prelude*, p. 510.

reject as "biased" any opinion that clashes with their own bias: they are fools endowed with a God Almighty complex. . . . Impartiality', Salvemini ran on, 'is either a delusion of the simple-minded, a banner of the opportunist, or the boast of the dishonest.'[17] This emphasis on history as a debate in which all (worthwhile) conclusions must remain arguable has sometimes been forgotten by those who have succeeded Salvemini in assessing the character of Fascist foreign policy. The words also carry a certain irony in his own case. Salvemini's career as a historian had begun in Liberal Italy and had, from its inception, combined scholarship with political commitment. An enemy of Giovanni Giolitti – he denounced the Liberal leader as one presiding over a 'Ministry of Crime'[18] – Salvemini wanted Italy to hasten on its journey towards democracy and modernity. He was also a patriot, one who worked for Italy's entry into the First World War, even if he wanted the result to be the extension of liberty and 'democracy' and not the building of an oppressive empire. In other words, Salvemini may have been critical of what he deemed to be Giolitti's manipulation of foreign policy for domestic ends, and he may have always opposed expansionist nationalism, but he certainly did not renounce the Italian national project. A self-confessed heir of Giuseppe Mazzini,[19] Salvemini wanted Italy to be a Great Power, but one in the service of what he regarded as the general good. All in all, then, there was something contradictory in Salvemini's analysis of Fascism's place in the world when he moved beyond an intentionalist denunciation of Mussolini. The King, the Pope and their friends were, in his eyes, culpable too; but somewhere in Italy, he maintained stoutly, there survived the virtue and the *virtù* of the Italian people and of the good Risorgimento's determination to spread liberty to the world.

In the aftermath of the First World War Salvemini had similarly preached these ideals, and had endeavoured to make the *Associazione Nazionale Combattenti* (the National Returned Soldiers' Association) their vehicle.[20] However, he and his friends had proved no match for Fascism, though Salvemini himself could rightly be deemed an anti-Fascist before the March on Rome. In 1925 Salvemini escaped from Fascist vindictiveness and bullying at his university, and for the next two decades remained one of the *fuorusciti*, operating outside Italy. In his flight he had been assisted by a young historian, Federico Chabod, who thereafter constructed a career within Fascist Italy and who would emerge in the 1950s as the most

17 G. Salvemini, *Prelude*, p. 9.
18 Salvemini's extensive works are available in a multi-volume Italian edition. In this particular case, see G. Salvemini, *Il ministro della mala vita e altri scritti sull'Italia giolittiana*, ed. E. Apih, Milan, 1962.
19 Mazzini's legacy has, of course, been disputed by very many heirs, who range from Fascists to the Far Left. In the most recent biography, Denis Mack Smith has depicted him as an imaginer of the European Union. See D. Mack Smith, *Mazzini*, New Haven, 1994.
20 For the standard account, see G. Sabbatucci, *I combattenti nel primo dopoguerra*, Bari, 1974.

prestigious and respected of liberal democrats, in quite a few minds a living symbol of the alleged fact that Italy had sloughed off its Fascist past. Chabod would work in a number of fields, but would gain special fame as the most intellectually innovative Italian analyst of foreign policy. Yet, as a student of Italy's place in the world, he, too, retained certain ambiguities.

Chabod's case has been revived in recent decades because his ghost has been summoned by the group of anti-Communist historians to join a national pantheon of the great and the good, helping thereby, even after his death, to rout the Marxists.[21] It is typical of this perceived posthumous relevance that Chabod's most celebrated book has, with the patronage of the Agnelli foundation, been belatedly translated into English.[22] In a welcoming preface to this edition, Charles Maier of Harvard has advised that Chabod's work can still be read in order to 'provide a revealing glimpse into how thoughtful, acutely responsible political historians envisaged a potential national society that might satisfy longings for community association without brutal chauvinism'.[23] Yet Chabod's history of Italian foreign policy in the period after 1870 had originally been conceptualised in Fascist Italy, with the approval and encouragement of the most prominent historian of the Fascist era, Gioacchino Volpe, and at a moment when Chabod himself was delighted at the idea that Fascism had conquered an African Empire for the nation. It cannot be automatically assumed that Chabod was always and utterly anti-Fascist. Indeed, his case raises the general question of how the historical profession behaved under the dictatorship. Moreover, what legacy did writing in the Fascist era have, for example in the later historiography of national diplomacy?[24]

Here controversy remains. The standard view is that the great majority of historians were not enslaved by Fascism. Even Volpe, we are these days told,[25] was not a real Fascist and, indeed, bravely resisted and circumvented the hostility of the regime; he should be remembered as 'one of the greatest

21 See e.g. the massive 721-page exploration of his career: B. Vigezzi (ed.), *Federico Chabod e la nuova storiografia italiana 1919–1950*, Milan, 1983. The contributors, who included De Felice and Republican Prime Minister and patriotic belle-lettrist historian Giovanni Spadolini, tended to be associated with that anti-communist and post-Christian-Democrat politics which would reach its doubtful pinnacle in the career of Bettino Craxi.

22 F. Chabod, *Italian foreign policy: the statecraft of the founders*, Princeton, 1996. The original Italian edition was entitled *Storia della politica estera italiana dal 1870 al 1896* and was published under the editorship of the *Istituto per gli studi di politica internazionale* in Milan in 1951. It was meant to be the first volume of a projected four, but the full work was never finished.

23 C. Maier, 'Foreword to the series', in F. Chabod, *Italian foreign policy*, p. xiii. It would thus, Maier said, be all the more relevant given the present rediscovery, presumably in the Balkans, of 'the pathologies of ethnic nationalism' (p. xii). Maier was talking about Chabod and work by socialist philosopher Norberto Bobbio and communist historian Emilio Sereni, each also being translated through the Agnelli-Princeton combination.

24 See e.g. De Felice's comment that anti-Fascists preserved much of a 'Fascist mentality'. R. De Felice, *Intervista sul fascismo*, ed. M. Ledeen, Bari, 1975, p. 7.

25 Perhaps the most balanced account is that by the Marxist G. Turi, 'Il problema Volpe', *Studi Storici*, 19, 1978, pp. 175–86.

and most resolutely modern historians of contemporary Italy'.[26] He is, we are also assured, best defined as a nationalist or patriot. By the 1980s and 1990s this commitment to the *patria* meant that he should be revered all the more, since the De Felices and Romeos of the Italian historical profession were arguing that what was wrong with their current Italy, and had been wrong with it since the fall of Fascism, was the lack of (good) nationalism.

Whatever the case, Volpe was but one part of the story of Italian history writing under Fascism, if only because he himself did not insist that his juniors automatically accept all of his own ideas. (Perhaps his openness should not be too naïvely praised. Even the ex-quadruumvir of the March on Rome, Cesare De Vecchi di Val Cismon, Minister of Education in 1935–6, can be found avowing the need for accurate and independent scholarship, while being sure that history was always best harnessed to the national cause.)[27] If the Fascists were less than tyrannous in their intrusions into the work of the younger generation of the historical profession, they had also not eliminated overtly anti-Fascist ideas. Thus, although Volpe himself was not a fan,[28] Benedetto Croce could, throughout the Fascist years, act as a surviving liberal beacon to the new generation. Crocean ideas, at least so it was said after 1945, percolated more readily than Fascist ones into the minds of the new cohort of Italian historians, who were thus likely to commit their souls to liberty even at that moment at which the Fascist regime was most determinedly and totalitarianly anxious to forge new Fascist men and women. At least in the history trade, it seems, the Fascist slogan of the 1930s, 'Make way for the young', prompted the commencement of many a non-Fascist career, based for the time on a newly professional commitment to 'science' and, by implication, ready for the world after 1945.

Those who researched the history of national foreign policy, so this version of the historiographical past avers, were particularly fortunate. They were armed against Fascist corruption and foolishness not only by the intellectual generosity of Volpe – he can readily enough be found urging better scholarship and a more acute understanding of the world outside

26 See R. Moscati, 'Ricordo di un maestro', in *Studi in onore di Gioacchino Volpe nel centenario della nascita (1876–1976)*, Rome, 1978, pp. 125–6. For a more recent example, see B. Vigezzi, 'Volpe, Croce, Chabod e la storia della politica estera dell'Italia liberale e la discussione sullo storicismo', *Storia contemporanea*, 22, 1991, pp. 397–418.
27 For the flavour of De Vecchi's historiographical leadership, see C. De Vecchi di Val Cismon, 'Esame di coscienza', *Rassegna Storica del Risorgimento*, 23, 1936, pp. 3–14; 'Per l'inaugurazione del XXVI congresso dell'istituto', *Rassegna Storica del Risorgimento*, 25, 1938, pp. 1319–26; 'La storia negli studi militari', *Rassegna Storica del Risorgimento*, 26, 1939, pp. 3–10; 'Ancora di Carlo Alberto', *Rassegna Storica del Risorgimento*, 28, 1941, pp. 607–14; 'Altezza di tono', *Rassegna Storica del Risorgimento*, 29, 1942, pp. 155–6. It is hard to distinguish between the views here expressed by De Vecchi and those of Volpe.
28 G. Volpe, *L'Italia in cammino: l'ultimo cinquantennio*, Milan, 1928 was written in response to the celebrated B. Croce, *Storia d'Italia dal 1871 al 1915*, Bari, 1967 (first published 1928). An English translation is available as B. Croce, *A history of Italy 1871–1915*, Oxford, 1929.

Italy[29] – and by the spiritual integrity of Croce. They also had an institutional base, the *Istituto per gli studi di politica internazionale* (ISPI), established in Milan in 1933,[30] and, eventually, presided over by Alberto Pirelli.[31] The books and journals published by ISPI, it is said, were serious and empirical pieces of scholarship,[32] cleansed of the Fascist aggression eddying around in the late 1930s and arguably 'anti-Fascist', at least in tendency. What ISPI well reflected was what nowadays is termed 'international best practice'. Its researchers, who included Enrico Serra[33] and many distinguished post-1945 historians, were granted access, otherwise forbidden by Fascist censorship, to the highest quality international work, for example that published by Chatham House in Britain. This privilege meant in turn that ISPI researchers were anxious to replicate such standards and, even more naturally, were led both to despise Fascist parochialism and crudity, and to prepare themselves to act as a new ruling élite as soon as the generation which Mussolini himself represented relinquished power. In sum, those who were lucky enough to work at ISPI were, by this reckoning, decontaminated of Fascist influences even as they accepted pay cheques from the regime.

Chabod's history of Liberal foreign policy appears to provide the final proof of the matter. It is intellectually wide-ranging and well ahead of its time in reviewing those 'unspoken assumptions' and that *Primat der Innenpolitik* which, as historians like Fritz Fischer and James Joll would remind students in the 1960s, have an immense influence on any diplomatic dealing. As Chabod put it in his preface, he would disclose the 'material and moral' bases of Italy's international situation:

> That is to say: passions and all forms of affect, ideas and ideologies, the situation of the country and of individuals – in a word everything that makes foreign policy a component or aspect of a much larger and more complex historical process that embraces the entire life of the

29 See e.g. G. Volpe, *Guerra dopoguerra fascismo*, Venice, 1928, p. 374, where he had proclaimed that 'the order of the day should be know the world, study the world'.

30 A. Montenegro, 'Politica estera e organizzazione del consenso. Note sull'Istituto per gli studi di politica internazionale', *Studi Storici*, 19, 1978, pp. 777–818.

31 For Pirelli, from the great Milanese industrialist family, see his important and revealing diaries, especially as read between the lines: A. Pirelli, *Taccuini 1922–1943*, Bologna, 1984 and the highly significant A. Pirelli, *Economia e guerra* (2 vols.), Milan, 1940. Each volume appeared under the ISPI imprint, Vol. 1 in May 1940, Vol. 2 in July.

32 For a contrary account, see R. Bosworth, 'Italy's historians and the myth of Fascism', in R. Langhorne (ed.), *Diplomacy and intelligence during the Second World War: essays in honour of F. H. Hinsley*, Cambridge, 1985, pp. 94–8.

33 For his own version see E. Serra, *Tempi duri: guerra e resistenza*, pp. 17–26. In Serra's account (p. 26) one of the most avowedly anti-Fascist among ISPI's historians was Carlo Zaghi. Both before and after Fascism, Zaghi's special area of expertise was the Empire. There he could be critical of the stupidity of certain politicians, for example that of Crispi before the Battle of Adua, but he certainly did not reject outright the idea of an Italian empire. See e.g. C. Zaghi, *Le origini della colonia Eritrea*, Bologna, 1934; *P.S. Mancini, l'Africa e il problema del Mediterraneo, 1884–5*, Rome, 1955; *L'Africa nella coscienza europea e l'imperialismo italiano*, Naples, 1973.

nation, defies any separation into watertight compartments, and binds
the field of foreign relations tightly and inseparably to its counterpart,
the internal life of the nation in its moral, economic, social, and
religious aspects.[34]

Chabod evinced pride, too, in Italy's liberal traditions: Cavour, in telling
contrast to Bismarck, was 'profoundly liberal'.[35] Left to its own devices,[36] it
seems from Chabod's account, it would indeed have been possible for Italy
to have become a force for good in the world.

Perhaps the cosiness of this version of the history of Italian history needs
probing, however. In the case of Nazism, the work of Michael Burleigh[37]
and others has illustrated that, at a very minimum, ostensibly respectable
German scholarship in the social sciences and related disciplines, including
history, contributed during the Third Reich to that atmosphere which
would produce the 'barbarisation of warfare on the Eastern front'[38] and
'Auschwitz'. What evidence is there that Italian historians under Fascism
were implicated in the aggression of the Fascist regime?

The answer to this question is undoubtedly that some evidence indeed
exists, even if it should be placed as scrupulously as possible in context.[39]
Take Volpe, for example. There can be no doubt that Volpe was a
nationalist, pledged to Italian expansion in an African empire and
elsewhere.[40] His very understanding of truth was that it had to be national.
As he wrote before 1922, 'A non-Italian, or non-German, or non-French,
teacher is, in Italy, or Germany, or France, a non-teacher.'[41] Once the
Fascists were in power Volpe was occasionally troubled by their cruder
elements, but he reserved his main derision for League of Nations
enthusiasts and all who clung to an internationalist ideal.[42] On a number of

34 F. Chabod, *Italian foreign policy*, p. xxxix.
35 F. Chabod, *Italian foreign policy*, p. 112.
36 Chabod himself is a little uncertain on the final motivation of foreign policy. For all his
    avowal of the power of ideas, he frequently ends up endorsing 'realism': 'Ideology
    evaporates,' he tells us, for example, 'and after the process of distillation there remains only
    the pure analysis of the element of power, of well-armed national entities driven only by
    their own self-interest and intent on fighting for hegemony in one area of the world or
    another.' F. Chabod, *Italian foreign policy*, pp. 44–5.
37 See e.g. M. Burleigh, *Germany turns eastwards: a study of 'Ostforschung' in the Third
    Reich*, Cambridge, 1988.
38 For the full implications of this usage, see the seminal work of Omer Bartov, including e.g.
    The Eastern Front, 1941–45: German troops and the barbarisation of warfare, London,
    1986 and *Murder in our midst: the Holocaust, industrial killing, and representation*,
    Oxford, 1996.
39 For my own earlier exploration of the matter, see R. Bosworth, 'Italy's historians and the
    myth of Fascism', pp. 85–105.
40 For further detail, see R. Bosworth, 'Italy's historians and the myth of Fascism', pp. 88–93.
41 G. Volpe, *Guerra dopoguerra fascismo*, p. 7. Conflict, he thought (p. 9), brought death but
    also life. He added, hopefully, that the Great War had set the entire Middle East in motion
    and that Alexandria was a 'half Italian city' (p. 113).
42 See especially G. Volpe, *Pacifismo e storia*, Rome, 1934. This 43-page pamphlet was
    published by the *Istituto nazionale fascista di cultura*.

occasions his work appeared implicitly or explicitly designed to sustain Fascist policy. For example, he deemed January 1939 a suitable moment at which to publish his *Storia della Corsica italiana* with ISPI. In this book he avoided the wilder claims then being voiced as part of Ciano's anti-French campaign for 'Tunis, Corsica, Djibouti and Nice'[43] and, instead, urged 'accuracy' and 'truth' as the watchwords for any study of the island.[44] None the less Volpe, indeed preferring a national truth, did provide what he regarded as conclusive evidence from geography and from historical thought and deed to demonstrate that 'Italian Corsica is not all of Corsica but is the greater part of it.'[45] He expressed his disappointment that the French had banned the work of the *Archivio Storico di Corsica* which he had set up in Milan in 1925, and disclaimed any aggressive intent. Yet it is hard to see that Paris was not reading him correctly. Certainly, at the very least, had some diplomatic or military chance brought Corsica into Italian hands Volpe's research could have been used to justify the island's retention by those masters who, his history stated, some time in the past had been its natural rulers.

Similarly, in May 1940 Volpe published his sometimes still lauded study of Italian 'public opinion' in 1914–15. Perhaps his motives were mixed; he dedicated the work to his sons, then approaching both manhood and war service. None the less, his preface suggested that he hailed much Fascist achievement. The counterproductive divisions and debates of the liberal era had, he wrote, been replaced by calm resolution. The rightful claims of the First World War – Trieste, Trento and the Adriatic – were now safe in Italian hands and were no longer matters of dispute. For the future there beckoned 'a greater sea, but one that was no less necessary'. Volpe's Italy was indeed 'on the march', and his phrases made it seem that the likely result would be territorial gain in the Mediterranean, won, inevitably and with his applause, from the liberal democracies of Britain and France.[46]

Nor were Volpe's commitments and beliefs altered when he knew the end of the story; that is, when he had seen the military and social disaster which the Second World War brought to Italy and the world, and had watched Italy renounce its empire in Africa, Albania and the Mediterranean and in its turn change into a liberal democracy. Since he was one of the very few Italians to lose his job in the usually lenient post-war purges,[47] Volpe may have had some personal justification for his intransigence. Certainly in the 1950s he was an intransigent. In his dreams Volpe hoped still that through

43 For an example of the wilder claims, see B. Pegoletti, *Corsica Tunisia Gibuti (dal taccuino di un 'inviato speciale')*, Florence, 1939.
44 G. Volpe, *Storia della Corsica italiana*, Milan, 1939, p. 289.
45 G. Volpe, *Storia della Corsica italiana*, p. 11.
46 G. Volpe, *Il popolo italiano tra la pace e la guerra (1914–1915)*, Milan, 1940, pp. 7–11. The book was published by ISPI and was based on writings first drafted in 1923–4.
47 For an English-language account of the background, see R. P. Domenico, *Italian Fascists on trial 1943–1948*, Chapel Hill, NC, 1991, though the book does not mention Volpe.

a 'new Risorgimento'[48] Italy would find a way to become a genuine Great Power. He had not even altogether accepted that the United States was both the Superpower and Italy's benevolent friend, as he summoned to his readers' view Gabriele d'Annunzio, 'a poet, an Italian poet'. The Archangel Gabriel[e]'s heroism in the Great War, Volpe recalled mistily, had occurred at a time when 'the greatest "liberators", the ultraliberators, the highest champions of "European and Christian civilisation", with their total bombing of defenceless cities even after the signing of armistices', had not been born.[49]

In the last few decades the conservative wing of the Italian history profession has cheerfully asserted that Volpe was the greatest historian produced in Italy this century.[50] Methodologically, empirically and ideologically, this is a highly arguable assertion. What is indicated, however, by Volpe's case, as well as by that of ISPI (this institution avoided linkage with the Salò Republic and, enjoying the blessing of Prime Minister Ferruccio Parri, soon resumed its activities after 1945),[51] and by Chabod and many members of that generation who, like Serra,[52] found their first academic employment under the Fascist regime is a marked continuity in the writing of the history of Italian foreign policy.

Historians may still be arguing whether it is proper to detect a continuity in the history of Italy from its unification through the Liberal and Fascist regimes and on to the Republic, but, with regard to Italian diplomatic historiography, the continuity is plain for all to see. In the decades after 1945, criticism of Mussolinian aggression would, of course, be possible and even the norm. However, for the great majority of students of Italian diplomacy, both intentionalism and the parenthesis thesis were taken as read. Any errors which might be detected in Italian behaviour during the inter-war period could thus be blamed on Mussolini and Fascism alone. Very few diplomatic historians either questioned the fundamental soundness of the national project of their state or objected to the main lines of its international actions since the Risorgimento. In their understanding,

---

48 G. Volpe, *L'impresa di Tripoli 1911–12*, Rome, 1946, p. 7.
49 G. Volpe, *Gabriele D'Annunzio: L'Italiano, il Politico, il Comandante*, rev. ed. Rome, 1981, p. 77.
50 For a series of eulogies, brought out under the Volpe family publishing house and at a moment in which history seemed to matter a very great deal, see the papers collected in *Studi in onore di Gioacchino Volpe nel centenario della nascita (1876–1976)*, Rome, 1978.
51 For Serra's autobiographical account of this revival, in which he played a major part as a leading young associate of Parri, see E. Serra, *Tempi duri: guerra e resistenza*, pp. 271–4.
52 For another classic case, cf. the successive works of Francesco Cataluccio, also sometime member of ISPI, and the biographer of Italy's Foreign Minister at the outbreak of the First World War. See F. Cataluccio, *Antonio San Giuliano e la politica estera italiana dal 1900 al 1914*, Florence, 1935; *Italia e Francia in Tunisia (1878–1939)*, Rome, 1939; *La 'nostra' guerra: L'Italia nella guerra mondiale*, Rome, 1940 (these last two works were released under the auspices of the *Istituto nazionale di cultura fascista*); *La politica estera di E. Visconti Venosta*, Florence, 1940; 'Problemi dell'emigrazione: emigrazione e "porta aperta"', *Nuova Antologia*, f. 1770, June 1948, pp. 192–7. By contrast, the leading anti-Fascist social historian Guido Quazza also found employment at ISPI during the war.

Italy was and should be a genuine Great Power, which must quite naturally pursue similar policies and ideas to those of other Great Powers. Only from 1922 to 1945, they averred, did the nation deviate from an ideal or predictable course.

The 'revisionist' works of, among others, Fritz Fischer in Germany, A. J. P. Taylor in Britain and Gabriel Kolko in the United States have, in those societies, normalised the view that a critical reading of national foreign policy is possible, and may even be a desirable part of that endless but passionate debate which, in a democracy, continues about all aspects of society. In Italy, however, there have been very few examples of this sort of 'revisionism'. When more critical readings of the national diplomatic past were attempted, they tended to come from non-Italian historians and could easily be written off, at least by major sections of the Italian historical profession, as the result of insufficient study and skill, or even as the manifestation of 'Italophobia: an English-speaking malady'.[53]

By the late 1960s, with the gradual opening of the archives, scholarly research into Fascist foreign policy had commenced. In the main, however, the messages of such scholarship were gentle. Whether written by Catholics,[54] moderate socialists,[55] Marxists[56] or, indeed, by foreigners,[57] the work was almost always posited on the assumption that Mussolini was himself to blame for Fascist aggression, that he was still the 'one man alone' who had committed Italy to the German alliance and capriciously entered the Second World War. Though the authors were not agreed on every aspect of their story, each painted an image of Italian diplomacy in which, at some time after the March on Rome, the healthy or commonplace traditions of Liberal Italy were ousted by a maleficent process of 'fascistisation'.[58] There were two especially symbolic moments in this story. One was the 'Corfu incident' of August 1923, when a dispute between Italy and Greece over the southern border of Albania provoked Mussolini to order his navy to shell the holiday island. In the words of a Canadian historian: 'Corfu disclosed the real

53 The phrase is that of the fine Canadian historian of emigration, Robert Harney. See the republication in his posthumously published collection of essays, R. Harney, *From the shores of hardship: Italians in Canada*, Welland, Ont., 1993, pp. 29–74.
54 See, notably, G. Rumi, *Alle origini della politica estera fascista (1918–1923)*, Bari, 1968.
55 See especially E. Di Nolfo, *Mussolini e la politica estera italiana, 1919–1933*, Rome, 1960. Very unusually, Di Nolfo has written evocatively of his own teenage years as a Fascist true believer and of the lights and shadows of the national *mentalité* at the end of the war. E. Di Nolfo, *Le paure e le speranze degli italiani (1943–1953)*, Milan, 1986.
56 See especially G. Carocci, *La politica estera dell'Italia fascista (1925–1928)*, Bari, 1969, but cf. F. D'Amoja, *Declino e prima crisi dell'Europa di Versailles: studio sulla diplomazia italiana e europea (1931–1933)*, Milan, 1967, which was more overtly structural in its approach.
57 The best example of a monograph is A. Cassels, *Mussolini's early diplomacy*, Princeton, 1970. Cf. also J. Barros, *The Corfu incident of 1923: Mussolini and the League of Nations*, Princeton, 1965.
58 For a very early analysis of the alleged fascistisation of the staff of the Italian Foreign Ministry, see the influential essay by F. Gilbert, 'Ciano and his ambassadors', in G. A. Craig and F. Gilbert (eds), *The diplomats 1919–1939*, Princeton, 1953, ii, pp. 512–36.

nature of Fascism's foreign policy. ... It constituted a veritable dress rehearsal of Mussolini's quarrel with the League over Ethiopia in 1935.'[59] The second was the dropping of Salvatore Contarini, the Secretary General of the Foreign Ministry (its bureaucratic head) in 1926; this action was followed shortly after by abolition of the office of Secretary General and thus, it is said, by the centralisation of policymaking into the hands of Mussolini or of his Minister of Foreign Affairs. In this version, the Mussolini of the 1920s was indeed bringing diplomacy under the totalitarian system and his own dictatorship, and readying his regime for the aggressive revisionism which would become more striking in the next decade. As Ennio Di Nolfo would put it, Italy was being pushed into a cleft stick: 'Mussolini thus backed revisionism [of the Treaty of Versailles] while not wanting actual revision.'[60] If his tactics were stupid, his methods were worse. Fascism was revolutionising and perverting the theory and the practice of Italian diplomacy.

In most senses, then, by the 1970s a consensus seemed to exist in the historiography of Fascist foreign policy. The surviving problem of research, most scholars suggested, was to fill in the detail rather than to grapple further with its meaning. No new questions needed to be asked, no new concepts deployed.

Yet, during the next years, the profound peace which had reigned over the historiography of Italian foreign policy was shaken, if not in the end broken. The challenges came from two very different directions. The first, and perhaps the most lasting and influential, originated within Italy. It was linked with a new willingness to express nationalist ideas of one kind or another, and exemplified a philosophical return to the beliefs, certainly of Volpe and ISPI and perhaps of Chabod and Croce, that the fundamental purpose of both good diplomatic history and good diplomacy lay in nation-construction. The second was occasioned by the publication of critical books by non-Italian scholars who translated into Italian non-Italian debates about aspects of the history of the twentieth century. Such criticism, occurring at a conservative turn in Italian culture, was out of kilter with the spirit of the times and, in the final analysis, had little perceptible impact on what remained the assumptions and conclusions of Italian writing about international relations.

The most blatantly new nationalist Italian historian of foreign policy was Rosaria Quartararo. Her main book addressed the character of Anglo-Italian relations from 1931 to the outbreak of war in 1940.[61] Documentary

---

59 A. Cassels, *Mussolini's early diplomacy*, pp. 125–6.
60 E. Di Nolfo, *Mussolini e la politica estera italiana, 1919–1933*, pp. 245–6.
61 R. Quartararo, *Roma tra Londra e Berlino: la politica estera fascista dal 1931 al 1940*, Rome, 1980. To some extent, cf. also D. Bolech Cecchi, *Non bruciare li ponti con Roma: le relazioni fra l'Italia, la Gran Bretagna e la Francia dall'accordo di Monaco allo scoppio della seconda guerra mondiale*, Milan, 1986. Bolech Cecchi is kinder to the British, but has some severe criticisms of French policy and generally treats 1930s diplomacy in 'realistic' vein.

evidence for this period, she contended, demanded an arch-realist reading of international behaviour. Fascist Italy's policies were 'absolutely *autonomous* [*sic*] in regard to internal policies'.[62] Pursuing the permanent national interest, Mussolini's Italy in its apparent flirtations with Nazi Germany was only seeking 'a mechanism for pressuring England towards a general accord'.[63] For Quartararo and, in her view, the statesmen of the 1930s, such an accord would have entailed a settlement in Europe along the lines of the praiseworthy Four Power Pact of 1933 and, beyond the seas, an arrangement which would admit Italy as a full Mediterranean power and acknowledge that the British could no longer rule an empire without limit. However, Quartararo explained, the British were dismayed by this imperial challenge, impressed as they were by Mussolini and Fascism, and alert to the seriousness of the Italian threat to their empire. All their policies, from 1935 to 1940, were coloured by their resultant hostility to Rome.[64]

During the successive crises of those years, Quartararo's account proceeded, Italy was frequently the crucial European state. Mussolini saved Europe from disaster at Munich: 'European war did not break out on 1 October [1938] only because Fascist Italy did not *want* to go to war *nor did it intend* [*sic*] to become involved in spite of itself'.[65] After Munich, however, Mussolini and Dino Grandi, still his ambassador in London and generally his most acute adviser, had to confront the deep 'anger and anxiety' of a Britain which pursued the 'encirclement' of Italy and Germany, and did so as 'the "legitimate defence" of a senescent empire, attempting to guarantee its own preservation against ... the rise on the continent of Germany and the expansion of Italy in the Mediterranean'.[66] In Quartararo's view the British now even contemplated preventive war in order to save their empire.[67] In August–September 1939 Britain, which was '*the real and only arbiter* [*sic*] of the crisis', bluntly rejected any mediation (by implication, from Fascist Italy) which alone could have avoided the great conflict.[68] While such acts were perpetrated, the British 'ideological mask – aiming at the destruction of the Nazi regime and the Fascist one – was too fragile to hide the imperialist motives which had driven London into the war'.[69]

Nor did Britain's vendetta against Fascist Italy end there. During the period of 'non-belligerency', the British repeatedly rejected Italian overtures and utterly failed to countenance the legitimacy and profundity of Italians' fears that Germany would invade them.[70] Only on 9 June 1940 did Mussolini

62 R. Quartararo, *Roma tra Londra e Berlino*, p. 32.
63 R. Quartararo, *Roma tra Londra e Berlino*, p. 35.
64 R. Quartararo, *Roma tra Londra e Berlino*, p. 150.
65 R. Quartararo, *Roma tra Londra e Berlino*, p. 399.
66 R. Quartararo, *Roma tra Londra e Berlino*, p. 404.
67 R. Quartararo, *Roma tra Londra e Berlino*, p. 406.
68 R. Quartararo, *Roma tra Londra e Berlino*, p. 500.
69 R. Quartararo, *Roma tra Londra e Berlino*, p. 536.
70 R. Quartararo, *Roma tra Londra e Berlino*, p. 545.

abandon his hope that he could make the British see reason and, given that Italy was the natural *peso determinante* (determining weight) in European diplomacy, decide that he must enter the war. Here, then, was what sounded like a ruthlessly 'realistic' reading, if not a return to a Fascist comprehension of the nature of diplomacy and of Italy's place in the international concert.

What is to be made of it? Quartararo herself has remained a relatively minor figure in the Italian academic world, and it might seem possible to discount her interpretation were it not for the fact that it was largely endorsed by Renzo De Felice himself. In the continuing volumes of his biography of Mussolini, De Felice frequently cited Quartararo's work approvingly in his footnotes.[71] He especially agreed with her positive understanding of the role in international diplomacy of Dino Grandi. Indeed, in the 1980s De Felice and his circle were involved in a scholarly campaign to publish autobiographical material made available by the elderly Grandi,[72] and generally to revive his image.[73] So effusive was the campaign that, according to the American historian Macgregor Knox, it included textual 'adjustments' in the editing process, apparently aimed at glossing over Grandi's responsibility for the darker side of Fascist policies.[74] Such a treatment of documents might seem highly undesirable, especially when undertaken by a school whose claim to historiographical pre-eminence rests very much on their superior documentary base and their scrupulously empirical reading of it. However, Knox's criticism was largely ignored by De Felice, though his footnotes did from time to time list the American as one who, along with Denis Mack Smith, had not done enough detailed research really to comprehend Italy.[75]

Though never quite as blunt or unsophisticated in his analysis as was Quartararo, De Felice himself, in the work which came out in the last years of his life, often expressed new nationalist ideas, even if, in his eyes, they were no more than 'science' and the 'truth'. For some time De Felice, originally a decidedly parochial figure, had taken up the cry that Italians must try to understand as much of the world outside Italy as possible (his own interest in those Italies beyond the *patria* which had resulted from emigration had never altogether been consummated).[76] An analysis of

71 See especially R. De Felice, *Mussolini il duce II. Lo stato totalitario, 1936–1940*, Turin, 1981. In the index (p. 942), 21 footnote references to her work are tabulated.
72 See e.g. D. Grandi, *La politica estera dell'Italia dal 1929 al 1932*, Rome, 1985 (preface by R. De Felice); D. Grandi, *Il mio paese: ricordi autobiografici*, ed. R. De Felice, Bologna, 1985.
73 See e.g. P. Nello, *Dino Grandi: la formazione di un leader fascista*, Bologna, 1987; *Un fedele disubbidiente: Dino Grandi da Palazzo Chigi al 25 luglio*, Bologna, 1993.
74 For the details of this alleged 'operation', see M. Knox, 'I testi "aggiustati" dei discorsi segreti di Grandi', *Passato e Presente*, 13, 1987, pp. 97–117.
75 See e.g. R. De Felice, *Mussolini l'alleato I. L'Italia in guerra 1940–1943*, Turin, 1991, pp. 86, 113, 595.
76 See e.g. R. De Felice, 'Alcuni temi per la storia dell'emigrazione italiana', *Affari sociali internazionali*, 1, 1973, pp. 3–10; 'Gli studi sull'emigrazione cinque anni dopo', *Affari sociali internazionali*, 6, 1978, pp. 7–14. *Affari sociali internazionali* was another of those scholarly journals very near the Ministry of Foreign Affairs.

foreign policy had always occupied an appreciable part of his biography of Mussolini, but now De Felice became alert to the policies which might have assisted a Fascist 'grab for world power', and which extended beyond the Mediterranean to the Arab world, India and even China. The conventional accounts of Salvemini and Mack Smith had ridiculed such evidence of Fascist hyper-ambition. De Felice, as usual preferring the literal evidence of documents to much reading between the lines, presented instead a Mussolini who genuinely envisaged Italy taking on the British Empire in its Indian heartland and who, for example, presided over a regime much better at understanding what De Felice called the 'Arab psychology' than were the *Duce*'s German allies.[77]

Such a view was then expanded in the last volume of the biography of Mussolini, covering the war years from 1940 to 1943, which De Felice would publish before his death. Here he narrated with his usual exhaustive detail what was indeed an Italian Second World War. It is a fairly unfamiliar one. According to De Felice, for a very long time Mussolini sought to impose his own, or Italy's, imprint on the conflict, wishing to engage in a 'parallel war'[78] rather than be subject to those Nazi German whims and wishes which the *Duce* correctly understood were often contrary to national best interest. After October 1940, the Greek fiasco brought a severe check to Italian hopes and reputation, but it did not represent the final failure of a Fascist war.[79] Rather, throughout 1940–2, Mussolini struggled manfully to direct a proper German attention to the Mediterranean theatre, which he rightly perceived to be the conflict's epicentre. He was regularly let down by the Germans, as was Italian business which had to confront 'unfair' German competition, for example in the Balkans.[80] It was typical, De Felice continued, that the Italians, free of any sense of racial superiority, maintained better diplomatic relations with the Japanese than did the Germans.[81] Similarly, Mussolini had an acute apprehension of the Eastern

77 R. De Felice, *Il Fascismo e l'Oriente: arabi, ebrei e indiani nella politica di Mussolini*, Bologna, 1988, p. 60.
78 R. De Felice, *Mussolini l'alleato I*, pp. 106–110 and *passim*.
79 As an illustration of the argument being presented, English-language readers will find useful the copious publications of the American historian James Sadkovich, whose work is regularly praised by De Felice in his footnotes. See e.g. J. J. Sadkovich, 'Understanding defeat: reappraising Italy's role in World War II', *Journal of Contemporary History*, 24, 1989, pp. 27–61; 'Of myths and men: Rommel and the Italians in North Africa', *International History Review*, 13, 1991, pp. 284–313; 'The Italo-Greek war in context: Italian priorities and Axis diplomacy', *Journal of Contemporary History*, 28, 1993, pp. 439–64; 'Italian morale during the Italo-Greek war of 1940–1941', *War and Society*, 12, 1994, pp. 97–123; *The Italian navy in World War II*, Westport, Conn., 1994. This last work includes what can only be described as an in-your-face preface, attacking critical foreign historiography about Italian policy (pp. xii–xx) and praising De Felice. Cf., in some contrast, Sadkovich's earlier book, *Italian support for Croatian separatism 1927–1937*, New York, 1987 which is highly 'realist' in its analysis of Italian policy. It thus discounts the influence of Fascist ideology in the erratic backing granted by Fascist authorities to Pavelić and his friends.
80 R. De Felice, *Mussolini l'alleato I*, p. 446.
81 R. De Felice, *Mussolini l'alleato I*, pp. 406–7, 470–81.

front. At first he accepted the idea of the German liquidation of the USSR on the grounds that it could lead to a compromise peace.[82] He regretted the German fixation with the war in the East, however, and, quite sensibly reversing his first assumptions, regularly suggested that they seek accommodation with the Soviets.[83]

By July 1943 the war would be lost. About that defeat De Felice had some unusual things to say, almost implying that another result would have been preferable. Certainly, he thought, the German and the Japanese middle classes had outperformed the Italian in their devotion to the war effort:[84] 'As Rosario Romeo frequently underlined, the Second World War revealed, on many occasions, the substantial weakness of Italy's ethical-political fabric, and especially the power of those psychological and cultural roots which bound Italians to their past before the Risorgimento.' According to De Felice, the 'best people' of Fascist Italy lacked an appropriate sense of national history. No wonder Mussolini grew irritated with them.[85]

Here, then, was 'a-Fascism', not to say amorality, of a spectacular kind. De Felice's Second World War had indeed lost any ethical impulsion for the Italy which, in the 1990s, was confronting another new world order. The war's only surviving message, it seemed, was to get on at last with nationalising the Italian masses and to remove the influence of those anti-Fascists who, in insisting on a moral conflict which it had been good for Italy to lose, had left the Republic after 1946 exposed to corruption, weakness and the alleged ills of *partitocrazia*.

At his death, in this as in other aspects of contemporary Italian historiography, De Felice commanded the majority view, or at least what was hailed by his powerful friends as the most authoritative interpretation of the past. None the less, in the conservative decades after 1978 some analysis had occurred which was more critical either of Italy's nationalist aspirations or of Fascist practice. The two main books in this regard were published in English by Cambridge University Press and then translated into Italian by Riuniti, the scholarly publishing house of the Italian Communist Party.[86]

---

82 R. De Felice, *Mussolini l'alleato I*, p. 396.
83 R. De Felice, *Mussolini l'alleato I*, pp. 1256–7. In this and similar passages, De Felice often acknowledged his debt to conservative and nationalist German historian Andreas Hillgruber.
84 R. De Felice, *Mussolini l'alleato I*, p. 959.
85 R. De Felice, *Mussolini l'alleato I*, p. 828.
86 See R. J. B. Bosworth, *Italy the Least of the Great Powers: Italian foreign policy before the First World War*, Cambridge, 1979 (for its translation, see R. J. B. Bosworth, *La politica estera dell'Italia giolittiana*, Rome, 1985); cf. also a more summary version, R. Bosworth, *Italy and the approach of the First World War*, London, 1983. M. Knox, *Mussolini unleashed 1939–1941: politics and strategy in Fascist Italy's last war*, Cambridge, 1982 (translation *La guerra di Mussolini 1939–1941*, Rome, 1984); cf. also Knox's follow-up accounts, e.g. his 'Conquest, foreign and domestic, in Fascist Italy and Nazi Germany', *Journal of Modern History*, 56, 1984, pp. 1–57; 'The Fascist regime, its foreign policy and its wars: an "Anti-Anti-Fascist orthodoxy?"', *Contemporary European History*, 4, 1995, pp. 347–65.

In 1979 I produced my own lengthy account of Liberal foreign policy in the years just before the outbreak of the First World War. My book earned censure from the conservative Rosario Romeo (in a review in the daily paper, *Il giornale nuovo*, he thought a possible inheritance from 'Botany Bay' might help to explain my opacity),[87] and from the liberal heir of Salvemini and Chabod, Roberto Vivarelli.[88] No doubt the limitations of my scholarship and style partially explain the vehemence of their critique. But ideology also played a part in it.

Romeo had, after all, just declared that the First World War amounted to 'the greatest triumph in our history ... and the final proof of the political strength and virtue of the state created in the Risorgimento'. Liberal foreign policy, he had added, 'brought advantage and was honourable'.[89] Vivarelli was less avowedly nationalist, but also believed that the Italian presence in the First World War could and should have had positive effects, and he strenuously justified the territorial settlement of 1918–19.[90] I, by contrast, was writing with a knowledge of the debates stimulated in the 1960s in West Germany by the research on Imperial German foreign policy completed by Fritz Fischer.[91] In Germany Fischer's book, whatever its author's original intention, had been read as implying a continuity thesis. The grab for world power attempted by the Imperial regime in the First World War was arguably not so different from that of Hitler and the Nazis in the Second. Nationalists of the 1960s, too, might be potentially responsible for the coming of a Third World War, if they did not favour an accommodation in the East and accept the division of Germany into two or more states for the foreseeable future.

My book implied that the situation was not completely dissimilar[92] in Liberal Italy. Already before 1914, Italians were seeking advantage in

---

87 See R. Bosworth, 'Italian foreign policy and its historiography', in R. Bosworth and G. Rizzo (eds), *Altro polo: intellectuals and their ideas in contemporary Italy*, Sydney, 1983, p. 65, and *Il giornale nuovo*, 13 November 1980.
88 *Journal of Modern History*, 54, 1982, pp. 599–602.
89 R. Romeo, *L'Italia unita e la prima guerra mondiale*, Bari, 1978, pp. 148, 157.
90 See e.g. R. Vivarelli, *Il fallimento del liberalismo: studi sulle origini del fascismo*, Bologna, 1981, pp. 113–21. Vivarelli also regularly deplored what he deemed to be the levity of foreign accounts of Italian history. See, notably, R. Vivarelli, 'Interpretations of the origins of Fascism', *Journal of Modern History*, 63, 1991, pp. 29–43.
91 See especially F. Fischer, *Germany's aims in the First World War*, London, 1967; *War of illusions: German policies from 1911 to 1914*, London, 1975.
92 In some ways nearer to the Bielefeld school, however, was the work of the American historian Richard Webster, who explored the evidence for the rise of 'social imperialism' in Liberal Italy. I was more doubtful of the specific responsibility of industrialists and bankers for pre-1914 new nationalism and believed such ideas were pervasive and, in the final analysis, scarcely novel. See R. A. Webster, *Industrial imperialism in Italy 1908–1915*, Berkeley, 1975; it was translated into Italian as *L'imperialismo industriale italiano 1908–1915: studio sul prefascismo*, Turin, 1974 and published by Einaudi, the same firm who were releasing the successive volumes of De Felice's biography of Mussolini. Latterly a French scholar, committed to empiricism and nothing else, has combined and extended Webster's and my work in an exhaustive description of the era. See D. J. Grange, *L'Italie et la Mediterranée (1896–1911). Les fondements d'une politique étrangère* (2 vols.), Rome, 1994.

Ethiopia, Albania, Asia Minor and the rest; already expansionist nationalist ideas flourished, especially among the younger intake of the Ministry of Foreign Affairs; already the myth of Rome and much of the rhetoric of the *mare nostrum* had been coined; already some Italians could carelessly contemplate war to bring the nation advantage. Here, then, were the lineaments of a continuity thesis. Had fascistisation really changed the norms of Italian diplomacy?[93] If it could be agreed that there was plenty that was unoriginal about Fascist diplomacy after 1922, what did that imply about Mussolini's own power and originality, and therefore about intentionalism and the 'one man alone' and parenthesis theses? Were there structural explanations which made it difficult for any Italian statesman from 1860 to 1945 to go far beyond the expected behaviour of the least of the Great Powers? And, rather than Mussolini's personality or the ideology of Fascism, was the real key to inter-war Italian policy the nation's position among the powers?

These are important questions, if ones which have not yet been fully addressed in subsequent research.[94] An exploration of the relationship between domestic affairs and Fascist foreign policy, for example of the type which Tim Mason long ago sketched out for Nazi Germany,[95] has not been attempted.[96] Indeed, ironically, the other non-Italian account of Italy's international behaviour which earned the ire of some conservative Italian historians was not very interested in these issues. What Macgregor Knox's *Mussolini Unleashed* and other works did instead was to emphasise the violence of the *Duce*. In great detail and with scrupulous archival research, Knox restated the case that Mussolini meant war, an ideological, fascist and totalitarian war.

Declaring with a neo-Rankean empiricism of his own that his aim was merely to explain 'what actually happened',[97] Knox began by stating that knowledge of the failure of Italy's military effort in the Second World War had produced a tendency 'to underestimate ... [Fascist Italy's] brutality, [and] the vigor and extent of its expansionist ambition'. In this sense, he concluded, 'Italy's weakness and Germany's strength explain the disparity between the two dictators' performances better than the usually alleged differences between their personalities.'[98] Knox had already noted that the

---

93 Virtually no Italian diplomats resigned in 1922. If Fascist contacts and their absence helped or hindered the careers of some after 1922, so contacts with a Crispi or a San Giuliano had helped and hindered careers before 1914 and Crispi, too, had abolished the position of Secretary General of the Ministry.

94 See the practical urging to get on with that research of S. C. Azzi, 'The historiography of Fascist foreign policy', *Historical Journal*, 36, 1993, pp. 187–203.

95 T. Mason, *Nazism, Fascism and the working class*, Cambridge, 1995, pp. 104–30, 295–322.

96 For my own brief structural account of Fascist foreign policy, see R. J. B. Bosworth, *Italy and the wider world 1860–1960*, especially pp. 36–53.

97 M. Knox, *Mussolini unleashed 1939–1941*, p. x.

98 M. Knox, *Mussolini unleashed 1939–1941*, pp. 1, 5.

aggressive aims of the Fascist regime had earned great domestic support 'until their price became fully apparent',[99] but in his subsequent pages he did little to explore the nature and effect of this backing. Thus, he suggested that 'industrialists had minimum influence' on Fascist diplomacy; 'Mussolini made policy, and from 1934–5 on lightheartedly risked state bankruptcy in pursuit of empire.'[100] In any case, Italy's fate had been sealed years earlier: 'By 1925–6, Mussolini's programme was set in all essential details.'[101]

In 1939–40, Knox continued, Mussolini was always restless because he was not at the front alongside his Nazi ally.[102] He was determined to have his own armed conflict because he wanted it to be 'a war of revenge on the Italian establishment'.[103] Somewhat inconsistently, Knox also emphasised that 'the Italian public was ready to partake of the spoils', with the universities (and, no doubt, their historians) being particularly pro-war.[104] As Mussolini had told Ciano: 'We will enter the war at Germany's side because the Italian people will never pardon me for having lost a chance like this.'[105] Thus Knox's interpretation bore major similarities with that drafted by Salvemini in 1953, though Knox omitted mention of the goodness which Salvemini always maintained was located somewhere in the Italian populace. For Knox, Mussolini was a dangerous and rogue dictator whose historical reputation should still place him among the wicked men of the twentieth century.

The idea of Italian niceness is hard to shake off, however. It has returned to the scholarship in analyses of the war itself and in examinations of Fascist Italy's part in the Holocaust. What, then, are the standard lines of interpretation of Fascist racism?

In regard to this matter, by the 1980s De Felice was again the plainest, if also the most exculpatory: 'I know that Italian Fascism is sheltered from the accusation of genocide, and quite outside the shadow [of guilt] for the Holocaust.'[106] Previous historians had been more doubtful, although, in their view, the question of the racial legislation which was promulgated in Fascist Italy in the autumn of 1938 and, thereafter, of the implementation of racist policies has usually seemed simple to explain. A certain degree of racism doubtless speckled Italian minds but, both in the Liberal era and in much of the Fascist one, Italy was the least anti-Semitic country in Europe. Rather, a fearful mimicry of Hitler drove Mussolini to dabble in anti-Semitism, despite the fact that in the past he had frequently derided it. As De Felice himself had put it in his pioneering account of the subject, even if

99 M. Knox, *Mussolini unleashed 1939–1941*, p. 1.
100 M. Knox, *Mussolini unleashed 1939–1941*, p. 12.
101 M. Knox, 'Conquest, foreign and domestic, in Fascist Italy and Nazi Germany', p. 11.
102 One small inconsistency in *Mussolini unleashed* is that Knox has Mussolini making his 'final decision' on a number of occasions. See pp. 83, 101, 107 and 116.
103 M. Knox, *Mussolini unleashed 1939–1941*, p. 102.
104 M. Knox, *Mussolini unleashed 1939–1941*, pp. 111–12.
105 M. Knox, *Mussolini unleashed 1939–1941*, p. 110.
106 *Corriere della Sera*, 27 December 1987.

Mussolini himself was never strongly pro- or anti-Semitic, he 'introduced state anti-Semitism in Italy, too, because of his basic conviction that, to render the Italian–German alliance iron-hard, it was necessary to eliminate every strident contrast between the two regimes.'[107] The *Duce's* gimcrack racism, the familiar story goes, was, however, rejected by the Church and the Italian people, who did their best to circumvent the law and who largely succeeded in doing so, except when the Salò Republic was reduced to a German puppet and its Jews, 9000 of whom were transported to the camps, became a prey to the SS.[108]

Even when they were conquering Europe, the mainstream account continues, Italians separated themselves from their German allies.[109] In an occupied Croatia, viciously beset by multiple civil wars, such unlikely heroes as Mario Roatta, a general accused of war crimes,[110] frustrated efforts certainly by the Germans and perhaps by the more extreme Fascist officialdom to lay hands on local Jews with murderous intent. The Cambridge historian Jonathan Steinberg has sought the hardest to find meaning in these events. In his interpretation, Roatta and others decided that 'the thing is just not possible' and thus came to 'the Italian determination to have no part in the German "final solution"'.[111] As Steinberg has explained, the motivation was complex: 'the vices of Italian public life made the virtues of humanity easier to practise. ... Habitual disobedience was so marked within Italian public bodies that even the army could not get [all] its orders obeyed.'[112] An amalgam of corruption and Christianity, machiavellism and maladministration, composed an Italian 'banality of good'.[113] In Steinberg's optimistic view, such essential goodness contrasted with that banality of evil which Hannah Arendt had detected in Eichmann and in the perpetrators of Auschwitz.[114] Italy, Steinberg emphasised, was not Germany.

Steinberg's conclusions were controversially reaffirmed in 1996 with the publication of Daniel Goldhagen's *Hitler's Willing Executioners*, whose author was certain that the key to the Holocaust lay in German history and

---

107 R. De Felice, *Storia degli ebrei sotto il fascismo*, Turin, 1961, pp. 79, 286. Cf. also the revised ed. of this work, published also in Turin in 1988.
108 For the standard accounts see M. Michaelis, *Mussolini and the Jews: German–Italian relations and the Jewish question in Italy 1922–1945*, Oxford, 1978; S. Zuccotti, *The Italians and the Holocaust: persecution, rescue, survival*, New York, 1987 and, in Italian, cf. also R. De Felice, *Ebrei in un paese arabo*, Bologna, 1978 (translated as *Jews in an Arab land: Libya 1835–1970*, Austin, Tex., 1985).
109 See e.g. D. Carpi, *Between Mussolini and Hitler: the Jews and the Italian authorities in France and Tunisia*, Hanover, 1994.
110 For his case see J. Steinberg, *All or nothing: the Axis and the Holocaust 1941–43*, London, 1990, pp. 4, 11, 34 and 41–3.
111 J. Steinberg, *All or nothing*, pp. 6, 11.
112 J. Steinberg, *All or nothing*, p. 170.
113 J. Steinberg, *All or nothing*, p. 6.
114 See H. Arendt, *Eichmann in Jerusalem: a report on the banality of evil*, rev. ed., New York, 1965.

in German history alone.[115] Goldhagen made no direct reference to Fascist Italy but, by implication, his concern to expose primordial German vice again acquitted Italy of the worst evil and removed from Mussolini's regime any guilt for Nazism's killing frenzy.

This is not the place to review in detail Goldhagen's often wrong-headed book. However, there is something rather too snug about the revival of concepts of *italiani brava gente* as a final summary of Fascist racial, imperial and foreign policies. It is a pity, for example, that Steinberg did not extend his narrative of Italian behaviour into the Salò Republic. Would he not then have found, in admittedly terrible times, a native Italian anti-Semitism and a participation, at least to a degree, in the Holocaust? What, too, might be made of the active approval of such apparently worthy Fascists as Bottai[116] of Fascist racism? When, in 1938, King Victor Emmanuel III deemed 'foreign Jews' of no matter,[117] was he not displaying a morality which has regularly been deplored in Pierre Laval or Philippe Pétain? What, too, of the anti-Semitism evident in Italian universities, and notably in the work of leading Fascist historians of the classical world, with their theses, for example, that Carthage stood for Semitism and that this racial inferiority caused its defeat by Rome?[118] Was the good not limited in extent, and very much prompted by the specific circumstances in which Fascism and the Italian nation found themselves in 1942–3, and in that sense too banal fully to define the Fascist record on race?[119]

More significant, perhaps, is another matter. Though he did not write in great detail on the subject, De Felice[120] can be found suggesting, predictably, that there has been too much moralising about Fascist policies in Africa and the rest of the Italian empire. The idea that Italians were always *brava gente* in their dealings with non-European peoples, however, still gets short shrift in most of the scholarly literature, because of the convincing and sustained attack on Italian imperialism written by the anti-Fascist historian Angelo Del Boca.[121]

115 D. Goldhagen, *Hitler's willing executioners: ordinary Germans and the Holocaust*, New York, 1996.
116 R. Finzi, *L'università italiana e le leggi antiebraiche*, Rome, 1997 underlines this point while also emphasising the blatant evasiveness in B. Bottai, *Fascismo familiare*, Casale Monferrato, 1997, on the matter.
117 G. Buffarini Guidi, *La vera verità*, Milan, 1970, p. 20.
118 For a succinct review of such work, see M. Cagnetta, *Antichisti e impero fascista*, Bari, 1979.
119 For a more critical Italian account, see M. Sarfatti, *Mussolini contro gli ebrei. Cronaca dell'elaborazione delle leggi del 1938*, Turin, 1994. Cf. for an introduction to the gypsy question in Fascist Italy, G. Boursier, 'La persecuzione degli zingari nell' Italia fascista', *Studi storici*, 37, 1996, pp. 1065–82.
120 R. De Felice, 'Preface' to L. Calabrò, *Intermezzo africano: ricordi di un Residente di governo in Etiopia (1937–1941)*, Rome, 1988, p. 6.
121 A. Del Boca, *Gli italiani in Africa orientale: dall'unità alla marcia su Roma*, Bari, 1976; *Gli italiani in Africa orientale: la conquista dell'impero*, Bari, 1979; *Gli italiani in Africa orientale: la caduta dell'impero*, Bari, 1982; *Gli italiani in Africa orientale: nostalgie delle colonie*, Bari, 1984; *Gli italiani in Libia: Tripoli bel suol d'amore 1860–1922*, Bari, 1986; *Gli italiani in Libia dal fascismo a Gheddafi*, Bari, 1988; in English, see only the brief A. Del Boca, *The Ethiopian war 1935–1941*, Chicago, 1969.

For this and other reasons, most notably the apparent irrelevance of a colonial past to an Italy which had indeed lost its empire, imperial history continues to hold a low profile in national historiography. However, over recent years its study has prompted an intriguing new thesis about the origins of Fascist racism. Luigi Goglia, another member of the De Felice school, has argued that Italian racism was a contagion caught in the empire and thence transported to Italy.[122]

Victory in the Ethiopian war, Goglia has explained, meant that the Fascist regime had to administer a much greater empire than ever before, and do so in the spotlight of international public opinion. In these circumstances racial legislation was the natural, if deplorable, result, as Italy sought to bear the 'white man's burden' in what it assumed was a gentlemanly way. Once promulgated, it was likely that such laws would be enacted in Italy itself and extend beyond coloured peoples to the Jews. In thus arguing, Goglia was, of course, endorsing the familiar De Felicean thesis that Fascist Italy constituted a regime *sui generis*. Even in its racism, Goglia urged, Mussolini's Italy did not just follow after the more fanatical and compelling Nazis.

It is hard to be utterly convinced by the thesis that Italian anti-Semitism had nothing in common with that of Nazi Germany, or the Jewish policies of 1930s Poland and Romania, for example. However, Goglia's research does carry the useful and important corollary that in racism, too, Fascist Italy was not just a fraud. The Fascist regime did not merely delude itself that it was governing; its citizens were not merely *brava gente*. Fascism did indeed pursue foreign, colonial and racial policies which may have carried the spirit of the times and which probably retained many national traditions; but those policies remained violent, aggressive, disturbing of the peace and frequently damaging to the peoples of both metropolitan Italy and its empire.

Ironically, the most conceptually sophisticated account of Italian foreign and colonial policy in recent times is a monograph about the at first sight insignificant topic of Italian administration of the Dodecanese.[123] In this study, Nick Doumanis has deployed with great subtlety the techniques both of oral history and of other approaches to popular culture and memory to read the relationship between the Italian occupiers of these 'Greek' islands and the population in all its texture and richness. As they expressed their own usable pasts to Doumanis, many of the islanders recalled Italian occupation more favourably than they did their experience of Turkish, British, French and German rule and, as long as they were not too educated into Greek nationalism, frequently averred that Fascist government could be contrasted favourably with Greek administration since 'liberation'. The

---

122 See e.g. L. Goglia, 'Note sul razzismo coloniale fascista', *Storia contemporanea*, 19, 1988, pp. 1223–66.
123 N. Doumanis, *Myth and memory in the Mediterranean: remembering Fascism's empire*, London, 1997.

'Blackshirts', especially as associated with the governorship of (that sometime historian) De Vecchi di Val Cismon after 1936, were bad, but ordinary soldiers and officials were often remembered as attractive and 'proper' human beings. Here it is not possible to review Doumanis more fully; suffice it to say that, in his account, Fascist Italy, once again, deserves the appellation the 'Italian dictatorship'. In the little world of the Dodecanese, as on the grander international and, as it shall soon be seen, domestic stages, traces of both the banality of good and the banality of evil can be located in the history of those Italians who experienced Fascist rule. And the study of Italy's empire, like the history of its foreign and racial policies, can scarcely be comprehended by focusing exclusively on the personality and policies of 'one man alone'. If historians are to advance knowledge of Fascism's place in the wider world, as well as carefully to review the nature of the *Duce*'s power, they will need to think through the numerous contexts in which Fascist Italy operated, and the manifold assumptions left unspoken there.

|5|

Fascist Politics and Economics: Mussolinism, Corporatism, Totalitarianism, Bureaucratism or Continuity?

As was noted toward the end of the last chapter, Angelo Del Boca has provided the best detailed account of the first years of Fascist government in its newly conquered Ethiopian empire. According to Del Boca, in this administration three men mattered – the *Duce* himself who, from time to time, telegraphed demands for greater, that is, more murderous, rigour, but varied these orders with plaintive suggestions that troops be sent home and costs cut; Alessandro Lessona, the Minister of Colonies, whose portfolio covered all of East Africa; and Rodolfo Graziani, the Governor General and then 'Viceroy', who commanded the Italian armies still engaged in 'pacifying' Ethiopia, and presided over the day-to-day actions of the new imperial bureaucracy. Del Boca regularly reveals that Lessona and Graziani each had one main purpose, and that was to outscore the other.[1] Both the Minister of Colonies and the Viceroy may have been Fascists, and both may have been accustomed to giving fulsome homage to their *Duce*. Such apparent commitment to an ideology and deference to a leader did not, however, mean that their personalities were similar, or that they shared an administrative ideal and purpose. Rather, they quarrelled, bickered, plotted, and sought to undermine each other's reputation. They kept doing so until, in November 1937, Mussolini sacked Graziani and replaced him as Viceroy with the not altogether Fascist figure of Amedeo, Duke of Aosta, the handsome *pukka sahib* (and tubercular) heir of the cadet branch of the Savoy dynasty. This change in personnel and image, however, represented but a pyrrhic victory for Lessona and, indeed, the Minister left office before

---

1 A. Del Boca, *Gli italiani in Africa orientale: la caduta dell'impero*, Bari, 1986, *passim*.

Graziani actually sailed for home.[2] On 27 November 1937 Lessona was replaced as 'Minister of East Africa'[3] by Benito Mussolini; he did not hold ministerial office again.

The departure of the two rivals did not, however, alter much. Having reached Ethiopia, the Duke of Aosta soon found himself embroiled in conflict with his deputy, Enrico Cerulli, with Ugo Cavallero, the military commander for Italian East Africa, and, inescapably, with Attilio Teruzzi,[4] the local representative of the Fascist party.[5] If this vignette of imperial government has meaning, Fascist Italy was not a regime possessed of a simple and reliable system of command, nor one in which its leading figures thought only of how best they might serve their ideology and nation.

Del Boca himself, like the overwhelming majority of Italian historians of Fascism, is an intentionalist; his Mussolini is still in charge. Yet contrary messages can be read in his tale. At least as far as East Africa was concerned, Mussolini's interventions were irregular; they often seemed capricious, or occasioned by reports of a particular event, either in Italy or in the empire. Although Ethiopia had been conquered, there was no semblance of a plan as to how it would be run, or how it might be financed, or how exactly it would relate to metropolitan Italy. Of course, this lack of serious planning may merely reflect Mussolini's levity as an executive; but any who have examined 'functionalist' analyses of the 'institutional Darwinism' of Nazi Germany might ask some different questions.[6] Was Lessona's and Graziani's small bureaucratic war emblematic of the way Fascist Italy worked? For all its pretensions to totalitarian uniformity, was the Fascist system in practice riven by personal, practical and ideological conflicts which the *Duce* was powerless to end (and which he may have fostered for utterly cynical reasons having to do with the protection of his own 'authority')? Despite all its talk of corporate unity and totalitarianism, was Fascist Italy a place in which executives scrambled past each other and, in their endless petty warfare, added both the ideology of Fascism and the possibility of contact with the *Duce* to the humdrum armoury of those who devote their lives to such matters? How different and how new was the behaviour of the men who helped to manage the Fascist state from 1922 to 1945? What, too, really constituted the social base of the movement? Were Fascism's followers true believers and did they come from specific classes and regions of Italy? Or was Fascist Italy, like Nazi Germany, a regime which illustrated that 'a

2 Lessona would live to a great age in the Republic, and would continue to maintain the virtue of Italy's imperial achievement. See A. Del Boca (ed.), *I gas di Mussolini: il fascismo e la guerra d'Etiopia*, Rome, 1996, p. 24.

3 The title change from the Ministry of Colonies to the Ministero dell'Africa Orientale had occurred in April 1937.

4 In October 1939 Teruzzi replaced Mussolini as Minister for AOI, an indication, no doubt, that the Empire had now lost almost all of its significance to Fascist government.

5 A. Del Boca, *Gli italiani in Africa orientale: la caduta dell'impero*, pp. 311–12.

6 For a very able summary of the historiographical line, see I. Kershaw, *The Nazi dictatorship: problems and perspectives of interpretation*, rev. ed., London, 1993.

house divided against itself *can* stand, provided, at least, that the occupants have no alternative place to go and the landlord pays attention to the wallpaper, if not to the walls'?[7] How, in sum, have historians assessed the political history of Fascist Italy, and have their answers to the above questions changed over time?

As has already been established in this book, it was only in the 1960s that academic historians began to turn their attention to Fascism and to a scholarly reading of Italy's 'long' Second World War. Until then, in many a mind both within Italy and elsewhere, 'contemporary history' was a contradiction in terms. For those Rankeans committed to the view that historians must necessarily separate themselves from their presents and scrupulously read the past in its own terms, a cooling-off period was indispensable before the past could be comprehended with proper empathy. If *ad fontes* was the battle-cry of a 'real' historian,[8] then there was a further difficulty in writing the history of the Fascist era. Most countries had a 30- or even a 50-year rule about the release of documents. Where the evidence had not been destroyed by bombing or by the civil disputes which afflicted Italy in 1920–2 and again in 1943–5, government archives were closed, or only just beginning to open. Private papers were also rarely available as yet, unless, like the Ciano diaries,[9] they had been released for political and personal reasons. As the decade of the 1960s began, there were many reasons both to explain the continuing fixation on Mussolini's biography and to justify the absence of thoroughgoing historical research on the rise to power and subsequent behaviour of the Fascist regime.

None the less, there were also signs of change. In the English-speaking world, Geoffrey Barraclough – in the aftermath of 'Auschwitz', a medievalist turned into an advocate of 'global history' – believed that the twentieth century possessed so many special and terrible characteristics that it needed to be read as a period on its own.[10] From the 1950s he campaigned for the term 'contemporary history' to be granted academic acceptance and respectability. Where Barraclough led, others followed. In 1966 the *Journal of Contemporary History* commenced publication, and its editors at once directed scholarly attention to the interpretation of generic fascism, a topic whose study the journal has never abandoned.[11] In Italy the same trend was apparent. The De Felicean *Storia contemporanea* published its first issue in

---

7 D. Schoenbaum, *Hitler's social revolution: class and status in Nazi Germany 1933–1939*, New York, 1966, p. 275.

8 For its evocation see G. Elton, *Return to essentials: some reflections on the present state of historical study*, Cambridge, 1991, p. 52.

9 The fullest version of these diaries is now that edited with characteristic attention to detail by De Felice. See G. Ciano, *Diario 1937–1943*, Milan, 1980.

10 See e.g. G. Barraclough, *An introduction to contemporary history*, Harmondsworth, 1967. Barraclough's book sprang from a paper he first gave at Oxford in 1956.

11 Indeed, understanding generic fascism remains the journal's most evident intellectual preoccupation, as is seen in its publication every decade of a special anniversary edition devoted to the subject. See vol. 1, 1966; vol. 11, 1976; vol. 21, 1986; vol. 31, 1996. For further on this matter, see Chapter 9.

1970,[12] its ideological rival to the left, *Rivista di storia contemporanea*, in 1972. A decade previously, in 1961, the first chairs in contemporary history had begun to be established in Italian universities. By the end of the 1960s, 'contemporary history', defined as the history of the origins and nature of the Fascist regime, had become, in Italy, the most prestigious and the most contested arena of historical research.

Here another context needs to be noted. It was in 1960 that the first uncertain attempt officially to legitimise neo-fascism was made, when a Christian Democrat government headed by Fernando Tambroni tried to rule with the 'external support' of the MSI (entailing a reliance on the MSI's votes in the parliamentary chamber, without actually giving neo-fascists seats in cabinet). The attempt failed in the face of massive, and what seem to have been spontaneous, popular demonstrations. The effect on Italian politics for the next decade and a half was a switch by the DC and its powerbrokers to the tactic of the 'Opening to the Left', that is, the inclusion in government coalition of the Socialist Party, previously reckoned an incorrigible ally of the PCI.

At the same time, the rejection of the MSI was also something of a historiographical statement. Whatever had been going on among academic historians in the realm of 'popular' history – for example, that published by the ex-Fascist radical-conservative journalist, Indro Montanelli,[13] or on the radio and television programmes of RAI[14] – the decade of the 1950s was marked by a profound silence about the failures, delusions and terrors of Fascism.[15] After all, this was the era not of anti-Fascism but of anti-communism, and any hint of a critical reading of Mussolini's rule could be attacked by the anti-Communist media as insulting the war dead and

12 Despite being such a leading proponent of *storia contemporanea*, De Felice, as he grew older, opposed post-1945 contemporary history on the classic grounds of too-evident political bias and too few archives. See P. Alvazzi Del Frate *et al.* (eds), *La ricerca storica: teorie, tecniche, problemi*, Rome, 1982, pp. 85–6.

13 For an example in English, see I. Montanelli, *Rome: the first thousand years*, London, 1962, pp. 369–70, in which he rejected Diocletian's 'socialism' and blamed assimilationism for bringing racial damage to the empire. In the 'De Felice affair' of the 1970s, Montanelli would prove a zealous defender of the historian against what he called a 'lynching' from the 'Left'. I. Montanelli, 'Ai comunisti fa comodo dare del fascista a tutti', *Oggi illustrato*, 27 October 1975, p. 7. In 1987, Montanelli again spoke up in De Felice's cause, declaring, with typical bravado, 'There have been two Fascisms: one was called Fascism and the other Anti-Fascism.' *Giornale nuovo*, 29 December 1987. In the 1950s, by contrast, Montanelli had, predictably, been among those who condemned neo-realist film (see Chapter 7) for lack of patriotism. See A. Gadda Conti, 'Equivoci e polemiche sul neorealismo nel cinema', *Nuova Antologia*, f. 1857, September 1955, p. 78.

14 See G. Crainz, 'I programmi: dalla Liberazione ai primi anni settanta', in G. Crainz, A. Farassino, E. Forcella and N. Gallerano, *La Resistenza italiana nei programmi della RAI*, Rome, 1996, pp. 43–52.

15 Once again, Italy was scarcely behaving idiosyncratically in this regard. Cf. e.g. the situation in France, as related with a certain residual patriotism by H. Rousso, *The Vichy syndrome: history and memory in France since 1944*, Cambridge, Mass., 1991.

'outraging'[16] the *patria*. Tambroni was thus hardly acting out of order in seeking to bring the MSI in from the cold.[17] To a naïve onlooker, all that he seemed to propose was an acceptance politically of what was already the norm in the functioning of the national economy, society and culture. In 1960, among those who venerated the ideology of anti-communism, Fascism did not seem such an evil memory (aside from the awkward fact that the Fascists had ingloriously lost the war in alliance with that Nazi regime, whose wickedness was hard to deny).

This tendency towards a patriotic, conservative and Whiggish version of Italy's recent past was, however, rudely shaken by the events surrounding the fall of Tambroni. Suddenly a fresh age began, in which the 'myth of the Resistance' and that of anti-Fascism were in vogue,[18] even if it remained distinctly possible to hold different interpretations of what these myths meant. In this new atmosphere, two young men emerged as rivals in the task of writing the first archival histories of Fascism. One was Roberto Vivarelli, who had begun his research at the Crocean *Istituto Italiano per gli Studi Storici* at Naples as early as 1956–7, under the direct encouragement of both Federico Chabod and Gaetano Salvemini. By 1967 a decade of work would indeed result in the publication of a first volume in what was announced would be his multi-volume and archivally informed account of the rise of Fascism.[19]

Vivarelli's competitor was Renzo De Felice, a student of Chabod and of Delio Cantimori,[20] this last having once been an intelligent Fascist, now turned intelligent Communist. De Felice, who had been born in 1929, had also become a Communist in his youth, but drifted away from the party in response to the crises and revelations of 1956. He seemed a junior figure compared with Vivarelli; but in 1961 it was De Felice who published a history of the Jews under Fascism, a study characterised by what would become his hallmarks of accurate documentary detail and impressive length.[21] Thereafter it became known that De Felice was writing a biography

16 One of the numerous pieces of Fascist legislation remaining on the statute book of the Republic was the crime of *oltraggio*, that is, insulting (or just demurring fom the views of) a public official.
17 For a detailed account see L. Radi, *Tambroni trent'anni dopo: il luglio 1960 e la nascita del centrosinistra*, Bologna, 1990.
18 See further Chapter 8.
19 R. Vivarelli, *Il dopoguerra in Italia e l'avvento del fascismo (1918–1922): I. Dalla fine della guerra all'impresa di Fiume*, Naples, 1967, p. viii. Here Vivarelli promised that he would replace Tasca and Salvemini not in interpretation but in wealth of archival detail.
20 With Cantimori De Felice had worked on Italian Jacobins but, ironically, he did not then display any sign of influence from or knowledge of the controversial work of Jacob Talmon. See e.g. R. De Felice, *Note e ricerche sugli 'Illuminati' e il misticismo rivoluzionario (1789–1800)*, Rome, 1960; D. Cantimori and R. De Felice (eds), *Giacobini italiani* (2 vols.), Bari, 1964. This last was a prosopographical study of the type favoured by conservative British historian Lewis Namier. In the former work, De Felice did already urge the need for the more rational present to be scrupulous in endeavouring to comprehend the genuine mysticism of some revolutionaries in the past. By the 1970s De Felice had realised, however, that Talmon was an appropriate reference. See R. De Felice, *Intervista sul fascismo*, ed. M. Ledeen, Bari, 1975, p. 105.
21 R. De Felice, *Storia degli ebrei sotto il fascismo*, Turin, 1961.

of Mussolini, a sort of life and times of the *Duce*. Methodologically, the book was likely to be conservative; it was, after all, to be a biography, a study of a 'Great Man', and one most concerned with political and diplomatic history. It would become a labour which would occupy its author all his life, and remains easily the most important and the lengthiest account of Italian Fascism.

The first volume, entitled *Mussolini il rivoluzionario*, appeared in 1965 under the imprint of the great Turin publishing house of Einaudi.[22] Delio Cantimori contributed a preface, welcoming this 'new type' of biography and praising De Felice's 'balance'.[23] However, Cantimori also had some words of caution as he watched his younger colleague embark on so huge a task. Perhaps, his old professor wrote, De Felice had a weakness for sociological or psychological readings; perhaps he was too inclined to lump together all 'socialists' as one and condemn too easily their failure to confront Fascism; perhaps there was something worrying in the suggestion that Mussolini remained a genuine revolutionary, even in 1920.[24]

None the less, for all his residual doubts, Cantimori hailed a great achievement and looked forward to the later volumes, already promised, which would cover Mussolini as 'Fascist', as '*Duce*', and as 'Ally'. In his own introduction, De Felice denied that he was endeavouring to write '*sine ira ac studio*', and, indeed, asserted (ironically given later developments) that 'a biography of Mussolini can only be "political" in our opinion'.[25] He added, however, in sentiments which would become more familiar with the passage of time, that he did not intend to write with a pro- or anti-Mussolinian, a Fascist or an anti-Fascist leaning: 'That would be an absurdity in the realm of history'.[26] Years and years of study, he predicted, would be needed fully to understand Fascism and, anyway, the movement was not singular. Rather, De Felice evoked Gramsci to argue that the Fascist phenomenon should best be comprehended as *fascismi*, more than one fascism: 'notwithstanding its apparently monolithic character and its totalitarian spirit, Fascism contained a number of different levels and, as Gramsci clearly understood, expressed within itself conflicts lying at the bottom of Italian society which could not come forward in other ways'. Fascism was an ideology and a regime 'in continuous tranformation'.[27] In any case, De Felice modestly reminded his readers, there was no doubt that

22 R. De Felice, *Mussolini il rivoluzionario 1883–1920*, Turin, 1965. It at once surpassed the descriptive L. Salvatorelli and G. Mira, *Storia d'Italia nel periodo fascista*, (2 vols.), Turin, 1964.
23 D. Cantimori, 'Prefazione' to R. De Felice, *Mussolini il rivoluzionario*, p. xviii.
24 D. Cantimori, 'Prefazione', pp. xviii–xx. The main English language critic, Stuart Woolf, ironically given later developments in the pages of the *Journal of Contemporary History*, was also troubled by this last issue. See S. J. Woolf, 'Mussolini as Revolutionary', *Journal of Contemporary History*, 1, 1966, pp. 187–96.
25 R. De Felice, *Mussolini il rivoluzionario*, p. xxi.
26 R. De Felice, *Mussolini il rivoluzionario*, p. xxi.
27 R. De Felice, *Mussolini il rivoluzionario*, p. xxii.

Fascism was too complex a matter to be defined merely through a knowledge of the *Duce*.

The biography was none the less worth writing, De Felice added, for two basic reasons. One was archival. The *Archivio Centrale dello Stato* (state archives) were open and their material deserved to be read, even if the search for additional documents could and must proceed.[28] The second reason was concerned with the need to gauge Mussolini's personality, to fathom, for example, that side of his character which sustained his revolutionary syndicalist tendencies, while also teasing out his recognisably machiavellian tactics and manipulations.[29]

De Felice began conventionally, with an account of Mussolini's birth and boyhood,[30] his intellectual training[31] and his gradual emergence as a prominent figure in Italy's socialist movement. Though told in a more detailed and scholarly way, De Felice's account was not particularly novel. Even at his most radical, De Felice explained, the *Duce* held views which were scarcely those of a simple believer in historical materialism. As the young Mussolini wrote in 1912: 'It is faith which moves mountains because it gives the illusion that the mountains move. Illusion is, perhaps, the only reality in life.'[32] By 1914, De Felice commented with some ambiguity, Mussolini was the most 'advanced' socialist in Italy and therefore the one most aware that Marxist principle might have to change with events.[33] It was no surprise, therefore, when he abandoned orthodox socialism for the war, even if his personality ensured that he did so with doubts and hesitations.[34] Similarly, in 1919, when he founded the *Fasci di combattimento*, Mussolini at first had little concept of what lay ahead;[35] only in 1920 would he opt for the Right, after the Left had demonstrated that it kept no place for him.[36] Indeed, De Felice maintained with increasing emphasis, Fascism was rising because of the many failures of local socialism.[37] The special arena of this defeat was the Po valley, where by 1920–1 a new sort of Fascism, 'squadrism', had become predominant. Its character was mixed: 'class hostility, a wish to complete a preventative counter-revolution in order to eliminate once and for all "the red peril", a desire for revenge and vendetta after a time of frustration and loss, a spirit

28 R. De Felice, *Mussolini il rivoluzionario*, pp. xxvi–xxix.
29 R. De Felice, *Mussolini il rivoluzionario*, pp. xxiv–xxv.
30 Perhaps the most amusing detail about him, given his history, is that the young *Duce* did not speak until the age of 3, a delay in maturation which occasioned parental alarm. See R. De Felice, *Mussolini il rivoluzionario*, p. 9.
31 It was predictable that the youthful revolutionary with intellectual aspirations would very early comment regretfully on his party's relative 'lack of culture'. R. De Felice, *Mussolini il rivoluzionario*, p. 52.
32 R. De Felice, *Mussolini il rivoluzionario*, p. 128.
33 R. De Felice, *Mussolini il rivoluzionario*, p. 218.
34 R. De Felice, *Mussolini il rivoluzionario*, pp. 248–62.
35 R. De Felice, *Mussolini il rivoluzionario*, pp. 459–60.
36 R. De Felice, *Mussolini il rivoluzionario*, p. 544.
37 R. De Felice, *Mussolini il rivoluzionario*, p. 616.

of adventure and emulation, self-interest and a hope to cut a dash in the political and social life' of the country – all such motives, De Felice noted, helped to compose 'the matrix of Fascism'. The movement's own propaganda emphasised 'a social content by no means restricted to class advantage, but, in the final analysis, what won out was this agrarian fascism, elemental and brutal'.[38] Moreover, De Felice added, by late 1920 those who composed the Fascist leadership had persuaded liberal-conservative Italy, as embodied in the great journalist and historian Luigi Albertini, the editor of *Corriere della Sera*, that they were worthy of the backing of big business and the rest of the established middle classes. At that moment, De Felice concluded in the last words of his first volume, 'triumphed . . . reaction and real Fascism was born'.[39]

A careful reader might thus be a little disconcerted that De Felice was able to characterise the *Duce* as some sort of continuing revolutionary at the same time that he seemed to accept that Fascism was an essentially reactionary force. However, De Felice's productivity hid this fuzziness in interpretation. Just a year after the first volume there came a second,[40] and then, in 1968, a third;[41] in all, they tallied more than 2100 pages, taking the story to 1929. When poor Vivarelli brought out his own first volume in 1967, a volume which, failing to reach the end of 1919, was published in-house, only specialists noticed.[42] His occasional quibble with De Felice – for example, Vivarelli stuck to the traditional line that Mussolini had lost any real feeling for the Left by 1917[43] – might be recalled in the odd footnote, but the scholarly contest in which the two had engaged was lost and won. Though, in a year when so much else was happening, or threatening to happen, it scarcely seemed a matter of great importance, by the end of 1968 Renzo De Felice had become the world expert on the history of Italian Fascism. It was a pre-eminence he would not surrender before his death in 1996.

The volumes on 'Mussolini the Fascist' which had appeared in 1966 and 1968 contained plenitudinous detail, but were not particularly controversial in their interpretations. According to De Felice, the story of the Fascist rise to power was clustered around the poles of the still-radical and perhaps 'revolutionary' Mussolini and the clearly reactionary agrarian fascists.[44] Moreover, much in the tale was adventitious; not even Mussolini had an apt plan to confront the complex of political and social difficulties through

38 R. De Felice, *Mussolini il rivoluzionario*, p. 617.
39 R. De Felice, *Mussolini il rivoluzionario*, pp. 661–2.
40 R. De Felice, *Mussolini il fascista 1. La conquista del potere 1921–1925*, Turin, 1966.
41 R. De Felice, *Mussolini il fascista II. L'organizzazione dello Stato fascista 1925–1929*, Turin, 1968.
42 The work (see n. 19 above) was published by the *Istituto italiano per gli studi storici*. Vivarelli spent 623 pages on the history of Fascism up to the start of the Fiume expedition. In other words, he hardly dealt with Fascism at all.
43 R. Vivarelli, *Il dopoguerra in Italia e l'avvento del fascismo*, pp. 230–1.
44 R. De Felice, *Mussolini il fascista I*, pp. 5–6, 16–17.

which the nation was passing.[45] By the summer of 1921, De Felice explained, Fascism drew authority from being a 'negative aggregation', but its 'real character remained quintessentially regional, provincial and often at heart local. . . . The real power and the real structure of Fascism were the *ras* and the local bosses and thus the squads.'[46]

None the less, De Felice suggested, Mussolini was never reduced to being their plaything. Rather, his political skills became steadily more obvious as he dealt adroitly both with potential opponents inside the Fascist movement and with members of the political world outside it, especially those from the Establishment, who thought that they could define Fascism as the 'liberalism of the age of the masses'.[47] The March on Rome was thus always understood, at least by Mussolini, to be aimed at augmenting the political pressure on the existing élite, rather than winning military or 'revolutionary' victory.[48] The masses, De Felice concluded, played no part in the formation of the first Fascist government, except in the sense that they were tired of social violence and could on occasion be attracted by the novelty and apparent strength and vitality of Mussolini and his movement.[49]

Nor did De Felice's interpretation express great novelty when he examined the period after 28 October 1922. In office as Prime Minister, Mussolini gained in status and authority, but the party did not; and its zealots were disturbed by what they viewed as the rapid onset of entangling compromises with the old order.[50] The *Duce* had much of the 'transformist' about him; that is, he replicated the eternal search, once associated with liberal politicians like Giovanni Giolitti and Agostino Depretis, for the middle ground. De Felice again emphasised that Mussolini, as a leader, lacked both a precise vision of the future and any genuine generosity of spirit; for the *Duce*, most issues ended up being reduced to a cynical question of the exercise of immediate personal power.[51] It was doubtful whether Mussolini was directly responsible for the Matteotti murder, De Felice decided after a careful and prolonged reading of the documents;[52] rather, this crime was just another incident in the continuing guerrilla war between the *Duce* and his less-than-loyal followers. It was this conflict which prompted Mussolini's declaration of a dictatorship on 3 January 1925, and the move to Fascist tyranny was therefore aimed as much against Fascists as anti-Fascists.[53]

There followed the construction of the 'Corporate' state; but, in De Felice's view, it did not proceed step by step either, and the most

45 R. De Felice, *Mussolini il fascista I*, pp. 113–14.
46 R. De Felice, *Mussolini il fascista I*, p. 115.
47 R. De Felice, *Mussolini il fascista I*, p. 226.
48 R. De Felice, *Mussolini il fascista I*, p. 348.
49 R. De Felice, *Mussolini il fascista I*, p. 389.
50 R. De Felice, *Mussolini il fascista I*, pp. 400–2.
51 R. De Felice, *Mussolini il fascista I*, pp. 462–8, 535–7.
52 R. De Felice, *Mussolini il fascista I*, pp. 622–3.
53 R. De Felice, *Mussolini il fascista I*, pp. 723–9.

pronounced and menacing opposition to Mussolini's own activities was regularly located within the Fascist movement.[54] The regime was thus 'classic' and 'authoritarian' in character, and, De Felice averred, should not be confused with the sort of 'totalitarianism' which would soon be manifested in Nazi Germany.[55] Mussolini was the dominant figure,[56] but he was frequently assisted by *fiancheggiatori* ('flankers', or fellow-travellers) from the old Establishment.[57] Juggling the interests and beliefs of radical Fascists like Roberto Farinacci and conservative Nationalist ones like Luigi Federzoni, while talking invitingly to Church, Army, big business and monarchy, the *Duce* cemented the position of his government and steadily weakened the appeal of the anti-Fascist opposition.[58]

The increase in the authority of Fascist or Mussolinian administration, De Felice added, brought requirements of its own, notably that expressed in the equation which stated that the nearer the regime was in real terms to the *fiancheggiatori*, the more it needed to theorise Fascism and to appear to demonstrate that it was proceeding on a path from theory to fact.[59] Tactics thus helped to explain the approach to what was called 'totalitarianism'; but, urged De Felice, the reality of totalitarianism lay in the political rather than the social or the economic world.[60] Moreover, the Fascist party, the PNF, was the foremost casualty of these processes, a circumstance which sharply distinguished Mussolini's regime from those of Hitler and of the Soviet Union.[61] By 1929 the *Duce* had grown even more cynical than in the past, and had decided that the great aim of his administration was to survive and to avoid crises, which, he continued to believe, were more likely to come from within Fascism than from anti-Fascism; Mussolini had abandoned whatever faith he had once possessed in the masses, and distrusted the élites. Indeed, he now believed only in himself, though he did talk glibly about forging a new and different generation among Italian youth.[62]

However, De Felice stated, if this was a hint that a spirit of revolt still lurked somewhere in the *Duce*'s psyche, it was a muted one, since Mussolini now moved with his accustomed cunning and phlegm to arrange the Lateran Pacts with the Vatican. Here he could boast a 'real success', if one that was neither original in concept nor likely to further a Fascist

54 R. De Felice, *Mussolini il fascista II*, pp. 3–4.
55 R. De Felice, *Mussolini il fascista II*, p. 9.
56 For a slightly later English-language version by a historian once from the Left, but who would eventually become a Berlusconian member of parliament, see P. Melograni, 'The cult of the Duce in Mussolini's Italy', *Journal of Contemporary History*, 11, 1976, pp. 221–37.
57 See e.g. R. De Felice, *Mussolini il fascista II*, pp. 31, 35, 43.
58 R. De Felice, *Mussolini il fascista II*, pp. 115–18.
59 R. De Felice, *Mussolini il fascista II*, pp. 264–6.
60 R. De Felice, *Mussolini il fascista II*, p. 297.
61 R. De Felice, *Mussolini il fascista II*, pp. 298–9. De Felice emphasised that Mussolini regularly backed the prefects, that is, the old state, against the *ras* (pp. 303–4).
62 R. De Felice, *Mussolini il fascista II*, pp. 357–61.

revolution.[63] Having signed the treaty and been rewarded with an overwhelming majority in the succeeding plebiscite, Mussolini could congratulate himself certainly on vanquishing all his enemies and perhaps on creating a 'new type of political regime'.[64] And yet, in De Felice's assessment, Mussolini had by no means won a total victory. Rather, De Felice wrote, in the uncharacteristically high-flown phrases which concluded his volume, anti-Fascist Italy lived on: 'Despite all its errors and limitations, this Italy not only was not dead in the hearts of Italians but rather represented still a variety of positives which seven years of Fascism had not succeeded in cancelling or in supplanting with other, more valid ideas.'[65] In 1968 it was widely accepted that De Felice was an indefatigible researcher and that he could write a thorough narrative, even if his prose style was and remained unwieldy.[66] What was not yet clear was whether he had become a 'De Felicean'. In the next two decades this term would come to signify a doughty opponent of an anti-Fascist 'vulgate'. But, presently, as he embarked on the first part of his study of 'Mussolini as *Duce*', De Felice still seemed a believer in the virtues of anti-Fascism and in what was commonly said to be the meaning of the Resistance.

Indeed, at the end of the 1960s, mainstream historiography could not be simply divided into the categories of anti-Fascist and anti-anti-Fascist. For example, a liberal conservative historian like Alberto Aquarone,[67] when he gave a legal-historical account of the *stato totalitario* and of the limited reality of 'corporatism',[68] was hard to distinguish in his interpretation from the consistently anti-Fascist Giorgio Rochat who, in 1967, published a rigorous account of Mussolini's manipulative dealings with the Army from 1919 to 1925. Rochat indicated that the result of this 'policy' was the shoring up of the dictator's personal 'power' and the rejection of any serious reform of the military in favour of the *status quo*.[69] Similarly, the authors of the numerous case studies of the rise of Fascism in different Italian towns

---

63 R. De Felice, *Mussolini il fascista II*, pp. 382–3, 437.
64 R. De Felice, *Mussolini il fascista II*, pp. 477–82. De Felice wondered, too, whether the *Duce* did not momentarily think of celebrating his victory by 'liberalising' his regime.
65 R. De Felice, *Mussolini il fascista II*, p. 483.
66 A De Felice sentence could run to a page and a half; a De Felice chapter rarely fell short of 100 pages.
67 For a eulogy, see R. Romeo, 'Alberto Aquarone: intellettuale intero', *Nuova Antologia*, f. 2155, July–September 1985, pp. 214–16. Here Romeo hailed a liberal great nephew of 'Italo Svevo', who had rightly rejected too many unfavourable comparisons between Italy's history and that of foreign states. Aquarone was the somewhat unlikely translator into Italian of Mack Smith and A. J. P. Taylor.
68 A. Aquarone, *L'organizzazione dello stato totalitario*, Turin, 1965. Aquarone noted that a certain judicial independence indeed survived in Fascist Italy (pp. 243–4), and thought that the Corporations by the late 1930s were best defined as 'useless' (p. 212).
69 G. Rochat, *L'esercito italiano da Vittorio Veneto a Mussolini (1919–1925)*, Bari, 1967. For another example of Rochat's consistently penetrating work, see e.g. his *Italo Balbo: aviatore e ministro dell'aeronautica 1926–1933*, Ferrara, 1979. For his eventual open rejection of De Felice, see G. Rochat, 'Il quarto volume della biografia di Mussolini di Renzo De Felice', *Italia contemporanea*, 28, 1976, pp. 89–102.

and regions[70] rarely engaged in a polemic with De Felice, but, rather, confirmed the image of a complex and contradictory set of *fascismi*. Everyone, it seemed, accepted that Fascism was an adaptable political movement which tended, as it approached the seats of power, to favour the conservative over the radical elements in its midst, at least as reliable a friend of the *fiancheggiatori* as of the Fascists.[71]

As De Felice had himself remarked, one of the key moments in the formation of the Fascist state occurred in 1926–7 during the so-called 'Battle for the Lira' (the issue under debate was the proper exchange value of the lira to the pound sterling or dollar).[72] De Felice, in his extended description of the matter, emphasised how Mussolini manipulated a financial debate to his own political ends.[73] However, this assessment was not the only one. The American historian Roland Sarti[74] read the currency valuation crisis as an indicator of Mussolini's preference for short-term political advantage over long-term ideological consistency,[75] but Sarti was also alert to the way in which the Italian 'industrial leadership' reacted to the matter. In his view, the industrialists cleverly safeguarded their own interests, so that, 'by the Second World War, [they] ... were more entrenched in the economic and social system than they were when fascism came to power', and what this entrenchment reflected was the possibility of 'the expansion of private power' in Mussolini's regime.[76] The industrialists remained mistrustful of Fascism but, in practice, were able to give as good as they got, notably in relation to that wing of the Fascist movement committed to syndicalism.[77] All in all, Sarti remarked, the industrialists belonged to the social group 'who yielded the least and gained the most' from Fascism.[78]

70 One early example, based on careful but patriotic scholarship, was E. Apih, *Italia: fascismo e antifascismo nella Venezia Giulia (1918–1943)*, Bari, 1966.
71 See Chapter 1.
72 R. De Felice, *Mussolini il fascista II*, p. 222.
73 R. De Felice, *Mussolini il fascista II*, pp. 222–64.
74 For more on Sarti's background, see Chapter 6.
75 R. Sarti, 'Fascist modernization in Italy: traditional or revolutionary?', *American Historical Review*, 75, 1970, p. 1038. Sarti did think Fascism had originally cut across class lines and that it tried thereafter to preserve a revolutionary purpose. Cf. also his 'Mussolini and the Italian industrial leadership in the battle of the lira 1925–1927', *Past and Present*, 47, 1970, pp. 97–8.
76 R. Sarti, *Fascism and the industrial leadership in Italy, 1919–1940: a study in the expansion of private power under Fascism*, Berkeley, 1971, p. 2. Sarti's views have been largely confirmed by F. H. Adler, *Italian industrialists from Liberalism to Fascism: the political development of the industrial bourgeoisie, 1906–1934*, Cambridge, 1995, though Adler is anxious to take the story back into the era before Fascism and to emphasise the continuity of a search for autonomy by Big Business.
77 R. Sarti, *Fascism and the industrial leadership in Italy*, pp. 89–92.
78 R. Sarti, *Fascism and the industrial leadership in Italy*, p. 136. In a more general work Sarti urged that Fascism should be viewed as 'a prolonged exercise in political equivocation'. R. Sarti, 'Introduction' to R. Sarti (ed.), *The ax within: Italian Fascism in action*, New York, 1974, p. 6. (This book contains some useful translation from the work, among others, of Rochat, De Felice and Aquarone).

What Sarti had to say was certainly not consistent with a totalitarianist reading of the regime, since believers in the model of totalitarianism had been particularly anxious to argue that totalitarians were people utterly opposed to the idea that the business of their country was business. Perhaps for this reason Sarti's ideas remained controversial, being rejected by the pronouncedly right-wing political scientist A. J. Gregor, who took to urging that Fascism[79] should best be comprehended as a 'developmental dictatorship', a rather benign variety of regime in a long-term economic sense.[80] Gregor was countered, in turn, by the economic historian J. S. Cohen, who agreed with Sarti and the De Felice of the 1960s in seeing the Fascist economy as more a place of opportunist manipulation than of ideological fanaticism.[81]

Another whose work seemed largely to endorse what De Felice had so far said was the English historian Adrian Lyttelton. He, too, thought that, in January 1925, Mussolini had been pushed by his own extremists into assuming an outright dictatorship.[82] He, too, delineated a complex, ambiguous and 'piecemeal' 'seizure of power',[83] while also emphasising a certain continuity – he cited with approval a Senator's comment that 'almost all the sons of the Liberals are in Fascism, with their fathers' consent'.[84] Similarly, Lyttelton depicted Fascism in office as a varied and changing movement. In the South, for example, the regime swiftly associated itself with those who had previously dominated society; in the North the pattern was not so constant and, despite Mussolini's public backing, the prefects actually did their best not to get offside with their own particular *ras*.[85] None the less, Lyttelton explained, although from 1925 the word 'totalitarian' came into frequent usage, authority still lay more with the state than the party.[86] 'Corporatism' was proving a dead letter, even if Fascist Italy was always a place in which a new bureaucracy could grow. However, the real challenge to the state came, Lyttelton concluded, from Mussolini's personal power which, by 1929, was tending to predominate.[87]

79 But cf. A. J. Gregor, *The Fascist 'persuasion' in radical politics*, Princeton, 1974, one of those period anti-anti-Vietnam books proclaiming that all radicals were Fascists at heart.

80 See e.g. A. J. Gregor, *The ideology of Fascism: the rationale of totalitarianism*, New York, 1969; and his *Italian Fascism and developmental dictatorship*, Princeton, 1979. And cf. Chapter 3.

81 See J. S. Cohen, 'Was Italian fascism a developmental dictatorship? Some evidence to the contrary', *Economic History Review*, 41, 1988, pp. 95–113; cf. his 'The 1927 revaluation of the lira: a study in political economy', *Economic History Review*, 25, 1972, pp. 642–54. V. Zamagni, *The economic history of Italy 1860–1990*, Oxford, 1993, pp. 243–55 concurs with Cohen.

82 A. Lyttelton, 'Fascism in Italy: the second wave', *Journal of Contemporary History*, 1, 1966, p. 81.

83 A. Lyttelton, *The seizure of power: Fascism in Italy 1919–1929*, London, 1973, p. 1.

84 Rolandi Ricci as quoted in A. Lyttelton, *The seizure of power*, p. 109.

85 A. Lyttelton, *The seizure of power*, pp. 162, 194–8.

86 A. Lyttelton, *The seizure of power*, p. 270.

87 A. Lyttelton, *The seizure of power*, p. 429.

In the early 1970s, then, a consensus seemed to have been reached aı. those who sought to interpret the politics of Fascist Italy. In this vı Mussolini was very much the fulcrum of his regime, even if lower down th scale of political, economic and social power lay a tangle of forces with a vitality of their own. At this secondary level operated the 'old order', those who had already possessed wealth and status in Liberal Italy; after 1922 they had been forced to make some compromises, but Mussolini had rarely changed their lives for the worse. By contrast, the more revolutionary pretensions of Fascism seemed hollow indeed, and the great majority of the masses remained offstage, where they had always been.

However, the new decade would prove a troubled one, politically, culturally[88] and historiographically. It was a time of generational turn, in which there came to adulthood the children of those Italians who had directly experienced the Second World War, the collapse of Fascism, the armed Resistance and the Salò Republic. The sometimes disunited student and worker demonstrations of 1968 seemed to promise that the post-war political settlement, and especially endless rule by the Christian Democrats, could no longer be taken for granted.[89] As if in admission of their own potential weakness, DC leaders took to bewailing the lack of a fully developed Catholic 'culture' and historiography.[90] The Communist party, by contrast, pressed forward with a tactic which it announced, with an ironical choice of words, as the 'historic compromise', hoping for 'legitimation' and a chance to join the governing coalition in Rome. In the successive years of 1974, 1975 and 1976 the PCI and its friends could celebrate victories. First the DC opposed a referendum approving divorce and, left only with the MSI as allies, suffered a severe political defeat, while exaggerating still further the sense that the DC was culturally bereft. Next, the PCI vote increased to more than 33 per cent in successive regional and national elections. Campaigning on the slogan *venuto da lontano* (come from afar), the PCI declared that it was struggling free from the heavy legacy of Stalinism, asserting that there was indeed an 'Italian road to socialism' and preparing itself for a future in government. Only a reiterated veto from the US embassy seemed to block the party's way.[91]

---

88 For a useful introduction to the problem of leftist culture and its complex relationship with the PCI, see N. Ajello, *Il lungo addio: intellettuali e PCI dal 1958 al 1991*, Bari, 1997.

89 For a contemporary English-language account, very much expressing the spirit of the times, see the characteristically entitled P. A. Allum, *Italy – Republic without a government?* New York, 1973. Many readers discounted the question mark.

90 See e.g. the peremptory comment of the right-Catholic philosopher, Augusto Del Noce, that the DC had no culture at all, as cited in *L'Espresso*, 30, 26 February 1984. Cf. the comment of the sometime Prime Minister Mariano Rumor that what the Catholic party above all needed was more culture. M. Rumor, *I Democratici Cristiani per il rinnovamento dello Stato, per lo sviluppo della democrazia, per la libertà e per la pace*, Rome, 1968, pp. 17, 40.

91 On 12 January 1978, for example, the embassy let it be known that the US attitude to Western European communist parties 'including the Italian, [had] not changed in any way'. See G. Andreotti, *Diari 1976–1979: gli anni della solidarietà*, Milan, 1981, p. 173.

Increasingly, however, another issue came to the surface – terrorism. Groups to the PCI's left,[92] like the *Brigate Rosse* (Red Brigades) and *Prima Linea* (First Line), began a physical, rhetorical and historiographical attack. In their efforts to 'strike at the heart of the state', which culminated in March–May 1978 in the kidnapping and brutal and deliberate murder of the hapless DC fixer, party secretary and many times Prime Minister Aldo Moro, the Left terrorists summoned the history and myth of anti-Fascism to their cause. They 'acted', they claimed, as once the partisans had done; indeed, they constituted the 'new Resistance'. By stripping the mask from a man like Moro, they would show up the Fascist tyranny which still lurked beneath the pleasing or confused surface of DC rule. They would lay bare the self-defeating 'reformism' entailed in any historic compromise, and even kill members of the PCI who got in their way. The terrorists of the Left would justify their bloody policy by reading history, politics, economics and sociology in a frighteningly literal way.[93]

Into this highly contested field stepped Renzo De Felice, the 'man from the archives',[94] the historian 'without an axe to grind', who opposed all 'rigid schematism'.[95] By December 1974 De Felice was ready to publish the first part of the next volume of his biography, the lengthiest so far, carrying the story of the Fascist regime from 1929 to 1936. It dealt as promised with 'Mussolini *il duce*', and was sub-titled 'the years of consensus'.[96]

Those of its findings relevant to foreign policy have been discussed in the previous chapter and will not be repeated here. In regard to domestic affairs, De Felice now turned his attention to the 'era of Achille Starace' as secretary of the PNF (1931–9) and the boasts of the regime that it was 'going to the people' and forging 'new men and women'. True to his title, De Felice duly emphasised that Fascism had now obtained a 'consensus' from its subjects.[97]

92 A right terrorism had long existed in Italy, and continued through the 1970s and 1980s. For its humdrum flavour see G. Salierno, *Autobiografia di un picchiatore fascista*, Turin, 1976, a 'revelation' which now also reads as a period piece.

93 The 'historic leader' of the Red Brigades was Renato Curcio, in his youth a student of sociology at the Catholic university of Trento. The best English-language introduction to the left-terrorist mind (and a friendly one) is A. Silj, *Never again without a rifle: the origins of Italian terrorism*, New York, 1979. A more scholarly literature with focus on the Moro murder continues to build. See e.g. D. Moss, *The politics of left-wing violence in Italy, 1969–85*, London, 1989; R. Wagner-Pacifici, *The Moro morality play: terrorism as social drama*, Chicago, 1986; R. Drake, *The revolutionary mystique and terrorism in contemporary Italy*, Bloomington, Ind., 1989; R. Drake, *The Aldo Moro murder case*, Cambridge, Mass., 1995.

94 De Felice was already beginning to publish monographs apart from the biography. See e.g. R. De Felice, *Il problema dell'Alto Adige nei rapporti italo-tedeschi dall'*Anschluss *alla fine della seconda guerra mondiale*, Bologna, 1973; R. De Felice (ed.), *L'Italia fra tedeschi e alleati: la politica estera fascista e la seconda guerra mondiale*, Bologna, 1973.

95 See the comments in this regard of Giovanni Spadolini, introducing a 'preview' of De Felice's next volume to the readers of the Establishment journal, *Nuova Antologia*, R. De Felice, 'Il Vaticano e il fascismo', *Nuova Antologia*, f. 2086, October 1974, p. 156.

96 R. De Felice, *Mussolini il duce I. Gli anni del consenso, 1929–1936*, Turin, 1974. Its longest chapter, on foreign policy, ran to 211 pages.

97 R. De Felice, *Mussolini il duce I*, p. 3.

He also seemed to evince a deeper sympathy for Mussolini than in the past, underlining his dislike of chatter, devotion to work, and concentration on his family as his chief diversion, while admitting that the *Duce* was mistrustful and unable to delegate sensibly, and, indeed, that he grew more isolated every year.[98] Moreover, De Felice added in what had been his usual refrain, Mussolini only rarely pursued a consistent political line, making his decisions 'suddenly, without adequate preparation'.[99] None the less, despite the apparent contradiction, De Felice accepted Mussolini's words about wanting to create a new generation, as though he were a scientist in a laboratory.[100] Hampered to some extent by the Depression, whose effects, even if relatively minor in Italy, could still be detected in 1938,[101] the *Duce* and his regime, according to De Felice, had considerable successes in this ambition.[102] However, the real opportunity to manufacture new Italians came most directly in the realm of foreign policy, which Mussolini addressed increasingly from 1933, partly out of irritation at the delays and inadequacies of what was occurring at home.[103] Even if the Fascist move against Ethiopia was not occasioned by domestic pressure, De Felice argued,[104] the war genuinely attracted the support of the 'Italian people'. The imperial victory constituted 'Mussolini's political masterpiece and greatest success'.[105]

Here were some controversial comments and phrases, and yet 'the De Felice affair', as it was soon being called, did not flare immediately into life. Rather, only a few days after the book's publication, a courteous exchange between De Felice and Giorgio Amendola, a leading Communist, who, given his family background, had plenty of claims to embody anti-Fascism, occurred in the pages of the radical democrat weekly *L'Espresso*. Amendola thought De Felice was somewhat inclined to overestimate the *Duce*, and De Felice grew more emphatic in his definition of Mussolini as the chief opponent of Hitler until 1936.[106] But in this peaceable debate there was little evidence of an impending historiographical storm. It would not really break until July 1975, with the publication, in the immediate aftermath of those regional elections in which the PCI had done so well, of an extended

98 R. De Felice, *Mussolini il duce I*, pp. 19–21, 174.
99 R. De Felice, *Mussolini il duce I*, pp. 23–4.
100 R. De Felice, *Mussolini il duce I*, p. 51. Even so, he admitted, again with seeming contradiction, that under Starace the party grew ever more bureaucratised and de-politicised in a way that destroyed the regime's ideological base (pp. 217–18).
101 R. De Felice, *Mussolini il duce I*, p. 58.
102 R. De Felice, *Mussolini il duce I*, p. 95. One important feature of the decade was 'ruralisation', a policy embarked on with great seriousness in De Felice's eyes. It was, however, a policy which ended, he admitted, in 'complete failure' (pp. 146–7).
103 R. De Felice, *Mussolini il duce I*, p. 179.
104 R. De Felice, *Mussolini il duce I*, pp. 613–14.
105 R. De Felice, *Mussolini il duce I*, pp. 616, 642.
106 See 'Tutti si aspettavano che il duce cadesse . . . Dialogo fra Giorgio Amendola e Renzo De Felice', *L'Espresso*, 20, 15 December 1974.

interview between De Felice and an American postdoctoral student named Michael Ledeen.[107] Before the holding of the national elections in June 1976 the *Intervista* had reached its sixth edition, stimulating reams of criticism and support.[108]

The 'De Felice affair' of this time is too familiar to need much recounting here.[109] Suffice it to say that, under Ledeen's respectful guidance,[110] the prolixity and complexity of De Felice's prose was swept away. Now, it seemed, the Italian historian had some very definite things to say, and every view was one which struck at the hopes of the PCI and at its version of the myth of the Resistance. Fascism, De Felice asserted, was based on a positive, not a negative force, and embodied the 'emerging middle classes'. In power there were doubtless many compromises, but they reflected the habits of 'Fascism regime'; this conservative strain never eliminated a radical element – 'Fascism movement' – whose central tenets Mussolini himself continued to uphold. Fascism's great aim remained a 'cultural revolution', and this purpose at home, combined with success in the empire, gave the Fascist regime a special vitality by the mid-1930s. Italian Fascism was also unique; its positive outlook contrasted starkly with the backward-looking aims of Nazism; the two movements were very different, and there was thus no credible 'model of fascism'. The era of fascism had ended in 1945 and would not revive. What was needed now, by means of scrupulous archival work, was serious, 'scientific' history, which would only become possible in a 'calmer' 'political atmosphere'. Then the 'communist cultural hegemony', which so scarred contemporary Italy, could be shaken off, and 'the abstractness and cultural conformism of many of our historians' would

107 R. De Felice, *Intervista sul fascismo*. The publishers, Laterza, were at the time issuing a series of such interviews and e.g. followed the one on Fascism with G. Amendola, *Intervista sull'antifascismo*, Bari, [February] 1976. In 1997 De Felice's book was republished with a highly apologetic new introduction by Giovanni Belarelli and an apologia on De Felice's own part from 1975. R. De Felice, *Intervista sul fascismo* rev. ed., Bari, 1997.

108 The most notorious or emblematic support within Italy came from the Big Business league, *Confindustria*, which in October 1975 bought up copies of the *Intervista* to distribute free. See N. Tranfaglia, *Labirinto italiano: radici storiche e nuove contraddizioni*, Turin, 1984, p. 344.

109 For my own main account, see R. J. B. Bosworth, *Explaining Auschwitz and Hiroshima: history writing and the Second World War 1945–1990*, London, 1993, pp. 135–7.

110 The American had begun his academic career with an article, M. A. Ledeen, 'Italian Fascism and youth', *Journal of Contemporary History*, 4, 1969, pp. 137–54. Later, he published two academic books: M. A. Ledeen, *Universal Fascism: the theory and practice of the Fascist International, 1928–1936*, New York, 1972; and *D'Annunzio a Fiume*, Bari, 1975 (English-language version, *The first Duce: D'Annunzio at Fiume*, Baltimore, 1977). In the latter Ledeen was notably effusive in his thanks to his old supervisor George Mosse (p. 3), and, indeed, he urged the seriousness of the cultural humus of Fascism and its 'third wave', even while admitting the regime's inconsistency or confusion. De Felice, too, would soon produce a study of D'Annunzio, taking the poet more solemnly than he deserves: R. De Felice, *D'Annunzio politico 1918–1938*, Bari, 1978.

end.[111] In the *Intervista* De Felice had set out the 'De Felicean' manifesto, from which his followers have never resiled.

Ironically, the most obvious result of this direct assault on the self-consciously leftist and anti-Fascist understanding of the Fascist past was a polarisation of the political history of Fascism which 20 years later has by no means been overcome. De Felice, then and later, could rely on the big battalions.[112] Though he was caustically reviewed by Denis Mack Smith,[113] De Felice had his cause strenuously defended by American experts, led by Ledeen[114] (in the pages of the *Journal of Contemporary History*) and by A. J. Gregor.[115] De Felice was also favoured by good fortune, or had understood the spirit of the times. The Moro murder closed the Left's window of political opportunity in Italy and the historic compromise lost its appeal, for both Communists and non-Communists. The 1980s became the era of the political 'realism' and 'good sense' of Craxi,[116] a time in which 'moderate' 'Western'-style socialism would seek to end the 'anomaly' of the continuing communist presence in Italian political life (even if, a little below the surface, it was also the decade of an avid desire for wealth, when greed was good and *Tangentopoli* in the making). Moreover, in this decade, 'new' politics as ever entailed new history, both academic and popular.

Given his fame in the media, it was predictable that De Felice should be drawn into a new world of 'infotainment', of popular exhibitions, TV documentaries and films, which now portrayed the Fascist era as an alluring

111 In English translation, see R. De Felice, *Fascism: an informal introduction to its theory and practice*, New Brunswick, NJ, 1976, pp. 113–15.

112 Laterza also cashed in on the affair by publishing a number of anthologies edited by De Felice. See R. De Felice (ed.), *Antologia sul fascismo: il giudizio storico*, Bari, 1976; *Antologia sul fascismo: il giudizio politico*, Bari, 1976. Something of the old De Felice came out in his next monograph, *Ebrei in un paese arabo*, Bologna, 1978, an austerely scholarly or historicist study of the small Jewish community of Libya.

113 See P. Meldini (ed.), *Un monumento al duce? Contributo al dibattito sul fascismo con i testi originali della polemica Mack Smith/Ledeen*, Florence, 1976. On 28 April 1976 RAI TV screened a lengthy debate between Mack Smith and De Felice to its prime-time audience.

114 M. Ledeen, 'Renzo De Felice and the controversy over Italian Fascism', *Journal of Contemporary History*, 11, 1976, pp. 269–83. By the time he published this article, Ledeen had become a frequent contributor to anti-Communist US journals, warning of the genuine threat to liberal capitalism posed by the PCI, and praising the young Socialist Bettino Craxi as a coming political figure. See e.g. M. Ledeen and C. Sterling, 'Italy's Russian Sugar Daddies', *New Republic*, 174, 3 April 1976, pp. 16–21; M. Ledeen, 'Roman roulette', *New Republic*, 175, 3, 10 July 1976, pp. 14–17; 'Inertia in Italy', *New Republic*, 175, 31 July 1976, pp. 14–16; 'Italian Communism at home and abroad', *Commentary*, 62, November 1976, pp. 51–4. His culminating denunciation was 'Italy in crisis', *The Washington papers*, 43, Beverly Hills, 1977, which appeared in Italy under the evocative title *Il complesso di Nerone* (The Nero complex). In *New Republic*, 7 January 1978, an article of his entitled 'Italy awaits Caesar' featured a photo of Mussolini with the caption 'Il Duce: the historical [sic] compromise of 1922'.

115 A. J. Gregor, 'Professor Renzo De Felice and the fascist phenomenon', *World Politics*, 30, 1978, pp. 433–49.

116 Apart from Ledeen, who gave up academic history, the most enthusiastic American scholarly proponent of Craxi and his antecedents was Spencer Di Scala. See S. M. Di Scala, *Renewing Italian socialism: Nenni to Craxi*, New York, 1988; and the slightly bemused S. M. Di Scala (ed.), *Italian socialism between politics and history*, Amherst, Mass., 1996.

time of pretty fashion and quaint but 'modernising' technology.[117] Similarly, he regularly gave press interviews, which interpreted the past – Fascist Italy bore no guilt for 'Auschwitz'; Italy, as a result of the Second World War, owed no debt to the USSR and communism – and explained the present – Fascism was no longer a credible idea; there was no need to veto the MSI from normal participation in national politics; anti-Fascism had lost its meaning and ethical thrust.[118] With the help of a younger colleague, he even published his own photographic studies of Fascism, which were typically serious in character, even if they did contain some delicious images that must have amused and attracted those students who flicked through the books' pages.[119]

However, it is hard to believe that this 'De Felice of the market' ever really overthrew the more familiar De Felice of the archives. Certainly he kept writing both the biography and other monographs,[120] and continued to seek out and, frequently, to publish documents.[121] And the centre of all his work remained his account of the life of Mussolini. In 1981, De Felice published the second part of *Mussolini il duce*, covering the period from the triumph in Ethiopia until the Italian intervention in the Second World War. The book's telling subtitle was *Lo Stato totalitario* (The Totalitarian State). Once again it was a work of immense and impressive archival detail.[122]

Though De Felice's prose remained tortuous, he was clear enough in setting out his main theses in his early pages. Already in 1936, he remarked,

117 The two great English-language accounts of this process are T. Mason, 'The Great Economic History Show', *History Workshop*, 21, 1986, pp. 3–35; 'Italy and modernisation: a montage', *History Workshop*, 25, 1988, pp. 127–47. The more direct organiser of the displays was Giano Accame, once a nostalgic for Salò. Accame, in the 1960s, had organised *incontri romani della cultura di destra* (Roman seminars in the culture of the Right). Among his speakers was A. J. Gregor. See P. Ignazi, *Il polo escluso: profilo del Movimento Sociale Italiano*, Bologna, 1989, p. 150, n. 39. See further Chapter 7.
118 Again, in English, see R. J. B. Bosworth, *Explaining Auschwitz and Hiroshima*, pp. 138–9. De Felice now took time to celebrate the career of his father-in-law, the liberal Guido De Ruggiero, in words which half-suggested that he was writing about himself. De Ruggiero, believing that there was no essential difference between Fascism and communism, stayed in Italy throughout the regime and devoted himself to scholarship (even if he did take the oath of allegiance and, in 1940, accepted a party ticket). In De Felice's eyes, De Ruggiero's purpose was always to influence the 'cultural and moral formation of the young' and so save them from Fascism. See R. De Felice, 'Il Magistero di Guido De Ruggiero', *Nuova Antologia*, f. 2161, January–March 1987, pp. 79–97; R. De Felice, *Intellettuali di fronte al fascismo: saggi e note documentarie*, Rome, 1985.
119 See R. De Felice and L. Goglia, *Storia fotografica del fascismo*, Bari, 1981; *Mussolini: il mito*, Bari, 1983 (and L. Goglia, *Storia fotografica dell'Impero fascista 1935–1941*, Bari, 1985).
120 Most had a focus on foreign policy, perhaps a topic for which it was easiest to find publication approval or subsidy. See e.g. R. De Felice, *Il Fascismo e l'Oriente: arabi, ebrei e indiani nella politica di Mussolini*, Bologna, 1988.
121 Probably the most important of these was the extensive diary of a true believer from below, the sometime Minister of Corporations, Tullio Cianetti. See T. Cianetti, *Memorie dal carcere di Verona*, ed. R. De Felice, Milan, 1983.
122 R. De Felice, *Mussolini il duce II. Lo stato totalitario 1936–1940*, Turin, 1981. Chapter 1, on Fascist 'totalitarianism', ran to 153 pages; Chapter 6, on 1939–40, to 172.

there was some evidence of the wartime crisis of the regime, and yet anti-Fascism was now feeble indeed, and the crisis in large part only reflected the fact that Fascism was itself changing. 'Without war and defeat Fascism would not have fallen,' he declared firmly.[123] Indeed, the confidence which Mussolini and his followers gained as a result of the conquest of Ethiopia had pushed them deeper into a 'totalitarianising process', in which the *Duce*, troubled by his health and sense of impending mortality, was particularly anxious to curtail the social power of the surviving old élites.[124]

It was true, De Felice admitted, that there were certain problems with the bureaucracy which back in 1923 Mussolini had called 'a huge, mysterious, powerful and inexplicable thing'.[125] Although it remained only superficially fascistised it continued to expand its numbers, and the *Duce* relied on it heavily for the stability it lent his regime.[126] None the less, Mussolini and some of the leading philosophers of Fascism also favoured a more pronounced politicisation and, indeed, a real totalitarianism.[127] The masses, De Felice suggested, were now at last being nationalised, and Mussolini was genuine in his pressing for a 'cultural revolution'.[128] Fascist initiatives to this end were not improvisations or absurdities, De Felice argued (in some contrast to his views in the 1960s), but were genuinely aimed at rooting out the 'bourgeois mentality'. He did acknowledge, however, that Bottai's allegedly 'Fascist' educational policies scarcely got past the blueprint stage, and he admitted that Fascism sought more to curry favour with the 'Italian family' than to bend it to its ideological will. He even agreed that, by the late 1930s, Mussolini did not devote to policy the sort of day-to-day attention which he once had done.[129]

Despite such admissions, De Felice continued to argue that the 'people' had broadly given their consent to the regime, its policies and ambitions.[130] The youngest members of the working class were, he claimed, notably inclined to believe Fascism's anti-bourgeois rhetoric.[131] So, too, was Mussolini, at least according to De Felice, although the nature of this belief was hard to ascertain amid the twists and turns of De Felicean prose. Doubtless the *Duce* was never a systematic thinker, De Felice stated; but he

123 R. De Felice, *Mussolini il duce II*, p. 4.
124 R. De Felice, *Mussolini il duce II*, pp. 7–15.
125 R. De Felice, *Mussolini il duce II*, p. 50. De Felice again repeated his familiar psychological diagnosis which revealed that the *Duce* became each year a more convinced pessimist about human nature (p. 59).
126 R. De Felice, *Mussolini il duce II*, pp. 57, 60–1.
127 R. De Felice, *Mussolini il duce II*, pp. 63–8.
128 R. De Felice, *Mussolini il duce II*, pp. 85, 88–9.
129 R. De Felice, *Mussolini il duce II*, pp. 90–3, 122–9, 269–72. De Felice thus now urged the serious character of the *Voi* and *passo romano* campaigns (p. 101). Especially the latter (the introduction of the goose-step into the Italian armed forces, while explaining that a goose was a Roman creature) had regularly been the butt of jokes for previous commentators.
130 R. De Felice, *Mussolini il duce II*, p. 156.
131 R. De Felice, *Mussolini il duce II*, pp. 192–3, 201.

was moving from 'a desire to last to a desire to dare', especially as he developed a national policy on colonial, racial and diplomatic questions.[132] Eventually there came the war and a German alliance which Mussolini did not want sundered, even while he sought to craft a Fascist 'parallel war' (and began to blame the Italian people for lacking an appropriate military spirit).[133] It would be Mussolini who would make the final and belated decision to take Italy into the conflict, but he would do so on tactical grounds and because of events at the front, and not out of a desire to build a Nazi–fascist new world order.[134]

The obsession with the Second World War was beginning to overwhelm both De Felice and all those who were currently writing the political history of Fascism. Another volume of the biography was in the making. 'Mussolini the Ally', part one, covering the three years from June 1940 to July 1943, would not appear until 1990. It would be printed in two volumes and exceed 1570 pages in length; in other words, it would average about one and a half pages for every day of Italy's war effort.[135] Because of its focus on foreign policy and war, *Mussolini l'alleato* has been discussed elsewhere in this book.[136] What might be presently noted is De Felice's reiteration in his preface that he had been fighting against 'historical journalism', which was in turn to blame for the 'mediocrity' of national culture, and his statement that his interpretation was 'the only possible and correct one both scientifically and in regard to the readership'.[137] He similarly declared his intention to rebut the arguments of those of his predecessors who had cheaply made Mussolini and Fascism the 'only scapegoats for the defeat', absolving or condemning other social forces out of ideology, not 'science'.[138]

Inevitably, De Felice narrated a complex story. As has already been noted, its chief burden was very much the war and Italo–German relations, in discussing which De Felice evinced a curiously parochial determination to treat the conflict as more a Mediterranean than an Eastern Front event. Often he seemed to accept the possibility of a 'parallel war', waged more for Italy's national interests than for ideology, and given its form by Mussolini's acute recognition that Italy should sit at the peace-table with its power as intact as possible.[139] According to De Felice, Mussolini was always in charge

132 R. De Felice, *Mussolini il duce II*, p. 301 (cf. p. 300).
133 R. De Felice, *Mussolini il duce II*, pp. 677–8, 691. With the greatest irony, Mussolini even repeated a metaphor Salandra had used in 1914–15, when he complained that it was awful to sit idle while 'others write history' (p. 687).
134 R. De Felice, *Mussolini il duce II*, pp. 843–4.
135 R. De Felice, *Mussolini l'alleato 1940–1945 I. L'Italia in guerra 1940–1943*, Turin, 1990. Chapter 2 on 'the short war 1940–1' ran past 300 pages, but De Felice reached his personal best in the last chapter, devoted to the crisis of 25 July 1943. It was 321 pages long.
136 See Chapters 4 and 8.
137 R. De Felice, *Mussolini l'alleato I*, pp. x–xi.
138 R. De Felice, *Mussolini l'alleato I*, p. 4.
139 R. De Felice, *Mussolini l'alleato I*, pp. 104–6.

of the war effort and did a reasonable job in the circumstances – he even asserts that the *Duce*'s incompetence in economics and determination to read every issue politically did not amount to an overwhelming drawback in the prosecution of Italy's war.[140] Instead, the villains of the piece are the Germans, who regularly fail to comprehend the worthiness of their ally,[141] and the Italian bourgeoisie, who lack an appropriate national spirit.[142] In any case, De Felice is emphatic that 'it was political-diplomatic and military matters which conditioned internal ones and not the other way round'.[143] A natural corollary was that organised anti-Fascism was very weak until 1943 and played no significant role in the collapse of the regime.[144] The most important criticism, by contrast, came from within Fascism and was aimed at reforming rather than eliminating the Fascist state.[145] In sum, De Felice's real preoccupation as he contemplated the war had become a desire to discover why, after 1945, the war effort could not be read in such a way 'as to induce a people to take proper account of its history, both in regard to itself and in comparison with other peoples'. How was it, De Felice asked in his stubbornly amoral way, that the Italian version of the Second World War brought out 'a substantial ethico-political weakness at the base of our national fabric', when the German, Soviet and Japanese campaigns did not?[146]

The controversial nature of De Felice's interpretation of the war linked well with the politics of the 'end of the First Republic', discussed above, and the general eclipse of the myth of the Resistance, to be reviewed in Chapter 8. It was also true that, by the 1990s, in the discipline of history itself political history had surrendered much ground both to social history and – after the historical discipline also showed some signs of acknowledging the 'linguistic turn' – to cultural and ethnographic history. Again as was noted earlier, the result in writing about Fascism has been the curious alliance between the De Feliceans, and especially Emilio Gentile, and American cultural and intellectual historians.[147] Occupying themselves in tracing the first usage of ideas expressed in a more mainstream way after 1922, these writers have concentrated their research on the question of the rise and

140 R. De Felice, *Mussolini l'alleato I*, pp. 536–7.
141 Perhaps De Felice's most remarkable comment was his view that Mussolini was not being unrealistic in contemplating a German–USSR separate peace, given Stalin's 'anthropological and geopolitical sensibility' (p. 1256). In expressing such ideas, De Felice noted his debt to the nationalist German historian Andreas Hillgruber.
142 See e.g. R. De Felice, *Mussolini l'alleato I*, pp. 538–59, in which De Felice seems to endorse the regime's complaints about the disorganisation of industry and agriculture and the low quality of planning in Italy compared with other combatants. Cf. also pp. 770–1, 825–9.
143 R. De Felice, *Mussolini l'alleato I*, p. 671.
144 R. De Felice, *Mussolini l'alleato I*, p. 680. De Felice was also unimpressed with the strikes in Turin and elsewhere in March–April 1943 (pp. 773–5, 938–9).
145 R. De Felice, *Mussolini l'alleato I*, p. 884.
146 R. De Felice, *Mussolini l'alleato I*, p. 959.
147 See Chapter 1.

origins of Fascism,[148] and have been much indebted to the work of George
Mosse. With the thesis that the cultural humus of Nazism gradually
developed in the aftermath of the French revolution, when the key issue
became the forging of a 'modernised' usable myth, Mosse argued that the
nation state needed the 'lay religion' of nationalism to act as a social glue,
replacing that 'dead' God who had propped up the social and political
structure of pre-modern societies. In his contention at least, the
'nationalisation of the masses' was the crucial process of nineteenth- and
twentieth-century existence.[149]

Gentile has prolifically injected these ideas into Italian historical
discourse. However, he has also written some more strictly political history,
commencing what promised to be a multi-volume history of the party which
might one day tell its story in the same detailed and detached way in which
De Felice had approached the *Duce*. The PNF, Gentile admitted in a first
volume which took the party's history to 1922, was usually dismissed as of
lesser influence than the dictator himself. However, this dismissal needed to
be reversed in the light both of recent research[150] and of the refurbishing of
the concept of 'totalitarianism'.[151] The PNF's real character, it emerged, was
cultural; this was an organisation which was 'always a *movement and a
militia*' [sic].[152] Its members were true believers in totalitarianism, which
meant that the PNF was never just another party.[153] Rather, Fascism was 'a
new state of mind', and Fascists themselves were utterly won over by the
liturgy, the rites and the ceremonial.[154] They really were the new crusaders.

In a second, shorter and more cursory volume reflecting on the party
after 1922, Gentile did acknowledge that majority opinion had described a
Fascist party which, by the early 1930s, had been bureaucratised and
depoliticised out of whatever significance it had earlier possessed.[155] It was a
majority view, Gentile again argued, which was also wrong; actually the
PNF represented 'the first experience for the Italian people of mass
organisation conducted through rigid, centralised and totalitarian principles

---

148 Somewhat ironically, the long-expected second volume of Roberto Vivarelli's promised
   history of Fascism similarly spent as much time talking about Liberal Italy (and about the
   alleged deficiencies of socialism) as about Fascism. For this lengthy, patriotic and
   intellectually disappointing book, see R. Vivarelli, *Storia delle origini del fascismo: L'Italia
   dalla grande guerra alla marcia su Roma*, Bologna, 1991.
149 See e.g. G. Mosse, *The nationalisation of the masses: political symbolism and mass
   movements from the Napoleonic wars through the Third Reich*, New York, 1975; *Masses
   and man: nationalist and fascist perceptions of reality*, New York, 1980.
150 E. Gentile, *Storia del partito fascista 1919–1922: movimento e milizia*, Bari, 1989, pp.
   79–80. Gentile agreed that it was an inter-class party, with considerable support from the
   'emerging middle classes'.
151 E. Gentile, *Storia del partito fascista 1919–1922*, pp. vii–ix. He dedicated his work to De
   Felice.
152 E. Gentile, *Storia del partito fascista 1919–1922*, p. 219.
153 E. Gentile, *Storia del partito fascista 1919–1922*, pp. 461, 543.
154 E. Gentile, *Storia del partito fascista 1919–1922*, pp. 518, 526–8, 533.
155 E. Gentile, *La via italiana al totalitarismo: il Partito e lo Stato nel regime fascista*, Rome,
   1995, p. 86.

with the aim of forming a collective identity and nationalising the masses'.[156]
Fascism, he claimed, adapting De Felice's views about 'regime' and
'movement', had two faces – one was 'authoritarian', the other genuinely
'totalitarian'; and, even if contradictions and inconsistencies remained, a
genuine totalitarianism was gaining ground during the 1930s under
Starace.[157] Adelchi Serena, Party secretary during 1940–1, aimed still more
directly at a 'permanent revolution'; it was only his sudden sacking that
prevented the party achieving this objective.[158]

Gentile's work has duly received the applause of his academic faction.
Non-De Feliceans, however, retain many doubts. Ironically, before Gentile's
arguments about a fascistised and totalitarianised society can carry real
conviction, they will need to be bolstered by more documentary evidence on
the actual state of mind of the peoples of the Italies throughout the regime.
As presently couched, Gentile's study of the PNF is too narrowly restricted
to political and intellectual history; he could learn from a reading of some of
the social history of Fascism to be discussed in the next chapter.

Before commencing that chapter, however, it is appropriate to essay some
general conclusions about the political history of Fascism and about the
achievement of Renzo De Felice as a historian during the long period of his
supremacy. One way to address the matter is to note briefly a further book,
published recently by Mauro Canali, another of De Felice's pupils. Canali's
monograph on the Matteotti murder is the best piece of Italian political
history to appear for some time, and well illustrates the strengths and
weaknesses of the neo-Rankean De Felice school.[159] Canali has been zealous
in tracing archives, both in Italy and abroad.[160] He also asks some new
questions, or probes old ones to greater effect than his predecessors had
done. Thus, the most fascinating part of his account of the background to
the murder is his reconstruction of the *tangenti cospicue* (sizeable bribes)
which were passing from US oil and other business interests to the
leadership of the Fascist party – here included were Mussolini and his
brother Arnaldo, Giacomo Acerbo and such familiar 'guilty men' of the case
as Aldo Finzi (another aspiring politician, assisted by a brother with good
contacts). Canali thus exposes at least three great structures of Italian
political and social life – 'corruption'; the Italian relationship with US
capital (Standard Oil, J. P. Morgan, Mellon, Guggenheim, Westinghouse
and many others); and the role of brothers (and the wider family) in
'success' and the broking which accompanies it.

---

156 E. Gentile, *La via italiana al totalitarismo*, p. 104.
157 E. Gentile, *La via italiana al totalitarismo*, pp. 136–7, 189–90.
158 E. Gentile, *La via italiana al totalitarismo*, pp. 254, 285–8.
159 M. Canali, *Il delitto Matteotti: affarismo e politica nel primo governo Mussolini*,
    Bologna, 1997. The work is dedicated to the deceased De Felice.
160 M. Canali, *Il delitto Matteotti*, p. 572 provides a nice case in which Canali rejoiced at
    finding a file which had eluded the search of De Felice (and which required some
    qualification of De Felice's views).

Regrettably, however, except for the occasional comment about the US, Canali leaves these matters for contemplation rather than analysis. He focuses instead on Amerigo Dumini and his team of killers, highlighting useful details about how, for example, the quaintly named Amleto Poveromo, a butcher by trade, would survive the scandal, and, after 1936, obtain significant trade and transport concessions in East Africa[161] (the Fascist equivalent of going out to govern New South Wales). In Canali's view, what Dumini's *Ceka* actually incarnated was something grandiose: a genuinely Fascist and Mussolinian (since the *Duce* is fully responsible for everything) preparation for a punitive secret police, and thus for a 'real' totalitarianism. Even as they kill, Dumini, Poveromo and the like, and their bosses among Mussolini's entourage, crusaders in their way from the 'party-militia', believe in the Fascist idea.[162]

In his reading both of the murderers' character and of the infant Fascist regime, Canali is on contestable ground; none of his documentary evidence eliminates a more cautious interpretation which would give greater place to opportunism and confusion. However, rather like his teacher, Canali is convinced that he has the answer and that it is the only answer. 'Marxist' or 'anti-Fascist' rivals he derides, both in his aggressive preface and in the text.[163] In particular, he ridicules the idea that anti-anti-Fascist history writing like his own serves the interests of the contemporary Right. Such allegations, he says, amount to 'a vulgate of pundits and self-interested *maîtres à penser*'.[164] Canali, it seems, has learned from his masters the neo-Rankean vulgate. In his eyes, the task of history is to find the answer, not to debate a point, and the truth detected in the documents has no direct relationship with the contemporary world.

What Canali asserts in his monograph, De Felice proclaimed in his lifetime of work, especially after his clarification of his theoretical position, with the help of American prompters, in the 1970s. His was, in most ways, a great achievement. No one can approach the political history of Italian Fascism without reading his work (and given that the biography concluded after 6425 pages,[165] and that it is only one of De Felice's books, plenty of reading is involved). No one can fail to acknowledge that, on many an issue of detail, the authority rests with De Felice. And yet his record also contains many negatives. Except when pinned down by an interviewer like Ledeen, De Felice frequently gave the sense of wanting to write a history without

161 M. Canali, *Il delitto Matteotti*, p. 522.
162 M. Canali, *Il delitto Matteotti*, p. 12. Canali duly acknowledges his intellectual debt to E. Gentile in his preface.
163 M. Canali, *Il delitto Matteotti*, pp. 10, 14, 415.
164 M. Canali, *Il delitto Matteotti*, p. 9.
165 The posthumously published and incomplete final volume of the biography R. De Felice, *Mussolini l'alleato 1940–1945 II. La guerra civile 1943–1945*, Turin, 1997, will be discussed in Chapter 8.

interpretation.[166] It has been noted that he repeated on more than one occasion Tasca's view that the history of Fascism could only be understood through its writing and research. Similarly, he told Ledeen that, in the 1970s, the comprehension of Fascism was at much the same stage of development that the history of the French revolution was at the time of Mme De Stael.[167] Perhaps this sense of the immensity of the historian's task made De Felice reluctant, in his scholarship if not his media statements, to reach too many, too definite, too consistent conclusions.

A greater issue in any assessment of De Felice's work is the quality of the questions he asked and his level of conceptual sophistication. Here his record is not good. In the early pages of this chapter, I raised a series of basic queries about the political history of Italian Fascism, linked to the problem whether it should be understood 'intentionally', that is, through Mussolini, or 'functionally', that is, through the meshing of self-interest, bureaucratism, the family and the other structures in the *longue durée* of Italian and human life. I did so knowing that, for at least a generation, these matters have stimulated a fruitful interrogation of many aspects of the history of Nazism, and that even Stalinism nowadays has occasioned a history 'from below'. Sadly, however, they are questions which Italian scholarship has not asked and is not asking. As has already been noted, we still lack a detailed study of the decision-making process of the domestic administration in Fascist Italy, and we cannot properly assess just how much freedom of will the *Duce* possessed. Similarly, although we have Gentile's assertions that the Italian 'people' had, to a considerable degree, become Fascist true believers, little direct evidence on this subject has yet been uncovered.

For this sort of fundamental absence, De Felice and his school must take much blame. Their neo-Rankeanism retains many of the positives and negatives evident in the career of Leopold von Ranke and his school in nineteenth-century Germany, even including an implicit involvement in nation-construction. Conceptually timid, De Felice and those of his school who are not open zealots of the Right have gone on stating that history's purpose is to be 'scientific', no more, no less, that the historian must find and read the archives, and, letting them in great part 'speak for themselves', report what they say. The De Felicean historians do not seem to recognise that 'scientific history', especially in its nationalised variety, 'went to

---

166 For a further example, see R. De Felice, 'Varieties of Fascism', in G. R. Urban (ed.), *Eurocommunism: its roots and future in Italy and elsewhere*, London, 1978, pp. 97–115. Urban was an editor for Radio Free Europe.

167 R. De Felice, *Fascism: an informal introduction*, pp. 36–7. It is highly ironic that one of the great books of post-1945 liberal democratic history writing is P. Geyl, *Napoleon: for and against*, Harmondsworth, 1965 (first published 1949). It demonstrates that, although historians continued after Mme De Stael to reflect on Napoleon's part in the revolution, they did not do so in a way which brought a steady, 'Whiggish' progress in understanding. Rather, their reflections illustrated the manner in which past and present continually penetrate each other.

Auschwitz'. In turn, this failure of recognition entails an inability to admit that the discipline of history, having surpassed Rankeanism, is now best devoted to avoiding final solutions to the understanding of this or that moment of past time.

6

Fascist Society: 'Totalitarian' Modernisation or Catholic/Peasant/Male Tradition?

In the immediate aftermath of the Second World War, the Torinese writer and anti-Fascist Carlo Levi[1] published *Cristo si è fermato a Eboli* (Christ Stopped at Eboli), an account of his experience during the Fascist regime. Levi had been sent into *confino*, that is, placed under house arrest at a remote country town.[2] In his case, the *paese* was Gagliano in the Basilicata, or Lucania, as this region was then more usually known. So powerful were Levi's images that the phrase about Christ (and civilization) not penetrating south of Eboli, a small town on the railway line some 50 kilometres from Salerno, has been etched deep into succeeding representations both of the 'Southern problem' and of the rural experience of Fascism.

Levi it was who described an all but timeless peasant world: 'hedged in by custom and sorrow, cut off from History and the State, eternally patient, ... that land without comfort and solace, where the peasant lives out his motionless civilization on barren ground in remote poverty, and in the presence of death'.[3] Rather than being 'modern' or ideologically driven, the Fascist party in Gagliano became the rallying place of the local bourgeoisie and gentry, landowners, doctors,[4] pharmacists and lawyers. The peasants, by contrast, 'were not Fascists, just as they would never have been Conservatives or Socialists, or anything else ... There are hailstorms, landslides, droughts, malaria and ... the State. These are inescapable evils;

---

1 For a recent study of Levi's philosophical and political background, see D. Ward, *Antifascisms: cultural politics in Italy, 1943–46: Benedetto Croce and the liberals, Carlo Levi and the 'Actionists'*, Madison, Wis., 1996.
2 C. Levi, *Christ stopped at Eboli: the story of a year*, New York, 1947.
3 C. Levi, *Christ stopped at Eboli*, p. 3.
4 C. Levi, *Christ stopped at Eboli*, pp. 16–17 notes the hereditary nature of the local medical profession.

such there always have been and there always will be.'[5] Nor did the 'myth of Rome', whether Fascist or not, much move the locals: 'To the peasants of Lucania Rome means very little; it is the capital of the gentry, the center of a foreign and hostile world. . . . [There is] Naples . . . [but] their other world is America. . . . New York, rather than Rome or Naples, would be the real capital of the peasants of Lucania, if these men without a country could have a capital at all.'[6]

Fascist celebrations were equally alien. Cries of *Duce! Duce! Duce!* issuing from a muffled loudspeaker to peasants forcibly assembled in the town piazza were heard as the imponderable *cedu, cedu, cedu*, and the official promise of land as the result of victory in the Ethiopian war left the peasants incredulous: 'Here in Gagliano I could see nothing [on the day of the invasion]. The peasants were quieter, sadder, and more dour than usual. They had no faith in a promised land which had first to be taken away from those to whom it belonged; instinct told them that this was wrong and could only bring bad luck.'[7] According to Levi, the peasants of the Basilicata possessed so visceral a sense of inferiority and inevitability that they were accustomed to remark: 'We're not Christians.'[8] In their minds Christ and His Spirit had not penetrated so far south, and never would.

Levi's book was influential because of its power, but also because the 'question' of the South – its continued poverty, violence and deprivation as compared with the rest of Italy – has remained a crucial one right up to our own time. The Fascist regime boasted that it had solved the 'Southern problem'. In the regime's aftermath, however, there was every reason to believe that it had not (even if it was also true that the electoral base of the neo-fascist MSI was always stronger in the South than in the North, as was a nostalgia for Mussolini the leader and his government). The South thus became a place which almost by definition seemed to be anchored in structures which had defeated politics or demonstrated that the doings of the great presented little more than a passing show. It is not surprising that Denis Mack Smith, the best known critical historian of his generation, should be the co-author of a history of Sicily, a place whose secular ills seemed indeed to exhibit the fatuousness of Fascist bluster about a totalitarian society and its nationalised masses.[9] It is equally predictable that many of Italy's leading conservative historians – Gioacchino Volpe from the Abruzzi,[10] Renzo De Felice, born in Rieti, Rosario Romeo from Sicily, and Emilio Gentile from the Molise – sprang from the southern middling classes.

 5 C. Levi, *Christ stopped at Eboli*, p. 76.
 6 C. Levi, *Christ stopped at Eboli*, p. 123.
 7 C. Levi, *Christ stopped at Eboli*, p. 133.
 8 C. Levi, *Christ stopped at Eboli*, p. 3.
 9 D. Mack Smith, *Medieval Sicily 800–1713*, London, 1968; *Modern Sicily after 1713*, London, 1968. These were the second and third volumes in a three-volume set, the first of which, on Ancient Sicily, was written by Moses Finley.
10 See his evocation in old age of his *paese*, Paganica: G. Volpe, *Ritorno al paese (Paganica): memorie minime*, Rome, 1963.

In their preoccupation with applauding or locating a state building process in Italy, they perhaps expressed the *mentalité* of what Gramsci called a 'Southern intellectual', a being anxious above all not to be confused with a southern peasant, and urgently determined to find a life north of Eboli.[11]

The meaning of the South was given another twist by a scholarly demarcation dispute. For many years after 1945, research on Southern society tended to be produced not so much by historians as by anthropologists.[12] Here appeared an immediate ambiguity in the representation of the peasantry and its history. Were rural dwellers 'others', so alien that they needed 'participant observation' to be understood? Given a general peasant illiteracy lasting well into the twentieth century, were they inaccessible to the techniques of historical research? It is well-known that Italians are inclined to think that 'Africa' starts in the region just south of their own. International scholarship seemed to agree, long treating the southern sections of the Italian peninsula as though they lay outside the rhythms and expectations of 'modern' society, a mere scrap of that third world in which the 'other' resided.

The most debated anthropological work written in the 1950s about Italy was Edward Banfield's *The moral basis of a backward society*, though nowadays it reads as a period piece. Despite being hampered by the fact that his 'own knowledge of the language [*sic*] was non-existent to start with and rudimentary later',[13] Banfield lived for 9 months with his wife and children among the villagers of a *paese* in the Basilicata, and from this microcosm drew the large generalisation that Southern Italians believed and practised the philosophy of 'amoral familism'.[14] Since 'in a society of amoral familists, the weak will favor a regime which will maintain order with a strong hand', Banfield explained, the locals recalled Mussolini with considerable fondness. 'I do not remember what it was the Fascists wanted,' one villager stated. 'I only remember that in those days one made out better than today.'[15] In Banfield's reckoning, the basic peasant alienation from the Great World had good and bad features. Cold Warriors could sleep comfortably enough; communism was just another modern ideology of utter and continuing irrelevance to a Southern peasant. On the other hand, Banfield did not foresee the rapid spread of a 'modern' civic sense in the Italian South: 'The change in outlook that is needed might conceivably come as the

11　See e.g. A. Gramsci, *The modern prince and other writings*, New York, 1957, pp. 43–7.

12　But see also e.g. E. R. Wolf, *The hidden frontier: ecology and ethnicity in an Alpine valley*, New York, 1974; cf. S. Silverman, *Three bells of civilization: the life of an Italian hill town*, New York, 1975.

13　E. C. Banfield, *The moral basis of a backward society*, New York, 1958, p. 15. Some comparison with Mack Smith's *Italy: a modern history* might well be instructive, given that each book brought rain on the parades being planned in 1959–61 for the centenary of the Risorgimento. The Italian translation of Mack Smith's work has been republished in an amplified edition in which the English historian is decidedly positive about developments in Italy in the 1990s. See D. Mack Smith, *Storia d'Italia*, rev. ed., Bari, 1997.

14　E. C. Banfield, *Moral basis*, pp. 83–4.

15　E. C. Banfield, *Moral basis*, pp. 93–4.

by-product of Protestant missionary activity,' he wrote naïvely. 'There is
little prospect, however, that Protestants will be permitted to proselytize in
southern Italy.'[16]

By the 1970s Banfield's rough and ready conclusions were modified,
notably by the research of the English anthropologist John Davis, who
produced a detailed study of another town in the Basilicata.[17] The society
which Davis delineated was scarcely 'nationalised' – 'some people [in the
paese] thought that English was another dialect [with a similar distant
relation to the national as their own], and indeed referred to Italian itself as
Florentine' – and the family, not the state, constituted the fundamental local
institution.[18] Southern society was also extraordinarily textured, with land
ownership being especially complex and bearing a long, contested and often
litigious history.[19] In this history it was possible to find echoes of national
politics – communal land sold in 1872 to assist railway construction had
been snapped up by the relatively wealthy among the locals,[20] that is, those
who had celebrated the Risorgimento as a time in which things changed in
order that they might remain almost the same. In Davis' account, the echoes
of Fascism were rather weaker; that era, it seemed, had in most senses
passed the peasants by.

The occasional portrait of peasants outside the South reinforced this
view. Of English-language studies, the most charming is the Italo-American
economic historian Roland Sarti's exploration of his village of family origin,
Montefegatesi, high in the Tuscan Apennines above the Puccinian resort of
Bagni di Lucca. Sarti noted drolly that another of the recurrent factors
differentiating political behaviour and attitudes among the Italian peasantry
is altitude.[21] The Tuscan peasants he described were liberals in the sense of
being both traditionally anti-clerical and in favour of modernity. Fascism
offered some promise of the latter, but its actual achievements were never
sufficient to challenge the myth of 'America', the real land of the blessed in
the local peasant mind.[22] 'Official indifference and neglect' were thus the
most obvious feature of Fascist rule, and were not especially resented; but
war was disliked, or at least was greeted with resignation and a fervent hope
that it prove short.[23] All in all, in most mountain peasants' comprehension,
Fascism was a matter of the plain and the city, in a basic sense not a
peasant's business. Fascism, Sarti advised, was, for Montefegatesi, 'a

16 E. C. Banfield, *Moral basis*, p. 162.
17 See, too, J. Davis, 'Morals and backwardness: a comment on *the Moral Basis of a
    Backward Society*', *Comparative Studies in Society and History*, 12, 1970, pp. 340–53.
    Banfield replied, pp. 354–8.
18 J. Davis, *Land and family in Pisticci*, London, 1973, p. 21.
19 J. Davis, *Land and family*, pp. 74–9.
20 J. Davis, *Land and family*, p. 79.
21 R. Sarti, *Long live the strong: a history of rural society in the Apennine mountains*,
    Amherst, Mass., 1985, p. 10.
22 R. Sarti, *Long live the strong*, pp. 193–228.
23 R. Sarti, *Long live the strong*, pp. 218–22.

movement of lowlanders and valley-bottom dwellers who could not resist the temptation to extend their dominion over all that their eyes could reach'.[24]

These images of peasant worlds moving with their own rhythms and purpose were reinforced by the belated publication of an anthropological study, actually carried out in the 1920s, of a Sicilian village (its author had then won local fame by being the first woman in history to enter the *paese* wearing slacks and carrying a camera).[25] Charlotte Gower Chapman's *Milocca* told of a place in which politics was best defined as a contest between 'Ins' and 'Outs'. Rather than being won over by a modern ideology or controlled by a totalitarian state, each faction adapted Fascism to its own history and world-view. The officials of Mussolini's regime went around renaming streets and piazzas, but the peasants interpreted the meaning of their environment for themselves. As Chapman noted: 'These high-sounding names [for example, the Via 4 Novembre or the Via Silvio Pellico] were used by no one, and known or understood by only a few, but they were felt to add an urban note, both suitable to the new dignity of the town and prophetic of greater things to come.'[26] In the referendum held after the Lateran Pacts in 1929 the villagers marched to the polls together, accompanied by the local band, and voted unanimously for the regime; but war and conscription remained unpopular, and Mussolini was defined by one cautiously vague *paesano* as 'a saint out of paradise'.[27] The history of the twentieth century, it seemed, was still unfolding and its meaning remained uncertain, but the previous century was remembered as *Quarant'ott*, 1848, a time of trouble and hope.[28] In Gower's version, her *paesani* enjoyed a greater agency than peasants had done in the accounts of Levi and Banfield; but the world they crafted was their own, and scarcely coterminous either with the national history of Italy or with the ideological story of modern times.

Whenever Sicily attracted scholarly investigators, one regular and indeed pressing theme was the presence there of the Mafia, another organisation which Fascism claimed to have suppressed and mastered, but which swiftly re-emerged once the regime had fallen. Here, too, was a topic for research by Northern European anthropologists. The German Henner Hess, for example, explored a 'Mafia', or, rather, *mafiosi*, who emerged in the interstices between a collapsing feudal order and the modern state.[29] Appearance mattered: 'A *mafioso* is not the man who regards himself as

24 R. Sarti, *Long live the strong*, p. 193.
25 P. Clemente, 'Paese/Paesi', in M. Isnenghi (ed.), *I luoghi della memoria: strutture ed eventi dell'Italia unita*, Bari, 1997, p. 31.
26 C. G. Chapman, *Milocca: a Sicilian village*, London, 1973, p. 9.
27 C. G. Chapman, *Milocca*, pp. 155–6.
28 C. G. Chapman, *Milocca*, p. 223.
29 H. Hess, *Mafia and mafiosi: the structure of power*, London, 1973 (first published in German, 1970), p. 14.

one,' Hess was told, 'but he who is regarded as one. It is the public that makes a *mafioso*.'[30] These were circumstances which Fascism and Cesare Mori, its 'mafia-busting' 'Iron Prefect', the official charged by the regime to end the Mafia, had understood. Then, however briefly, the state had 'vigorously asserted its monopoly to the use of physical force'.[31] Whether Fascism had extirpated Mafia culture was another matter.

More nuanced was the work of a Dutch anthropologist Anton Blok, whose study of a Mafia *paese* appeared in English with a foreword from the social historian Charles Tilly.[32] The peasants in Blok's account were poor – his was a *latifondo* village – and suspicious. Asked 'How are you?' they habitually replied: 'We are resisting or struggling.'[33] There may have been some political change under Fascism, but local methods of agricultural production had altered not a jot, and the village greeted 1945 with few intimations of modernity.[34] This lengthy survival of a sort of post-feudalism had been made possible because the anti-Mafia campaigns launched by the Fascists had only inconvenienced lower-ranking *mafiosi*, leaving intact the more powerful figures and the social structure which underpinned all Western Sicilian society.[35] Blok ended with a certain degree of optimism. Since there was no single organisation of the Mafia, but rather individuals, families and *cosche* (cells or branches; the word literally means the leaves of an artichoke), and since the real explanation of the Mafia's authority was structural, an eventual arrival of modernity would be likely to entail its disappearance. Then the peculiar Sicilian version of 'backwardness' could be overcome.

By the time that Davis, Hess and Blok were writing, the historical profession was turning its attention to 'social history' with a new enthusiasm. After the publication and critical and commercial success of E. P. Thompson's *The making of the English working class* (1963),[36] a generation of historians began seeking to rescue a huge variety of the 'subaltern classes' from 'the enormous condescension of posterity'. Though already by the 1980s the short-lived empire of the social historians was having to endure forays from the increasingly triumphant cultural historians, social history

30 H. Hess, *Mafia and mafiosi*, p. 51.
31 H. Hess, *Mafia and mafiosi*, p. 175.
32 C. Tilly, 'Foreword' to A. Blok, *The Mafia of a Sicilian village, 1860–1960: a study in violent peasant entrepreneurs*, Oxford, 1974, pp. xiii–xxiv. Blok lived in his village and engaged in participant observation for two and a half years. He also used the techniques of historical research to locate evidence about the *paese* going back to the Risorgimento and beyond. Cf. also J. Boissevain, *Friends of friends: networks, manipulators and coalitions*, Oxford, 1974.
33 A. Blok, *The Mafia of a Sicilian village*, p. 48.
34 A. Blok, *The Mafia of a Sicilian village*, p. 73.
35 A. Blok, *The Mafia of a Sicilian village*, pp. 184–6.
36 E. P. Thompson, *The making of the English working class*, London, 1963. Thompson had a direct connection with Italy and the Resistance, having participated as a tank commander in the liberation of Perugia. See his evocative piece, E. P. Thompson, *The heavy dancers*, New York, 1985, pp. 183–205, with its claim that Thompson and the Umbrian peasantry knew that they were part of a just and anti-fascist war (pp. 199–200).

for a time seemed to have gained acceptance as the best and most wide-ranging way to explore the human condition, and to have all but wiped out 'old-fashioned' political history. What, then, was the impact of this new social history on the special field of Italian Fascism?

The answer is that its effect was slighter and more ambiguous than might have been expected (the fact that Fascism was itself a political category and one which, at least until the 1990s, remained of apparently direct continuing political significance made it hard to write much Fascist history 'with the politics left out'). It is thus regrettably true that, even today, there exists no full-scale social history of the Fascist era in Italian or any other language. Instead, the literature offers occasional glimpses of the social lives of the inhabitants of Italy under the regime.

One topic which has kept its salience is the 'Mafia' – after all, the anthropologists investigating the subject in the 1970s were already utilising the theories of Marxist social historian Eric Hobsbawm on bandits and other forms of 'primitive rebels'.[37] Hobsbawm apart, the work of two other historians deserves special mention. In 1989 the English historian Christopher Duggan wrote a detailed study of Sicily in the Fascist period concluding, in what was now a somewhat common refrain, that the 'Mafia' was more an idea than an organisation[38] and that Fascist anti-Mafia activism did little to alter the fundamental structures of local life. Cesare Mori, himself a Northerner, was reported to believe 'vendetta is firstly a duty, and secondly, a pleasure and a right',[39] and all political campaigns directed at Sicily rapidly acquired a Sicilian gloss. Factional politics was one key – Duggan cited C. G. Chapman with approval[40] – the social order the other. Moreover, by the end of the 1920s the regime had lost its zeal for reform: 'What was distinctive about Sicily in the 1930s was not that the mafia had been destroyed, but that the authorities could not use the word to describe the chaos.'[41] Fascism's Sicilian policies and responses, Duggan concluded, fitted into ancient patterns, displaying anew the ongoing weakness of the state in relation to local society. There was no Sicilian 'parenthesis' before or after Fascism. In Duggan's explanation, the return of the Mafia along with the liberating US army was a fact before it happened and, in Sicilian history, Sicily conquered all.

Perhaps the greatest expert on the Mafia, however, is the Italian sociologist and anti-Mafia campaigner Pino Arlacchi. By the mid-1980s translations of his research were spreading the depressing message that, contrary to the predictions of Blok and others, the Mafia had indeed found

37 See e.g. E. Hobsbawm, *Primitive rebels*, Manchester, 1959 (pp. 30–56 focus on the Mafia); *Bandits*, London, 1969.
38 An American couple of anthropologists urged that it should be viewed as 'broker capitalism' and thus an economy rather than the polity which Blok had perceived. See J. and P. Schneider, *Culture and political economy in Western Sicily*, New York, 1976, pp. 8–10.
39 C. Duggan, *Fascism and the Mafia*, New Haven, 1989, p. 179.
40 C. Duggan, *Fascism and the Mafia*, p. 152.
41 C. Duggan, *Fascism and the Mafia*, p. 264.

ways to modernise itself, tighten its organisation and make its 'entrepreneurship' more ruthless, 'productive' and 'global'.[42] Arlacchi also wrote a detailed historical account of the Mafia in Calabria, which demonstrated yet again how risky generalisation about Italian history is. Arlacchi showed that Calabria possessed at least three separate and diverse socio-economic systems which in turn favoured different and distinct political, economic and criminal behaviour. Fascism had penetrated very superficially into this complex world, favouring for a while the largest and most exploitative landowners, and exacerbating the social crisis through its mistaken autarkic economics in the 'Battle for Wheat' and its unplanned venture into the Second World War.[43] Arlacchi's conclusions in this regard were further endorsed in a history by Enzo Ciconte of the *'ndrangheta*, that is, the alleged Calabrian equivalent to the Mafia in 'organised crime'. In Ciconte's view, Calabrian history could only be comprehended in the *longue durée*. His *'ndrangheta* members manipulated Fascism for their own ends, while the widespread social injustice and violence accompanying the regime further assisted this Mafia-style group to preserve its social base and self-confidence into the post-war world.[44]

All in all, then, students of the Italian South[45] and its experience of Fascism have tended to endorse the view that a regime which only lasted a generation was too superficial and fleeting in its authority greatly to amend the long-standing and multiple structures of local peasant life. Whereas Carlo Levi had seen a world of timeless oppression, more recent analysts, replicating the findings of other social historians about other places and other times, have instead depicted a populace which was differentiated and knew itself to be differentiated. In this populace many an apparently subaltern person retained a degree of agency somewhere beyond those places where the power of *Duce*, or state, or police, or party, or landowners, or criminal organisation, or the local version of patriarchy, or Church intersected.

---

42 See especially P. Arlacchi, *Mafia business: the Mafia ethic and the spirit of capitalism*, London, 1986.
43 P. Arlacchi, *Mafia, peasants and great estates: society in traditional Calabria*, Cambridge, 1983, pp. 192–6; cf. also J. Steinberg, 'Fascism in the Italian South: the case of Calabria', in D. Forgacs (ed.), *Rethinking Italian Fascism: capitalism, populism and culture*, London, 1986, pp. 83–109. Steinberg was the translator of Arlacchi's book into English.
44 E. Ciconte, *'ndrangheta dall'Unità a oggi*, Bari, 1992, pp. 216–36. The book has an approving preface written by the leading anti-Fascist historian Nicola Tranfaglia. If very succinct, an English-language account of the Neapolitan criminal organisation, the *Camorra*, further endorses Ciconte's findings. See T. Behan, *The Camorra*, London, 1996, p. 25.
45 The main English-language account of Puglia traces the rise to power of Fascism there rather than exploring the regime in office. Its theme of local interests reinforcing their class position through the new ideology, and adapting Fascism rather than being adapted by it, does not conflict with the general image of the South's meeting with the regime. See F. M. Snowden, *Violence and the great estates in the South of Italy: Apulia 1900–1922*, Cambridge, 1986. (For some anthropological work on Puglia, see e.g. A. L. Maraspina, *The study of an Italian village*, Paris, 1968; A. H. Galt, *Far from the church bells: settlement and society in an Apulian town*, Cambridge, 1991). There is of course a massive regional literature in Italian on Fascism in the South. For a pioneering example, see S. Colarizi, *Dopoguerra e fascismo in Puglia (1919–1926)*, Bari, 1971.

Another group who might be expected to be drawn into focus by social history is composed by Italian emigrants. In their regard the boast of the Fascist regime was again straightforward: Fascism would both end the humiliating requirement for Italians to emigrate, and would be more solicitious and demanding of its citizens beyond the national borders than its liberal predecessors had been.[46] Once more, however, the literature indicates that there are many reasons to be sceptical about such claims. Emigration was curtailed under the regime, but rapidly returned to something like its pre-Fascist heights after 1945 before finally ending after the 'economic miracle'. Italians stopped leaving their country, in other words, because of the effect of an eventual movement in a secular structure rather than in response to the ideology or policy of a government. Although there is quite a lot of evidence that Italians abroad hailed Mussolini as a great leader, few seem to have rallied to the Fascist war effort in 1940. After Pearl Harbour, for example, American-Italians expressed their American patriotism to an unparalleled degree, and historians of Italo–America regularly claim that the war marked a major milestone in the 'Americanisation' of the immigrants.

The scholarly literature devoted to exploring the behaviour and ideas of Italians outside Italy is varied in quality and purpose. Demography and economics get better coverage than do *mentalités* and social patterns.[47] 'Problem-solving' social scientists are likely to outnumber historians in the field, all the more because the great questions of migration and its associated politics – assimilation, integration and multiculturalism – mattered so immediately to host societies after 1945. Anthropologists are again prominent, with a mixed return for historians: the author of one of the more distinguished American accounts of a century-long emigration from a Southern Italian town cannot distinguish between the 'Italian socialist movement' and the MSI.[48]

Nonetheless, with Renzo De Felice himself issuing a clarion call for the writing of emigrant history,[49] recent decades have seen the production of a number of monographs about Fascism (and anti-Fascism) in certain emigrant communities.[50] From this research it has been possible to learn

46 For my own summary of the regime and migration questions, see R. J. B. Bosworth, *Italy and the wider world 1860–1960*, London, 1996, pp. 114–58.

47 The two most evident general histories are E. Sori, *L'emigrazione italiana dall'Unità alla seconda guerra mondiale*, Bologna, 1979 and Z. Ciuffoletti and M. Degl'Innocenti (eds), *L'emigrazione nella storia d'Italia 1868–1975*, 2 vols., Florence, 1978. The latter is a documentary collection. Both have a top-down approach.

48 See W. Douglass, *Emigration in a South Italian town: an anthropological history*, New Brunswick, NJ, 1984, p. 22.

49 See R. De Felice, 'Alcuni temi per la storia dell'emigrazione italiana', *Affari Sociali Internazionali*, 1, 1973, pp. 3–10; 'Gli studi sull'emigrazione cinque anni dopo', *Affari Sociali Internazionali*, 6, 1978, pp. 7–14.

50 The fullest in English is G. Cresciani, *Fascism, Anti-Fascism and Italians in Australia*, Canberra, 1980. An Italian translation of this book appeared as *Fascismo, antifascismo e gli italiani in Australia 1922–1945*, Rome, 1979. The publishing house was Bonacci, which thereafter published a number of such books under the series editorship of De Felice.

much about the organisation of the Fascist party and its anti-Fascist rivals among emigrants resident in Detroit[51] or North Queensland,[52] Canada[53] or Belgium.[54] But such studies have still very much been political histories, and have made only slight attempts to explain what the social effect on individual emigrants of commmitment to some sort of Fascism may have been. Similarly, the emigrant 'community', often glibly and with evident political purpose portrayed as united, but actually always engaged in disputation, must have had its behaviour and self-understanding amended by Fascism. However, little research has appeared to explain the detail of such amendment.

There have, of course, been many social histories of migration, but by tradition they strenuously ignore politics, even when it involves a regime which proclaimed itself totalitarian.[55] Typically, the multi-volume study of emigration financed by the Agnelli foundation altogether avoids the Fascist dimension of the history of Italians abroad.[56] Equally, John Zucchi's neat account of the rise of an 'Italo-Torontan' identity makes only brief and unsatisfactory mention of Fascism.[57] From Zucchi we can learn intricate detail of marriage patterns, piety, entrepreneurship and patron–client networks, all of which are linked to the emigrants' changing self-understanding as Italians dwelling in a Canadian city. Of the role of Fascism we hear far less: a Fascist activist and war hero tries to make the vice-consulate the centre of community activities from 1929 and public attacks are duly launched against local anti-Fascists, but formal politics, it seems, are not a central part of emigrant lives. As Zucchi concludes ambiguously: 'Except for very few individuals, Italian immigrants in Toronto did not embrace fascism even though they supported the vice-consul and his colleagues.'[58]

51 P. V. Cannistraro, 'Fascism and Italian-Americans in Detroit', *International Migration Review*, 9, 1975, pp. 29–40.
52 W. A. Douglass, *From Italy to Ingham: Italians in North Queensland*, St. Lucia, 1995. For my own accounts of a fervently Fascist vice-consul in Perth (and his ambiguities), see R. Bosworth, 'Luigi Mistrorigo and *La Stampa*: the strange story of a Fascist journalist in Perth', in R. Bosworth and M. Melia (eds), *Aspects of ethnicity: Studies in Western Australian history*, Nedlands, 1991, pp. 61–70; 'Renato Citarelli, Fascist Vice Consul in Perth: a documentary note', *Papers in Labour History*, 14, 1994, pp. 91–6.
53 L. Bruti Liberati, *Il Canada, l'Italia e il Fascismo*, Rome, 1984.
54 A. Morelli, *Fascismo e antifascismo nell'emigrazione italiana in Belgio (1922–1940)*, Rome, 1987.
55 For some of the many examples, see M. Cohen, 'Changing educational strategies among immigrant generations: New York Italians in comparative perspective', *Journal of Social History*, 15, 1981–2, pp. 443–66; R. F. Harney, *Dalla frontiera alle Little Italies: gli italiani in Canada 1800–1945*, Rome, 1984; G. R. Mormino and G. E. Pozzetta, *The immigrant world of Ybor City, 1885–1985*, Urbana, 1990; R. A. Orsi, *The Madonna of 115th street: faith and community in Italian Harlem, 1880–1950*, New Haven, 1985; R. Pascoe and P. Bertola, 'Italian miners and the second generation "Britishers" at Kalgoorlie, Australia', *Social History*, 10, 1985, pp. 9–35.
56 M. Pacini (ed.), *Gli euroamericani*, 3 vols., Turin, 1987; cf. also the belated volume on Australia, which has similar omissions: S. Castles *et al.*, *Australia's Italians: culture and community in a changing society*, North Sydney, 1992.
57 J. E. Zucchi, *Italians in Toronto: development of a national identity, 1875–1935*, Kingston, 1988.
58 J. E. Zucchi, *Italians in Toronto*, p. 197.

This omission is all the odder because, after all, for emigrants in Canada, Australia and Britain even a flirtation with Fascism brought eventual punishment. In each country quite a few Italian settlers were interned as potential fifth-columnists during the course of the Second World War. In these years the most credulous believers that the tentacles of a totalitarian state reached out to control the minds of humble emigrants turned out to be the governments of host societies. However, again we await a proper history of the way in which this distant meeting with Italy's state ideology was absorbed into emigrant lives and *mentalités*.[59]

As was noted above, one aspect of the emigrant experience which has produced serious work is that of religion. Partly, emigrant piety has been a topic of research because of the missionary role of the Scalabrinian brothers, an organisation which commenced its welfare and proselytising work among emigrants before 1914 under the apposite slogan *religione e patria*.[60] In more recent times, members of this order have muted their once-strident nationalism and, through Gianfausto Rosoli, until 1997 the director of the *Centro Studi Emigrazione* in Rome, have fostered much high quality historical research.[61] Rosoli himself has been well aware of the connection between the Fascist regime and the Church authorities, and has written sensibly on the subject, though he is better at exposing formal structures than at mapping the emigrant mind.[62]

In regard to Italy itself there is similarly an appreciable volume of material examining the relationship between Catholicism and Fascism. Still unsurpassed in many ways (and certainly so in English) is D. A. Binchy's *Church and State in Fascist Italy*, originally published in 1941 for the Royal Institute of International Affairs.[63] Given the date of its publication it is no surprise to find that this book is in essence a political history, recounting, for example, the background to and effects of the Lateran treaties in 1929, the quarrels over *Azione Cattolica* and the troubled Church response to racial legislation. Binchy accepts that quite a number of the Church hierarchy from time to time made approving pronouncements about Fascist policies – celebrating the 'saving' of heretical Coptic Ethiopia from its own priesthood and from malevolent Protestant missionaries in 1936, for example – but he also argues that Catholicism had not sold its soul to Fascist totalitarianism.

59 But see R. Perin's forthcoming comparative book of essays on this subject.
60 For an account, see R. J. B. Bosworth, *Italy the least of the Great Powers: Italian foreign policy before the First World War*, Cambridge, 1979, pp. 114, 339.
61 See the house journal *Studi emigrazione*, and G. Rosoli, *Un secolo di emigrazione italiana: 1876–1976*, Rome, 1978; and his *Insieme oltre le frontiere: momenti e figure dell'azione della Chiesa tra gli emigrati italiani nei secoli XIX e XX*, Caltanissetta, 1996. This work is a collection of Rosoli's own essays over the last couple of decades, including a number of pieces with a focus on Fascism.
62 See e.g. his review article, G. Rosoli, 'Santa Sede e propaganda fascista all'estero tra i figli degli emigrati italiani', *Storia contemporanea*, 17, 1986, pp. 293–315.
63 This remarkable book was republished in 1970 with a new preface. D. A. Binchy, *Church and State in Fascist Italy*, Oxford, 1970.

Binchy observes that the lower clergy especially were unlikely to have been fully won over by the regime. But his evidence on this topic is less than scholarly, being drawn chiefly from Silone's novels[64] and from Binchy's resultant sense that rural life in Italy had not yet been profoundly penetrated by Fascist or any other version of modernity.[65]

In succeeding decades there has been much additional research on the Church–State relationship, but the picture which Binchy drew has not been drastically modified. Of English-language authors, John Pollard has done the most detailed work. For example, he has effectively traced those conflicts which emerged after Pius XI had hailed Mussolini as his 'Man of Providence', that is, after the signature of the Lateran Pacts had formally ended most of the unresolved political and economic conflicts between Church and state left over since the Risorgimento. Pollard has made the important point that neither the Church nor Fascism was a monolithic organisation[66] and that therefore any account of their relationship must be aware of nuance and process. The treaties, he notes, sprang from secret negotiations at the top. The successful resolution of the Church–State conflict greatly surprised most Italians and annoyed more than a handful of them, especially traditionalist clergy and anti-clerical Fascists.[67] Nor did the agreement bring real peace and amity. Mussolini, according to Pollard, remained an 'instinctive and lifelong anti-clerical,'[68] while the Church continued to separate its own interests from those of both Fascism and the Italian nation state.

Nor were Fascist–Church relations a simple story of Fascist aggression being regularly blunted by a defensive wall of tradition. Pius XI (died 1939) had a forward policy of his own, both internationally, where his ambitions and his fervour sometimes outran Mussolini's,[69] and domestically. In their own way, the Pope and his Church were pursuing an 'aggrandising and clericalising policy' and preparing among the faithful young a new ruling class which would eventually come into its own with such post-war Christian Democrats as Amintore Fanfani,[70] Aldo Moro and Giulio Andreotti.[71] One way to apprehend the uneasy relationship between

---

64 See Chapter 7.
65 D. A. Binchy, *Church and State*, pp. 680–1.
66 J. F. Pollard, *The Vatican and Italian Fascism, 1929–1932: a study in conflict*, Cambridge, 1985, pp. 3–4.
67 J. F. Pollard, *The Vatican and Italian Fascism*, pp. 48–54.
68 J. F. Pollard, *The Vatican and Italian Fascism*, p. 101.
69 For more on the Church's international policy, see J. F. Pollard, 'Il Vaticano e la politica estera italiana', in R. J. B. Bosworth and S. Romano (eds), *La politica estera italiana*, Bologna, 1991, pp. 197–230; cf. also P. C. Kent, *The Pope and the Duce: the international impact of the Lateran Agreements*, London, 1981.
70 For an introduction to the young Fanfani's curious mixture of economics, clericalism and Fascism, see M. Losito and S. Segre, 'Ambiguous influences: Italian sociology and the fascist regime', in S. P. Turner and D. Käsler (eds), *Sociology responds to fascism*, London, 1992, pp. 56–7.
71 J. F. Pollard, *The Vatican and Italian Fascism*, p. 172.

Fascism and Catholicism is to see it as a meeting between a long-sighted Church[72] and a short-sighted regime.

The robust and stubborn Pius XI was succeeded by Pius XII, whose pontificate coincided with the appalling events of the Second World War[73] and who remains, as a result, a highly controversial figure. However, the historiographical debates which rage over the morality and efficacy or otherwise of Pius XII's reaction to 'Auschwitz' generally concentrate on the Church's policy towards Nazism.[74] Comment on Pius' response to the other combatants is more muted. The British historian Owen Chadwick has argued, not altogether convincingly, that Pius' Church was really a friend of the Allies in the war.[75] There is plenty of other evidence, however, that many in the Church viewed Mussolini, for all his failings, as one of their favourite sons; Italy, for all its sins, as one of their most cherished places; and Fascism, for all its crudities, as by no means the worst ideology of the twentieth century. In many an episcopal mind in wartime, Fascism as a governmental system and philosophy was preferable certainly to communism, socialism and Nazism, and perhaps to liberal capitalism.[76]

Once again, however, there is a striking omission in the literature, and to go beyond the world-views of popes and cardinal-archbishops is difficult. No social history of Italian religiosity has been published, nor is there any serious account of the impact Fascism might have had on the religious beliefs and practice of Italians. All that a historian can conclude is that the weight of present evidence suggests that Catholicism retained a framing power over many an Italian mind until well after 1945 and thus, in its way, successfully resisted Fascism.

Research into the history of primary education, a sphere in which the Church was particularly active under the regime, does, for example, disclose the survival in many schoolrooms of a Catholic piety which rivalled any credulity about Fascism and may indeed have undermined it, at least potentially.[77] The Fascist regime was typically slow to intrude deeply into elementary schools in the South, where, late in the 1930s, the real deficiency

---

72 Some think it significant that future Prime Minister Alcide De Gasperi spent his time as an internal exile under Fascism in the Vatican library introducing the cataloguing system of the Library of Congress. See M. R. Catti De Gasperi, *De Gasperi: uomo solo*, Milan, 1964, p. 143.

73 Somewhat ironically, especially given the vulgar Marxist understanding of Fascism, this Pope indeed came from a background in finance capital, since the Pacelli family were prominent in the management of the Banco di Roma.

74 See, notably, the celebrated and accusatory play, R. Hochhuth, *The deputy*, New York, 1964. The *Catholic Historical Review* is the first place to look for rebuttals of such attacks.

75 See O. Chadwick, *Britain and the Vatican during the Second World War*, Cambridge, 1986; cf. also his 'Bastianini and the weakening of the Fascist will to fight the Second World War', in T. C. W. Blanning and D. Cannadine (eds), *History and biography: essays in honour of Derek Beales*, Cambridge, 1996, pp. 227–42.

76 For a detailed and wide-ranging account of the Church throughout Pius XII's pontificate, which lasted until 1958, see A. Riccardi (ed.), *Le chiese di Pio XII*, Bari, 1986.

77 See e.g. T. M. Mazzatosta, *Il regime fascista tra educazione e propaganda (1935–1943)*, Bologna, 1978. This book came with an endorsing preface by R. De Felice.

remained an all-but-complete absence both of equipment and of a local 'national' culture.[78] The first construction of the totalitarian state had, for example, included a decree in 1928 asserting governmental control over elementary school textbooks, but only in 1939 was a *Commissione permanente del libro di Stato* established.[79] Its achievements were few. State texts seem to have been feeble vehicles for ousting the teachings of the Bible and psalter from Italian souls. None the less, historians need a fuller understanding of what was doubtless the changing impact of religion on the identity, behaviour and thoughts of Italians who lived under Mussolini's dictatorship.

The women and children of Italy are two social groups very likely to have remained influenced by some sort of Catholicism. They are also the typical subject matter of the new social history.[80] It is of course a cliché that Fascism was preoccupied with the young.[81] Similarly, Fascist Italy was nothing if not a place of organisation and parade, in which young bodies donned Fascist uniforms and young minds were tutored in thoughts unfamiliar at home. Mussolini frequently trumpeted the fact, notably in the 1930s, that his regime was forging 'new' men and women. To join the *Balilla* or the *Le Figlie della lupa* (the Daughters of the She-Wolf), the regime surmised, was to enter the 'factory' in which 'consensus' was being made.

Philip Cannistraro, Marzio Barbagli and Victoria De Grazia are only three of the scholars who have worked creatively in this field. In 1975 Cannistraro, for example, published his study of Fascism's efforts to harness the mass media to its cause and to complete some sort of 'cultural revolution'. He was driven to conclude that its victory was no more than partial, even under the renewed fanaticism of the Salò Republic;[82] it was, he

---

78 For a splendid example, see T. M. Mazzatosta, *Il regime fascista*, pp. 200–1.

79 Its chief was the egregious (but usually ineffective) E. M.Gray (T. M. Mazzatosta, *Il regime fascista*, p. 94). For more details on Gray's career, see R. J. B. Bosworth, 'Tourist planning in Fascist Italy and the limits of a totalitarian culture', *Contemporary European History*, 6, 1997, pp. 8–12.

80 For an English-language historiographical review of Italian material, see M. De Giorgio, 'Women's history in Italy (nineteenth and twentieth centuries)', *Journal of Modern Italian Studies*, 1, 1996, pp. 413–31.

81 For an instructive study of one issue in this regard, see A. Scotto di Luzio, *L'appropriazione imperfetta: editori, biblioteche e libri per ragazzi durante il Fascismo*, Bologna, 1996 on the not always coherent policy of Fascism towards children's books. Scotto di Luzio concludes that both the capitalist interests of the publishers and the popular fondness for pre-Fascist and for foreign books conditioned the regime's totalitarian ambitions in this area. There is a rather naïve English-language study of youth organisations: T. H. Koon, *Believe Obey Fight: political socialization of youth in Fascist Italy 1922–1943*, Chapel Hill, 1985. Cf. also the work of Bruno Wanrooij, who approaches Fascism as a generational issue, notably in B. Wanrooij, 'The rise and fall of Italian Fascism as a generational revolt', *Journal of Contemporary History*, 22, 1987, pp. 401–18.

82 See P. V. Cannistraro, *La fabbrica del consenso: fascismo e mass media*, Bari, 1975. The book is another to have earned a preface from De Felice. Unfortunately there is no English-language version, but, for some summary, see P. V. Cannistraro, 'Mussolini's cultural revolution: Fascist or Nationalist?' *Journal of Contemporary History*, 7, 1972, pp. 115–39.

remarked, a *rivoluzione culturale mancata*.[83] Mussolini, Cannistraro's pages tell a reader, was no Mao. But, although Cannistraro ably indicates some of the limitations of politicians' achievements in Fascist Italy, he is much weaker when it comes to unveiling the intimate thoughts and beliefs of the Italian people. His 'factory of consensus' is populated with Fascist officials and intellectuals rather than with 'ordinary' Italians.

In any case, Cannistraro's particular focus is countered by the structural research into Italian education undertaken by Barbagli.[84] In a book which should be required reading for any who are too easily convinced by the current 'culturalist' approach to Fascism, Barbagli studies Italian teaching and learning in the *longue durée*. His comprehension of the 'emerging middle classes' is qualified by his knowledge of the overproduction of lawyers in post-1919 Italy – one commentator then bewailed the 'patho-logical elephantisis of the forensic orders'.[85] Barbagli notes, too, the school-teachers' union UMN's preoccupation before 1922 with their loss of social status, and argues that the élitism of the Gentile, 'most Fascist', reform of education was generated by the desire to calm the 'intellectual classes', using the classic method of reducing intellectual unemployment through limiting production.[86] By 1931, only 3 per cent of university students sprang from the working class.[87] Whatever the ideological views which coursed through them, concluded Barbagli, Fascist universities scarcely reflected a mass society.

Joining Barbagli in being wide-ranging in her approach to the history of everyday life and sceptical of the boasts of Fascist sources is Victoria De Grazia in her study of the mass organisation of leisure.[88] De Grazia explains that she had commenced her research as a believer in 'awesome' 'totali-tarian' power which she wanted to probe from on high. However, her topic increasingly persuaded her to examine the 'depoliticized underside of Fascism'.[89] With a comparative perspective frequently absent in other interpreters of the Fascist era, De Grazia noted the need to set events in Italy in the global context of the new age of 'an expansive, consumer-oriented, organized capitalism'.[90] The idea behind the Fascist *dopolavoro* (after-work) organisation, for example, she learned, owed much to Mario Giani, who had developed his model while working for a Westinghouse subsidiary

83 P. V. Cannistraro, 'Mussolini's cultural revolution', p. 7. De Felice also praises Cannistraro for the insight that Fascism 'oscillated continuously between a traditional culture and a modern culture' (p. x).
84 It is available in translation as M. Barbagli, *Educating for unemployment: politics, labor markets, and the school system: Italy, 1859–1973*, New York, 1982.
85 M. Barbagli, *Educating for unemployment*, p. 114.
86 M. Barbagli, *Educating for unemployment*, p. 129.
87 M. Barbagli, *Educating for unemployment*, p. 138.
88 V. De Grazia, *The culture of consent: mass organization of leisure in Fascist Italy*, Cambridge, 1981.
89 V. De Grazia, *The culture of consent*, pp. vii–viii.
90 V. De Grazia, *The culture of consent*, p. 1. De Grazia acknowledged an intellectual debt to Charles Maier (cf. Chapter 9).

established at Vado Ligure.[91] If the world of capitalism was one side of the story, the realities of Italian life were the other. The Fascist authorities, De Grazia explained, were 'not inclined to expend excessive energy regulating groups that posed no obvious threat to their rule'.[92] Even during the populist campaigns mounted by the PNF secretary Achille Starace in the 1930s,[93] Fascism had an uneven presence in society. As late as 1936, still only 20 per cent of workers and 7 per cent of peasants, according to official figures, were enrolled in the *dopolavoro*.[94] In much of agricultural Italy, Fascism rejected 'thorough-going modernization out of deference to the traditional landed élites and for fear that the ensuing rural landfight might swell already high rates of unemployment'.[95] After more than ten years of Fascist rule, a commentator on Matera remarked: 'Nothing, absolutely nothing, had been done to give the local people a tangible sign of the fascist era'.[96] Even outside the South, De Grazia contended, the *dopolavoro* and other party organisations mainly fostered 'passivity, ignorance, individualism, traditionalism [and] evasion'.[97] In its appeal to its masses Fascism was neither entirely original nor entirely credulous, nor consistently successful nor committed. Mussolini himself believed cynically that winning over the population was a fragile and impermanent act: 'Consent,' the *Duce* admitted as late as the 1930s, 'is as unstable as the sand formations on the edge of the sea.'[98]

If the youth of Italy were unreliably Fascist, what of Italian women? What does social history reveal of what Fascism did to them and what they did to Fascism? By now we know quite a lot about the history of the 'gender order' under Fascism. Women in a particular factory,[99] women and demographic policy,[100] women and abortion,[101] women and Fascist culture,[102]

91 V. De Grazia, *The culture of consent*, pp. 24–6.
92 V. De Grazia, *The culture of consent*, p. 20.
93 Mussolini had set as 'an order for the day' in 1931 'the going decisively towards the people'. P. V. Cannistraro, *La fabbrica del consenso: fascismo e mass media*, p. 70.
94 P. V. Cannistraro, *La fabbrica del consenso*, p. 55.
95 P. V. Cannistraro, *La fabbrica del consenso*, p. 94.
96 P. V. Cannistraro, *La fabbrica del consenso*, p. 122. For a moving account of the timelessness and hopelessness of the cave-dwelling urban population there, see C. Levi, *Christ Stopped at Eboli*, pp. 85–7. The children of the town were typically a prey to trachoma and malaria. According to a 'confined' anti-Fascist in a local *paese* the news was still announced by a crier with a trumpet. A. Gobetti, *Camilla Ravera: vita in carcere e al confino con lettere e documenti*, Rome, 1969, p. 289.
97 V. De Grazia, *The culture of consent*, p. 224.
98 V. De Grazia, *The culture of consent*, p. 225.
99 P. R. Willson, *The clockwork factory: women and work in Fascist Italy*, Oxford, 1993.
100 L. Caldwell, 'Reproducers of the nation: women and the family in Fascist policy', in D. Forgacs (ed.), *Rethinking Italian Fascism*, pp. 110–41; cf. also the fuller account of C. Ipsen, *Dictating demography: the problem of population in Fascist Italy*, Cambridge, 1996.
101 P. R. Willson, 'Flowers for the doctor: pro-natalism and abortion in Fascist Milan', *Modern Italy*, 1, 1996, pp. 44–62. Cf. also P. R. Willson, 'Women in Fascist Italy', in R. Bessel (ed.), *Fascist Italy and Nazi Germany: comparisons and contrasts*, Cambridge, 1996, pp. 78–93.
102 See the essays in R. Pickering-Iazzi (ed.), *Mothers of invention: women, Italian Fascism and culture*, Minneapolis, 1995.

women and the Fascist construction of reproduction,[103] women and the Salò Republic,[104] Mussolini's most intellectual mistress[105] – all have found their historians, even in English.[106] Moreover, as noted in Chapter 1, we also possess De Grazia's finely wrought account of how Fascism ruled women, with her emphasis, yet again, on the gap between Fascist theory and practice, and on the ways in which women, especially young ones of the 'Fascist generation', were engaged in making their own history, even as Fascism sought to foist its world-view on them.[107] De Grazia's work is amplified by that of Michela De Giorgio, author of a history of Italian women since the Risorgimento.[108] De Giorgio writes as a social and cultural historian who ignores or underplays the chronology of political events. References to Fascism in her work are thus scattered, and, indeed, readers of her study will learn as much about the history of washing and of beauty, its aids and fluctuating definition,[109] as about the direct impact of the dictatorship. De Giorgio commences with the assertion that 'the symbolic frontiers of the difference between men and women [in Italy] have been continuously re-affirmed, re-modelled and re-defined', and her understanding of the process of identity construction is evident throughout her work.[110] Similarly, her Italy is anything but a homogeneous or 'primordial' place; age, geography and class (and the possibility of emigration) are all important ingredients in differentiating one woman's life from another's. In her analysis, probably the most important influences on women, at least those who see themselves as at the forefront of their sex, come from the United States (though Catholicism retained an immensely powerful hold, especially on the 'silent majority').[111] Fascism, by contrast, was too contradictory in the signals which it gave to be effective in nationalising or fascistising its female masses.[112] In the *longue durée* of the history of gender in Italy,

103 See the highly Foucaultian, D. G. Horn, *Social bodies: science, reproduction and Italian modernity*, Princeton, 1994. Rather more wide-ranging in reading through statistics is S. Patriarca, *Numbers and nationhood: writing statistics in nineteenth century Italy*, Cambridge, 1996, but Patriarca's work only makes indirect reference to the Fascist period.
104 M. Fraddosio, 'The Fallen Hero: the myth of Mussolini and Fascist women in the Italian Social Republic (1943–5)', *Journal of Contemporary History*, 31, 1996, pp. 99–124.
105 P. V. Cannistraro and B. R. Sullivan, *Il Duce's other woman*, New York, 1993.
106 On women in the South, there are in English the marvellous accounts by the non-professional anthropologist, Ann Cornelisen. Fascism plays no part in her story, but perhaps its absence is telling, too. See A. Cornelisen, *Torregreca: life, death, miracles*, New York, 1969; *Women of the shadows*, London, 1976. Emigrant women are also not well treated in the literature and where they are the connection with Fascism is scarcely made. For some comment, see F. Iacovetta, 'Writing women into immigration history: the Italian Canadian case', *Altreitalie*, 9, 1993, pp. 24–47.
107 V. De Grazia, *How Fascism ruled women*, Berkeley, 1992.
108 M. De Giorgio, *Le italiane dall'Unità a oggi: modelli culturali e comportamenti sociali*, Bari, 1992.
109 See e.g. M. De Giorgio, *Le italiane dall'Unità a oggi*, pp. 169–74.
110 M. De Giorgio, *Le italiane dall'Unità a oggi*, p. ix.
111 M. De Giorgio, *Le italiane dall'Unità a oggi*, pp. 197, 306.
112 M. De Giorgio, *Le italiane dall'Unità a oggi*, p. 514.

Fascism could not really compete either with the traditions of religion or the modernity of consumerism.

If De Grazia and De Giorgio, though pursuing somewhat different methodologies, none the less come to similar conclusions about the impact of Mussolini's regime on Italian women, their research still operates on a rather generalised level. The most detailed study of the everyday lives of Italian families under the dictatorship is Luisa Passerini's account of the housewives of working-class Turin.[113] Utilising both a wide-ranging conceptual apparatus and her own intimate interviews (frequently conducted in dialect) with those who lived in Turin during the inter-war period, Passerini delineates a working class which possessed its own social and urban identity, but which also had a definite and not particularly friendly attitude towards Fascism. Women could find the regime 'traditional' in its endorsing of purblind Catholic policies, especially in matters of reproduction. In any case, both sexes understood that Mussolini's was a low-wage regime and accepted the fact that the working-class family's standard of living contradicted much Fascist rhetoric, prevented too overt a political commitment[114] and left the populace in a state of at best passive dissent. It was simply not in the interests of the families of Turin to behave or to think otherwise. If the Fascist regime tried to impose the 'language of totalitarianism' it could easily enough be subverted by jokes, dialect and parody.[115] In this limited, but realistic and powerful sense, Turin, in Passerini's explanation, was a site of anti-Fascism and Resistance; its soul never fell to Fascism;[116] as soon as there was the glimmering of a chance, its working class would act to improve their pay and conditions, and eliminate Fascism from their lives.[117]

It may well be that Turin, the city of Gramsci and Togliatti and the possessor of an established working-class culture before 1922, is scarcely comparable with other Italian towns, and that historians must wait for social histories of different parts of the peninsula to be written with Passerini's insight.[118] It is a particular shame that Passerini's acute accounts

---

113 L. Passerini, *Fascism in popular memory: the cultural experience of the Turin working class*, Cambridge, 1987 (first published in Italian in 1984); cf. L. Passerini, 'Italian working class culture between the wars: consensus to Fascism and work ideology', *International Journal of Oral History*, 1, 1980, pp. 3–27; 'Work ideology and working class attitudes to Fascism', in P. Thompson (ed.), *Our common history: the transformation of Europe*, London, 1982, pp. 54–78.

114 L. Passerini, *Fascism in popular memory*, p. 130 notes that women seem to have liked the uniforms more than working-class men did.

115 L. Passerini, *Fascism in popular memory*, pp. 75–9.

116 Cf., by contrast, the much less textured and more literal 'De Felicean' account of public opinion under the regime. S. Colarizi, *L'opinione degli italiani sotto il regime 1929–1943*, Bari, 1991.

117 Turin was, indeed, the site of the first, largely spontaneous strike in Axis-occupied Europe in March 1943. For an account in English, see T. Mason, 'The Turin strikes of March 1943', in his *Nazism, Fascism and the working class*, Cambridge, 1995, pp. 274–94.

118 One historian has, however, shown that the regime never developed a consistent rental policy. See F. Bortolotti, *Storia della politica edilizia in Italia: proprietà, imprese edili e lavori pubblici dal primo dopoguerra ad oggi (1919–1970)*, Rome, 1978, p. 41.

of male reaction to the regime have not been further pursued in the literature. Here, indeed, was a regime which flaunted a certain type of masculinity; yet we know little about the origins of its *gallismo* (cock-ism), whether or not it was novel, and what its legacy may have been. As is often true at the current historiographical moment, it is easier to discover what it meant to be female in Fascist Italy than what it meant to be male.

For women, and more especially for men, Fascism was a regime which promised to harden and develop the body[119] through government-sponsored sporting activity. But while research has revealed quite a bit about the official organisation of Fascist sports, there is, again, only trifling reference to what sport, its promise or its narration meant to Italians of the Fascist generation. An occasional survey of the sporting past is available,[120] but a genuine social history exploring the relationship between sport and Fascism has not yet been written.

One slightly paradoxical element in the life of both Italians and visiting foreigners in Mussolini's Italy was tourism, which remained Italy's most remunerative industry, even when autarky became the official national economic line. A totalitarian state which favours international tourism is something of a contradiction in terms. Stalin's USSR did not aim to attract visitors unless it could utterly control them, and Nazi Germany alleviated some of its harsher and more controversial policies during the Berlin Olympic Games in 1936. What, it might be asked, happened in that Fascist Italy in which the *Duce* himself was well aware of the advantage to the national exchequer brought in by tourists? This topic, too, needs further exploration, but the evidence we do possess points unsurprisingly to the tendency for 'corruption' and the relaxed ways associated with tourism contradicting and undermining Fascist xenophobia and ideological rigour.[121] Here was another area in which middle-class Italians were reminded that their natural contacts were with France and the civilization and modernity of the 'West', and in which they were reinforced in their assumption that, in the best of worlds, the pursuit of national power should always be accompanied by peace. Thus, despite its decorous adoption from time to time of Fascist rhetoric and its reiterated commitment to the nation,

119 K. Pinkus, *Bodily regimes: Italian advertising under Fascism*, Minneapolis, 1997, though marred by the jargon of cultural studies and vague in its definition of Fascism, contains much fascinating detail on constructions of the body under the regime, including information about the Facist–Futurist impact on defecation (pp. 98–107).

120 A. Papa and G. Panico, *Storia sociale del calcio in Italia: dai club dei pionieri alla nazione sportiva (1887–1945)*, Bologna, 1993 is, despite its title, disappointingly superficial. Descriptive but still fundamental as an account of Italian football is A. Ghirelli, *Storia del calcio in Italia*, Turin, 1967. For a brief English-language introduction to the history of golf under the regime, see R. J. B. Bosworth, 'Golf and Italian Fascism' (forthcoming).

121 See R. J. B. Bosworth, 'Tourist planning in Fascist Italy and the limits of a totalitarian culture'; 'The *Touring Club Italiano* and the nationalization of the Italian bourgeoisie', *European History Quarterly*, 27, 1997, pp. 371–410; T. Syrjämaa, *Visitez l'Italie: Italian state tourist propaganda abroad 1919–1943, administrative structure and practical realization*, Turku, 1997.

a massive organisation like the *Touring Club Italiano* of Milan, with a membership of more than half a million, was always as much Milanese and bourgeois as it was Fascist. To be sure, the leadership of the *Touring Club* were accustomed to emphasise their patriotic and nationalising purpose. Moreover, as well as welcoming foreigners, the national tourist industry hoped to 'make Italy known to Italians'; but its clients tended still to be more middle-class than peasant, and more from a northern city than a southern *paese*. Tourism was another cranny of Italian life into which a Fascist totalitarianism did not fully penetrate.

Another social group who accepted that they belonged to the nation but tried to define it on their own terms were public servants. In an important recent book, Mariuccia Salvati has examined their relationship with Fascism and discovered, once again, a history of nuance.[122] Petty bureaucrats grew used to being the object of Fascist campaigns emphasising zeal and efficiency and talking cheerfully of reform. In practice, however, most clerks sought to manipulate the system to their own advantage, and their preference for immobility (and the expansion of their numbers) was strengthened by the anxiety which the more extreme Fascist rhetoric inspired. Here was yet another group of Italians who may well have possessed a party ticket, but who had scarcely surrendered their world-view and self-interest to Fascism.

In an authoritative article, John Davis, perhaps the leading English-language social historian of modern Italy,[123] complained that the focus on 1922 has obscured Italy's 'path to the twentieth century'.[124] The obsession with the politics of Fascism should, Davis argued, be replaced with a longer view. Only then would the great and lasting issues of the Southern problem, the nature of the family, the character of the Italian bourgeoisie and the weakness of the national state be set in a proper context. There is, of course, as any student of the philosophy and politics of Fernand Braudel might be persuaded to admit,[125] a danger in the conclusion that history is timeless, or at least that it always works in the *longue durée*. And so Davis' caution might be rephrased to suggest that it is a poor history of Fascist Italy which does not seek to elucidate the relationship there between politics and society. As Passerini's work on Turin demonstrates, for example, Fascism, for all its frailty, levity and contradiction, could affect its populace even in such unlikely areas as what they deemed to be funny. At the same time, any student of the social history of Italy must also agree that, time and again, and in many a different place and social setting, the practice of Fascism

---

122 See M. Salvati, *Il regime e gli impiegati: la nazionalizzazione piccolo-borghese nel ventennio fascista*, Bari, 1992.
123 See especially his wide-ranging J. A. Davis, *Conflict and control: law and order in nineteenth century Italy*, London, 1988.
124 J. A. Davis, 'Remapping Italy's path to the twentieth century', *Journal of Modern History*, 66, 1994, pp. 291–320.
125 For my own view, see R. J. B. Bosworth, *Explaining Auschwitz and Hiroshima: history writing and the Second World War 1945–1990*, London, 1993, pp. 104–7.

varied, as the ideology and its practitioners met up with the multiple histories of Italy and the Italies. As soon as the peoples who lived in Italy, or could somehow be defined as Italian, are brought into the equation, it is hard indeed to think of Fascist Italy as a place in which a modernising totalitarianism overwhelmed all.

In his last years Mussolini would frequently complain about the recalcitrance and 'ungovernability' of the people of Italy, remarking in disgust in July 1943 at the time of his fall: 'In half an hour the people change the entire course of their thoughts, their sentiments and their history.'[126] What the *Duce* was actually expressing was the bafflement of one who wanted to provide a political top-down history with a simple and set reading, and who thus ignored the fluctuating multiplicities of the human experience. More than half a century later the great advantage of social historians' interpretations of the Fascist past is their reminder that, as well as the history of a dictatorship, the histories of the Italies are located there.

126 B. Mussolini, *Storia di un anno: il tempo del bastone e della carota*, Milan, 1944, p. 108.

|7|

The Traces of Fascism in Music, Film, Literature and Memory: A Fascist Cultural Legacy?

When I lived in Rome during a period of study leave in 1972 and again in 1975–6, a musical battle was being fought on the streets of the city. At that time, when the histories of Fascism and anti-Fascism seemed to matter so much, the discordant sounds of the recent past still floated through the air. Or, to be more accurate, vendors of vinyl discs of Fascist or anti-Fascist music were located on many a street corner. I bought what they had to sell, and assembled a considerable collection of records with titles like *Otto milioni di baionette* or *La Resistenza*. I even acquired, courtesy of a man in a three-wheeler truck spruiking his goods outside a suburban branch of the neo-fascist MSI, a two-disk set of Mussolini's speeches.

When I went home to the Antipodes I became incapable of giving a lecture without a suitable musical introit. If hard-pressed, I could always sing the words of *Giovinezza*, the Fascist anthem, or the *La badoglieide*, the spendidly scabrous and interminable song which recalls the many corruptions and incompetencies of Pietro Badoglio, Field Marshal, Prime Minister and sometime Duke of Addis Ababa.[1] I was not alone in this behaviour and interest. Another of the left-wing songs, revived in the 1970s all the more because of its apparent feminism, was *Sebben che siamo donne*. In a memorable scene in his movie *1900*, first screened in 1976, Bernardo Bertolucci displayed women socialists from the Po Valley singing

---

1 There is also a certain literature, usually dating to the 1970s, which records the lyrics of these songs and, to some extent, analyses them. See e.g. A. V. Savona and M. L. Straniero (eds), *Canti dell'Italia fascista (1919–1945)*, Milan, 1979; G. Vettori (ed.), *Canzoni italiane di protesta (1794–1974)*, Rome, 1975.

it as they bravely repelled the tyrannous and phallocentric forces of law and order.[2]

What the retailing of this music from truck and screen and my own purchases best reflect is the spirit of the 1970s, that decade when (a change in) the future of Italy seemed to be being decided through interpretation of the past. But 20 years later, when old passions are spent and the understandings of the previous generation seem exhausted, what do scholars say can be learned about Fascism from an examination of its musical and other cultural leftovers and from the reaction of national culture to this past since 1945?

In the 1990s this question seems all the more important because of the rise of that culturalist approach to the history of Fascism outlined in Chapter 1. In turn, the new emphasis on the 'fascination' of Fascism and on the hypocrisy of some of the myth of anti-Fascism owes something to the strenuousness with which the Italian intelligentsia, at least after 1968, denied any contamination from the Fascist past. The socialist philosopher Norberto Bobbio put the matter most drastically (and incredibly): 'Where there was culture there wasn't fascism, where there was fascism there wasn't culture. There never was a fascist culture.'[3] Such an assertion is quite plainly wrong, as well as being evidently self-interested, as it asserts both the purity of the intelligentsia and its holy significance for the mere mortals who are its acolytes.

Thus it did not take prolonged research or thought to demonstrate that an intellectual life had existed under Fascism, and that cultural figures enjoyed and required the regime's subsidies and praise. This conclusion, however, does not necessarily imply, as some historians maintain, either that Fascist culture was especially glittering or, more importantly, that the culture expressed in Italy from 1922 to 1945 was Fascist and nothing else. Rather, the message, which may be becoming predictable for a reader of this book, is that, to 1945, music, literature, film, art, architecture and 'memory' resonate more with the cadences of an Italian dictatorship than with those of a stentoriously Fascist one; and that after 1945 they display the influence of the (changing) circumstances in which they were composed.

Intentionalists, however, will be pleased to learn that Mussolini himself is hard to expel from the story. *Professor* Mussolini, linguist extraordinaire (at least in his own mind), art critic of (fairly) advanced tastes, author of plays,

2 Typical of the sexuality of this film was the fact that the women blocked their enemies by lying on the ground, thus inviting and rejecting rape by the wicked or nonplussed reactionaries. The song urges women to get behind the union and includes a nice verse: *E voi altri signoroni/ che ci avete tanto orgoglio/ abbassate la superbia/ e aprite il portafoglio.* (And you other big bosses who are so blown up with pride, humble yourselves and open up your wallets.) See G. Vettori (ed.), *Canzoni italiane di protesta*, pp. 103–4.
3 As cited in *L'Espresso*, 28, 26 December 1982.

novels[4] and histories,[5] patron of the cinema, of museums, framer of memory, was, at least according to official piety, particularly interested in culture and particularly anxious to be recognised as cultivated by its intellectual producers. It was thus typical that the regime's propaganda machine wanted the *Duce* to be heard musically as in other arenas. So, in the 1920s, it was explained to ideally credulous readers that the young *Duce* sprang from a musical family and, as a boy, 'in the solitude of the countryside, . . . nourished a special sympathy for birds'.[6] When he grew to manhood, this account proceeded, and was driven into emigration, Benito carried along his precious violin. 'Played with increasing expertise, the violin became his invisible comrade.' Returned to Italy and in power, he continued his love affair with this instrument. As his musical biographer would conclude, modestly: 'In the strict sense of the word Mussolini is not a musician nor a virtuoso on the violin. He is something greater and better – a musician in his very heart and soul.'[7]

Despite such tales of skill and dedication, it is none the less clear that Mussolini's own abilities and interests do not exhaust the history of music under his regime. Rather, the organisation and performance of music during the Fascist years possessed a certain complexity, if one in which many familiar refrains redounded amid the well-publicised attempts to 'fascistise' music and its practitioners. An American historian has put it well: 'Study of Italian music under fascism reveals a picture of workaday infighting and intrigue in abundance, much grotesque opportunism, occasional examples of naïve good faith in the government, and very little real political opposition.'[8]

The story grows repetitive. Even if composers and performers sometimes had things other than high politics on their minds, the musical establishment greeted the rise to power of the Fascists with widespread applause. Giacomo Puccini, for one, took out a well-publicised party ticket before his death and posthumous triumph in *Turandot* in 1924.[9] By 1926–7 the musical bureaucracy was duly inducted into the Corporate State, with the creation

4 Available in English is the period anti-clerical bodice ripper (in which, in other words, the ripping remains genteel), B. Mussolini, *The Cardinal's mistress*, London, 1929.
5 See e.g. his curious study of Jan Huss, the Czech heretic-protestant, with its overt anti-clericalism and its tinges of nationalism. B. Mussolini, *Giovanni Huss: il verdico*, Rome, 1948 (first published, 1913).
6 R. De Renzis, *Mussolini musicista*, Mantua, 1927, p. 13. The implications of the *Duce* being a new St Francis are evident. Predictably enough, Mussolini's ideological and ethical rival, Antonio Gramsci, would also 'love birds'.
7 R. De Renzis, *Mussolini musicista*, pp. 17, 22.
8 H. Sachs, *Music in Fascist Italy*, New York, 1988, p. 10.
9 Puccini's world-view was always that of a whingeing reactionary. In the First World War, he did not hide his sympathies for that law and order which he thought prevailed in Imperial Germany. In its aftermath, with his usual insecurity and opportunism, he composed a 'Hymn to Rome' in order to refurbish his patriotic credentials. Unsurprisingly, it was later taken up by the Fascist regime. English-language readers can get a very partial introduction to Puccini's mind in G. Adami (ed.), *Letters of Giacomo Puccini mainly connected with the composition and production of his operas*, New York, 1973.

of the 'National Fascist Federation of Theatrical, Cinematic and Related Industries'; although a further reshuffling occurred in 1930 with the foundation of the 'Corporation of Entertainment'. A National Fascist Union of Musicians was also created, to be headed by Giuseppe Blanc, the worthy composer of *Giovinezza*. He was assisted in his task by such better-renowned and less overtly Fascist musical figures as Umberto Giordano and Riccardo Zandonai.[10]

The totalitarian form, however, hid the usual vortex of dispute in which the personal and self-interested usually outweighed the ideological. Composers typically cherished protecters in the Fascist hierarchy, but the resultant networks were rarely straightforward, either politically or ideologically. Thus the most radical of composers, Alfredo Casella, once a Futurist, linked himself with Giuseppe Bottai, while the more conservative faction gave fealty to Farinacci. Of the more internationally famous and productive classical musicians, Ottorino Respighi was courted by the regime but preserved a certain independence from it, while Pietro Mascagni, who had exhausted most of his creativity in *Cavalleria rusticana* (1890), kept composing and reacted to the regime with a characteristic blend of blatant obsequiousness and irritable idiosyncrasy.

After 1938 the racial legislation did gradually affect music without much protest from within the industry. By then the most prominent musical anti-Fascist was the conductor Arturo Toscanini. Also a highly idiosyncratic figure, Toscanini in 1929 abandoned his position at La Scala in Milan and went into a well-publicised exile, though he sometimes returned to Italy, and retained property there. Much about the regime, or at least about the behaviour and *mentalité* of its leaders, was summed up in a concert which Toscanini conducted at Lucerne in August 1938. For this event the wives of Alfieri, Volpi, Marconi, De Martino and Borletti and Crown Princess Maria-José herself ignored the sounds of impending war reverberating from the Sudetenland, and crossed the border into Switzerland so that they could hear the maestro's music or be seen at his concert.[11] The Italian secret police recorded these ladies' moral defection from the Fascist cause, but without any obviously deleterious subsequent effect on their lives or on the careers of their husbands.

If a bureaucratic history of music under the Fascist regime carries many an equivocation, so, too, the music of Fascist songs did not always beat out a single message. The words could indeed be bloodthirsty and 'fascist', with much emphasis on the *santo manganello* (holy club) and the struggle to the death. The *Canto delle donne fasciste* (Song of Fascist women), for example, cheerfully invoked the prospect of a vengeful female stabbing of their non-Fascist adversaries.[12] It was typical, however, of the local basis of

10 H. Sachs, *Music in Fascist Italy*, pp. 28–30.
11 H. Sachs, *Music in Fascist Italy*, p. 230.
12 A. V. Savona and M. L. Straniero (eds), *Canti dell'Italia fascista*, pp. 181–2.

much Fascism that many party 'hymns' had alternative versions which were sung selectively in this town or that. As the regime solidified certain songs were given primacy, with *Giovinezza* acquiring the status of a national anthem and typically being played on official occasions alongside the established *Marcia reale* or Royal March. Here, too, compromise was evident – a totalitarian state with more than one national anthem is not quite as bracing in its uniformity as might be expected.

Similarly, more than one strain could often be detected in the music itself – the emphatic words of the song *Squadristi a noi* (Squadrists, ready)[13] were, for example, accompanied by a tea-dance tune. After 1922, it and other similar pieces frequently resounded from the instruments of those mellifluous or eager bands, accustomed each Sunday or *festa* to play in the piazzas of Italy's many beautiful cities and towns, there to foster an air of ease and contentment in which, it may be surmised, the audience frequently heard the music and forgot or disregarded the words.

The best symbol of this fundamental contradiction in the very sounds of Fascist Italy was, however, the enormously successful song *Faccetta nera* (Little Black Face), top of the pops during the Ethiopian war. Hinting at the possibility of love between a Fascist soldier and a female Ethiopian slave (presumably an updated Aida), the song celebrated the fact that the Italians would bring 'another king and another law' to the peoples of East Africa.[14] Its sentiments would not be imitated in soldiers' songs of the *Wehrmacht* or the SS as they carried Nazi German barbarisation to the Eastern front after 1941.

Anti-Fascist music possessed equivocations of its own, especially when re-sung in the 1970s. In that decade you might hear revived at a left-wing *festa*, for example, a song from the period of the Fascist rise to power, *Se arriverà Lenin* (If Lenin Comes). The message was practical and even bloodthirsty, again somewhat in contrast to its pleasant tune:

Se arriverà Lenin faremo una gran festa:	If Lenin comes we'll have a great festa:
andremo dai signori, gli taglierem la testa.	We'll go to the bosses and cut off their heads.
Oilì oilà la lega la crescerà.	Ha, ha, the [peasant] union will grow.
Le guardie regie in pentola le fanno il brodo giallo,	The royal police we'll boil into soup

---

13 For the translation into English of this and some other Fascist songs, see G. Cresciani, 'Political songs of modern Italy', *Teaching History*, 12, 1978, pp. 30–43.
14 A. V. Savona and M. L. Straniero (eds), *Canti dell'Italia fascista*, pp. 270–1. The full chorus ran *Faccetta nera/ bella abissina/ aspetta e spera/ già l'Italia s'avvicina./Quanno staremo/vicino a te/ noi te daremo un'antra legge e un antro Re.* (Little black-face/ beautiful Ethiopian girl/ who waits and hopes./ Italy is coming close to you/ When we are up close/ we shall give you another law and another King.) The song met with official disapproval from 1937.

| *carabinieri in umido e arrosto il maresciallo.* | We'll steam the carabinieri and roast the police. |
| *Oilì oilà e la lega crescerà.*[15] | Ha, ha, the [peasant] union will grow. |

Anti-Communists would also think it telling that the most famous of all Resistance songs, *Fischia il vento*, should be based on a Russian air.[16] 'Real' 'Italian' folk songs, meanwhile, both before and after 1945, continued habitually to be sung in dialect.[17] At their most intimate they would express the traditions of the Italies and deny that the nationalisation of the masses had progessed far. Their ubiquity and popularity again imply that Italians had not yielded musically to the ambitions of the totalitarian state. So also does the fact that the most popular 'Italian' music-making of all was that coming from Italo-America. In music, as in so many other cultural forms, American-style consumerism was what entranced the young, and its influence was marking Italian lives even while, whether as consenting or dissenting Fascists, they wore black shirts. Not Giuseppe Blanc nor Alfredo Cassella, but Perry Como, Mario Lanza, Frank Sinatra, Dean Martin and, eventually, Madonna were the way of the future.

If music thrums with the message that Italian history is complex and fluid, and that Italian society is composed of individuals who, under Fascism, retained quite a degree of personal agency, what is revealed by a study of other aspects of cultural life during the regime and after 1945, when film, literature and 'memory' joined professional historians in offering a continuing meaning to the past?

Film is one of the more celebrated areas of the Fascist venture, all the more because of the critical and commercial success of Italian film-making after 1945 and what is now widely accepted to have been the pronounced continuity between the Republic's film industry and that which had developed under the Fascist regime. Cinema production had begun in Italy before the First World War, with about 500 films being released each year between 1909 and 1914[18] in what is commonly called Italian cinema's 'golden age'. Though patriotism was already a common topic for screen presentation, the early cinema had a raffish, aristocratic and cosmopolitan character which it would never altogether lose.[19] For this and other reasons, it was soon beset by demands for censorship, from the Church as well as the Italian state which, in 1913–14, required that films should avoid moral offence and not impugn 'the reputation and sense of decorum of the nation'.[20]

---

15 G. Vettori (ed.), *Canzoni italiane di protesta*, pp. 126–7.
16 For the lyrics, see G. Vettori (ed.), *Canzoni italiane di protesta*, pp. 153–4.
17 For one collection of lyrics, see G. Vettori (ed.), *Canti popolari italiani*, Rome, 1974.
18 P. Leprohon, *The Italian cinema*, London, 1972, p. 23.
19 For the basic narrative, see G. P. Brunetta, *Storia del cinema italiano 1895–1945*, Rome, 1979.
20 G. P. Brunetta, *Storia del cinema italiano 1895–1945*, p. 64; A. Bernardini, 'Industrializzazione e classi sociali nel primo cinema italiano', *Risorgimento*, 2, 1981, p. 164.

Entry into the First World War brought an end to this 'golden age', and the *dopoguerra* was characterised by a severe financial crisis which would last well beyond the March on Rome. Gradually, however, the Fascist authorities began, like politicians of diverse political persuasion in other countries at the time, to see the enormous potential power of film.[21] In 1926, as part of the first construction of the Corporate State, cinemas were obliged to screen the newsreels being produced on national or Fascist themes by the *Istituto Nazionale LUCE* (*L'unione cinematografica educativa*), founded two years previously and dependent on government subsidy.[22] LUCE became one of the major propaganda institutions of the regime, though it never quite possessed a monopoly of film information. In October 1926, for example, Catholic interests inaugurated their own documentary service as a friendly rival to the established body.[23] The Church was already fostering a network of parish cinemas which would remain a typical venue for the viewing of films, especially in the South, even after 1945.

From the 1920s, then, the Fascist regime took a pronounced interest in film – indeed, in 1926, the party ideological journal *Critica fascista* hailed cinema as potentially the most Fascist of all the arts – but it did so in a less-than-overbearing way. As the eminent director Alessandro Blasetti, a patriot[24] whose career would outlast Fascism, put it: 'A state film industry would come into existence with one and only one major aim – propaganda. And it would fail. The products of such an industry, whether or not bearing the stamp of the Fascist state, would inexorably be boycotted [by audiences], rejected by business, [and] banned by foreign censors.'[25] Film, Blasetti advised (and Bottai endorsed his views)[26] was an industry in which the market, and the coterie of film-makers, must decide what should be exhibited on Italian screens. Even in the late 1930s Blasetti was still urging that 'the people consider, and must always consider, cinema as a kind of diverting entertainment', while declaring that cinema was 'the most

21 For an introduction, see P. V. Cannistraro, *La fabbrica del consenso: Fascismo e mass media*, Bari, 1975, pp. 273–322.
22 G. P. Brunetta, *Storia del cinema italiano 1895–1945*, p. 238. From time to time, Mussolini intervened personally in its productions, requesting further shots of a short-skirted female ice-skater and forbidding accounts of political assassinations. See E. R. Tannenbaum, *Fascism in Italy: society and culture 1922–1945*, London, 1973, p. 267.
23 G. P. Brunetta, *Storia del cinema italiano 1895–1945*, p. 323. The Catholics also had their own journals of film criticism. Meanwhile Catholic censorship remained rather more oppressive than Fascist, being troubled, for example, by Tarzan and Laurel and Hardy movies, and preferring that Disney cartoons be viewed only by adults. See G. P. Brunetta, 'Con i fascisti alla guerra di Spagna', *Bianco e Nero*, 47, 1986, p. 31.
24 In the 1920s, in writings which sedulously followed the Fascist style, Blasetti urged that films be made 'above all for love of the *patria*' and that they should avoid '*americanume*' and '*tedescheria*'. He also believed that each 'race' (*razza*) should express itself cinematographically. A. Blasetti, *Scritti sul cinema*, Venice, 1982, pp. 92, 99.
25 A. Blasetti, *Scritti sul cinema*, p. 119; cf. G. P. Brunetta, *Storia del cinema italiano 1895–1945*, pp. 212, 243.
26 G. P. Brunetta, *Storia del cinema italiano 1895–1945*, p. 248.

powerful force of all' and urging, by implication, that its budget should not be cut in preference for greater military expenditure.[27]

At that time Blasetti had reason to be worried. The Great Depression had shrunk the market, in Italy as elsewhere. Confronting a decline in production, Mussolini's regime from 1931 pursued a more interventionist line, and the film industry grew to rely on government subsidy. The activism of these years culminated on 21 April 1937 (the Fascist holiday for the 'Birth of Rome') with the opening of *Cinecittà* (Cinema city), a technolgically advanced set of studios favourably positioned on the edge of the nation's capital. This complex was presided over by the *Duce*'s eldest son, Vittorio, who acted as patron to a group of young men-about-town, rich or independent enough to involve themselves in the cinema industry and, as often as not, natural admirers of the United States and natural critics of what they saw as the curtailing crudities of Italian Fascism.[28] Vittorio Mussolini was attracted by the US, too, and in 1936 had expressed the wish that Fascist films imitate the 'technical virtuosity and fluid narrative styles' of Hollywood rather than favouring 'heavy-handed German trauma' or French 'trite farce and *double entendre*'.[29] However, as the 1930s wore on direct contact with the US became more difficult, and pressure increased for the cinema industry to obey the rules of autarky being imposed on the rest of the Italian economy. Cinema, too, must go it alone, the official line maintained, as the government anxiously endeavoured to ensure that Italian films were the first choice for every audience.[30]

Even at the height of the campaigns for a genuinely Fascist society, films none the less remained 'a reservoir of contradictions',[31] both directly in the sense that the majority of productions were comedies and light romances,[32] and indirectly. In this latter regard a recent study has shown how multiple and sometimes unintended were the messages which an Italian audience could draw from a film made in full Fascist orthodoxy. In 1940, for example, audiences were laughing at the naughtiness of *Maddalena, zero in condotta* directed by the sometime radio comedian and man of parts, Vittorio De Sica.[33] Maddalena was not really a bad girl, audiences learned

27 A. Blasetti, *Scritti sul cinema*, pp. 156–7, 163.
28 The classic account of a move by one in this circle from a very cosy dissent to a more serious anti-Fascism is R. Zangrandi, *Il lungo viaggio attraverso il fascismo: contributo alla storia di una generazione*, Milan, 1962. See further Chapter 8.
29 V. De Grazia, 'Mass culture and sovereignty: the American challenge to European cinema', *Journal of Modern History*, 61, 1989, p. 73.
30 None the less, in 1938 Amercian films still took 73.5% of box office receipts. V. De Grazia, 'Mass culture and sovereignty', p. 285.
31 M. Landy, *Fascism in film: the Italian commercial cinema, 1931–1945*, Princeton, 1986, p. ix.
32 The genre was given the charming title of 'white telephone movies' because, some time during them, an alluring lady clutched a white telephone and breathed heavily. For examples see E. R. Tannenbaum, *Fascism in Italy: society and culture 1922–1945*, p. 274.
33 M. Landy, *Fascism in film*, pp. 6, 51. Perhaps attracted by such glimpses of provocation, film audiences increased in number by 30% from 1938 to 1942.

by the end of the film, but before that denouement her story did place on the screen generational and gender difference. Considering this and other productions, an English-language historian has concluded that the films of the era gave little 'sense of a mobilised society' and presented life as 'refreshingly normal', if with a 'Hollywoodian'[34] ethos – 'no distinctively Fascist ideology in a political sense emerges in the majority of the films'.[35] Indeed, quite a lot of evidence suggests that Italian audiences, from the *Duce* (himself a fan of Laurel and Hardy) down, preferred the products of American consumer capitalism, and watched national movies as a second best option.

The populist appeal of American movies proved to be the dominant influence on Italian cinemagoing in the aftermath of Fascism. None the less, for a number of decades following the war the Italian film industry became Hollywood's chief competitor across the globe, in critical acclaim if not in box-office success. Especially in the years of 'neo-realism', the Italian cinema was praised for bringing a new 'honesty' and 'truth' to film representation, and some of this representation was historical. What, then, more than a generation later, can be learned from post-war Italian film depiction of (the myths of) Fascism and anti-Fascism and thus their re/visioning[36] of history on the cinema screen?[37]

Of course the great majority of films produced in post-war Italy avoided both history and overt political comment.[38] Even so, there are still too many 'historical' films to be reviewed in a book of this length. My focus will therefore fall on four major movies of the 1970s, Bertolucci's *1900* (1976), Marco Leto's *La Villeggiatura* (1972), Pier Paolo Pasolini's *Salò* (1975) and Federico Fellini's *Amarcord* (1973). I shall then note more briefly the fate of historical re/presentation on Italian screens after 1978, given the conservative or anti-anti-Fascist turn in the culture of those years.

Before examining film versions of history from the 1970s, however, some comment must be made about neo-realism. Even while warfare raged across the Italian peninsula, film-makers were at work. Commencing in 1943, or, more likely, under the regime itself, Italian cinema entered its 'season' of

34 G. P. Brunetta, 'The conversion of the Italian cinema to fascism in the 1920s', *Journal of Italian History*, 1, 1978, p. 452. Brunetta asserted that the US cinema had a greater influence in Fascist Italy than did such Soviet film-makers as Sergei Eisenstein.

35 G. Nowell-Smith, 'The Italian cinema under Fascism', in D. Forgacs (ed.), *Rethinking Italian Fascism: capitalism, populism and culture*, London, 1986, p. 151.

36 For this typically postmodern pun and some theoretical comment, see R. A. Rosenstone, *Visions of the past: the challenge of film to our idea of history*, Cambridge, Mass., 1995; R. A. Rosenstone (ed.), *Revisioning history: film and the construction of a new past*, Princeton, 1995.

37 This question is all the more relevant because films make such a wonderful aid to teaching, especially in a world in which the borders between history and cultural studies grow ever more blurred.

38 For my own more detailed summary, see R. J. B. Bosworth, 'Film memories of Fascism', in R. J. B. Bosworth and P. Dogliani (eds), *Italian Fascism: history, memory and representation* (forthcoming).

neo-realism, which would last until the early 1950s.[39] In this 'springtime'[40] of achievement, a score or so movies were made which retain their status as classics. Included on most critics' lists are Luchino Visconti's *La Terra trema* (1948), an account of the travails of the fisherfolk of Acitrezza, near Catania, with a soundtrack full of the impenetrable dialect of the town;[41] Giuseppe De Santis' *Riso Amaro* (also 1948), a sensual, *cinema noir* depiction of the harsh life of rice-harvesters near Vercelli;[42] De Sica's *Bicycle Thieves* (again 1948), offering a touching insight into the perils of unemployment for a young family in post-war Rome.[43] With *La Terra trema* being the extreme case, each of these films depicted the sufferings of 'ordinary' people and implied that such pain needed urgent political amendment. Each claimed to be 'true' in the sense of avoiding the accustomed magic, sentiment or 'wromance' of film – there is not a white telephone in sight, and even 'stars' are generally absent or held in check. Each may be viewed as a commentary on the inadequacy of Fascism in addressing Italy's social problems and in provoking a devastating war, though none directly confronted the Fascist past. The neo-realist movies which most directly reworked contemporary history were the 'war trilogy' of Roberto Rossellini: *Germania: Anno Zero* (1947), *Paisà* (1946) and *Roma: città aperta* (1945).[44] In the literature, these films, and especially *Rome: open city*, are often viewed as expressing that new Italy which, its humanism and sense of reality intact, had emerged from the dark years of the dictatorship.

Accepting for the moment that Rossellini's trilogy forms part of the neo-realist venture, on the most cursory reflection it also indicates that there is something troubling about that director's career. As with Visconti, De Sica,

39 For some introduction, see R. Armes, *Patterns of realism*, South Brunswick, 1971; C. Lizzani, *Il cinema italiano 1895–1979* (2 vols.), Rome, 1979; M. Marcus, *Italian film in the light of neo-realism*, Princeton, 1986; J. J. Michalczyk, *The Italian political filmmakers*, Rutherford, 1986, and especially M. Liehm, *Passion and defiance: film in Italy from 1942 to the present*, Berkeley, 1984.

40 For a translation of some of the key documents of the era, see D. Overbey (ed.), *Springtime in Italy: a reader on neo-realism*, London, 1978. Given Fascism's emphasis on the *primavera di bellezza* in *Giovinezza*, there is something ironical about the choice of metaphor.

41 The dialogue is available in translation in L. Visconti, *Two screenplays: 'La Terra trema', 'Senso'*, New York, 1970; cf. also L. Visconti, *Three screenplays: 'White knights', 'Rocco and his brothers', 'The job'*, New York, 1970. One of Visconti's collaborators on the film was Franco Zeffirelli, whose politics thereafter would move well to the right. See F. Zeffirelli, *Zeffirelli: the autobiography*, New York, 1986.

42 For further detail, see A. Vitti, *Giuseppe De Santis and postwar Italian cinema*, Toronto, 1996.

43 The film was loosely based on a sententious novel which has been translated into English. L. Bartolini, *Bicycle thieves*, London, 1977. For useful commentary on De Sica, see P. V. Cannistraro, 'Ideological continuity and cultural coherence', *Bianco e Nero*, 36, 1975, pp. 14–19.

44 For their texts see, in English translation, R. Rossellini, *The war trilogy*, New York, 1973. Federico Fellini collaborated in the production of *Rome: open city* and *Paisà*.

De Santis, the great Marxist script-writer Cesare Zavattini,[45] and such younger figures as Federico Fellini,[46] Rossellini had made his mark in cinema well before the collapse of the Fascist regime in July 1943. Indeed, when Badoglio and the King took over in Rome, Rossellini had only just finished another, earlier, 'Fascist' war trilogy: *La Nave bianca* (1941), *Un Pilota ritorna* (1942) and *L'Uomo della croce* (1943).[47] These films, while being anti-Soviet and Catholic Nationalist rather than Nazi-fascist in their ideology, evoked a certain verisimilitude on their own account. None the less, they form what a naïve reviewer might regard as a somewhat surprising backdrop to *Rome: open city*, if that film is accepted as an 'honest' 'documentary attack on the questions of the day' and a straightforward expression of anti-Fascism.[48] Commentators regularly aver that *Rome: open city* is 'the most important film in Italian cinema history'.[49] What, however, is its place in Italian historiography?

The most common answer to this question is that Rossellini's film set a historical course which would long be the norm, and that *Rome: open city* opened the 'vulgate' of anti-Fascism. After all, as a communist critic maintained in the 1970s, to many the film portrayed 'reality as collectively lived in those months by millions of Italians'.[50] An American scholar has added that, in cinema history, the film acted as a sort of 'April 25, the day on which a new Italy was born and with it a new realism'.[51]

In the 1990s, however, *Rome: open city* deserves more critical scrutiny. Perhaps it does express a myth of anti-Fascism, but the greater myths which it purveyed, ones especially appropriate in 1945, were a populist myth of the Italian nation and of the nationalisation of the Italian masses, and the liberal one of Fascism being a mere parenthesis in Italy's positive national history. On 8 September 1943 the Italian nation state had collapsed and, in fleeing for their lives, King Victor Emmanuel III, Marshal Badoglio and his leading ministers had acknowledged that they and the 'ruling class' to which

---

45 For introduction to his (manipulative) understanding of neo-realism, see C. Zavattini, 'Some ideas on the cinema', *Sight and Sound*, 23, 1953, pp. 64–9. Michelangelo Antonioni was another leading director who worked with the Fascists in the 1930s.

46 For a detailed English-language study, see P. Bondanella, *The cinema of Federico Fellini*, Princeton, 1992.

47 For a review focusing especially on the last of the three, see P. Bondanella, *The films of Roberto Rossellini*, Cambridge, 1993, pp. 32–44; cf. also P. Brunette, *Roberto Rossellini*, New York, 1987.

48 W. C. Makins, 'The film in Italy', *Sight and Sound*, 15, 1946, pp. 126–7.

49 P. Brunette, *Roberto Rossellini*, p. 41. Unlike most neo-realist cinema, it was a considerable box-office success, topping the national takings in 1946–7. Of the others to do well commercially, *Bicycle Thieves* came 11th in 1948–9 and *Riso Amaro*, scandalously assisted by the legs of Silvana Mangano, 5th in 1949–50. See V. Spinazzola, *Cinema e pubblico: lo spettacolo filmico in Italia 1945–1965*, Milan, 1974, p. 19. The nationalism in neo-realism had a more practical side than usual as the Italian cinema industry strove to keep itself afloat against what seemed overwhelming competition from the USA. From 1949, the situation eased somewhat as the Christian Democrats brought in protective legislation.

50 C. Lizzani, *Il cinema italiano 1895–1979*, Rome, 1979, ii. p. 107.

51 M. Liehm, *Passion and Defiance*, p. 59.

they belonged could not carry out the fundamental task of any government – to feed the people and provide them with a minimum of security. Thereafter, a basic question requiring consideration would be what sort of nation state could and should be reconstructed.

One simple way out of the terrible dilemma posed by a nation in disarray was to cover over the facts with history and, in particular, to give a lineage which went back before 1922 and which said as little as possible about Fascism to any future Italy. Hence the *fastidio* of Croce and his view that Fascism was too boring and tawdry to deserve study. And hence *Rome: open city* in its 'national populism' (that is, its promotion of the idea of primordial *italiani brava gente*) and its commercial success. Much more powerfully than Croce, and well before literary constructions of the Fascist past,[52] Rossellini and his film were developing a history in which Fascism did not really matter, and was not, in any case, 'Italian', and in which, therefore, there had been no authentic national collapse.

A brief narration of the plot will establish this point. *Rome: open city* depicts the 'resistance' of a Communist, 'Manfredi', and a Catholic priest, 'Don Pietro', both of whom die heroically at the hands of the Gestapo. In their rather different modes of resistances, these two stalwart partisans possess a 'genuine popular base'. It is composed of men, women and children of the people (the most activist boy resister is called Romoletto, as he doubtless waits to refound Rome). Local Fascist police are on the people's side. There is no sign of class (or regional) difference. The only collaborator with the Germans is a showgirl whom the Gestapo have trapped with drugs, a fur coat and sex, and, in the end, she too sees the error of her ways. Not even the Germans really approve of Nazi deeds. Those who incarnate evil in this movie are but two people, the Gestapo commander Bergmann and his lesbian assistant, Ingrid.

It has been rightly remarked that in *Rome: open city* Bergmann appears as a 'stage queer',[53] fond of leather and thigh-high boots, aroused by torture and death. This bracketing of Nazism with deviant sexuality was another of the distancing features of the movie. Really bad Fascists were 'not like us' in their sexual preference and, presumably, in all aspects of their lives. In adopting this motif, Rossellini again was well ahead of his time; he would live to see his views replayed in such celebrated later movies as Visconti's *The Damned* (1969), Bertolucci's *The Conformist* (1970), Lina Wertmüller's *Seven Beauties* (1975)[54] and Pasolini's *Salò* (1975). The link

---

52 P. A. Sitney, *Vital crises in Italian cinema: iconography, stylistics, politics*, Austin, Tex., 1995, p. 29.

53 P. A. Sitney, *Vital crises in Italian cinema*, p. 36.

54 Of recent directors, the moderate and eventually Craxian socialist Lina Wertmüller was perhaps the cheapest in her marriage on the screen of film and sex. But then she cheerfully explained, 'I don't make films about the fascist era, but films about us, today.' See G. Bachmann, ' "Look Gideon –": a talk with Lina Wertmüller', *Film Quarterly*, 30, 1977, pp. 2–11.

with sexual 'abnormality' would also become a staple of psycho-historical theorising about 'fascism' (by which is usually meant Nazism) and of the construction of the past forged in such artefacts of popular culture as the comic book and rock music. The idea that fascists are abnormal (whatever that might mean) is, of course, a highly dubious one and directly conflicts with the argument that 'Auschwitz' expressed the 'banality of evil'.[55] In other words, what is obvious about *Rome: open city* is that the film did not demand of contemporary Italians any genuinely critical reckoning with the misdeeds and calamities of their own Fascist past.

The fact that *Rome: open city* was actually a highly conservative film in its depiction of the social (and intellectual)[56] order and the nation state was disguised by the history of Italian film and Italian culture from 1948 on, that is, once the Cold War had settled over Italy and the rest of Europe. In the 1950s Christian Democrat Italy became reluctant to discuss anything with too much rigour – Visconti for one got into trouble with the censors for proposing in *Senso*[57] a film account of the Risorgimento which would depart from the official heroic *rivoluzione nazionale* line. Though the occasional movie, notably Florestano Vancini's *La lunga notte del '43* (1960),[58] was given a Fascist setting, it would not be until the decade after 1968 that Italian film-makers could again confront the issues of the dictatorship in a major way.

As has already been demonstrated in this book, the 1970s were an unusual time in which the history of Fascism, if read aright, promised to light up the way to a better future. The decade thus saw the production of a large number of films 'about' Fascism, ranging from *The Conformist* and *The Garden of the Finzi-Continis*[59] in 1970 to Liliana Cavani's *The Skin* (1981) and the Taviani brothers' *The Night of the Shooting Stars* (1983), when a new political and cultural atmosphere was becoming apparent.

If one film had to be chosen to represent the 1970s, it would be Bernardo Bertolucci's *1900*, a movie which has also stimulated a greater degree of commentary than any other.[60] At the very beginning of the 1970s, Bertolucci

---

55 See further Chapter 9.
56 It ought to be evident that one of those escaping from the past in this movie is Rossellini (along with much of the Italian intelligentsia).
57 Visconti had to adopt this title as a second choice when he was banned from calling the movie 'Custoza', after the less-than-glorious battle fought there in 1866. For an account of his difficulties, see J. Doniol-Valcroze and J. Domarchi, 'Visconti interviewed', *Sight and Sound*, 28, 1958, p. 145; V. Spinazzola, *Cinema e pubblico*, p. 138.
58 D. Ward, 'Fascism and Resistance in the films of Florestano Vancini', *Italian Culture*, 10, 1992, pp. 227–42.
59 Vittorio De Sica was the controversial director of this beautiful movie, based on Bassani's novel of the same title. Similarly, *The Conformist* gave screen presentation to the Moravia novel and Cavani's film sprang from the one written by Malaparte.
60 For some English-language examples see, among others, R. P. Kolker, *Bernardo Bertolucci*, London, 1985; T. J. Kline, *Bertolucci's dream loom: a psychoanalytic study of cinema*, Amherst, Mass., 1987; R. Burgoyne, *Bertolucci's 1900: a narrative and historical analysis*, Detroit, 1991; and my own R. J. B. Bosworth, 'Bernardo Bertolucci's *1900* and the myth of Fascism', *European History Quarterly*, 19, 1989, pp. 37–61.

had already made two films exploring the problem of Fascism. Taking its basic plot from Alberto Moravia's novel of the same title, *The Conformist*[61] recounted the way in which Fascism was the upshot of a 'fear of freedom' (Erich Fromm's psychological theorising about Nazism was the ultimate inspiration of both novel and film).[62] Less overtly commercial, but much more subtle in its exploration of the meaning of Fascism, history and memory was *The Spider's Strategem* (1970). In using a plot which owed something to a Borges short story, Bertolucci here prefigured much postmodernism by exhibiting the labyrinthine complexity of any attempt to reckon with the past.[63] By the time he directed *1900*, however, Bertolucci read history with less artfulness. In his depiction of peasant life in the Po valley from 1900 to 1945 and beyond, Bertolucci now boasted that he would bring to the screen the definitive history of peasant Italy (or at least that from around his own birthplace of Parma). There can be no doubt that he produced a marvellous film, and one of great visual opulence, even if it was not a box office winner.[64] As a piece of historical reconstruction, however, Bertolucci's 'version of the class struggle has,' as one critic put it, 'all the complexity of a Punch and Judy show'.[65]

The plot entails a struggle between the Berlinghieri family of landowners and their peasantry. After the First World War, and with the current *padrone* a fan of modern technology and law and order, Fascists appear to help keep the peasants in check. Attila, with his evocative name, is depicted as both very violent and not very bright. He is also sexually deviant, raping and murdering a small boy at a symbolic moment in his rise to power. Later he would do the same to a landowner's widow. His Fascists by the 1930s would impose an outright reign of terror, shooting peasants, including a pregnant woman, into the mud. Attila is bad. Anti-Fascism has its exemplum, too, in the form of Olmo, a 'socialist with holes in his pocket' (for more ready masturbation). Olmo has good sex and is a hero. Driven off by Attila as a subversive, he returns in triumph in 1945 and presides over the execution of the Fascist and his wife, 'Regina' (her name implies that she embodies the monarchy and other *fiancheggiatori*). The film has a curious coda, however. In it, the liberal landowner and Olmo are still wrestling in a class struggle 30 years after the war is over. They are, it seems, waiting to hear the results of the 1970s' 'crisis of the Italian crisis'.

61 A. Moravia, *The Conformist*, London, 1952.
62 See E. Fromm, *The fear of freedom*, London, 1942 and cf. Chapter 9.
63 For a deconstruction see F. Flanagan, 'Time, History and Fascism in Bertolucci's films', *The European Legacy* (forthcoming).
64 Especially when compared with his recent triumph (1972) in *Last Tango in Paris*. After *1900*, Bertolucci's movies would become increasingly beautiful and increasingly silly, a decline which *Stealing Beauty* (1995) showed no signs of arresting.
65 L. Quart, ' "1900": Bertolucci's Marxist opera', *Cineaste*, 8, 1976, pp. 14–17.

Undoubtedly the most drastic 1970s filmic reading of the Fascist past was Marco Leto's *La Villeggiatura* (*The Holiday Camp*).[66] Shot in a grainy black and white, its images seemed very much those of a resumed neo-realism. Its plot, however, broke radically from that national consensus which underpinned *Rome: open city* and, very unusually in Italy, probed the role of the intellectual in society. The story went thus: a young liberal-democrat historian, '*professor* Francesco Rossini', a pupil of Salvemini and Croce, and the son of a liberal philosophy professor, was sent into *confino* on an island off the Italian coast as a punishment for his anti-Fascist ideas. There, he found three forces at work – ordinary (communist) cadres, Fascist gaolers and 'Commissario Rissuto', the prison director, just one bureaucrat among others, and, it is soon plain, an embodiment of the continuity of national history. The real contest, it gradually becomes clear, is one fought between the communists and the *Commissario* for Rossini's soul. Rissuto talks mistily of his debt to Rossini's father, under whom he had studied (liberal) philosophy at university. He treats the son as a case apart and, as one intellectual to another, offers access to books, classical music, wife and child – a combination of scholarly and family life and thus a holiday camp indeed. The *Commissario* also gets Rossini's father and a leading regime historian, [Gioacchino] 'Volpe', to write persuasively about the good sense and opportunity involved in a renunciation of political activism. There is a cost, however. This 'normal' life can only be regained if the *professore* avoids further contact with the Italian people as incarnated by the imprisoned cadres; in other words, if he betrays them. Here, then, is the film equivalent of those historians who saw all Italian history summed up in the word 'continuity', and those political commentators who believed that Christian Democrat Italy had never renounced the Fascist heritage.[67]

The continuity which audiences of *La Villeggiatura* viewed on the screens was a continuity of evil, in which the *fiancheggiatore*-style, liberalish bureaucrat served the Fascist tyranny more truly and more criminally than did the Blackshirts. Indeed, it is the *Commissario* who is the real author of the 'Fascist' murder of the most intransigent imprisoned Communist. As Leto explained, he was trying to mount a 'visceral challenge' to a comfortable history of Italy by engaging in an analysis of 'a Fascism which never ends', that, for example, which could presently be detected in the

---

66 Ironically, the historian and anti-Fascist Leo Valiani would twice describe his experience of *confino* on Ponza as a sort of *villeggiatura*. See L. Valiani, *Sessant'anni di avventure e battaglie: riflessioni e ricordi raccolti da Massimo Pini*, Milan, 1983, p. 32 ('*una villeggiatura diversa*'); L. Valiani, *Tutte le strade conducono a Roma*, Bologna, 1983, p. 49 ('*un anno di villeggiatura*').

67 For an extreme case, see the 'revolutionary socialist' and sometime leader of PSIUP (a party to the left of the PCI), Lelio Basso's view that Christian Democracy (and its capitalist masters) constituted a variety of 'totalitarianism'. A *Fondazione Lelio Basso* was established in 1973 to favour his memory and ideas. See L. Basso, *Fascismo e Democrazia: due regimi del capitalismo italiano*, Milan, 1975 (a good year for the re-publication of such extreme ideas).

'white shirts' of the Republic's bourgeoisie and its Christian Democrat leaders.[68] If there was one film which understood history in the way that the Red Brigades and other left-wing terrorists of the decade did, it was *La Villeggiatura* (and it is thus no surprise to learn that it was singled out for attack in *Rinascita*, the theoretical weekly of the PCI).[69]

Still more controversial was Pier Paolo Pasolini's *Salò o le 120 giornate di Sodoma*, a film which was ready for release at the end of 1975, shortly after Pasolini's squalid murder, and was indeed then shown in Paris, but was seized by the Italian censors and only distributed in a somewhat modified version in 1977. Pasolini, a novelist and film-maker of great talent and sensibility,[70] was an aggressive and open homosexual.[71] His last film went out of its way to outrage 'respectable' audiences as it depicted beautiful young males and females pent up in a villa and forced by their elders to engage in perversions, torture and murder. They banquet on shit, for example (a paralleling with Fascist ideology which Bertolucci repeats in a notable scene in *1900* in which the peasants literally give back to 'their' Fascists the bullshit retailed by the regime). Pasolini sets his action in 1944–5 during the Salò Republic; but at first sight the historical reference takes a secondary place to contemporary preaching. And yet, as one reviewer acutely noted, 'The morbid fascination of *Salò*'s images of sadistic sexual violence far outweighs – and ultimately undermines – his [Pasolini's] recondite and prosaic critique of capitalism.'[72] Reading a film too literally is usually a mistake on a historian's part. The different and subtle assumptions of the medium prompt caution. But it is hard not simultaneously to conclude that *Salò* and, indeed, all attempts by the cinema to link fascism and sexual perversity weaken rather than augment historical understanding of the fascist era. Indeed, they suggest that an essentially escapist understanding of that past is being marketed to the viewer.

More pleasurably interested in sex, surreal rather than 'real', but with a wonderful comprehension of provincial life, is Federico Fellini's *Amarcord* (*I remember*) (1973). Fellini's works regularly offer an artful glimpse of the relationship between art and society and between province and metropolis. Frequently, under Fellini's direction, the two seeming alternatives tend to merge. Though prominent in an industry in which, even after its time of flowering, intellectual respectability was often linked to 'neo-realism',

68 P. Pintus, *Storia e film: trent'anni di cinema italiano (1945–1975)*, Rome, 1980, pp. 117–20.

69 P. Pintus, *Storia e film*, p. 118.

70 For a recent study in English, see S. Rohdie, *The passion of Pier Paolo Pasolini*, London, 1995.

71 For some introduction see, in English, E. Siciliano, *Pasolini: a biography*, New York, 1982; in Italian, G. C. Ferretti, *Pasolini: l'universo orrendo*, Rome, 1976; E. Golino, *Pasolini: il sogno di una cosa*, Bologna, 1985 and, on his murder, M. T. Giordano, *Pasolini: un delitto italiano*, Milan, 1994.

72 J. R. Macbean, 'Between kitsch and fascism: notes on Fassbinder, (Homo)sexual politics, the exotic, the erotic and other consuming passions', *Cineaste*, 13, 1984, p. 17.

Fellini remarked archly: 'The word "real" gives me great discomfort. I have to admit that I don't actually know what that word means.'[73] It is thus predictable that his most overtly political memories as represented in *Amarcord* scarcely provide a straightforward comprehension of Fascism. What the film does gently depict are those gaps between theory and practice which mark everyone's life. Fascism is present, and threatening to a degree – the semi-autobiographical narrator's father is dosed with castor oil after refusing to attend a Fascist event – but so, too, are the Church, the family and the cohort of friends maturing to uncertain manhood (Fellini is always better at depicting men than women). The Italians of the seaside town portrayed in the film – Fellini grew up in Rimini – are most moved by the passing of the transatlantic liner *Rex*, which must have been heading to or from the USA (and Hollywood). With typical ambiguity of message, Fellini exhibits the image of a plainly fake *Rex*, floating massively on what is obviously a sea composed of black plastic. Can it be, despite appearances, a ship with no conclusive destination?

Plenty of other fine movies of the 1970s were set in the Fascist period and formed a backdrop to the passionate historiographical debates of that time. By the end of the decade, however, the conservative turn in Italian politics and culture was evident in film, and in succeeding years the new atmosphere would become more pronounced. One major reason for this change in approach was undoubtedly the fact that the end of RAI, the state radio and television company's monopoly, meant the rise of private television, especially that associated with Silvio Berlusconi and his firm, Fininvest. In 1978 RAI still enjoyed a 90 per cent audience share. Four years later it had declined to 50 per cent, and it has not revived.[74] Similarly, attendance at cinemas fell steeply in this period, while the ubiquity of film on television – in 1990 more than 5000 movies were screened[75] – blunted the impact of cinema's political and intellectual thrust. Reflecting on the impact of these changes in media output, one commentator concluded that the 1980s were 'Italy's stupidest decade'.

None the less, to some extent film continued to influence the remembrance of the Fascist past. Very much preoccupied with 'memory' and its construction were the Taviani brothers in *La Notte di San Lorenzo* (*The Night of the Shooting Stars*) (1983). To some, this film is the most subtle of all cinema accounts of the Fascist story. Robert Rosenstone, the leading American expert on film and history, has written that the Tavianis directed a movie 'less to entertain an audience or to make profits than to

73 G. Bachmann, 'A guest in my dreams: an interview with Federico Fellini', *Film Quarterly*, 47, 1994, p. 10.
74 P. Schlesinger, 'The Berlusconi phenomenon', in Z. G. Baranski and R. Lumley (eds), *Culture and conflict in postwar Italy: essays on mass and popular culture*, London, 1990, p. 274.
75 M. Morandini, 'Paradise lost', *Sight and Sound*, 1, 1991, p. 19.

understand the legacy of the past'. It was, however, Rosenstone claimed, a fresh understanding, since it questioned

> the comfortable, traditional heroism of the Italian (and, by extension, European) resistance to fascism by telling its story from the viewpoint of a young girl. Rather than a conventional tale of unblemished bravery, the story becomes one of cowardice, political indifference, opportunism, cruelty, and random violence – not exactly the sort of heritage cherished by national narratives of liberation.[76]

It is true that the movie is full of modishly postmodern hints about the framing being engaged in by film-makers and audience, the mutability of memory, and the greater seriousness, for most people, of the little world of everyday life compared with the menace and caprice of high politics. Similarly there can be no doubt that *The Night of the Shooting Stars* contains many beautiful depictions both of 'San Martino' ('really' San Miniato) and Tuscany, and of the human condition. But the Tavianis go beyond the point which Fellini had made in *Amarcord* to suggest that the conflict being fought in 1944 was no more than a civil war. In this sense their movie needs to be set in two contexts. One is that of their own work. Their most subtle film is undoubtedly *Padre Padrone* (1977), an astonishingly articulated study of the Sardinian peasantry, if also one favouring to some extent the nationalisation of the masses, and suggesting a possible comfort in resting in the arms of the Italian state. After 1983 these existing hints of a certain social conservatism transmute into a confused endorsement of the virtue of the blood and soil of Tuscany, if not of Italy as a whole, in such dismal efforts as *Good Morning Babylon* (1987) and *Fiorile* (1992). In the former, the Tavianis muse self-indulgently on the history of cinema and the ties between Italy and Hollywood, in order to display a heroic (and non-racist) D. W. Griffiths and to claim that the very soil of Tuscany throbs with artistic creativity. The second context within which to set *The Night of the Shooting Stars* is, of course, that of Italian culture in general. In that regard, the Tavianis' film should certainly be seen as fitting what, by 1983, was becoming the spirit of the times.

Given that Bertolucci had retreated to compose beautiful and archetypally vapid movies about China, North Africa and India before his limp return to Italy (or, rather Tuscany!) as a subject in *Stealing Beauty* (1995), the next significant films about Fascism would be made by a new generation of directors. With helpful investment from Berlusconi or his friends, the two most celebrated of these became Giuseppe Tornatore's *Cinema Paradiso* (1989) (which earned the Academy award for best foreign film in 1990) and Gabriele Salvatores' *Mediterraneo* (1991) – it won the same prize in 1992.[77] The films have much in common. Whether set in a

---

76 R. A. Rosenstone (ed.), *Revisioning history: film and the construction of a new past*, pp. 6, 9; cf. also the great French film historian Pierre Sorlin's even more ecstatic account of the film in the same book. P. Sorlin, 'The night of the shooting stars', pp. 73–87.

77 Tornatore was born in 1956, Salvatores in 1950.

small town in Sicily or on one of the Dodecanese islands to be occupied by the Germans after September 1943, each film carries a message of nostalgia and little else. They are films for the end of history, and for a time when there is no ethical position worth adopting any more about Fascism. They are films in which Italians are, and have been since the beginning of time, *brava gente*. They are films which give unsurprising proof of the fact that cinema's historicisation of Fascism was replicating what was occurring in academic history writing.

The relationship between Italian literature and Fascism is not so different from that outlined above in regard to music or cinema. There is, for example, the same equivocal evidence of fellow-travelling under the regime by writers who, after 1945, emerged as anti-Fascists of one kind or another. Typical is the case of Alberto Moravia, a hugely popular post-war author[78] and a cousin of the martyred heroes of the Resistance, Carlo and Nello Rosselli. Under the Republic, Moravia would successfully construct himself as the Grand Old Man of dissenting literature.[79] His expertise would embrace the Fascist past, feminism and Mao's China,[80] while the novel which he had written under the regime, *Gli indifferenti*, would win fame as a scathing exposure of the bourgeois corruption and boredom of the Fascist years.[81]

In 1946 Moravia declared that he himself had always been an anti-Fascist, as had 'almost all of his literary peers'.[82] There are problems with this statement, however. *Gli indifferenti* had raised issues that were also Fascist preoccupations; and, indeed, Moravia had begun publishing it in a radical Fascist journal whose masthead bore the inscription: 'Mussolini is our God'. As late as 1933 Moravia can be found praising the *Duce*'s view that writers should 'immerse' themselves in life. As the most acute student of the continuity between Fascist and post-war culture has remarked in regard to Moravia and others: 'Throughout the thirties, the ideological construct of the third way would serve as a conveniently vague emblem of Fascist identity that allowed a wide variety of political discourses to be expressed within the framework of the regime.'[83]

---

78 Moravia was a pseudonym. The writer's family name was Pincherle. For more of his work in English translation, see e.g. A. Moravia, *The woman of Rome*, Harmondsworth, 1952; *Roman tales*, Harmondsworth, 1959; *A ghost at noon*, Harmondsworth, 1964; *The two of us*, St. Albans, 1974; *1934*, London, 1985. Moravia's novels had the further commercial value of being a little salacious, another case of Fascism and sex being brought together.

79 See e.g. the typically entitled A. Moravia, *Intervista sullo scrittore scomodo* (ed. N. Ajello), Bari, 1978 and cf. A. Moravia, *Impegno controvoglia: saggi, articoli, interviste: trentacinque anni di scritti politici*, Milan, 1980.

80 A. Moravia, *The Red Book and the Great Wall: an impression of Mao's China*, Bungay, 1968.

81 A. Moravia, *The Time of indifference*, Harmondsworth, 1970. It was first published in Italian in 1929.

82 R. Ben-Ghiat, 'Fascism, writing, and memory: the realist aesthetic in Italy, 1930–1950', *Journal of Modern History*, 67, 1995, p. 663.

83 R. Ben-Ghiat, 'Fascism, writing, and memory', pp. 632, 645, 653.

Ironically, the most plainly anti-Fascist novelist of the 1930s was
Secondo Tranquilli, who is better known under his pseudonym Ignazio
Silone. He wrote two spare denunciations of the Fascist exploitation of the
peasantry in his home region of the Abruzzi.[84] Silone had been gaoled by the
regime as a Communist and then gone into exile. However, he left the party
in 1930 and in the post-war period became a 'god-that-failed' anti-
Communist,[85] with his last major publication being a curious play about
Catholic spiritualism.[86]

By that time a pile of novels about Fascism had been published, especially
from writers near the PCI; and they had been associated, in the years
immediately after 1945, with the school of 'social realism'. The most
celebrated of these authors was that agonised if sexist figure, Cesare Pavese
(born 1908). He had stayed in Italy under the dictatorship, doing much
translating of American literature, and had been gaoled as an anti-Fascist in
1935. He finally joined the PCI in November 1945. His short novels, *The
Comrade* and *The Moon and the Bonfire*, offered heartfelt, if sometimes
over-wrought, accounts of anti-Fascist political commitment. In August
1950, Pavese committed suicide, leaving behind his moving diary.[87] More
crudely following the party line was Vasco Pratolini's *A Tale of Poor Lovers*
(1947), set in the back streets of Florence, where honest workers faced
Fascist violence, corruption and murder.[88] Much harder to generalise about
was the work of Curzio Malaparte, sometime radical Florentine Fascist,
turned Communist and, before his death in 1957, a convert to Maoism. In
1949, Malaparte published *The Skin*, a scabrous account of the US
liberation of Naples.[89]

The season of such novels ended at much the same time as did that of
neo-realist cinema. Thereafter, Fascism turned up from time to time as a

84 I. Silone, *Fontamara*, London, 1934 (first published in Italian, 1930); *Bread and wine*,
London, 1962 (first published in Italian, 1937). For an anthropological account of the
Abruzzi and thus the setting of these novels, see C. White, *Patrons and partisans: a study
of politics in two Southern Italian towns*, Cambridge, 1980.
85 See I. Silone's chapter in A. Koestler (ed.), *The god that failed: six studies in communism*,
London, 1950, pp. 83–120.
86 I. Silone, *The story of a humble Christian: a biography in dramatic form*, London, 1970.
There is also an autobiography available in English as I. Silone, *Emergency exit*, London,
1969. Cf. too the curious work I. Silone, *The school for dictators*, London, 1939, a
denunciation of both Mussolini and Stalin.
87 C. Pavese, *This business of living*, London, 1964; cf. also e.g. his *The moon and the bonfire*,
London, 1952; *The comrade*, London, 1965; *The political prisoner*, London, 1966; *The
devil in the hills*, Harmondsworth, 1967. The last of these is an 'apolitical' novel,
confronting the problem of alienation and the failure of communication, always major
issues for Pavese.
88 V. Pratolini, *A tale of poor lovers*, London, 1949.
89 Malaparte (the name was a pun on Buonaparte) was another pseudonym, this time of the
writer Kurt Erich Suckert. Malaparte had been the most brilliant and the most unreliable
of the war correspondents of any country in the Second World War. Some of his pieces were
made available in English in the post-war years, with his *Kaputt* especially containing
images of an unparalleled power. See C. Malaparte, *Kaputt*, London, 1948; *The skin*,
London, 1952; *The Volga rises in Europe*, London, 1957.

literary theme, but without the earlier urgency or direct political sponsor-
ship. The most significant pro-Fascist novelist was Giose Rimanelli, whose
The Day of the Lion was an account of the 'accidentalism' that could lead a
young man to fighting for the Salò Republic. Rimanelli's characterisation
prefigured much 1990s-style 'revisionist' 'memory' of that era.[90] Also
focusing on the war with a belated realism was *History* (1974), a lengthy
novel by Elsa Morante, who was then married to Alberto Moravia.[91] More
subtle were the studies of racism by the Jewish-Italian authors, Giorgio
Bassani and Primo Levi. In *The Garden of the Finzi-Continis* (1962) Bassani
produced a novel set in Ferrara and exploring both the onset of the anti-
Semitic legislation and the issue of political and social isolation and
commitment. This fictional work contains perhaps the most memorable
statement in post-war Italian literature concerning the banality of racism.
The words are those of a young and shallow non-Jewish woman
contemplating the intrusion of Fascism into her young life:

> Something 'very unpleasant' had happened, she told me ... Maybe I
> didn't know, but in the tournament that was just over at the tennis
> club, she and Bruno had got right into the finals no less – which was
> something neither of them had ever even dreamt of. Well then: the
> final match was in full swing, and once again things had begun taking
> the most incredible turn (enough to make everyone goggle, quite
> honestly: Desirée Baggioli and Claudio Montemezzo, two real stars at
> the game, in trouble with a couple of non-classed players: even to the
> point of losing the first set ten-eight, and being outmatched in the
> second as well!), when suddenly marchese Barbicinti, who was judge
> and umpire of the tournament on his own initiative interrupted the
> match. It was six o'clock admittedly, and they couldn't see too well.
> But not so dark that they couldn't have carried on for at least another
> two games! Heavens, what a way to behave! At four-two in the second
> set of an important match, no one had the right to shout 'stop' out of
> the blue, to march on to the court waving his arms and declaring the
> match suspended 'because of the darkness', and putting the whole
> thing off till the following afternoon. Besides, the marchese wasn't
> acting in good faith at all, that was perfectly obvious. And if she,
> Adriana, hadn't noticed him, at the end of the first set, in an excited
> huddle with that creep Gino Cariani, secretary of the GUF [Gruppo
> Universitario Fascista]. (They'd moved a bit away from the crowd,
> next to the little building where the changing rooms were); and
> Cariani, perhaps so as not to be noticed, had his back turned to the
> tennis court as if to say: 'Carrry on, carry on with your game, it's not

90 G. Rimanelli, *The day of the lion*, London, 1956. For Rimanelli's idiosyncratic positioning
    in Italian literature, see G. Rimanelli, *Il mestiere del furbo: panorama della narrativa
    italiana contemporanea*, Milan, 1959.
91 E. Morante, *History*, Harmondsworth, 1980.

you we're talking about': all she'd have needed was the marchese's face as he bent down to open the gate into the courts, so pale and bewildered she'd never seen anything like it – a real proper death's head! – to guess that the gathering darkness was only a pretext, a feeble excuse. Anyway, how could you possibly doubt it? The interrupted match was never even mentioned, as next morning Bruno got exactly the same express letter as I'd had, the one I'd wanted to show her. And she, Adriana, had been so disgusted by the whole business – so outraged apart from everything else, at anyone having the bad taste to mix sport and politics – that she's sworn never to set foot in the *Eleonora d'Este* club again. Suppose they'd got something against Bruno, well, they could have forbidden him to take part in the tournament; said frankly: 'Things being the way they are, we're terribly sorry, but we can't accept you for it'. But once the tournament had started, in fact was nearly over and he was within a hair's breadth of winning one of the matches they just shouldn't have behaved the way they did. Four-two! What pigs! The sort of piggery you might expect from Zulus, not from anyone supposed to be educated and civilised![92]

Still finer was the writing of Primo Levi and especially his autobiographical account of his transportation from the Salò Republic to Auschwitz, *If This is a Man*.[93] It is a book of universal significance and of universal importance.

Proponents of the culturalist strand in the contemporary historiography of Fascism have been busily highlighting other aspects of Mussolini's regime, such as its art and architecture.[94] It has always been clear that Fascism lacked Nazism's retrograde vision of art, and that Mussolini, in his capacity as an aspirant intellectual, seems generally to have enjoyed the idea that his Italy should encourage a certain degree of cultural freedom. Rival schools could thus compete, so long as they paid lip-service to the ideals of the regime. For every spartan portrait of a militant *Duce* or of his new legionaries, a later art historian can find countering examples of non-representational art. Fascism ruled the art world lightly and, apart from the most blatantly propagandist works, it is hard to see much of a specifically Fascist high artistic legacy.

Architecture, by contrast, left a definite Fascist imprint on the Italian peninsula, both because the regime was in office for a generation and because it was committed to public works. Few urban settings in Italy today

92 G. Bassani, *The Garden of the Finzi-Continis*, Harmondsworth, 1962, pp. 64–5; cf. also his *The gold-rimmed spectacles*, London, 1960, a gentle study of the difficulties faced by a homosexual under Fascism.

93 P. Levi, *If this is a man*, London, 1969. Levi also wrote a number of other accounts of his experiences, often in short-story form. See e.g. P. Levi, *The monkey's wrench*, New York, 1986; *Moments of reprieve*, London, 1987 and cf. further Chapter 8.

94 For one example see D. Ghirardo, *Building new communities: New Deal America and Fascist Italy*, Princeton, 1989.

do not contain some physical reminder of Fascism, though sites are rarely 'pure' historically and tend best to reflect the continuity of Italian taste from one era to another and the placement of Italian work in the corpus of cosmopolitan architectural practice. So prominent an architect as Marcello Piacentini was only one of those who pursued his career both under Mussolini and under Christian Democrat goverments. The popular effect of Fascist architecture awaits its analyst, though a maximum of sterility (and a certain degree of beauty) is evident in Rome's EUR, the new suburb erected for the Great Exhibition or *Esposizione Universale Romana*, planned for 1942 and, nowadays, the site of party congresses, empty museums and the state archives.[95]

Two further examples of the Fascist architectural heritage are the *Foro italico* (once the *Foro dell'impero*), on the opposite side of Rome from EUR, and the Piazza Vittoria in Brescia, though the popular reading of the two seems to have been diverse. The *Foro italico* is located outside Rome's main football ground (and very near the Republic's Ministry of Foreign Affairs, a building originally constructed to be the Fascist party headquarters). As they stream into or away from the stadium, fans have made a habit of adding their own, generally crude, graffiti about sport or sex to the marbled blocks of the Fascist monument, which were originally designed to bear inscriptions celebrating this (unlikely) victory or that (over the Mafia, for example, or in the 'battle of the births'). In exhibiting such cheerful levity towards the messages of the past, the fans' behaviour is not unique. When Fascism fell, Rome's politicians, rather than bulldozing the site, simply added some blocks of their own, marking Mussolini's departure on 25 July 1943, the end of the war in April 1945 and the election of the Republic on 2 June 1946. Here, then, is a highly desacralised space which in its combination of openness and the humdrum provides a striking contrast to the nervous secrecy and falsehood evident in, say, post-war Germany's treatment of its Nazi architectural past. Nor is the *Foro italico* the only such instance. Rather, on many an Italian building for many years after 1945, an alert onlooker could see Fascist slogans only partially blotted out, still half-preaching such messages as *Noi tireremo diritto* or *Mussolini ha sempre ragione*.

However, architectural remembrance is not always cosy. Piacentini's square in Brescia, which contains an outdoor rostrum designed for a Fascist orator, was by the 1970s the object of continuing political contestation. Such conflict culminated murderously in May 1974, when neo-fascists exploded a bomb there and killed eight bystanders. Mussolini's own *paese* of Predappio has also had its moments of disputation, although they have

95 Its opening was prevented by the war and some of the buildings were finished after 1945. For a rather naïve account of one aspect of the exhibition, see M. Fuller, 'Wherever you go, there you are: Fascist plans for the colonial city of Addis Ababa and the colonizing suburb of EUR '42', *Journal of Contemporary History*, 31, 1996, pp. 397–418.

been less violent than bathetic. This little town in the foothills of the Apennines had, by the 1930s, been changed into a cult site. Since its liberation in October 1944 Predappio has been governed by the Left, with the result that official memory there has usually fitted into the ideas and interpretations of the 'myth of the Resistance'. However, the burial of Mussolini's remains in the local cemetery in 1957 has ensured that Predappio has also become a place of Fascist pilgrimage, with at least some visitors inscribing their hope that, eventually, 'history will prove us right'.[96]

In one of his more pompous statements concerning the meaning of *1900*, Bernardo Bertolucci declared that 'cinema is really a kind of reservoir of the collective memory of this century'.[97] In the two decades since Bertolucci spoke, the study of memory, whether collective or not, has achieved a high historiographical profile, especially as pioneered by the French historian, Pierre Nora.[98] The French focus on 'memory' has frequently carried unnerving echoes both of nostalgia for an allegedly lost, peasant, *Gemeinschaft* past and of a semi-racial nationalism, anxious, for example, to erase from the past the France of ethnic minorities. Italian work on the subject has been more belated[99] and, so far, seems politically eclectic, with just the occasional hint of a desire to employ memory as a bulwark against the uncertainties that hang over nation states in the current world order.[100] Most Italian commentators on the subject have been aware that memory is almost always open to manufacture, manipulation and change, and is, indeed, like the discipline of history itself, never 'primordial', a 'process and not a thing'.[101]

'Heritage' is another topic requiring more research. Work is now becoming available on the Fascist deployment of history, for example that of the Middle Ages and Renaissance as marketed for commercial and political reasons to both local and cosmopolitan tourist consumers by the regime in Florence, Siena and other 'historic' cities.[102] However, perhaps because the

96 M. Baioni, 'Predappio', in M. Isnenghi (ed.), *I luoghi della memoria: simboli e miti dell'Italia unita*, Bari, 1996, p. 510.
97 B. Bertolucci, 'The poetry of class struggle', in D. Georgakas and L. Rubinstien (eds), *Art Politics Cinema: the Cineaste interviews*, London, 1985, p. 144.
98 For an English-language introduction see P. Nora, *Realms of memory: rethinking the French past*, New York, 1996, a sample from the multi-volume *Les lieux de memoire*, Paris, 1984–92.
99 The major work is collected in two volumes edited by M. Isnenghi (ed.), *I luoghi della memoria: simboli e miti dell'Italia unita*, Bari, 1996, and M. Isnenghi (ed.), *I luogi della memoria: strutture ed eventi dell'Italia unita*, Bari, 1997. They include chapters from such well known anti-Fascist historians as Angelo Del Boca, Patrizia Dogliani, Anna Bravo, Nuto Revelli and Giorgio Rochat.
100 For example, see M. Isnenghi, *Le guerre degli italiani: parole, immagini, ricordi 1848–1945*, Milan, 1989.
101 The best work in this field has been done in the US and has no direct connection with Italy. See e.g. J. R. Gillis (ed.), *Commemorations: the politics of national identity*, Princeton, 1994; E. T. Linenthal, *Preserving memory: the struggle to create America's Holocaust Museum*, New York, 1995.
102 See e.g. M-D. Lasansky, 'Tableau and Memory: the Fascist revival of the Medieval/Renaissance festival in Italy', *The European Legacy* (forthcoming).

Italian Republic so notoriously controls, or thinks that it controls, such a high percentage of humanity's 'artistic patrimony', there is as yet no Italian equivalent to David Lowenthal's deconstructions of the 'heritage crusade', and, despite his world-ranging interests, Lowenthal himself rarely draws on Italian examples.[103]

What, then, in summary, are the main traces of Fascism which can be detected in the post-1945 cultural history of Italy, and what do they imply about the historicisation process of this significant part of the Italian past? The first point must be that of continuity. In the realm of culture, as in every other aspect of Italian life, the idea of a 'parenthesis' fully bracketing off post-Fascist history from that which went before or came after is simply ludicrous. In music, literature, film, art, architecture and memory, Italians did not slough off Fascism at a stroke, but rather adapted to its fall as, very frequently, they had adapted to Fascism itself. In a pattern which is not at all uncommon in those other countries which had just survived the horror of the Second World War and glimpsed the meaning of 'Auschwitz', an initially ardent, if superficial, desire to understand was replaced, notably in the 1950s, by the cosier alternative of a denial and a forgetting of the graver aspects of the dictatorship and its wars. However, especially in the moments of high political and social contestation in the 1970s, Fascism returned after a generation, at least in mythical form, to play a major part in Italy's culture and politics.

The murder of Aldo Moro in 1978 and the accompanying failure of the 'historic compromise' to legitimise the PCI and its version of a Left duly heralded the more conservative decades which have followed. Already in the 1980s, a nostalgic return to 'everyday' life under Fascism was evident, a process in which what was important was no longer the tyranny but the gadgets, the catchy advertisements and the other ephemeral aspects of 'modernity', prompting the reviewer of one such exhibition to remark in *Corriere della Sera*: 'Never before has the extraordinary vitality of our country in the inter-war years been made so clear'.[104] As an English observer concluded prophetically: in future 'only pedants and anachronistic zealots will become involved in heated, divisive arguments about history and the diffusion of historical ideas', now that 'Anti-fascism is thus made synonymous with prejudice, lack of historical curiosity, fighting yesterday's battles, finger-wagging moralism and being gratuitously divisive today.'[105]

Thereafter the eclipse of anti-Fascist culture quickened. By the 1990s, the logic certainly of postmodernism and perhaps of the 'end of history' ensured that cultural parity would be granted to the 'victims' of anti-Fascism, directly in the alleged 'triangle of death' in the Romagna and those *foibe* (or

---

103 See especially D. Lowenthal, *The past is a foreign country*, Cambridge, 1985; *Possessed by the past: the heritage crusade and the spoils of history*, New York, 1996.
104 Quoted by T. Mason, 'The Great Economic History Show', *History Workshop*, 21, 1986, p. 26.
105 T. Mason, 'The Great Economic History Show', pp. 27–8.

caverns) which stud the hills above Trieste, or indirectly in reversing the opprobrium visited, at least publicly, at least in the 1970s, on those who had served the Salò Republic. To a cynical eye it seemed only a matter of time before the Fascists who ruled in Tripoli or Addis Ababa would become the latest 'others' to be brought in from the historiographical cold. Indeed, in 1996, President Oscar Scalfaro himself went out of his way to ensure that official Italy did not acknowledge the centenary of the First Battle of Adowa,[106] and culturalist historian Mario Isnenghi warned, in the cliché of the moment, that Italian colonialists of the Liberal era should not be lightly condemned since they, too, must be treated on their own terms.[107] At present, the culture of Fascism carries an uncertain glamour and 'authenticity' from a past which is composed of a jumble of bright images. One culture among many others, it now frequently lacks a clear ethical message for the present or future, except 'buy and be happy'.

106 See Angelo Del Boca's introduction to the conference papers collected as A. Del Boca (ed.), *Adua: le ragioni di una sconfitta*, Bari, 1997, pp. 5–7. Eventually the efforts of historian Gian Giacomo Migone, the PDS head of the Senate's Commissione Esteri, ensured that there was at least some Italian witness to the Ethiopian commemoration of the Italian invasion.
107 M. Isnenghi, 'Il colonialismo di Crispi', in A. Del Boca (ed.), *Adua: le ragioni di una sconfitta*, p. 72.

8

Resistance or Civil War
1943–1945?

In 1995–6 Angelo Del Boca achieved at least partial success in a campaign which had lasted more than 30 years. Faced with overwhelming documentary evidence, the Italian Ministries of Defence and Foreign Affairs finally accepted that Fascist forces had deployed poison gas in Ethiopia and had deliberately covered up its deployment thereafter. While he was fighting for this truth to emerge,[1] Del Boca had grown used to condemnation, both from returned soldiers' and settlers' organisations and from so individualist but passionately anti-Communist a journalist and popular historian as Indro Montanelli.[2] Indeed, even when he finally accepted the case that terror bombing had occurred, Montanelli refused to abandon his general belief that Italian colonialism had not been as 'inhumane' as that practised by other imperial powers.[3] On African issues, as on those involving the north-eastern border where, during the war, the young Fascist party secretary Aldo Vidussoni had talked carelessly about the 'extermination' of all local Slovenes,[4] official Italy,[5] rather like official Japan[6] and, indeed, following the

---

1 Perhaps as a result of Del Boca's campaigns, in November 1997, on an official visit to Addis Ababa, the Italian President Oscar Luigi Scalfaro apologised (in that generic way which has recently become popular among politicians) for the Fascist invasion of Ethiopia.

2 Montanelli, as he was fond of recounting, had served as a 20-year-old in Ethiopia and could recall, for example, such happy times as when he bought and sold a 12-year-old 'wife'. See A. Del Boca, 'Una lunga battaglia per la verità', in A. Del Boca (ed.), *I gas di Mussolini: il fascismo e la guerra d'Etiopia*, Rome, 1996, p. 30.

3 A. Del Boca (ed.), *I gas di Mussolini*, p. 45.

4 E. Apih, *Italia: fascismo e antifascismo nella Venezia Giulia (1918–1943)*, Bari, 1966, p. 419.

5 See J. Walston, 'History and memory of the Italian concentration camps', *Historical Journal*, 40, 1997, pp. 169–83. Walston contrasted Italian silence with that of the French and found the former more profound.

6 For Japan, see the endless Saburō Ienaga case as summed up in R. J. B. Bosworth, *Explaining Auschwitz and Hiroshima: history writing and the Second World War 1945–1990*, London, 1993, pp. 167–90, and 'Nations examine their past: a comparative analysis of the historiography of the "Long" Second World War', *The History Teacher*, 29, 1996, pp. 499–523. In August 1997 Ienaga won his court case, at least on one major count, against the

public line taken by most combatants in the Second World War except Germany, has only reluctantly acknowledged the cruel violence in which it once engaged.

In the late 1990s Del Boca's small victory ran against the norm in Italy. Nowadays, in most Italian discourse, a different sort of revisionism from his is at play. It is a revisionism which is anxious to emphasise neither the evils of Fascism, nor the crimes of the nation, but rather the moral failings of anti-Fascism, both during the last stages of the war and as a historiographical legacy. The pundit Ernesto Galli della Loggia is only the most fervent proponent of the idea that the myth of anti-Fascism should bear chief responsibilty for post-war Italians' alleged lack of civic sense and appropriate level of patriotism.[7] The 'First Republic', he warns, was constructed on a lie about the past and, he implies, Italy can only rise again when the truth is restored. Galli della Loggia himself is particularly anxious to see an admission of guilt from Italy's ex-communists, who presently adjust to the hegemony of the market as members of the Democratic Party of the Left. One incident which he thinks especially deserves notice is that which occurred at Porzûs, where communist partisans assaulted the *Brigata Osoppo*, a non-communist Resistance unit, slaughtering some 20 victims whose only vice was to want to retain the national border in the north-east.[8] (He, like other revisionists, strenuously refuses to acknowledge the bitter history of conflict on the frontier; in fact, a sort of ideological and ethnic 'civil war' was raging there from early 1942.[9])

Galli della Loggia's words were soon reinforced by images on a cinema screen. In 1997, the most debated film of the year was *Porzûs*, directed by Renzo Martinelli and screened at the Venice film festival (without winning a prize). Some questioned the film's quality as a piece of cinema, but the liberal democrat commentator Giampaolo Pansa praised it for forcing Italians to face up to the sanguinary side of the Resistance.[10] Another leftist writer, Antonio Padellaro, asked why that pre-eminent anti-Fascist of the last generation and sometime President, Sandro Pertini, had granted clemency to the partisan perpetrator of the crime, Mario Toffanin, who,

---

Ministry of Education's efforts to eliminate any discussion of murderous Japanese policies. In Germany there was also plenty of reticence about the genocide of the Jews, but some silence also survives about the barbarisation of war in the East.

7　See E. Galli della Loggia, *La morte della patria: la crisi dell'idea della nazione tra Resistenza, antifascismo e Repubblica*, Bari, 1996; cf. his briefer version in G. Spadolini (ed.), *Nazione e nazionalità in Italia: dall'alba del secolo ai nostri giorni*, Bari, 1994, pp. 125–61.

8　G. Spadolini (ed.), *Nazione e nazionalità in Italia*, p. 61.

9　For an account see P. Spriano, *Storia del partito comunista italiano IV. La fine del fascismo: Dalla riscossa operaia alla lotta armata*, Turin, 1973, pp. 107–8, 270. Spriano notes that a combined Fascist militia and Army raid in August 1942 employed 10 000 men without stamping out the local partisans. Cf. also, as a case study of Resistance in a local *paese* (and of the strengths and weaknesses of pro-Resistance historiography), C. Perco Jacchia, *Un paese. La Resistenza: testimonianze di uomini e donne di Luninico Gorizia*, Udine, 1981.

10　See e.g. G. Pansa, 'I fantasmi di Porzûs', *L'Espresso*, 43, 14 August 1997 in a debate headlined *Assassinio nella Resistenza* (Murder in the Resistance); and his further article, 'Ma fateci andare al cinema, bigotti d'Italia!', *L'Espresso*, 43, 11 September 1997.

according to newspaper accounts, had survived into old age at Capodistria in independent Slovenia as an unreconstructed Communist. That amnesty, Padellaro declared from the perspective of the 1990s, was carrying mercy and partisanship too far.[11]

Had not the Communist party worked against the national interest and been willing to 'betray' Italy to Jozef Tito and the Yugoslavs, allegedly sacrificing Italians to the advantage of 'Slavs', such revisionists asked (even if they thus exhibited a characteristic blindness towards the moral ambiguities long present on Italy's contested north-eastern border)?[12] Had not Tito's Yugoslavia, after 1945, persecuted and expelled its Italian subjects and destroyed their culture?[13] Moreover, had not violent anti-Fascism, after the end of the war, and notably in the 'triangle of murder' in Emilia-Romagna, been responsible for hundreds, or even thousands,[14] of spontaneous executions, the perpetrators of which sometimes used a pretext of Fascism to cover the settling of personal scores or the winning of financial or other private advantage?[15] Had not the Resistance killed and maimed with a will, too? Many a political crime, Italians were regularly told, in the 1990s, had been papered over by a historiography dominated by anti-Fascist *parti pris* and managed in the interests of the PCI.

The present, it was asserted, should, by contrast, be the occasion for new voices,[16] or at least for the expression of points of view suppressed for two generations. The wound of dishonesty, which had suppurated in the national collective memory unremarked for 50 years, should at last be salved. Even those who had fought for Salò should be given a voice in narratives of the past. So should that great majority which had just wanted to wait out the war.[17] Indeed, everybody should speak and be heard in a postmodern, multi-vocal reckoning with the many-stranded past. It is thus no surprise to find that one of the publications to appear in Italy in 1996 was *La Franchi*, an account by Edgardo Sogno of his own independent (and

11 A. Padellaro, 'Troppa grazia, san Pertini', *L'Espresso*, 43, 25 September 1997.
12 For acute analyses of the hiding of the past in this border region, see G. A. Sluga, 'The Risiera di San Sabba: Fascism, anti-Fascism, and Italian nationalism', *Journal of Modern Italian Studies*, 1, 1996, pp. 401–12; 'Trieste: ethnicity and the Cold War, 1944–54', *Journal of Contemporary History*, 29, 1994, pp. 285–303.
13 For an account of this 'tragedy' in even a left-leaning journal, see R. Pupo, 'L'esodo degli italiani da Zara, da Fiume e dall'Istria (1943–1956)', *Passato e presente*, 40, 1997, pp. 55–81.
14 For an account of the battle over numbers, so typical (and macabre) a part of historiographical controversy about aspects of the Second World War, see G. E. Rusconi, *Resistenza e postfascismo*, Bologna, 1995, who puts the death toll between April and July 1945 at 15 000 (p. 164). For more detail, cf. N. S. Onofri, *Il triangolo rosso (1943–1947): la verità sul dopoguerra in Emilia Romagna attraverso i documenti d'archivio*, Rome, 1994.
15 N. S. Onofri, *Il triangolo rosso (1943–1947)*, p. 41. Onofri noted, however, that ex-Fascists were also among the post-war killers (see p. 162).
16 Even though the old and bitter Fascist historian Gioacchino Volpe had, in 1952, already summed up the history of the Resistance as 'in nine tenths of its reality, a bloody story of civil war'. G. Volpe, *Nel regno di Clio*, Rome, 1977, p. 100.
17 G. E. Rusconi, *Resistenza e postfascismo*, pp. 9, 164.

staunchly anti-Communist) partisan brigade between 1943 and 1945.[18] Under the Republic, Sogno had pursued an idiosyncratic path and, indeed, was occasionally rumoured to be engaged in plots to overthrow the current regime for patriotic and ideological reasons.[19] *La Franchi* was slated to be launched with an introduction written by Renzo De Felice, but the conservative historian[20] died before the project was complete. The actual book thus appeared with two introductions. One, by Sogno, was predictable in its intransigence. Thanking De Felice for his 'warm encouragement', Sogno declared that the facts which he related would help terminate 'the rigid cultural conditioning which has dominated Italian historiography until today', and diminish the power of what De Felice had rightly called the (leftist) 'vulgate'.[21] To Sogno's mind, all proper understanding of the Resistance had been overwhelmed by misleading ideas of the 'forces of the revolutionary left', among which he numbered the PCI, 'maximalist' socialists and even the (liberal democrat) *Partito d'Azione*.[22] He was sure, he added, that De Felice would have agreed with him over the matter.[23]

Whether or not Sogno was right in this conclusion must necessarily remain a matter of speculation. However, the publishing house with which he was dealing, the moderate but certainly not left-wing *Il Mulino*, had its doubts; they provided a second, anonymous introduction in which it was emphasised that Sogno's 'polemical style' went well beyond *Il Mulino*'s custom. The publishers believed that Sogno had a right to print his views, but asserted that they had a responsibility to express their dissent from them.[24]

In other words, what this book and a whole series of other recent works demonstrate is that, ever since the fall of the Berlin Wall and the accompanying collapse of what had seemed the post-war Italian political and cultural settlement, a special controversy has raged over the meaning and legacy of both the Resistance and its opponents in the Salò Republic. Why, then, is there this preoccupation with the period from September 1943 to 1945, which some write off as no more than a 'civil war'? What are the issues? Have they remained the same since 1945? Or, like other controversial questions examined in this book, was their history, too, a process subject to fluctuation and change with the passage of the years and with the alteration of the intellectual climate?

18 E. Sogno, *La Franchi: storia di un'organizzazione partigiana*, Bologna, 1996.
19 See e.g. R. Minna, 'Il terrorismo di destra', in D. Della Porta (ed.), *Terrorismi in Italia*, Bologna, 1984, pp. 49–50.
20 In 1994 De Felice attended the same conference at which Galli della Loggia spoke about the death of the *patria*. See G. Spadolini (ed.), *Nazione e nazionalità in Italia*, pp. 37–44. So, too, did Emilio Gentile (pp. 65–124). If they expressed themselves in a less strident manner, each of these academic authorities basically endorsed Galli della Loggia's views.
21 E. Sogno, *La Franchi*, p. xi.
22 E. Sogno, *La Franchi*, p. xii.
23 E. Sogno, *La Franchi*, pp. xii, xvi.
24 E. Sogno, *La Franchi*, p. viii.

Listening to some of the historiographical debates of the 1990s, and especially to the claim that the Italian past has long been controlled by a 'vulgate' of anti-Fascism, it would be easy to conclude that this last question should be answered in the negative, that both academic history and public memory since 1945 have been dominated by approving accounts, whether ingenuous or manipulative, of the Resistance. Such a conclusion would, however, bear little relationship to reality. It is, after all, obvious that the contest against Nazi-fascism and the victory of anti-Fascism, however defined, were rapidly succeeded by another conflict; for Italy, in its capacity as a border territory of the West, played a particularly important role in the Cold War. In the 1948 elections its people, prompted by Marshall aid and by the combined propaganda forces of the US government and the Vatican, were 'saved' from communism by their own vote.[25] The nation joined NATO in 1949, and, over the next two years, the US financed the re-equipping of the Italian armed forces. American bases became and remained an important presence in such different cities as Naples and Padua, while the secret services of Italy and the USA began planning *Operazione Gladio*, a 'stay-behind' scheme by which loyal, armed anti-Communists were to carry on the fight, even after a hypothetical communist seizure of Italy.

The 1950s, then, was a decade characterised by a pervasive anti-communism and a time in which those who had opposed Mussolini were frequently viewed with suspicion, especially if they were susceptible to the charge that they had been soft on communism. Occasional voices sought to remind Italians of the anti-Fascist cause,[26] but it was predictable that, when state television began broadcasting in 1954, it did its best to avoid contemporary history and, on occasion, screened messages about the patriotic unity of the past in which anti-Fascism was ignored or obscured.[27] Those memorials which were erected to the victims either of the Fascist regime or of the civil conflict from 1943 to 1945 were the products of local initiative.[28] Even though ex-*Partito d'Azione* Prime Minister Ferruccio Parri presided in 1949 over the creation of the *Istituto nazionale per la storia del movimento di liberazione in Italia* (The national institute for the history of the liberation movement in Italy), still today there is no national monument

25 For a detailed English-language account, see J. E. Miller, *The United States and Italy, 1940–1950: the politics and diplomacy of stabilization*, Chapel Hill, 1986, pp. 213–71.
26 For an example, see P. Calamandrei, *Uomini e città della resistenza: discorsi scritti e epigrafi*, rev. ed., Bari, 1977 (first published, 1955). The re-publication, 20 years after the author's death, was more fitting of the time than had been the original date of issue. Calamandrei said that the Resistance had stood for a new morality and his sort of people from circles near Parri saw themselves as 'the forerunners of a new ruling class', who were then betrayed by the Christian Democratic Republic (p. 23).
27 G. Crainz, 'I programmi: dalla liberazione ai primi anni settanta', in G. Crainz, A. Farassino, E. Forcella and N. Gallerano (eds), *La Resistenza italiana nei programmi della RAI*, Rome, 1996, pp. 37–47.
28 See e.g. P. Dogliani, *La premiata resistenza: concorsi d'arte nel dopoguerra in Emilia-Romagna*, Bologna, 1995.

to the Resistance.[29] It was true that 25 April, 'Liberation Day', occasioned parades and celebrations, but from 1948, if not before, there were already signs of dissent and contestation over the meaning of such events.[30] For example, Piazzale Loreto, the square in Milan at which the bodies of Mussolini, Claretta Petacci and some executed Fascist bosses were publicly displayed on 25 April 1945, was recalled in different and often sharply contrasting ways, all the more because Salò *repubblichini* had executed 16 hostages there on 10 August 1944.[31]

It was similarly no surprise that Primo Levi, the author of *If this is a man*, the most extraordinary and moving of all Auschwitz memoirs, should have had difficulty finding a major publisher. In fact, only in 1958, when Einaudi released the book under its imprint,[32] did Levi's work begin to sell[33] – its tardy success a testimony both to its quality and to a new climate enveloping Italy, in which it was becoming just possible to disagree with the verities of Cold War ideology. Levi, who, in his life after 1945, thought of himself as an anti-Fascist but one without party affiliation, had been captured by the Salò militia on 13 December 1943. Convinced that its soldiers were interested in him as a member of the liberal democrat organisation *Giustizia e Libertà* (Justice and Liberty), only belatedly would he understand that it was his Jewishness which would decide his immediate fate.[34]

Back in 1953 another ex-member of *GeL*, Roberto Battaglia, had provided the first detailed narrative of the Resistance experience in a book that was regularly thereafter republished.[35] In his preface, the author wondered whether his 'burning devotion for our Resistance Movement has occasionally prevented me from seeing events in their true historic perspective', and admitted that 'my outlook has sometimes been too personal, not sufficiently objective'.[36] Battaglia's tale was certainly characterised by

29 For a fuller account see A. Ballone, 'La Resistenza', in M. Isnenghi (ed.), *I luoghi della memoria: strutture ed eventi dell'Italia unita*, Bari, 1997, pp. 405–13.

30 A. Ballone, 'La Resistenza', pp. 413–15.

31 See M. Dondi, 'Piazzale Loreto', in M. Isnenghi (ed.), *I luoghi della memoria: simboli e miti dell'Italia unita*, Bari, 1996, pp. 487–99. Dondi notes the silence of the great Milanese paper *Corriere della Sera* over the matter (p. 491).

32 P. Levi, *Se questo è un uomo*, Turin, 1958 (English-language version *If this is a man*, Harmondsworth, 1979, published in a combined version with *The truce*, Levi's superb account of his slow return to Italy via a chaotic, ruined and humane USSR. *La tregua* was first published by Einaudi in 1963).

33 It exhausted its modest first run of 2000 in a few weeks. M. Cicioni, *Primo Levi: bridges of knowledge*, Oxford, 1995, p. 26.

34 P. Levi, *If this is a man*, p. 19.

35 R. Battaglia, *Storia della Resistenza italiana (8 settembre 1943–25 aprile 1945)*, Turin, 1953; *Breve storia della Resistenza*, Rome, 1955. A version drawn from both of these works was also made available in English: R. Battaglia, *The story of the Italian resistance*, London, 1957. It would be characteristic of the moment that, in 1974, another version of Battaglia's work, as re-edited by Giuseppe Garritano, would be be distributed free to any who took out an annual subscription to the PCI daily *L'Unità*. See R. Battaglia and G. Garritano, *La resistenza italiana: lineamenti di storia*, Rome, 1974. This edition also came with a preface from Gian Carlo Pajetta of the PCI's central committee.

36 R. Battaglia, *The story of the Italian resistance*, p. 9.

clear, strong, political and moral lines. The strikes of March 1943, he wrote, demonstrated that the 'Italian people' had by then lost faith in Fascism, being especially disgusted by the German alliance.[37] Salò, in Battaglia's estimate, entirely lacked a popular base; its supporters were no more than 'a dismal crew of crazy phantoms whirling madly round amid the havoc they had created and determined to precipitate the little that still remained intact into the vortex'.[38] It was true that the old order of wealth and status in Italy was somewhat troubled by events, Battaglia added, even if the church hierarchy, for example, did little directly to oppose the Nazi-fascists. There were also problems in the South, where the US-led liberators were only too ready to deal with ex-Fascist or with trimmers (*trasformisti*).[39] But, he averred, the heart of the nation was sound – the lower clergy wanted nothing to do with Salò, since they retained both their humanity and their patriotism, and they deserved congratulations for ensuring that the peasantry did not fall victim to *repubblichino* propaganda.[40]

Battaglia admitted the existence of *attendismo* (*attentisme* or the desire to wait out the conflict and wish a plague on the house of all the active contestants), but thought it both defeatist and the refuge of those who, if not sympathetic with Fascism, wanted to restore the Liberal state.[41] The 'real people', by contrast, were spontaneous in their rejection of Hitler's friends. The extent of their activity[42] necessarily varied with opportunity; the regional diversity of Italy was as relevant as ever in the Resistance.[43] The pro-Resistance political parties, however, were, in most senses, united; where there was conflict, it was easily explained and did not have too negative an effect. Undoubtedly, the communists played a major role in the campaign against the Nazi-fascists, and behaved reasonably on most occasions, despite attempts at provocation, but in the heart of the Armed Resistance lay patriotism.[44] The anti-Fascist movement culminated in 1945 in a 'national uprising'. Then, workers and peasants 'acquired for the first time an understanding of the part they would be called on to play in the [democratic] future of their country'. Then, too, on 'the international plane, the Resistance redeemed the honour of Italy which had been so vilely besmirched by the Fascists'.[45]

Many of Battaglia's themes would become part of the first generalised 'myth of the Resistance', which in the 1960s would begin to win some official endorsment after the failure of the Tambroni experiment and with

37 R. Battaglia, *The story of the Italian resistance*, pp. 31–2.
38 R. Battaglia, *The story of the Italian resistance*, p. 169.
39 R. Battaglia, *The story of the Italian resistance*, pp. 100–1.
40 R. Battaglia, *The story of the Italian resistance*, pp. 130–2.
41 R. Battaglia, *The story of the Italian resistance*, pp. 77–8.
42 R. Battaglia, *The story of the Italian resistance*, p. 89, using the March 1944 strikes as his example.
43 R. Battaglia, *The story of the Italian resistance*, pp. 117–20.
44 R. Battaglia, *The story of the Italian resistance*, pp. 147–9.
45 R. Battaglia, *The story of the Italian resistance*, p. 281.

the adoption of the tactic of the 'Opening to the Left'. Battaglia's work was amplified by the publication of some detailed histories of anti-Fascism, not merely in war but throughout the Mussolini regime. The best of these was written by the American historian Charles Delzell, who defined himself as a J. F. Kennedy-age Democrat, rejecting 'totalitarianism' of whatever hue. He also explained in his preface that he thought that the *Resistenza Armata* had been particularly effective, capping the history of anti-Fascism both at home and abroad.[46] In his text he wrote a detailed political narrative of the array of movements which had stubbornly maintained their objection to Fascism: Catholics, socialists, liberals, as well as communists, all had played a part. Delzell was notably anxious to defend the *fuorusciti*, those who had gone into exile, in the face of doubts raised about them by Croce and others. The exiles' staunch anti-Fascism had helped prepare the way for the rejection of the regime by the populace in 1942–3.[47] Croce's anti-Fascism was also real, Delzell added disarmingly; a humanist national tradition survived in Italy, despite Fascism's best efforts to liquidate it.[48]

Delzell did admit that the anti-Fascist movement was rent by its own internal divisions, and he noted that Carlo Rosselli, for one, twisted and turned in his own ideas.[49] However, such complications and contradictions had faded into insignificance with the onset of the great crisis. The Fascist entry into the Second World War soon precipitated evidence of a popular alienation from the regime[50] and, from the summer of 1941, the PCI, too, joined the general 'battle for democracy'.[51] Even though its fighting force constituted only a fraction of the population, the 'Armed Resistance' deserved to be called the 'Second Risorgimento', and, Delzell argued, was far more genuinely popular than had been the First.[52] In sum, the anti-Fascist idea was crucial in the making of a new and democratic Italy. It was anti-Fascism that connected the Republic with the nation's best traditions (just as Fascism was the putrid fruit of all that was worst in national history).

Delzell published his book in 1961, during the continuing celebrations of the centenary of Italian unification and its accompanying historiographical debate about the relationship of the Italian present to an Italian past.[53] At

---

46 C. F. Delzell, *Mussolini's enemies: the Italian anti-Fascist resistance*, Princeton, 1961, pp. vii–viii; cf. the much narrower F. Rosengarten, *The Italian Anti-Fascist press (1919–1945) from the legal opposition press to the underground newspapers of the Second World War*, Cleveland, OH., 1968; and J. K. Wildgen, 'The liberation of the Valle d'Aosta, 1943–5', *Journal of Modern History*, 42, 1970, pp. 21–41. Rosengarten endorsed the view that the Resistance had been the moment at which both the peasantry and women first played an active part in Italian political life.
47 C. F. Delzell, *Mussolini's enemies*, pp. 44–5.
48 C. F. Delzell, *Mussolini's enemies*, pp. 87–94. Gramsci's *Letters from prison*, he thought, were another demonstration of this native humanism (p. 120).
49 C. F. Delzell, *Mussolini's enemies*, pp. 60–2.
50 C. F. Delzell, *Mussolini's enemies*, p. 182.
51 C. F. Delzell, *Mussolini's enemies*, p. 207.
52 C. F. Delzell, *Mussolini's enemies*, p. 295.
53 For some context see R. J. B. Bosworth, *Italy and the wider world 1860–1960*, London, 1996, p. 11.

that time, antagonistic historical interpretations could be expressed rather more readily about the Risorgimento than about Fascism and anti-Fascism. Prominent in the lists were the champions of the nation led by Rosario Romeo and Giovanni Spadolini, with their view that the Risorgimento had benefitted the Italian people, and the followers of Antonio Gramsci, who, by contrast, asserted that the unification had only marked a *rivoluzione mancata*.[54]

The position which Gramsci obtained posthumously as a historian of the Risorgimento owed much to the increasingly enthusiastic efforts by the PCI to market its 'martyred' ex-leader. Especially in the light of the revelations of the Twentieth Party Congress of the USSR in 1956, Gramsci's writings and personality seemed to guarantee the 'diversity' of Italian communism.[55] 'The myth of Gramsci' proved that Italian communism could indeed pursue its own path to socialism, and that it would be a happy road avoiding the spectre of Stalinism. By the 1970s, Gramsci's image shone in the political and cultural firmament and, despite the doubts of old Right and New Left,[56] he seemed, on occasion, to have ousted Dante from his accustomed position as the most admired intellectual of national history, while also proving an attractive export to those cultural worlds outside Italy, in which, it sometimes seemed, each buyer consumed a different Gramsci.[57]

Along with the selling of Gramsci as a Great Intellectual whose guidance could illuminate past, present and future, went a communist commitment to history as a discipline.[58] Often the two matters were conjoined. Not for nothing was the PCI's cultural institute named the *Istituto Gramsci*. Not for nothing, either, did this institute become known more and more for its 'openness', for the accessibility of its archives, for the welcome which it gave to scholars even when they did not bear a party card. The USSR was notorious for being a closed society whose single reading of history was narrow and obsessive. The USSR was the place where the (changing) truth was expressed in uncontestable and lapidary fashion in the pages of the various editions of the *History of the CPSU (Bolshevik): short course*.[59] By

54 Equally celebrated (or condemned) at the time was Denis Mack Smith, *Italy: a modern history*, Ann Arbor, 1959, which, whether consciously or not, seemed to argue a Gramscian line.
55 G. Liguori, *Gramsci conteso: storia di un dibattito 1922–1996*, Rome, 1996, p. 96, dates 1956 as the 'watershed' year in readings of Gramsci.
56 G. Liguori, *Gramsci conteso*, p. 153, 172–4. It would be appropriate that the new edition of Gramsci's works, as re-edited by Valentino Gerratana, would appear in 1975 under the copyright of the *Istituto Gramsci*.
57 For some introduction see G. Eley, 'Reading Gramsci in English: observations on the reception of Antonio Gramsci in the English-speaking world 1957–82', *European History Quarterly*, 14, 1984, p. 441; cf. E. Hobsbawm, 'The Great Gramsci', *New York Review of Books*, 21, 18 April 1974.
58 For an account of some of these processes in the early aftermath of the war, see D. Betti, 'Il partito editore: libri e lettori nella politica culturale del PCI 1945–53', *Italia contemporanea*, 175, 1989, pp. 53–74.
59 For some introduction to these matters, see R. J. B. Bosworth, *Explaining Auschwitz and Hiroshima*, pp. 142–66.

contrast, its proponents proclaimed, the PCI had accepted that history was an argument and that its truths were fragile at best. By acknowledging the plurality of the past, the party would assert the genuineness of its commitment to a plural society, should it ever obtain office in Rome.

The historian who most evidently symbolised this communist new course was Paolo Spriano.[60] Back in the 1950s, he had already commenced research on a massive study of Italian communism from its birth in January 1921 to the fall of Fascism, starting with an investigation of the 'worker city' of Turin.[61] By 1964 he had moved to writing a full party history. The first instalment of this work appeared with Einaudi in 1967 and, for a time, the succeeding volumes, which ranged widely across the general themes of the national story, tracked the publication of De Felice's biography of Mussolini,[62] offering, as it were, a shadow of that better Italy which communists and anti-Fascists had kept alive despite the Fascist tyranny.[63]

Just like De Felice, if a little belatedly, Spriano gave an *intervista* in the series being published by Laterza – his interlocutor was the De Felicean historian Simona Colarizi, whose political base lay close by that of the socialists. Spriano explained that, as a youth, he had been a *GeL* partisan, fighting alongside Paolo Gobetti, the son of the 'liberal socialist' martyr to Fascism, Piero Gobetti, about whom, after the war, Spriano wrote his thesis.[64] By then Spriano had joined the PCI, working at first in the Turin regional office of the party daily *L'Unità*, where he discovered Gramsci and thereafter remained immensely influenced by him. Spriano always considered Palmiro Togliatti, who headed the PCI through tumultuous years until 1964, a man of political finesse; Gramsci, by contrast, was, in his mind, the 'long-sighted one who could see matters far off better than those in front of him and who comprehended the gravity of a situation by placing it in historical perspective'.[65]

---

60 G. Amendola, *Intervista sull'antifascismo*, Bari, 1976, p. 4. Spriano was certainly not the only case of his kind; see e.g. Paolo Alatri, another from *GeL*, who went over to the PCI in 1948. P. Alatri, 'Minima personalia', *Belfagor*, 41, 1986, pp. 462–3; cf his *Le origini del fascismo*, Rome, 1962, providing a fairly straightforward Marxist account of the rise of Fascism at the behest of the old élites.

61 P. Spriano, *Storia di Torino operaia e socialista: Da De Amicis a Gramsci*, Turin, 1958. Liguori has noted Spriano's determination to separate Gramsci's ideal of revolution from that of Lenin. See G. Liguori, *Gramsci conteso*, p. 121.

62 It is perhaps appropriate that conservative De Feliceans have, after their master's death, launched an attack on Spriano's alleged dishonesty in obscuring the extent to which, in their view, the PCI remained the puppet of Stalin. See E. Aga Rossi and V. Zaslavsky, *Togliatti e Stalin: il PCI e la politica estera staliniana negli archivi di Mosca*, Bologna, 1997, p. 20. This book is dedicated to De Felice and his wife Livia De Ruggiero.

63 See P. Spriano, *Storia del partito comunista italiano 1. Da Bordiga a Gramsci*, Turin, 1967; *Storia del partito comunista italiano II. Gli anni della clandestinità*, Turin, 1969; *Storia del partito comunista italiano III. I fronti popolari, Stalin, la guerra*, Turin, 1970; *Storia del partito comunista italiano IV. La fine del fascismo: Dalla riscossa operaia alla lotta armata*, Turin, 1973; *Storia del partito comunista italiano V. La Resistenza. Togliatti e il partito nuovo*, Turin, 1975.

64 P. Spriano, *Intervista sulla storia del PCI* (ed. S. Colarizi), Bari, 1979, pp. 3–4.

65 P. Spriano, *Intervista sulla storia del PCI*, pp. 7, 54, 98–9, 128, 133.

The crisis of 1956 had been ethically taxing, but Spriano had come through it and had begun to devote his life to history. In the party's story, he mostly found good. Stalin was a problem, but Spriano defended Togliatti's role in the Moscow of the 1930s and at other times (and, at least for the moment, ignored the PCI's own victims in the purges who, naturally enough, are presently being remembered).[66] Back in 1921–2, Spriano declared, the PCI did not deserve blame for dividing the Italian left.[67] Similarly, the party's course after 1945 had not been forced on it, but represented rather 'the fully matured experience of worker anti-Fascism'.[68] In so far as the discipline of history was concerned, the PCI had been saved from Zhdanovism by the 'antidote' of Gramsci's legacy and by the never sundered contacts with such anti-Fascist and non-Communist historians as Franco Venturi and the great French experts on 1789.[69] In sum, even before 1956 the Italian Communist party had favoured the expression of 'a pluralism of voices' and of more than one Marxism.[70] By contrast, Spriano noted wryly to clinch his point about the PCI's special history, as late as 1979 Gramsci's work had still not been published in a serious edition in the USSR.[71]

In the 1980s, with the political climate turning sour, Spriano none the less endeavoured directly to confront the issue of Stalin, hoping also to illuminate the background to the 'involutions' evident in those states which composed the world of 'actually existing socialism'.[72] Spriano's emphasis was on the totality of Stalin's power – this was no history from below – and on the ignorant and parochial world of the Stalinist secret police: he repeated, for example, the story of the arrest of Paolo Robotti, a cousin of Togliatti who in 1938–9 was arraigned as a terrorist for his planned actions against the Fascist regime. According to Robotti, the NKVD man did not understand the meaning of the word Fascist, but did know that secret policemen must revile terrorist acts.[73] If a little coy on the Ribbentrop–Molotov pact, Spriano agreed that it had caused consternation among non-Soviet communist leaders, and suggested that the party line approved on

66 See e.g. R. Caccavalle, *La speranza Stalin: tragedia dell'antifascismo italiano nell'Urss*, Rome, 1989; *Comunisti italiani in Unione Sovietica: proscritti da Mussolini, soppressi da Stalin*, Milan, 1995. None the less, the first of these works is dedicated to Spriano, who had promised to write an introduction but died before its completion. Recording his debt to Spriano's 'habitual scrupulousness' (p. xx), Caccavalle thought that the Italian victims of the purges numbered some 200, of whom he estimated 15% lived to tell the tale. In his second work, *Comunisti italiani in Unione Sovietica*, Caccavalle is scathing about contemporary anti-communist attempts to whip up more moralising on the matter than it deserves (pp. 14–16).
67 P. Spriano, *Intervista sulla storia del PCI*, p. 50.
68 P. Spriano, *Intervista sulla storia del PCI*, p. 146.
69 P. Spriano, *Intervista sulla storia del PCI*, p. 179.
70 P. Spriano, *Intervista sulla storia del PCI*, p. 180.
71 P. Spriano, *Intervista sulla storia del PCI*, p. 181.
72 P. Spriano, *I comunisti europei e Stalin*, Turin, 1983, p. x.
73 P. Spriano, *I comunisti europei*, pp. 42–5.

25 August 1939 was always 'fragile and embarrassed'. He added that Togliatti, for one, did not desist in its aftermath from attacking Mussolini and his regime.[74] The rank and file, Spriano argued, were also anxious to make active their opposition to Fascism, but it was only the beginning of Operation Barbarossa that fostered a 'real leap in quality' in so far as resistance was concerned.[75] By 1943–4 Togliatti and the party members and even Stalin (if for strictly realistic reasons to do with the devastated state of the USSR) did not want to lose contact with the 'West' and its humanist and revolutionary heritage.[76] The Cold War blighted all from 1946,[77] but a history of popular fronts in 1935–7, 1941–3 and 1945–7 taught lessons for the present, and suggested a way out of the sterility of endless bipolar conflict.[78]

In his interview with Colarizi, as in his more scholarly works, Spriano thus embodied a communist historiography which certainly honoured the party's past, but which did agree that there were issues to debate and research to be done. In such work he was joined by other avowedly Communist historians.[79] Prominent among them was Renato Zangheri, a major analyst of the peasantry who could be relied on to defend the Gramscian interpretation of the Risorgimento against Romeo, and track with pleasure the rise of peasant unionism;[80] from 1970, he would also become PCI mayor of Bologna, the party's 'show-case city'.[81]

Similarly, Giuliano Procacci, a PCI senator, wrote prolifically about the origins of socialism,[82] as well as publishing a translated general history of Italy which appeared in English under the popular Penguin imprint. From Procacci it was possible to learn that non-Communist anti-Fascists were

---

74 P. Spriano, *I comunisti europei*, pp. 94, 133. For Spriano's earlier reading of this crucial period, see P. Spriano, *Storia del partito comunista italiano IV*, pp. 3–59. Here, he omitted much serious discussion of the effect of the pact on the PCI, while also taking pains to recall the major role, played in Italy after June 1941, of the image of Stalin and of the Soviet people's resistance to the invaders (pp. xiii–xiv).

75 P. Spriano, *I comunisti europei*, p. 167.

76 P. Spriano, *I comunisti europei*, pp. 178–9, 212.

77 P. Spriano, *I comunisti europei*, p. 268.

78 P. Spriano, *I comunisti europei*, p. 294.

79 The journal *Studi storici*, established in 1959, was the special vehicle for party scholarship and gained wide recognition as one of the best publications on national history. Cf. also the work of Enzo Santarelli, e.g. his *Fascismo e neofascismo: studi e problemi di ricerca*, Rome, 1974.

80 R. Zangheri, *Agricoltura e contadini nella storia d'Italia: discussioni e ricerche*, Turin, 1977, pp. 131–2, 189–240. Zangheri's ideological precursor was the great communist historian of rural life, Emilio Sereni (died 1977). For Zangheri's own early work, see R. Zangheri, *La proprietà terriera e le origini del Risorgimento nel Bolognese*, Bologna, 1961.

81 For an English-language example of Zangheri's pushing of this line, see the interview with him in M. Jäggi, R. Müller and S. Schmid, *Red Bologna*, London, 1977, pp. 187–207. Zangheri there ascribed Italy's post-war social gains, evident especially in his city, to the legacy of the 'mass participation of the population in the anti-Fascist resistance' (p. 192). In Italian, cf. his account of the 'event' of 1977, when his city was occupied by far left radicals. R. Zangheri, *bologna '77: intervista di Fabio Mussi*, Rome, 1978 (Bologna was not capitalised as a gesture of anti-authoritarianism).

82 See e.g. G. Procacci, *La lotta di classe in Italia agli inizi del secolo XX*, Rome, 1970.

inclined to 'amateurish activism', while the PCI 'had flung itself into the anti-Fascist fight with all its strength'.[83] Moreover, 'of all the anti-Fascists the Communists were those who [through Gramsci] took the analysis of Italy's political and social reality in the light of Fascist victory deepest, and produced a new and articulate programme of the forces and directions of the Italian revolution'.[84] It was natural, Procacci concluded, that communists should lead the Resistance, 'an anti-Fascist and anti-German [popular] front'.[85] It was natural, too, that these forces should win. The Resistance 'was above all a very wide political movement. It had been the achievement not only of the workers who had sabotaged and the men of the military formations who had fought, but also of the peasants who had fed them and the priests who had hidden them'.[86] The Resistance, in Procacci's eyes, possessed a 'genuine mass base', not solely composed of communists. Re-emphasising the messages of such academic work were party memoirs such as those of the Pajetta brothers[87] and, especially, of Giorgio Amendola, a member of the PCI's central committee.[88] Amendola, indeed, published histories of his own; as has already been noted, he was the 'expert' chosen by Laterza to give an interview on anti-Fascism in reply to De Felice's and Ledeen's on Fascism.[89]

In all this work, anti-Fascism held centre stage. Its principles and practices in the past had 'proved' the genuineness of the PCI's current enthusiasm for intellectual openness, and simultaneously promised the PCI a glorious future.[90] At the same time, anti-Fascism illuminated the indomitable virtue which coursed through the Italian people and implied that the Italian state, for all its present travails, could be reformed into a more honest and 'real' democracy. Nor were communists the only ones to pursue this line. The independent leftist Leo Valiani was only one of a number of academic historians prominent in public life who, then and later,

---

83 G. Procacci, *History of the Italian people*, London, 1970, p. 361.
84 G. Procacci, *History of the Italian people*, p. 361.
85 G. Procacci, *History of the Italian people*, p. 372.
86 G. Procacci, *History of the Italian people*, p. 374.
87 See e.g. the autobiographical histories: Giuliano Pajetta, *Douce France: Diario 1941–2*, Rome, 1971; *Ricordi di Spagna: diario 1937–9*, Rome, 1977; Giancarlo Pajetta, *Il ragazzo rosso va alla guerra*, Milan, 1986. The most recent instance of this genre is A. Natta, *L'altra resistenza: i militari italiani internati in Germania*, Turin, 1997.
88 See e.g. G. Amendola, *Fascismo e movimento operaio*, Rome, 1975; *Gli anni della repubblica*, Rome, 1976; *Storia del partito comunista italiano 1921–1943*, Rome, 1978.
89 G. Amendola, *Intervista sull'antifascismo*. Amendola began characteristically by arguing both that the history of Fascism mattered directly to the Republic of the 1970s and that this Republic, with all its faults, had nonetheless presided over a rise in well-being of a previously unimagined kind (pp. 1–2).
90 In an elegant set of essays illustrating Spriano's cultural breadth, he recalled that, in September 1947, Togliatti told the Chamber of Deputies: 'We come from a long way back and we shall go a long way forward' (while deputies from the Right yelled: 'Yes, from Russia. And you'll go back there'). P. Spriano, *Le passioni di un decennio 1946–56*, Milan, 1986, p. 66.

spoke up in the cause of anti-Fascism and seemed to favour a sort of historiographical popular front.[91]

Moreover, a series of important memoirs were helping to build support for the cause. Notable were the works of Nuto Revelli. The first and most celebrated was *La guerra dei poveri*, published by Einaudi in 1962.[92] Revelli was another who had fought as a partisan and, in 1945, backed the *Partito d'Azione* of Ferruccio Parri in its short-lived attempt to carry the ideals of anti-Fascism into government. But Revelli united the history of the Armed Resistance with what had gone before, notably recounting the horror of the Eastern Front; it was there that he and the other *poveri cristi* serving in the Fascist forces began to understand the issues of the Second World War.

In September 1939, despite recognising the occasional squabble between the Army and the Fascist party, Revelli had entered the officers' school at Modena, confident in the quality of both the regime and the nation's military. Together, he had believed, they guaranteed that Italy would win any war.[93] However, as soon as he reached the USSR in the summer of 1942, the confident and credulous world of his youth collapsed: 'At once, no sooner had we camped in a large wood, we learned to fear the [Soviet] partisans and to hate the Germans'.[94] The retreat west constituted the first part of the 'poor people's war', and, in their suffering, Revelli and his comrades learned about the levity of Fascism, and the injustice of the invasion mounted by the Nazi Germans. The second part of Revelli's war came after his return to Italy and after the collapse of Fascism. At first he was deeply mistrustful of politics. His diary entry for 26 July 1943 read: 'Everyone an anti-Fascist; too many anti-Fascists. The real truth is this: there were very few anti-Fascists in Italy. To curse about Fascist dress, to tell jokes: that was not anti-Fascism. It was moral confusion.'[95] The royal government's attempt to change sides on 8 September was an even more disgraceful event, during which Revelli only saw chaos, looting and *sauve*

---

91 See e.g. L. Valiani, *Dall'antifascismo alla Resistenza*, Milan, 1959; L. Valiani, G. Bianchi and E. Ragionieri, *Azionisti, cattolici e comunisti nella resistenza*, Milan, 1971; L. Valiani, *Tutte le strade conducono a Roma*, Bologna, 1983; L. Valiani, 'Il dibattito sul fascismo', *Nuova Antologia*, f. 2165, January–March 1988, pp. 167–71 (in debate with R. De Felice). In 1980, Valiani was elected a Senator for life and sat with the Republicans but he did not take out a party ticket. In 1945 Valiani had belonged to that leadership group of the Resistance who decided that it would be better for Mussolini to be executed than put on trial. Among his colleagues in this decision were Pertini, Longo, and historian Emilio Sereni. L. Valiani, *Sessant'anni di avventure e battaglie: riflessioni e ricordi raccolti da Massimo Pini*, Milan, 1983, pp. 98–100, 133.

92 N. Revelli, *La guerra dei poveri*, Turin, 1962. Another very typical publication of that moment was R. Zangrandi, *Il lungo viaggio attraverso il fascismo: contributo alla storia di una generazione*, Milan, 1962, which told of a resistance growing within Mussolini's own family entourage – Zangrandi had been a schoolboy friend of the *Duce*'s eldest son, Vittorio. By 1939 Zangrandi's group had set up a fledgling 'Revolutionary Socialist Party' in disgust at the hypocrisy which they had discerned in the 'Fascist Revolution'.

93 N. Revelli, *La guerra dei poveri*, pp. 4–5.

94 N. Revelli, *La guerra dei poveri*, p. 14.

95 N. Revelli, *La guerra dei poveri*, p. 129.

qui peut. Ten days later, he had taken to the hills. 'We did not want to hear anyone talk about politics. We were still soldiers. The Army was something more than and better than Fascism. It could be re-born in the aftermath of 8 September. . . . The people [too] were with us since every family had a son wandering somewhere. But they were with us prudently.'[96] Only as a partisan did Revelli realise that he was fighting for the reconstruction of Italy, for a new Italy, committed to 'moral rigour', to 'sacrifice' and to a 'future without war', to a Republic, to the final defeat of Fascism, to the *Partito d'Azione* and to the rejection of the corruption and compromise of the Italian South.[97] Revelli's life history became still more compelling as he revealed how he had been severely wounded in a fight and been taken off to Paris to have his face reconstructed: 'They tell me that I have acquired a nose [again]. I want to see myself, to know myself.'[98]

This moving account of the wars of the poor was followed by later oral histories in which Revelli continued to add the people's history to his own, revealing more about both the appalling experience of the Fascist armies in the USSR and peasant detachment from and hostility to the Italian nation state.[99] Each book in its way was a classic of humanist anti-Fascism, and was praised as such by reviewers. None the less, even as Revelli told of horror and suffering, of resistance and victory, his message had a soft side. His image of Italy remained, or at least could easily be read as, a populist one. The humble soldiers on the Eastern Front were victims of the Germans and of the ideology of Nazi-fascism, not of themselves. The partisans, fighting heroically for a better Italy, killed and maimed their enemies, but they only did so in a noble cause and using their weapons justly. They fought, too, as Italians; in September 1944 Revelli noted in his diary the arrival of US equipment, but added that it was still a partisans' war in which he served.[100] For Revelli, anti-Fascism was the cause of the (just) nation as much as anything else.

This historiographical popular front had its enemies: on the Right, of course, but also, as early as the 1960s, on the 'new Left'. The best-known denunciation of the too-cosy unanimity of 'anti-Fascist progressivism' was a literary history by the critic and philosopher Alberto Asor Rosa.[101] Daring even to doubt the 'great Gramsci', Asor Rosa warned that 'national populism' had been given too large a place in the past and declared that the resultant snugness was obscuring the path which ran from present to future.[102] The Resistance, and its portrayal, Asor Rosa argued, had had a

96 N. Revelli, *La guerra dei poveri*, pp. 127–8.
97 N. Revelli, *La guerra dei poveri*, p. 165.
98 N. Revelli, *La guerra dei poveri*, p. 314.
99 N. Revelli, *La strada del Davai*, Turin, 1966; *L'ultimo fronte. Lettere di soldati caduti o dispersi nella seconda guerra mondiale*, Turin, 1971 and *Il mondo dei vinti*, Turin, 1977.
100 N. Revelli, *La guerra dei poveri*, p. 291.
101 A. Asor Rosa, *Scrittori e popolo: il populismo nella letteratura italiana contemporanea*, Rome, 1972, p. vii. (This book was first published in 1965.)
102 A. Asor Rosa, *Scrittori e popolo*, pp. 3–4.

particularly negative effect when, for example, workers had been described as saving their factories for the nation rather than fighting for their class.[103]

No mainstream historian wrote a similar denunciation. But, very much expressing the spirit of 1968, Renzo Del Carria did produce a two-volume general history of Italy, *Proletari senza rivoluzione*. In a book which De Felice would later imply gave comfort to terrorists,[104] Del Carria depicted a nation which had only ever experienced *rivoluzioni mancate*.[105] In his reckoning, the Resistance was a spontaneous revolt, but this spontaneity was duly challenged and controlled by the PCI and the old order, and neutered into a *rivoluzione interrotta*.[106] The responsibility of the present, Del Carria implied, was not to seek out 'historic compromises', but to resume this interrupted revolution.[107]

Nor was his the only hard voice as the decade of the 1970s began. Published by Feltrinelli in Italian,[108] Giovanni Pesce's tough-minded memoir of the Resistance preached messages rather different from those of Revelli. Pesce's account fitted his title; he was one neither to seek nor to give quarter: 'In partisan warfare, objectives do not fall; they are destroyed. Enemy forces are not encircled; they are eliminated.'[109] The Resistance was not a time of nicety: 'A partisan was a fighter who never betrayed his [sic] companions. ... In every case, when a man became a potential danger to us, he automatically became an enemy.'[110]

Faced with these attacks from the Left, anti-Fascist commentators now made a number of attempts to tighten the definition of the Resistance and to abandon the solacing line, common in the 1960s, that the Resistance had been a victory of the whole people. The 'historic compromise' was envisaged, no doubt, as some sort of revived popular front, but somewhere to the right there were elements outside it. In his interview Giorgio Amendola was

---

103 A. Asor Rosa, *Scrittori e popolo*, pp. 157–8. 'Stalinists', he added, also favoured the idea of a general alliance. Though never a slavish follower of the party line, Asor Rosa would reconcile himself with the PCI, and, as communism fell, was acting as the last editor of the PCI's weekly theoretical magazine *Rinascita*. He would also be a key figure in the publication of the multi-volume Einaudi history of Italian literature and perhaps influence Einaudi's similar venture on history, the *Storia d'Italia*, a massive work of social and cultural history, with a frequent leaning to the left.

104 R. De Felice, 'Italian historiography since the Second World War', in R. J. B. Bosworth and G. Cresciani (eds), *Altro polo: a volume of Italian studies*, Sydney, 1979, p. 176. He would cite Spriano as agreeing with him.

105 R. Del Carria, *Proletari senza rivoluzione: storia delle classi subalterne italiane dal 1860 al 1950*, 2 vols., Milan, 1966. The book was republished in a number of different editions thereafter.

106 R. Del Carria, *Proletari senza rivoluzione*, ii. pp. 359–61.

107 Del Carria thought genuine revolutions could be located in China, the USSR, Cuba, Bulgaria and even Albania (R. Del Carria, *Proletari senza rivoluzione*, i. p. 16, n. 2).

108 Giangiacomo Feltrinelli, from the publishing family, was one of the odder figures of the time. He would die in March 1972, attempting to attach high explosives to an electricity pylon near Milan.

109 G. Pesce, *And no quarter: an Italian partisan in World War II: memoirs*, Cleveland, OH., 1972, p. 61.

110 G. Pesce, *And no quarter*, p. 243.

not, therefore, being especially original when he acknowledged that anti-Fascism must be understood as a movement which did not possess the unanimous support of the nation.[111] None the less, throughout the 1970s the PCI leadership did seek to picture the Resistance past as a time in which all progressive forces had banded together in the single cause. The comments of 1960s party leader and Spanish Civil War veteran Luigi Longo that, from the moment of its foundation, the PCI had led and dominated the whole cause of anti-Fascism were underplayed.[112] The fact that, in 1975–6, the Christian Democrats sought renewal through the figure of Benigno Zaccagnini, once a fighting partisan, was emphasised.[113] At communist morale- and fund-raising *Feste dell'Unità*, which were typical of the decade, a watermelon became an easy symbol of the nation. Like the national flag, it was green, white and red (or pink!). Naturally, it was the red part which offered the real nourishment. If there were black (Fascist) pips, destined to be spat out into the trash-can of history, they were few and easily detectable. Here, indeed, history was being manufactured as folklore, and a past of death and destruction had been reworked for its charm and contentment. It is not surprising that anti-Communists and their friends, and even some communist sympathisers, gagged at the mixture.

The PCI, like most Italian political movements, had always possessed its regional heartlands – its vote was usually highest in the Emilia-Romagna, Tuscany and Umbria, and, although in the aftermath of the 1975 regional elections communists took over the mayoral office in Rome and Naples, the centre-North would remain the party's redoubt as, from 1979, the electoral cycle turned against the PCI. Ironically, the lineaments of regional difference can also be detected in the historiography. De Felice and his school were making Rome their home; it was thence that they launched their assault on what they declared was an anti-Fascist hegemony (even though a prosopography would almost certainly demonstrate that the majority of chairs in history at Italian universities during the 1970s was held by an assortment of Crocean liberals, conservative patriots and other non-Communists). The opponents of De Felice, with Guido Quazza and Nicola Tranfaglia prominent, were instead based in the North, notably at the University of Turin, the *alma mater* of Gramsci and Togliatti. It is tempting to suggest that, just as once the Armed Resistance had been confined to the North, so the defence of anti-Fascism and the Resistance became, from 1975, the cause of 'northern intellectuals'.

111 G. Amendola, *Intervista sull'antifascismo*, pp. 169–70.
112 L. Longo, *Un popolo alla macchia*, Rome, 1965, pp. 11, 22. A third edition of this book
      was brought out in 1975.
113 See e.g. the autobiographical article about his experiences in the Ravenna Resistance in L.
      Bergonzini (ed.), *La resistenza in Emila-Romagna: rassegna di saggi critico-storici*,
      Bologna, 1976, pp. 315–30.

Guido Quazza, like Nuto Revelli, was another who had fought in the Resistance,[114] an experience he remembered fondly as a time in which his partisan band had acted as a 'microcosm of direct democracy',[115] and who had hoped greatly in Ferruccio Parri and the *Partito d'Azione*.[116] Just a month before the crucial 1976 national elections, Quazza, who was a leading member of the editorial board of the *Rivista di storia contemporanea*,[117] published a detailed reflection on the place of the Resistance in national history. He recalled 1968 as marking a 'watershed' in the efforts to comprehend the partisan war. Partly there had been a radical surge critical of what was perceived as the passivity of the left-wing parties. However, these attacks had in turn stimulated further research, which had resulted in a much more intricate picture of the whole experience of the Resistance.[118]

Despite his acceptance of the complex nature of the human condition, Quazza still preached that the message of the past was a need to continue the struggle: 'there has never been a time like the present in which [in the Gramscian formula] the pessimism of the intelligence and the optimism of the will are the essential conditions to comprehend both the history of the Resistance and the successive history of contemporary Italy'.[119] There had been no parenthesis in 1945, and many of the 'forms' of Fascism had survived. The Constitution, framed for the Republic in 1947, had a fictitious rather than a real relationship with the Resistance (and quite a lot of the fault for that lay with the compromises of Togliatti's PCI).[120] Militancy directed against the established order was still a good idea. After all, he stated clearly, the historiographical conflicts of the 1970s were 'in many senses a paradigm for [Italy's] entire national life'.[121]

Nor did Quazza change his views in the years which followed. In 1985, for example, he underlined how 'contemporary' the history of Fascism and its opposition remained: 'In the historiography there has never been a moment of peace and quiet about Fascism because there has never been a moment of peace and quiet about Fascism in the economic, social, political

---

114 C. Pavone, *Una guerra civile: saggio storico sulla moralità nella resistenza*, Turin, 1991, p. 14. See also his evocation of Ferruccio Parri, G. Quazza *et al.* (eds), *Ferruccio Parri: sessant'anni di storia italiana*, Bari, 1983.
115 C. Pavone, *Una guerra civile*, p. 130 citing G. Quazza, *Resistenza e storia d'Italia: problemi e ipotesi di ricerca*, Milan, 1976.
116 De Felice and the more extreme among his school seem to have reserved a greater animus against these 'traitors within the gates' than against more straightforward communists. See e.g. R. De Felice, *Intervista sul fascismo* (rev. ed.), Bari, 1997, p. 135.
117 Among his colleagues were Enzo Collotti, Giorgio Rochat and, for a time, Nicola Tranfaglia.
118 G. Quazza, *Resistenza e storia d'Italia*, pp. 19–20.
119 G. Quazza, *Resistenza e storia d'Italia*, p. 21.
120 G. Quazza, *Resistenza e storia d'Italia*, pp. 438–53.
121 G. Quazza, 'Il Fascismo: l'esame di coscienza degli italiani', in G. Quazza *et al.*, *Storiografia e fascismo*, Milan, 1985, p. 7.

and cultural struggle.'[122] With evident reference to De Felice, he added that those who inculcated ideology under the mantle of objectivity were behaving in the most manipulative way imaginable.[123] Even as the Berlin Wall fell, Quazza had no doubts: 'One can say with security that the ethical and civil progress of Italy finds its nerve centre . . . in anti-Fascism'.[124] In the new post-Communist world, he predicted optimistically, anti-Fascism would prove more alive than ever.[125] Quazza went to his death in July 1997 a convinced believer in the continuing morality of the Resistance.[126]

As prominent in the defence of the virtue of the history of anti-Fascism was the younger figure of Nicola Tranfaglia. He had been born in Naples in 1938, but had obtained a posting in Turin in 1976 and had stayed there. His first major book, a sympathetic study of the early career of Carlo Rosselli as an ideologue of anti-Fascism, had appeared in 1968.[127] Tranfaglia also rapidly made a name as a reviewer – in the pages of *Studi storici*, he was a very early critic of De Felice[128] – and as an editor.[129] His interest both in politics[130] and historiography made him especially alert to the role of recent history in the Italian Republic, and throughout the 1970s, 1980s and 1990s he regularly tried to rebut De Felice and his school, and resist their revision of the history of Fascism and anti-Fascism.[131] De Felice, Tranfaglia remarked, was frequently far too literal in his reading of his documents; when 'they spoke for themselves' they spoke misleadingly. De Felice thus

122 G. Quazza et al., *Storiografia*. This book was composed of chapters by members of the *Istituto nazionale per la storia del movimento di liberazione in Italia*.
123 G. Quazza et al., *Storiografia*, p. 23. Also criticising the rival conservative school in this volume were such well known Anti-Fascist historians as Enzo Collotti, Gianpasquale Santomassimo and Massimo Legnani.
124 G. Quazza, 'L'antifascismo nella storia italiana del Novecento', *Italia contemporanea*, 178, 1990, p. 5.
125 G. Quazza 'L'antifascismo', p. 16. Cf. also G. Quazza, 'Storia contemporanea nell'Università: la didattica come ricerca', *Rivista di storia contemporanea*, 17, 1989, pp. 477–516, asserting the primacy of the University of Turin in contemporary historical research.
126 For a studied obituary, see G. Perona, 'Guido Quazza, la storia come autobiografia', *Passato e presente*, 41, 1997, pp. 107–29.
127 N. Tranfaglia, *Carlo Rosselli dall'interventismo a 'Giustizia e Libertà'*, Bari, 1968. Cf. also N. Tranfaglia, *Dallo stato liberale al regime fascista: problemi e ricerche*, Milan, 1973.
128 N. Tranfaglia, 'Dalla neutralità italiana alle origini del fascismo', *Studi storici*, 10, 1969, pp. 335–86. Cf. also, 20 years later, his praise of Salvemini by contrast with De Felice, N. Tranfaglia, 'Gaetano Salvemini storico del fascismo', *Studi storici*, 29, 1988, pp. 903–23.
129 For example, he was to write the history of the Italian press with Valerio Castronovo, the director of a multi-volume project. See especially N. Tranfaglia, P. Murialdi and M. Legnani, *La stampa italiana nell'età fascista*, Bari, 1980. Cf. also N. Tranfaglia (ed.), *L'Italia unita nella storiografia del secondo dopoguerra*, Milan, 1980. Among the contributors here (they had originally spoken at a conference in Palermo in 1978) was, somewhat surprisingly, Rosario Romeo, who declared that 'the study of contemporary history is never merely an academic matter' (p. 293).
130 See e.g. N. Tranfaglia (ed.), *Mafia, politica e affari nell'Italia repubblicana 1943–1991*, Bari, 1992, which documented 'structural' evil, and a continuity in Italian history.
131 For a typical example see N. Tranfaglia, 'Fascismo e mass media: dall'intervista di De Felice agli sceneggiati televisivi', *Passato e presente*, 3, 1983, pp. 135–48.

underestimated Fascist coercion and forgot that, as an anti-Fascist stated in January 1935, 'death is called Fascism'.[132] He was also wrong to discount anti-Fascist sources, which retained both perspicacity and power.[133] Then as in more contemporary times, it was silly to over-generalise about the Left, since by definition it was variegated. During the 1970s, for example, Left historiography was as influenced by the *Annales* and sociology as it was by a simple dedication to anti-Fascism.[134]

After the publication in 1995 of De Felice's second interview,[135] Tranfaglia again tried to defend anti-Fascism against the idea that all the sins of the 'First Republic',[136] and notably the *partitocrazia* (domination by the parties), had sprung from it.[137] The real key to Fascism, he believed, was the *compromesso autoritario* (authoritarian compromise) of 1922–5. After 1926–7 Mussolini controlled the party for his own manipulative ends rather than to produce a cultural revolution. Similarly there was no real parenthesis in 1945, given that the Christian Democrats took over many of the laws and cultural attitudes of Fascism.[138] Togliatti and his party doubtless had their faults, but such limitations should not be allowed to obscure the DC's parochialism and its objection to free debate of any kind, which lasted certainly to the Tambroni affair and perhaps beyond.[139]

Indeed, at any time, Tranfaglia complained, serious debate about Italian history remained difficult to achieve. De Felice might possess great strengths as a researcher (even while there were many evident problems in his interpretations and his fixation on Mussolini as a Great Man), but would not discuss his ideas with any except his ideological friends. From 1987, his anti-communism, fitting easily into the new political mood and favoured by the old powers that be, led him to use history to justify the so-called *sdoganamento* (the end of the quarantine) of the neo-fascist MSI, which thus now possessed a present, a past and, presumably, a future.[140] But De Felice would not acknowledge the political effect of his work either. In the circumstances, Tranfaglia maintained stoutly, anti-Fascist historians and historians of anti-Fascism must go on asserting their own views, denying, for example, that 8 September represented the end of the Italian nation.[141]

132 N. Tranfaglia, *Labirinto italiano: radici storiche e nuove contraddizioni*, Turin, 1984, pp. 86–7, 111–12, 118.
133 N. Tranfaglia, *Labirinto italiano*, pp. 345–6.
134 N. Tranfaglia, *Labirinto italiano*, p. 223.
135 See above, pp. 17–19.
136 It was appropriate at this time that Tranfaglia should mourn Sandro Pertini who had died at the age of 94, unreconstructedly proud of a life spent fighting fascism. See N. Tranfaglia, 'La battaglia contro il fascismo', *Ventesimo secolo*, 5, 1995, pp. 219–25.
137 N. Tranfaglia, *Un passato scomodo: Fascismo e postfascismo*, Bari, 1996, p. ix. Cf. his own attempt to write a general history of Fascism, at least up to 1938. N. Tranfaglia, *La grande guerra e il Fascismo (1914–1938)*, Turin, 1995.
138 N. Tranfaglia, *Un passato scomodo*, pp. 9, 17.
139 N. Tranfaglia, *Un passato scomodo*, pp. 36–7.
140 N. Tranfaglia, *Un passato scomodo*, pp. 65–7, 79–80, 97–8.
141 N. Tranfaglia, *Un passato scomodo*, pp. 91–2.

It has been noted above that this interpretation of the resistance as a 'civil war' has been regularly preached by anti-anti-Fascist historians in contemporary Italy – indeed, in newspaper interviews, De Felice had been using the term since the early 1980s.[142] The fullest presentation of their case appeared in the incomplete final volume of De Felice's biography of Mussolini, published posthumously in 1997 through the efforts of Emilio Gentile, Luigi Goglia and others of the De Felice school.[143]

Somewhat appropriately, the biography ends in mid-stream, in January 1944, when Mussolini had just accepted the show trial and execution of his son-in-law Ciano, a vengeance demanded by the leaders of the 'radical' *Partito Fascista Repubblicano* (Republican Fascist Party), by Rachele, the *Duce*'s tough-minded wife, and by political self-interest (it is now that Mussolini uttered the direly narcissist cry: 'it is my singular destiny to be betrayed by everyone, even by my daughter').[144] In reaching this point, De Felice on his death had characteristically used more than 500 pages to advance the story by some six months, and had left uncovered more than a year of his subject's life.

In the sections he did complete, De Felice evinced a certain sympathy for the restored dictator, deciding charitably that Mussolini's motivations in accepting the leadership of the Salò Republic included both a desire to leave some form of Fascist revolutionary idea as a legacy to 'history'[145] and a belief that, if he did not interpose his body as a shield against Nazi German wrath, Italy would be treated 'like Poland' by its erstwhile allies.[146] De Felice also made plain some of the internal conflicts which had riddled Salò – it was a time when Fascist quarrelled with Fascist, Army fought against Militia, the Germans had little respect or patience to waste on their half-allies and more-than-half-puppets, the Anglo-Americans held no love for Italy as they advanced slowly from the south, while, De Felice concluded, for Mussolini 'the most dangerous enemy of all was the party [PFR], but he understood that he could not govern without it.'[147]

---

142 See e.g. *L'Espresso*, 30, 5 August 1984.
143 R. De Felice, *Mussolini l'alleato 1940–1945 II. La guerra civile 1943–1945*, Turin, 1997. An anonymous preface writer notes that the book remained incomplete and that 'it is not possible to say how many and what chapters the author foresaw himself composing to end the volume' (p. ix). De Felice had left no plan in what had become a story of unfinished sympathy between historian and Mussolini.
144 R. De Felice, *Mussolini l'alleato 1940–1945 II*, pp. 522, 527.
145 For at least a decade De Felice had made plain his belief that honourable and radical men had backed Salò. See e.g. R. De Felice (ed.), 'Dalle "Memorie" di Fulvio Balisti: un dannunziano di fronte alla crisi del 1943 e alla Repubblica Sociale Italiana', *Storia contemporanea*, 17, 1986, pp. 469–516. Cf. also De Felice's use of the memoirs, which are indeed fascinating, of an upright career official, G. Dolfin, *Con Mussolini nella tragedia: diario del capo della segretaria particolare del Duce 1943–1944*, Cernusco sul Naviglio, 1949.
146 R. De Felice, *Mussolini l'alleato 1940–1945 II*, pp. 64–9, 343–5.
147 R. De Felice, *Mussolini l'alleato 1940–1945 II*, p. 510.

However, the main part of this last volume of De Felice's work is centred on one short and one long chapter in which Mussolini hardly appears and which analyse instead 'the national catastrophe of 8 September' 1943[148] and 'the drama of the Italian people caught between Fascists and partisans'.[149] Now it is that De Felice argues the case of a 'civil war' with disastrous and lasting effects on Republican Italy. 'Foreigners', he says sadly, still carry an image of Italy coloured by the ruin of Badoglio, King Victor Emmanuel III, the Army and the other institutions of the nation state. The bourgeoisie as a whole bore special responsibility for this catastrophe; and the result of their dereliction and that of others was that Italians after 1945 could not 'construct the bases of a national moral and material unity'.[150]

The most obvious competing parties in the civil war, in De Felice's eyes, could not be separated either morally or practically. Each began spontaneously, but each was then dominated by forces connected with foreign powers, the *repubblichini* (De Felice avoids the term) by Nazi Germany and communist partisans by the USSR. Each was capable of violence (even if De Felice noted on a couple of occasions that Salò moderates, including the *Duce*, were frustrated by the deliberate provocations of the communists, who knowingly unleashed Salò Fascist retribution on the populace at large).[151] Similarly deplorable, at least according to De Felice, were non-Communist partisans like Ferruccio Parri and Sandro Pertini. Parri, in particular, deserved blame for the mistaken views that pre-Fascist Italy had not been a democracy and that, at the end of the Second World War, a social revolution was necessary. This sort of historical error damaged the formation of the Republic and freed too great an ideological space for the PCI.[152]

While fanatics, cynics and the unlucky battled out their unrewarding conflict, the populace at large, De Felice reiterated, had wished a plague on both their houses. Ordinary Italians sought simply to survive from one day to the next and prayed for the warring to cease. It was thus 'not possible to define the Resistance as a popular mass movement'.[153] In turn, De Felice argued these terrible events and the suppression of their 'true' history scoured the path of the nation thereafter. Moreover, despite the minority nature of the conflict, De Felice added with some contradiction, 'Italy then knew a civil war of a dimension and significance unparalleled in any other country except perhaps Yugoslavia'.[154] Here, with a curious combination of parochialism and moralising amorality, ended the De Felice lessons. If his interpretation was to be believed, there was no right or wrong in the Second

---

148 R. De Felice, *Mussolini l'alleato 1940–1945 II*, pp. 72–102.
149 R. De Felice, *Mussolini l'alleato 1940–1945 II*, pp. 103–342.
150 R. De Felice, *Mussolini l'alleato 1940–1945 II*, pp. 87, 99.
151 R. De Felice, *Mussolini l'alleato 1940–1945 II*, pp. 125, 173–5, 184, 323–7.
152 R. De Felice, *Mussolini l'alleato 1940–1945 II*, pp. 168–9.
153 R. De Felice, *Mussolini l'alleato 1940–1945 II*, pp. 178, 275.
154 R. De Felice, *Mussolini l'alleato 1940–1945 II*, p. 340.

World War, just competing interests, and the real casualty of the war had been the noble commitment of the better sort of Italians[155] to the nation.

It was natural that, from time to time in his text, De Felice should condemn what he perceived as the failings of 'anti-Fascist historiography'.[156] As was noted at the beginning of this book, the major non-De Felicean account of the period is Claudio Pavone's essay *Una guerra civile* (1991), on the 'morality' of the Resistance.[157] It goes without saying that, although Pavone had used the term 'civil war' and argued forcibly for a more textured reading of the period from 1943–5 which would take into account its ideological, national, patriotic and class aspects, his views remain widely separated from those of De Felice. For the self-consciously anti-Fascist Pavone, the Second World War was still a 'good war', one in which virtue won and evil was defeated. Similarly, Pavone was scarcely a convert to the De Felice school's opaque lucubrations about the death or wounding of the Italian nation during the fall of Fascism. Rather, anti-Fascism remained a cause in which to believe and which still connected the past to a good future.

To a very considerable extent, the debate between the De Feliceans and their rivals was and is a dialogue of the deaf, having little impact on the history of those Italian people who, at one time or another and in one way or another, rejected the basic theses of Fascism. However, it would be a mistake to conclude that it amounts to a historiographical black hole. The fine efforts of Luisa Passerini to understand the 'passive dissent' of the housewives of Turin and of Roger Absalom to comprehend the reaction of northern peasants to Allied escapers after 8 September 1943 have already been noted,[158] and those two are not the only historians to have attempted a history from below of anti-Fascism and Resistance.

In the histories of the Resistance, women, for example, have long been accorded a place. However, the rise of feminism has increasingly made it seem a subordinate and inadequate place, which by no means automatically led to an improvement in women's role in Italian society during the first decades of the Republic. The sense that Italy's experience of the Second World War should be examined as a time when women, though 'unarmed', endured the conflict has stimulated research.[159] The most wide-ranging social history of the Resistance (in peace if not in war), Giovanni De Luna's account of anti-Fascism in national society from 1922 to 1939, pays special

155 Inevitably, among these is numbered Giovanni Gentile. R. De Felice, *Mussolini l'alleato 1940–1945 II*, pp. 483–4.
156 R. De Felice, *Mussolini l'alleato 1940–1945 II*, pp. 163, 235–6.
157 C. Pavone, *Una guerra civile*, Turin, 1991 and see Chapter 1.
158 See Chapters 1 and 6. Cf. the cultural history of the war written by Mario Isnenghi, which emphasises, perhaps with some exaggeration, the commonality of vocabulary of the rival sides. M. Isnenghi, 'La guerra civile nella pubblicista di destra', *Rivista di storia contemporanea*, 18, 1989, pp. 104–15 and, more generally, M. Isnenghi, *Le guerre degli italiani: parole, immagini, ricordi 1848–1945*, Milan, 1989.
159 See A. Bravo and A. M. Bruzzone, *In guerra senza armi: storie di donne, 1940–1945*, Bari, 1995.

attention to the experience of women. Utilising the records collected by the Fascist Special Tribunal, De Luna has sought to recreate the everyday life of its victims, some hundreds of whom were women. De Luna follows the methods of *Alltagesgeschichte* in evoking their pains and their joys, and in comprehending what he calls their 'existential', not their 'political' anti-Fascism.[160] In his view, politics and ideology were secondary matters for the great majority. Spirit, soul, love, the family, all might make an individual take the step from a generic anti-Fascism to membership of the Communist party, or *Giustizia e Libertà*, or some other anti-Fascist grouping. The humanity came first, the political commitment later: 'Only with difficulty did one start as a Communist or a member of *GeL* and turn into an anti-Fascist. Rather the contrary was always true. One was an anti-Fascist and hence looked for a contact with the organised parties in order to activate a choice which in its first origin was not exclusively political.'[161]

De Luna suggests, somewhat boldly, that his approach can represent a way around what he calls 'the interminable game of historiographical ping-pong' between anti-Fascist and anti-anti-Fascist readings of the past.[162] Certainly De Luna's detail is interesting and significant and, in general, his book takes the reader closer to the minds and sentiments of the subjects of Fascist Italy than do many other accounts. It is also another antidote to any idea that Fascism achieved its totalitarian intent. In De Luna's account of Italian society, the family, the Church, the market, love, opportunity for advantage and tradition render totalitarianism contradictory in practice and impossible of realisation.[163] None the less, the 'everyday' history approach always carries the risk of designing a Fascism with the Fascism (and anti-Fascism) left out, and of privileging a crude populism in which the meek and only the meek are always blessed, and those who make ideas, or exercise political, social and economic power, do not matter at all.

It is appropriate to end this survey of the historiography of anti-Fascism in a state of some equivocation. Those who constructed a heroic and overtly didactic history of anti-Fascism, and used it both to justify the existence of the Italian Republic and to urge its reform in a leftwards direction, are plainly out of tune with politics after the 'end of history'. The Italian Communist party is no more and, having lost its future, it scarcely needs a past to cheer its members, to allure its friends and to affright its enemies. At the same time, although the PCI has followed the USSR into the shadow world, the social and ethical forces which gave the PCI a special place certainly in Italian and perhaps in international history are, arguably, not yet completely exhausted. In a new millennium it will be important to understand that anti-Fascists were as frail and divided as human beings

160 G. De Luna, *Donne in oggetto: l'antifascismo nella società italiana 1922–1939*, Turin, 1995, p. 11.
161 G. De Luna, *Donne in oggetto*, p. 117.
162 G. De Luna, *Donne in oggetto*, p. 20.
163 G. De Luna, *Donne in oggetto*, pp. 35–8.

generally are, and that they were capable of both cruelty and fatuity as well as of courage and selflessness. It will be a shame, however, if those who remained unconvinced by the Fascist regime between 1922 and 1940, and who stubbornly imagined its downfall, do not retain some historical recognition. It will be worse still if the period from 1943 to 1945 is read as no more than a civil war, in which it is utterly impossible to distinguish the virtue and vice of the combatants. After all, it is still true that, as one sympathetic historian put it: 'Historically, anti-Fascism acted as the bridge across which Italy could pass to a modern democracy.'[164] It similarly remains true that, in a democracy, a history which does not draw lessons from the past is of more menacing potential than a history which does.

---

164 N. Gallerano, 'Memoria pubblica del Fascismo e dell'antifascismo', in G. Calchi Novati *et al.*, *Politiche della memoria*, Rome, 1993, p. 18.

9

Italian Fascism and Models of Fascism

In 1930 Plinio Salgado, an army officer's son in his forties, returned to his native Brazil after a visit to Fascist Italy. He had been impressed by what he saw: 'The Italian man [today] stands in the fullness of his integrity. He is a complete man.' Indeed, Salgado added prophetically, 'the concept of Fascism will be the light of the new age'.[1] As if to prepare for this happy event, Salgado set up the Brazilian integralist movement, or AIB, on the admired Roman model. By 1934 he claimed to have attracted 180 000 members, and had designed for them a green shirt with black or blue armbands featuring the letter sigma. By that time he expected his followers to goose-step when on parade, while he himself had acquired a small tooth-brush moustache and was given to anti-Semitic pronouncements.[2] In 1937 Salgado, expecting the chance to make an integralist revolution, helped Getulio Vargas, the military-backed president, stage a coup. However, within a month Vargas had betrayed him, banned political parties and cemented his own position as dictator. Accepting these changes meekly enough, Salgado, after a brief flirtation with local monarchists, went into exile the following year in Portugal.[3]

This small story suggests how perplexing it can be to place Mussolini's regime within any model of generic (or small f-) fascism. The *Duce* and his tame philosophers and historians may have declared that fascism was the ideology of the twentieth century. The Fascist regime may even for a time have sponsored a fascist International, paying subsidies to, and attracting the interest of, such luminaries as the Dutchman Simon Ooms, the Swiss Colonel Fonjallez[4] and the fertile English writer and resident in Florence,

1 R. M. Levine, *The Vargas regime: the critical years, 1934–1938*, New York, 1970, p. 81.
2 R. M. Levine, *The Vargas regime*, pp. 83–5.
3 R. M. Levine, *The Vargas regime*, pp. 159–64.
4 M. Ledeen, *Universal Fascism: the theory and practice of the Fascist International, 1928–1936*, New York, 1972, p. 84.

James Strachey Barnes.[5] However, none of these individuals proved to be a historical winner, and the idea of an International under the guidance of Rome soon dissipated. Certainly, in the 1990s the triumph of market liberalism is so overwhelming that any fascist pretensions to universality and durability are hard to take seriously. Even in the 1930s, there was something risible about fascist internationalism, as Salgado's moustache suggested. Once Nazism had made its appearance on the historical stage, who would bother to look to Rome? From 1933, to use that public-school vocabulary easily adopted by certain English politicians, was not Hitler dictator major and Mussolini dictator minor?

This political reality was promptly replicated in scholarship. During the 1930s and thereafter, was not the key purpose in examining Italian Fascism frequently that of trying to get better purchase on Nazism and those of its policies which took the world to 'Auschwitz'? Are not all non-Italian historians of twentieth-century Italy, in a sense, the pensioners of Adolf Hitler, relying on his 'charisma', which has proved so durable after his death, to send them students and readers? As, in these next pages, I assess the significance which Italy has assumed in the various models of generic fascism, one question will be insistent: Did the Italian fascist regime and ideology matter in themselves, or were they regularly treated only as a yardstick with which to measure the achievement and wickedness of Nazi Germany?

Before reviewing the academic work, however, it is worthwhile briefly pondering any generalisations about Fascism which were made in the 1920s, when the Nazis were only one among a number of German rightist groups to receive unreliable sympathy and subsidy from Rome.[6] During that decade, figures on the right, impressed by talk of a fascist philosophy, or by events in Italy, or, most significantly, by glad tidings of the routing of the Bolshevik devil,[7] took to borrowing the word 'fascist' from Italian and deploying it in their own language, with somewhat uncertain effect. Among them were Miss Rotha Linthorn-Orman, a spinster and Field-Marshal's granddaughter, and Brigadier-General R. G. D. Blakeney, once the manager

5 M. Ledeen, *Universal Fascism*, p. 86 notes that, from 1928, Barnes headed a *Centre international d'études sur le fascisme* which published work by Gioacchino Volpe, Luigi Villari and others. For more on Barnes, see his own explanations of Fascism, J. S. Barnes, *The universal aspects of Fascism*, London, 1928; *Fascism*, London, 1931, and his autobiography, *Io amo l'Italia: memorie di un giornalista inglese*, Milan, 1939, in which he modestly listed himself as another among the throng who, at one time or another, was considered for the throne of Albania (pp. 129–31).
6 For some droll detail see A. Cassels, *Mussolini's early diplomacy*, Princeton, 1970, pp. 166–74, 353–5. The Nazis of Bavaria in 1922–3 let at least their Italian interlocutors believe that they defined themselves as 'fascists'.
7 For a splendid and typical period piece, see 'Sir' Percival Phillips, *The 'Red Dragon' and the Black Shirts: how Fascist Italy found her soul: the true story of the Fascisti movement*, London, 1923. It was, of course, W. S. Churchill who found the most fervent words about the Mussolinian victory over 'the bestial appetites and passions of Leninism'. C. Hibbert, *Benito Mussolini: the rise and fall of the Duce*, Harmondsworth, 1962, p. 96.

of the Egyptian state railways and now her rival at the head of the 'British Fascisti'. Whoever assumed the mantle of its leadership, however, this organisation scarcely secured a mass base; but it did count among its converts A. E. R. Gilligan, sometime England fast-bowler and cricket captain, as well as, eventually, a renowned BBC cricket commentator.[8] By Gilligan's definition, 'Fascisti-ism' sounded a bit like muscular Christianity. As he explained in an article for the Fascisti bulletin: 'On cricket tours it is essential to work solely on the lines of Fascism, i.e. a team must be good friends and out for one thing, and one thing only, namely the good of the side, and not for any self-glory'.[9]

Somewhat more subtle in his intellectualising was Georges Valois, who in 1925 proclaimed himself the leader of the French Fascists, or *Faisceau*.[10] Valois despised hedonism and endorsed Social Darwinism, while also seeking a genuine fusion of nationalism and socialism. His movement peaked early, however, and the *Faisceau* then lost ground in the complex conflicts of the myriad of grouplets on the French right. After being assaulted by a young *Camelot du Roi*, Valois drifted left, favouring the Resistance during the war and dying a prisoner of the Nazis.

Most effusive in his worship of the light shining from Rome was the Spanish military and monarchist dictator General Miguel Primo De Rivera. This corrupt old soldier told Mussolini in 1923: 'Your figure is not just an Italian one. You are the apostle of the world campaign against dissolution and anarchy.' 'Fascism,' Primo added piously, 'is a universal phenomenon that ought to conquer all nations. ... Fascism is a living Gospel.'[11] Thereafter he sought to apply some populist lustre to his regime by invoking a 'Latin fascism'; but, in practice, his government failed either to 'nationalise' its masses, or even minimally to carry through a fascist 'revolution'.

However, the real theorisers of a generic fascism in the 1920s came not from the right but the left. For Marxists, the international context of Italian Fascism was set by those authoritarian and 'counter-revolutionary' regimes which had prevailed in Hungary and other parts of Eastern Europe after 1919, and which may have been prefigured in that gathering of the right defeated in 1917 in the Kornilov affair and thereafter in the Russian Civil War. Thus the Hungarian Djula Sas published in German in 1923 an account of Italian Fascism, emphasising that the movement acted in the interests of big capital and 'was not a speciality of Italy alone but rather of

8 A. Moore, 'The "Fascist" cricket tour of 1924–5', *Sporting Traditions: Journal of the Australian society for sports history*, 7, 1991, pp. 164–74. F. C. Toone, the manager of the MCC team on this tour, also belonged to the Fascisti.
9 A. Moore, 'The "Fascist" cricket tour', p. 167.
10 For a defence of this group, see A. Douglas, 'Violence and Fascism: the case of the *Faisceau*', *Journal of Contemporary History*, 19, 1984, pp. 689–712; and his *From Fascism to libertarian communism: Georges Valois against the French Republic*, Berkeley, 1992.
11 S. Ben-Ami, *Fascism from above: the dictatorship of Primo de Rivera in Spain 1923–1930*, Oxford, 1983, pp. 131–2.

the most immediate relevance on the international plane'.[12] Sas, as a good communist of his time, went on to blame Italy's 'social democrats' for the 'political' defeat which had permitted the Fascist rise to power. He admitted, however, that Mussolini had secured the support of many petits bourgeois and peasants, and even some workers.[13] In his eyes Fascism did possess a mass base, and he warned that a similar project was conceivable throughout Central Europe unless communists actively prosecuted revolution there. Moreover, he concluded ominously, Fascism's triumph there 'would entail the victory of Fascism in the whole capitalist world'.[14]

In June 1923 the Comintern, accepting that events in Italy were bringing to the surface international structures and not just Italian ones, agreed on a definition of fascism which did not depart far from Sas' line.[15] Even if the issue of a mass base caused continuing debate, Marxists continued to view fascism as possessing a significance beyond Italy.[16] Indeed, the word became a sort of shorthand term for all enemies of the ('genuine') left. By the end of the 1920s, communists would be notoriously obliged to accept the thesis of 'social fascism', which maintained that any whose politics were placed to the right of the Party were fascists at heart, the running dogs of capital, the 'objective' agents of the bourgeoisie.[17] This theory would in turn explain the practice of the German communists in not opposing the rise of the Nazis with complete conviction. The KPD had loyally espoused the 'worse the better' principle, believing that the Nazis would at last reveal the 'real' character of the bourgeoisie and its governance, and thus of 'social fascism'.

As has already been noted, however, the Nazis' accession to power vastly diminished the apparent significance of the Italian regime in elucidating the meaning of generic fascism. Leon Trotsky was one who, while affirming the view that Mussolini had risen by exploiting petit bourgeois fears and ambitions, and had then done nothing to satisfy them in office except to create a personal and bureaucratic regime, now thought that it was Germany which mattered more. Revolutionary Marxists like himself, he noted, were interested in divining when Mussolini might fall. But, he predicted in January 1932, 'without venturing into the risky business of setting dates, one can still say that Hitler's victory in Germany would mean a new and long lease of life for Mussolini. Hitler's crash will mean the

---

12 D. Sas, 'Il Fascismo italiano', in R. De Felice (ed.), *Antologia sul fascismo: il giudizio politico*, Bari, 1976, p. 70. The book's original version was G. Aquila (pseudonym), *Der Faschismus in Italien*, Hamburg, 1923.
13 R. De Felice (ed.), *Antologia sul fascismo*, pp. 75–6.
14 R. De Felice (ed.), *Antologia sul fascismo*, p. 79.
15 See R. De Felice, *Le interpretazioni del fascismo*, Bari, 1971, pp. 70–3.
16 For examples see G. Sandomirskij, 'Il fascismo' and M. Rákosi, 'Il fascismo italiano', as excerpted in R. De Felice (ed.), *Antologia sul fascismo*, pp. 81–105. Both were originally published in the USSR, Sandomirskij in 1923, Rákosi in 1925.
17 For the background, see L. Ceplair, *Under the shadow of war: Fascism, Anti-Fascism and Marxists, 1918–1939*, New York, 1987, pp. 47–51.

beginning of the end for Mussolini.'[18] Once the Nazis achieved office, Trotsky warned against underestimating them; the history of Italian Fascism, he observed, had already indicated that a fascist dictator could avoid carrying out the more 'fantastic' parts of his programme, especially those which promised some form of social justice.[19] He surmised, none the less, that the pace of history was accelerating: 'German fascism operates at a speedier tempo than Italian fascism – not only because Hitler can take advantage of the experience of Mussolini, but primarily because of the higher-level social structure of Germany and the greater acuteness of its contradictions.'[20]

A more thorough 'Trotskyist' account of generic fascism (one destined to be regularly reprinted) was provided by the French journalist, Daniel Guerin, in 1936.[21] Guerin was unusual in treating the histories of Germany and Italy as equivalent, but he was also convinced that the Italian origins of fascism were somewhat accidental; the ideology and the policies it favoured were 'universal'.[22] In his eyes, both Italy and Germany were 'backward', latecomers in the imperialist thrust for a 'place in the sun'. As a result, their heavy industrial and banking sectors were all the more 'anxious', resorting compulsively to fascism when there were threats to their profits.[23] Everyone was a little surprised, however, that the hiring of armed bands resulted in a fascist seizure of state power, and, thereafter, both the 'parvenu' fascist leaders and the capitalist groups remained notably suspicious of each other.[24] Even in the mid-1930s, the divisions and fears which eddied through the class base of each of the fascist regimes offered hope and opportunity to their genuinely revolutionary Marxist opponents, those who realised that the permanent enemy was not so much fascism as capital.[25] Guerin remained uncertain whether fascism meant war, but was convinced that capitalism did. In other words, he explored generic fascism less to understand it than to throw light on what he already knew to be the pernicious nature of capitalism.

Marxists were not the only ones who believed that any explanation of fascism assisted the comprehension of the world order (and in their accounts, non-Marxists, too, frequently revealed more about themselves than about the subjects they purported to study). As has been noted throughout this book, the main anti-Marxist approach to fascism was the 'model of totalitarianism', the fundamental ideas of which were already extant before 1939, even though the formal model had to await its crafting

18 L. Trotsky, *The struggle against fascism in Germany*, Harmondsworth, 1975, p. 166. Trotsky did reject the 'social fascist' line and blamed it on Stalin (see p. 451).
19 L. Trotsky, *The struggle against fascism in Germany*, p. 417.
20 L. Trotsky, *The struggle against fascism in Germany*, p. 423.
21 D. Guerin, *Fascism and big business*, rev. ed., New York, 1973.
22 D. Guerin, *Fascism and big business*, p. 21.
23 D. Guerin, *Fascism and big business*, pp. 22–4.
24 D. Guerin, *Fascism and big business*, p. 62.
25 D. Guerin, *Fascism and big business*, p. 288.

by Friedrich and Brzezinski in 1956.[26] During the 1950s[27] and again during the 1980s and 1990s, totalitarianist theory was pervasive in the 'West', both in the academy and in public discourse, the absence of totalitarianism in that sphere being frequently viewed as the proof of virtue of liberal, free-market 'democracy' – while the Second World War was still being disputed the 'rationalist' economist F. A. Hayek had decreed that any form of social planning carried totalitarian tendencies.[28] The other great purpose of most totalitarianist theory was to implicate either 'Stalinism' or the Russian revolution as a whole in the evident crimes of Nazism. Explaining Nazi Germany, and, certainly, elucidating the history of Fascist Italy were no more than corollaries of what increasingly became a conservative political operation in the ongoing Cold War. Because the emphasis given to Germino's utilisation of the theory in the 1950s, and De Felice and Gentile's subsequent revival of it, has been scrutinised in earlier chapters, further comment on totalitarianism is unnecessary here. But a reader should recall that many of the post-1956 attempts to define 'generic fascism' have been influenced by a desire to amplify, shore up or replace the explanatory power of the model of totalitarianism.

Friedrich and Brzezinski were political scientists, not historians, and their work is a reminder of the fact that the crisis of the twentieth century has attracted the attention of a great variety of social scientists. For example, the 1930s saw the birth of 'psychological theories of fascism'. As the decade began the American psychologist Harold Lasswell was already wondering about the relationship between 'psychopathology' and politics.[29] In 1933, he moved naturally to discuss the 'psychology of Hitlerism', blaming events in Germany on 'the psychological impoverishment of the lower middle classes' there.[30]

Pushing the evidence further and more speculatively was Wilhelm Reich who, in that portentous year of the Nazi accession to power, published his zany work, *The mass psychology of fascism*. Despite his title, Reich argued that the real key to fascist behaviour was psychosexual. Linking the ideas of Marx and Freud, he urged that fascism, 'the most extreme representative of political and economic reaction', had 'become an international reality', outstripping its rivals on the left.[31] Fascism was, he added, not ascribable to either Mussolini and Hitler as Great Men, but amounted instead to the 'expression of the irrational structure of mass man [sic]'.[32] However, when

---

26 See Chapter 2.
27 In Italy it was easy enough to find droll examples of PCI spokespersons in the 1950s worrying about the 'clerical totalitarianism' which they thought that the DC may have been plotting through, for example, the *legge truffa*. M. Flores, 'L'Antifascismo all'opposizione', in M. Argentieri *et al.*, *Fascismo e antifascismo negli anni della Repubblica*, Milan, 1986, p. 52.
28 F. A. Hayek, *The road to serfdom*, Chicago, 1944, p. xiv.
29 H. D. Lasswell, *Psychology and politics*, New York, 1960 (first published, 1930).
30 H. D. Lasswell, 'The psychology of Hitlerism', *Political Quarterly*, 4, 1933, pp. 373–84.
31 W. Reich, *The mass psychology of fascism*, rev. ed., London, 1972, p. 3.
32 W. Reich, *The mass psychology of fascism*, p. xx.

it came to focusing his analysis, Reich concentrated almost exclusively on Germany, as he explored the impact of the Depression on German lives, expectations and sexuality. The *Führerprinzip*, racism, the swastika – all were examined and explained as manifestations of the kinks and repressions in Germany's 'sex economy'. The Italian case, however, was either assumed or ignored; indeed, in the later editions of his work Reich was most interested in what his theorising could demonstrate about the 'totalitarian' experiences of Germany and the USSR.

The outbreak of the Second World War opened further opportunities for psychologists, the most notorious of whom belonged to an American team which set out to psychoanalyse Hitler in his absence.[33] These experts suggested that the *Führer* was a 'neurotic psychopath',[34] who was deeply troubled sexually: Hitler, they averred, liked watching scantily clad actresses through powerful opera glasses, and especially when they bent over.[35] Mussolini, whose sexual appetites may have seemed depressingly 'normal', at least for an Italian male of his era, was not the object of such fascinated scrutiny, although the Americans did transport some of his brain tissue to the USA in 1945 and then took 20 years to restore it to Rachele, his wife. Eventually, 'the tissue was delivered in six test tubes in a wooden box, with the compliments of the American ambassador in Rome'.[36] However, rather than searching for more exotic forms of psychopathology, the interest of US scientists seems to have lain in discovering whether the *Duce* was syphilitic.

The war had also seen the publication of Erich Fromm's *The fear of freedom*, a work which, as has been noted above, had a considerable resonance in Italy because of its apparent influence on Moravia's novel, *The Conformist*, and the subsequent Bertolucci film of the same title.[37] Fromm was another who began with the thesis that fascism and the general 'crisis of democracy' did not constitute 'a peculiarly Italian or German problem'. The trouble, it seemed, was but part of the fate of 'modern man' and his 'sado-masochistic' fear of being genuinely free.[38] When, however, Fromm presented his evidence, he made no serious reference to Italy. Rather, he again defined fascism as a German product, or at least gave primacy to the German case – Fromm thought that Luther and the Reformation had quite

33 For an account both of Hitler and the process involved, see W. C. Langer, *The mind of Adolf Hitler*, London, 1973. Cf. also E. Erikson, 'Hitler's imagery and German youth', *Psychiatry*, 5, 1942, pp. 475–94. Here Erikson urged that Hitler and his Germans should be regarded as 'delinquent adolescents' who had allowed themselves to be carried away by 'hysterical abandon'. The Japanese, Erikson added, though operating in a 'different setting', were 'of equal suggestibility and of equal hateful defensiveness' (p. 492).
34 W. C. Langer, *The mind of Adolf Hitler*, p. 17.
35 W. C. Langer, *The mind of Adolf Hitler*, p. 94.
36 J. P. Diggins, *Mussolini and Fascism: the view from America*, Princeton, 1972, p. xv.
37 See Chapter 7.
38 E. Fromm, *The fear of freedom*, London, 1942, pp. 3, 200.
39 E. Fromm, *The fear of freedom*, pp. 62–77.

a lot to answer for in regard to German fearfulness,[39] but it was hard to see how they had generated Italian Fascism.[40]

Nor did this situation change when, from the 1970s, psychohistory became an academically popular undertaking. Both Kaiser Wilhelm II and Hitler[41] had their lives explained by psychohistorians, but Mussolini did not. Peter Loewenberg sought the origins of the 'Nazi youth cohort' in German adolescents' experience of the First World War, especially during the 'turnip winter' of 1916–17 when, he averred, young boys were damagingly deprived of fathers, food, comfort, love and hope.[42] The comparative question – whether Germans' experiences were different from those of their age group in other embattled countries – was an obvious one, but Loewenberg did not ask it; and certainly no historian of Fascist Italy has endeavoured to read the psychic health of its citizens, let alone provide a separate diagnosis of each class, region, age cohort and gender. Apart from the basic and established point that the experience of the front in the First World War had an influence on those who returned, a theme recently re-emphasised by Emilio Gentile with his ideas about Fascism-as-holy-militia, psychohistory has cast little light on the history of Italian Fascism. In some sort of reciprocation, this history has been treated by psychohistorians as too outlandish or insignificant to be worthy of their major attention.

Other social scientists were also active in applying the skills of their disciplines to the understanding of fascism. Among sociologists,[43] the most prominent early figure in the Anglo-Saxon world was Talcott Parsons, a student of the twentieth-century crisis of the middle class. Parsons had direct experience of Germany[44] – he was an exchange student there, gaining

40 Similarly, the 'Frankfurt school' in emigration in the USA were interested both in Nazism and in their new environment in the United States, but not in Italy, though Herbert Marcuse in the early 1960s thought that the practical moderation of the PCI gave (alarming) evidence of the creation of 'one-dimensional man'. See H. Marcuse, *One-dimensional man: studies in the ideology of advanced industrial societies*, London, 1964, pp. 20–1. Cf., by contrast, the pioneering work of T. W. Adorno *et al.*, *The authoritarian personality*, New York, 1950, which is preoccupied with Germany, the USA and the USSR, but which ignores Italy.

41 The most credulous example is R. G. L. Waite, *The psychopathic God: Adolf Hitler*, New York, 1977.

42 See e.g. P. Loewenberg, 'The psychohistorical origins of the Nazi youth cohort', *American Historical Review*, 76, 1971, pp. 1457–502; 'Psychohistorical perspectives on modern German history', *Journal of Modern History*, 47, 1975, pp. 229–79.

43 For further exploration of the background, see R. C. Bannister, 'Principle, politics, profession: American sociologists and fascism', in S. P. Turner and D. Käsler (eds), *Sociology responds to fascism*, London, 1992, pp. 172–213.

44 German sociologists had begun to review Fascism in the 1920s. Their most renowned figure was the half-Italianised Roberto Michels, who in 1928 took the chair in political science at the new Fascist University of Perugia. Before 1933 most German sociologists, including Michels, were not convinced that Fascism was replicated by Nazism. For a review, see D. Käsler and T. Steiner, 'Academic discussion on political guidance: social-scientific analyses of fascism and National Socialism in Germany before 1933', in S. P. Turner and D. Käsler (eds), *Sociology responds to fascism*, pp. 88–100.

a Ph.D. from Heidelberg in 1927[45] – and explaining Nazism became one of his major scholarly aims. When he thought comparatively he was one of a number of scholars who wanted to trace the difference in the path to modernity traversed by Germany, Britain and the United States. To be sure, during the Second World War he did make some attempt to explore generic fascism, urging that the movement should be understood as a 'radicalism of the Right', possessing a mass base, dependent on the 'irrational' for its appeal, nurtured by the pervasive sense of anomie afflicting modern man, and, above all, not being a product of capitalism.[46] Aside from an acknowledgement to Pareto, however, Parsons did not make direct reference to Italy in coming to his views.

Rather more detailed in his research was Seymour Lipset, notably in *Political man*, first published in 1959. In arguing that fascism was often an 'extremism of the center', Lipset gave most credence to evidence about Nazism, underlining, for example, the almost complete disappearance of the middle-class 'liberal' parties during the Nazis' rise to electoral success from 1928 to 1933.[47] In Lipset's view, 'center fascists' came typically from those sections of the middle class anxious to resist what they saw as the tyranny of both capital and labour. In pursuing his analysis Lipset made reference to fascist movements in Argentina, Austria and Italy, while also examining McCarthyism in the USA and newly (re-)installed Gaullism in France; indeed, it was the 1958 'coup' against the Fourth Republic which he acknowledged to be the immediate stimulus for his work.[48] None the less, Lipset's comments on Italy were brief and trite – he had drawn, he noted, on the *Encyclopedia of the Social Sciences* for his factual information about the character of Fascism in the Po valley.[49] The Italian variant of fascism, he thought, featured an uneasy combination of the centre and the right. In the course of the regime the conservative section of the movement often dominated, but when the Salò Republic took over 'the more genuinely fascist part' re-emerged.[50] None the less, Lipset remarked elsewhere, Mussolini had been adept at 'fostering leftist demagoguery, while basically maintaining the existing system of privilege'.[51] Under Lipset's scrutiny, the *Duce* seemed more an opportunist than a maker of new men and women.

Implicit in much of the sociologists' analysis was the issue of 'modernisation', a somewhat nebulous term often meaning little more than the

45 T. Parsons, *Politics and social structure*, New York, 1969, pp. 59–60.
46 T. Parsons, *Politics and social structure*, pp. 82–3, 91.
47 S. M. Lipset, *Political man: the social bases of politics*, New York, 1960, pp. 138–48.
48 S. M. Lipset, *Political man*, p. 127.
49 S. M. Lipset, *Political man*, p. 165. He spent rather more time looking at the MSI, even if it, too, he feared, was anomalous in its fit with the expected pattern of neo-fascism (pp. 166–8).
50 S. M. Lipset, *Political man*, pp. 165–6.
51 S. M. Lipset, *The politics of unreason: right-wing extremism in America, 1790–1970*, New York, 1970, p. 195. Lipset compared Mussolini in that regard with Huey Long, governor of Louisiana.

present beneficent condition of the United States. In modernisation theory the big question was usually comparative – what road did a certain society follow in integrating, or seeking to integrate, the masses into its political and economic system and arriving at a happy present? Perhaps the most grandiose such study was Barrington Moore's *Social origins of dictatorship and democracy* (1966). Moore sought to track the paths of Britain, France, the USA, China, Japan and India from a peasant world to 'modernity'. Though he did not devote a separate chapter to Germany, this country none the less played an important part in his analysis, since, he concluded, after the model of Anglo-Saxon liberalism, 'the second main route to the world of modern industry [which] we have called the capitalist and reactionary one, [was] exemplified most clearly by Germany and Japan'. This road, he explained further, was paved by the methods of 'fascism from above' (Moore remained vague about how and when an 'authoritarian' regime, marrying the interests of big industry and big agriculture, turned into a fascist one).[52]

To a degree Moore did seek to join Italy to his model; it was, after all, the country in which 'fascism was invented',[53] and all Moore's work was given impetus by the desire to bring peasants in from the scholarly cold to which Marxist theorising had allegedly consigned them. Despite this standpoint, Moore did not allow the detail of Italian history to divert him too much. At one and the same time he endorsed Edward Banfield's assertion that Southern Italian peasants were corrupted by 'amoral familism',[54] while also approving the view that pre-Fascist Italy had been some sort of democracy. Fascism of any kind, he contended, was 'inconceivable without democracy', since a fascist movement endeavoured 'to make reaction and conservatism popular and plebeian'.[55] At the same time, he added, fascism carried a great cost because it entailed conservatives abandoning their approval of freedom and embracing 'blood and death' as exuding erotic appeal. Such moralising apart, Moore concluded that fascism was 'the product of both the intrusion of capitalism into the rural economy and of strains arising in the post-competitive phase of capitalist industry'. It 'developed most fully in Germany'[56] (though the argument that fascism arose at this time might have worked better in distinguishing the powerful Fascism of the Po valley from its feebler variants in Sicily). But, in the final analysis, Moore could not take Italy too seriously. 'Cynical opportunism', he remarked, was 'more blatant' in Italy than in Germany or Japan.[57] Moore joined that long list of com-

52 B. Moore, *Social origins of dictatorship and democracy: lord and peasant in the making of the modern world*, Harmondsworth, 1967, p. 433.
53 B. Moore, *Social origins of dictatorship and democracy*, p. 436.
54 B. Moore, *Social origins of dictatorship and democracy*, p. 477. For more on Banfield, see Chapter 6.
55 B. Moore, *Social origins of dictatorship and democracy*, p. 447.
56 B. Moore, *Social origins of dictatorship and democracy*, p. 448.
57 B. Moore, *Social origins of dictatorship and democracy*, pp. 451–2. Silone and Salvemini were Moore's cited Italian sources.

mentators who have concluded that the Italian version of fascism was nearer to airy persiflage than a world-shattering ideology.

By the time Moore was writing, academic historians had also begun to examine the problem of fascism (the first issue of the *Journal of Contemporary History* was published in the same year as *Social origins of dictatorship and democracy*). Politically, the decade of the 1960s had opened in the spirit of a new era in which the verities of the (first) Cold War might no longer hold. As if on cue, the historiography of the meaning of the 'long' Second World War also moved in a radical direction, with the publication of the controversial books by Fritz Fischer, A. J. P. Taylor and Hannah Arendt.[58] None of these works was of direct significance to Italian history, except in the sense that each implied that it was no longer possible to limit the responsibility for Nazi evil to Adolf Hitler as a person, or to the 'totalitarian state'. Still more unsettling to the discipline of history, at least in the English-speaking world, was the publication of E. H. Carr's *What is history?*, a durable manifesto for those who regard truth, in some sense, as a relative matter, and the task of the historian as having as much to do with stimulating debate as coming up with final answers.[59]

With controversy about the meaning of both history and the Second World War in the air, it was an appropriate time for the publication of a breakthrough book on generic fascism, even if, in retrospect, it was odd that this work should be a study, in by no means limpid prose,[60] by the German Heideggerian cultural historian Ernst Nolte. Entitled *Der Faschismus in seiner Epoche*, and focusing on the history of ideas, it came out in 1963. Two years later it appeared in translation under the certainly catchier and perhaps more telling title of *Three faces of fascism*.

Nolte devoted quite a few of his pages both to the analysis of Italian Fascism and, once he had defined it as 'normal fascism', to the rehearsal of its history. And yet, of the three movements he was investigating, it was clear that, despite its alleged normality, Italian Fascism was the least significant. Often, indeed, the self-consciously intellectual Nolte could scarcely suppress a sneer when it came to taking the Italians into account. Italian Fascism, he typically wrote, was possessed of an 'often wavering, continuing evolving doctrine', which was 'not on the same plane' as the 'precise, self-contained' ideology of *Action Française*. 'Hence the Action Française is to [Italian] fascism – however much both are simultaneously practice and theory – what philosophy is to life: just as life is more colorful, rich, and complex, so it is also less equipped with, and more needful of, direction.'[61]

58 See Chapter 2.
59 E. H. Carr, *What is history?*, London, 1961.
60 For a fine demolition of Nolte's theses, see M. Kitchen, *Fascism*, London, 1976, pp. 36–45.
61 E. Nolte, *Three faces of fascism: Action Française, Italian Fascism, National Socialism*, New York, 1965, p. 193.

Nolte's 'first level' definition of generic fascism,[62] however, made great play of the link between fascism and Communism (he had by no means cast aside the theses of totalitarianism, so commonly accepted in the 1950s). In turn, Mussolini's socialist background became a key matter. Nolte argued that it

> is correct that Mussolini's thinking was mercurial, fragmentary, and often liable to fluctuation. But if we proceed, as today we must, from his Marxist youth, we cannot fail to perceive a continuous and highly significant thread, and we are forced to admit that never has the path of any outstanding European politician been more closely and variously affiliated with the intellectual evolution of his time.[63]

The *Duce* was thus a man possessed of serious and influential ideas: 'His command of contemporary philosophy and political literature was at least as great as that of any other contemporary European political leader.'[64] Under the *Duce*'s leadership Italy experienced a 'National Fascist Totalitarian Development Dictatorship', in which the draining of the Pontine marshes, for example, engaged the souls of the populace as never before.'[65] By 1937–8, however, the regime had lost its autonomy and become the 'satellite' of Nazi Germany.[66]

As his footnotes confirm,[67] Nolte was much more interested in Mussolini's philosophy than he was in the practice of Italian Fascism. And yet the *Duce*'s ideas, for all their flair, were, as noted above, not as original or fully developed as were those of Charles Maurras and his followers in *Action Française*. Nolte's emphasis on the French movement carried other very important messages. Even if the inter-war period constituted an 'era of fascism', and both the First World War and the Russian Revolution were crucial factors in the precipitation of the new movement, the origins of the ideology of fascism could be traced back before 1914. Nolte's 'third-level' definition of fascism – as a 'metapolitical phenomenon' embodied in a 'resistance to transcendence' (concepts which critics have puzzled over ever since)[68] – was, by contrast, sprung mainly from his comprehension of 'radical fascism', that is, the German Nazi variety. Germany was thus both the epicentre of fascism, and also, paradoxically, it became more and more clear in Nolte's later writings,[69] not alone 'responsible' for its crimes.

62 E. Nolte, *Three faces of fascism*, p. 40.
63 E. Nolte, *Three faces of fascism*, pp. 42–3.
64 E. Nolte, *Three faces of fascism*, p. 200.
65 E. Nolte, *Three faces of fascism*, pp. 280, 286.
66 E. Nolte, *Three faces of fascism*, p. 294.
67 They make repeated acknowledgement to Mussolini's *Opera omnia*. Nolte scarcely uses secondary sources, but where he does he is in some debt to D. L. Germino.
68 E. Nolte, *Three faces of fascism*, p. 538. By this last term Nolte seems to have meant something rather like a 'fear of freedom'.
69 See R. J. B. Bosworth, *Explaining Auschwitz and Hiroshima: history writing and the Second World War 1945–1990*, London, 1993, pp. 82–6.

Whatever political bias lurked in Nolte's work, there can be no gainsaying the fact that publication of *Three faces of fascism* set off a flurry of attempts to provide an alternative analysis of generic fascism. Partly the explanation for the new interest in exploring the definition of fascism lay in chronology. The spirit of the 1960s affected the world of scholarship, too, and the thaw in the Cold War rendered unstable for a time the hegemony of the totalitarianist model in non-Marxist versions[70] of the history of twentieth-century Europe. If the totalitarianist account would not do, it was natural for liberals and others to seek to craft an alternative model, especially one which would not replicate the Marxist line.

One assemblage of new work was a lengthy series of essays on the 'European Right' edited by the American-based emigré historians Hans Rogger and Eugen Weber. It did not, however, take interpretation very far. In his conclusion, Rogger judged the radical Right an incoherent and intellectually unsophisticated force, its leaders men of 'banality and pettiness'. Even though Mussolini had undoubtedly 'furnished a model for many rightists', his 'antics' meant that levity was usually his most evident characteristic.[71] Thus, Rogger concluded, since liberalism was, after all, the far Right's 'greatest enemy', the Right was an unsuitable vehicle to transport the world to the pleasures of liberal modernity: 'Is it too much to say that the whole history of the new or radical Right is one of failure, and that it failed most when it succeeded best?'[72]

For all its limitations, the book edited by Rogger and Weber did alert historians to the existence of a radical right in countries outside Italy and Germany, the two classic venues of fascism. Moreover, Nolte's interest in France had stimulated researchers to reflect further on 'minor' fascist movements. Eugen Weber, for example, began a long campaign to remind the scholarly world about the history of the Legion of the Archangel Michael in Romania. In the 1930s this group, under their charismatic and eventually murdered leader C. Z. Codreanu, won considerable electoral support – the Legion seemed a fascist movement both with a mass base in the peasantry and with a genuinely millenarian rhetoric of great conviction and appeal. Did its members compose the real 'third face' of fascism? What did the practice of the Romanian movement prove about fascist pretensions to be revolutionary, and about the vulgar Marxist insistence that fascists,

70 Prominent in Italian scholarship were the rightists, Domenico Settembrini and Augusto Del Noce, though their greater animus came in their assault on Marxist accounts rather than in their own positive construction of an understanding of fascism. See e.g. D. Settembrini, 'Mussolini and the legacy of revolutionary socialism', *Journal of Contemporary History*, 11, 1976, pp. 239–68. Del Noce had long urged that fascism was a totalitarian 'secular religion', occasioned by the sin of the war and the death of God. For a brief introduction, see R. De Felice (ed.), *Le interpretazioni del fascismo*, Bari, 1971, p. 88.

71 H. Rogger, 'Afterthoughts', in H. Rogger and E. Weber (eds), *The European Right: a historical profile*, London, 1965, pp. 580–1. The specific chapter in the collection on Italy (S. Saladino, 'Italy') is of some use as a narrative, but is deferentially totalitarianist in its analysis.

72 H. Rogger, 'Afterthoughts', p. 589.

whatever their party speeches and manifestos might proclaim, were 'objectively' reactionaries?[73]

While a literature grew on fascism in Iceland,[74] Lithuania[75] and New South Wales,[76] other researchers more ambitiously sought to capture the meaning of fascism as a whole. John Weiss was one scholar who constructed a typology of fascism. However charged with their respective national characters, fascist movements he deemed to be both essentially anti-liberal and detectable as early as in the immediate aftermath of 1789.[77] The conservative aspects of fascism, he maintained stoutly, should not be overlooked. Fascism only ever came to power with the assistance of an old conservative élite and, in office, 'Both terror at home and terror abroad . . . were attempts to resolve political, economic and social problems without the sacrifice of conservative and reactionary values.' Weiss attacked a history of ideas concentrating on the search for 'great precursors' as being likely to hide this political reality.[78] He contended, moreover, that it was a mistake both to read fascist rhetoric too literally, and yet to deny that fascist regimes had, on occasion, transformed social institutions in radical ways.[79] The final reality of fascist power was, however, war; for both Italy and Germany, countries with quite a lot in common since their belated unifications in the nineteenth century, international conflict was the

---

73 See e.g. E. Weber, 'Romania', in H. Rogger and E. Weber (eds), *The European Right*, pp. 501–74; 'The men of Archangel', *Journal of Contemporary History*, 1, 1966, pp. 101–26; 'Revolution? Counterrevolution? What revolution?', *Journal of Contemporary History*, 9, 1974, pp. 3–47. Cf. also the useful little book of documents and commentary, E. Weber (ed.), *Varieties of fascism*, Princeton, 1964. In it, Weber argued, 'Mussolini's movement, . . . then, appear[s] as the prototype of modern Fascism, which is in effect an opportunistic activism inspired by dissatisfaction with the existing order, but unwilling or unable to proclaim a precise doctrine of its own and emphasizing rather the idea of change, as such, and the seizure of power' (p. 28). A book concentrating on Italy came out in this same series, S. W. Halperin (ed.), *Mussolini and Italian Fascism*, Princeton, 1964.

74 A. Gudmundsson, 'Nazism in Iceland', in S. U. Larsen *et al.* (eds), *Who were the fascists: social roots of European fascism*, Bergen, 1980, pp. 743–51. The membership of this grey-shirted movement peaked in 1936 at 300 (p. 748). The essays collected by Larsen *et al.* cover an enormous variety of fascist movements. From its pages it is possible to learn about Polish, Lithuanian, Latvian and Slovak admirers of Italian Fascism (J. W. Borejsza, 'East European perceptions of Italian Fascism', pp. 354–66), about the psychic state of the Legion of the Archangel Michael (Z. Barbu, 'Psycho-historical and sociological perspectives on the Iron Guard', pp. 379–94), and about the attractions of fascism to some Swiss technology institute students (B. Glaus, 'The National Front in Switzerland', pp. 467–78). Wearing grey shirts with black ties, these last were accustomed to chant 'We have no program, we are the program' (p. 476).

75 See e.g. R. J. Misiunas, 'Fascist tendencies in Lithuania', *Slavonic and East European review*, 38, 1970, pp. 88–109.

76 K. Amos, *The New Guard movement 1931–1935*, Melbourne, 1976.

77 J. Weiss, *The fascist tradition: radical right-wing extremism in modern Europe*, New York, 1967, pp. xi–xii.

78 J. Weiss, *The fascist tradition*, pp. 3, 6–7, 11.

79 J. Weiss, *The fascist tradition*, pp. 9, 92.

'inevitable' result of fascism.[80] None the less, Weiss concluded in ambiguous aphorism, 'each nation . . . generates the fascism it deserves'.[81]

In 1968, Stuart Woolf, a distinguished historian of pre-Risorgimento Italy based at the University of Reading,[82] and the translator into English of Primo Levi, brought together a range of historians and political scientists to review the model of fascism. Two volumes of papers resulted, but the interpretations expressed in them were hard to reconcile.[83] Norman Kogan, an American expert on the structures of Italian foreign policy, started with the affirmation that 'Italy under fascism was not a fascist state'.[84] A. F. K. Organski argued, by contrast and with special reference to Italy and Argentina, that fascism was a 'stage in modernization', occasioned by the tensions which developed between the 'modern' and the 'non-modern'.[85] George Mosse, though as yet without providing serious Italian examples, urged that fascist intellectuals and their ideas deserved proper study.[86] Stuart Woolf himself did not much resolve these contradictory stances, agreeing, for example, that a single fascist economic system was hard to map,[87] but claiming that, while no 'single, all-embracing' fascism could be readily defined, there was plenty of overlap between the various movements. An onlooker of inter-war Europe, he stated, could swiftly detect 'patterns' of fascism.[88]

80 J. Weiss, *The fascist tradition*, pp. 110–11. Weiss took seriously the idea that Italian Fascist racism was 'native', in the sense of being already manifested in attitudes expressed in the Italian empire (p. 114).
81 J. Weiss, *The fascist tradition*, p. 128.
82 See especially S. J. Woolf, *A history of Italy 1700–1860: the social constraints of political change*, London, 1979.
83 S. J. Woolf (ed.), *The nature of fascism*, London, 1968; S. J. Woolf (ed.), *European fascism*, London, 1968. Somewhat confusingly, this latter book was later republished as S. J. Woolf (ed.), *Fascism in Europe*, London, 1981.
84 N. Kogan, 'Fascism as a political system' in S. J. Woolf (ed.), *The nature of fascism*, p. 16. For examples of Kogan's other work, see N. Kogan, *Italy and the allies*, Cambridge, Mass., 1956; *The politics of Italian foreign policy*, London, 1963; *A political history of postwar Italy*, London, 1966; N. Kogan et al., *Realtà e immagine della politica estera italiana*, Milan, 1980.
85 A. F. K. Organski, 'Fascism and modernization', in S. J. Woolf (ed.), *The nature of fascism*, p. 23. Some years later the conservative American historian Henry Turner picked up this idea. See H. A. Turner, 'Fascism and modernization', in H. A. Turner (ed.), *Reappraisals of fascism*, New York, 1975, pp. 117–39.
86 G. L. Mosse, 'Fascism and the intellectuals', in S. J. Woolf (ed.), *The nature of fascism*, pp. 205–25. Cf. P. Vita-Finzi, 'Italian fascism and the intellectuals' (pp. 226–42), a conventional account of a fatal attraction, allegedly weakening by the 1930s. On this topic, see, too, A. Hamilton, *The appeal of fascism: a study of intellectuals and fascism*, London, 1971, a rather racy history of intellectuals of the right, giving pride of place to Italian ones, but which began by terming fascism 'that thoroughly ambiguous ideology' (p. xii).
87 S. J. Woolf, 'Did a fascist economic system exist?' in S. J. Woolf (ed.), *The nature of fascism*, p. 120.
88 S. J. Woolf, 'Introduction', in S. J. Woolf (ed.), *The nature of fascism*, p. 6. Cf. also Woolf's own most detailed account of Mussolini's regime, S. J. Woolf, 'Italy', in S. J. Woolf (ed.), *European fascism*, London, 1968, pp. 39–60. Also emphatic that fascism possessed 'universal features', however concealed by national traditions, was Michael Hurst, another

The possible basis of these patterns was growing steadily more intricate. Heinz Lubasz treated Japan as another candidate for the third face of fascism, while admitting that the proferred explanations of a generic fascist ideology and a generic fascist practice remained unsatisfactory.[89] Paul Hayes, by contrast, implied that Nordic variants of fascism needed closer study. He declared pessimistically that 'fascism is one of those "-isms" for which every person will find his own definition', even if he agreed that the Italian case was 'the fascist prototype'.[90] Mussolini and his regime, he added, did aim at inter-class 'revolution' and were differentiated from the old élites, but they were also failures. Citing Mack Smith with approval, Hayes emphasised the limitations of the Italian Fascist effort in the Second World War compared with the Liberal achievement in the First.[91] Mussolini, Hayes stated in familiar vocabulary, was ruled by whim; Italy was a country given to 'chaos'.[92] In Hayes' analysis, yet again, Nazi Germany was the place which really mattered. Alan Cassels, on the other hand, returned to the view that Italian Fascism and German Nazism were the two chief examples of the ideology. The world of fascism, he thought, could be readily split in two, with 'advanced countries' tending to imitate Germany and being 'backward-looking' in their philosophy, and less developed societies following Italy in treating fascism as a potentially modernising force.[93]

Rather more conceptually sophisticated or ambitious than Lubasz, Hayes and Cassels was the Parisian New Left sociologist Nicos Poulantzas, who, in 1970, had published *Fascisme et dictature*, a work which appeared four years later in English translation as *Fascism and dictatorship*. Whereas the liberal commentators had insisted that fascism was viscerally anti-liberal, Poulantzas accepted the mainstream Marxist view that the purpose of any fascist movement was to attack the interests of the working class. Fascism did indeed mark out one of the forms of the 'exceptional Capitalist state'; Germany and Italy followed next behind Russia as weak links in the 'chain of imperialism'.[94] At the same time Poulantzas rejected the simple 'instrumentalist' view that fascists were no more than the agents of finance capital. Italian Fascism was armed with a modernising wing; it was always nearer to Northern business interests than to Southern agriculture.[95]

---

who wanted to argue that fascism's greatest enemy was not Marxism but liberalism. M. Hurst, 'What is fascism?', *Historical Journal*, 11, 1968, pp. 167, 176. Fascism, he added in something of a circular argument, could not come to power in 'strong democracies'. Similarly, he declared, the existence of the Vatican and the monarchy made the idea of an Italian Fascist totalitarianism laughable (pp. 180–1).

89 H. Lubasz (ed.), *Fascism: three major regimes*, New York, 1973.
90 P. M. Hayes, *Fascism*, London, 1973, pp. 13, 135–40.
91 P. M. Hayes, *Fascism*, pp. 140, 147–9.
92 P. M. Hayes, *Fascism*, pp. 157, 160.
93 A. Cassels, *Fascism*, Arlington Heights, Ill., 1975, p. x.
94 N. Poulantzas, *Fascism and dictatorship: the Third International and the problem of fascism*, London, 1974, pp. 11, 25. Poulantzas had been born in Athens, but made a career in France, teaching at the Universities of Vincennes (and Frankfurt).
95 N. Poulantzas, *Fascism and dictatorship*, pp. 114–19.

Moreover, although its petit bourgeois base was fragile, and although a lot of the regime's policies simply feather-bedded the bourgeoisie, Fascism retained a certain populism. It was, of course, anti-socialist, but it kept looking to the working class for some sympathy and, in office, did not assault workers' interests with the same consistency with which it afflicted the peasantry and even some of the petite bourgeoisie.[96] Fascism, and by this term Poulantzas meant the regimes in Italy and Germany (which he distinguished from the more traditional military and reactionary forces dominant in Spain, Hungary and Romania), possessed its own distinctive characteristics and was neither simply bourgeois nor simply 'Bonapartist'.[97] It was thus 'exceptional', a term which seemed to mean interventionist, in the sense of being a tyranny, while, at the same time, being paradoxically a regime which wanted somehow to embrace its populace.

Less intellectualist in his emphases was Arno Mayer, a historian of the 'German problem'.[98] Though explaining what he called the 'Judeocide' would prove his ultimate obsession, Mayer during the 1970s did seek to look beyond Germany and scan the long-term history of the European lower middle class.[99] In so doing he was seeking to identify the 'dynamics of counter-revolution', a term which allowed him to link inter-war fascism with what he thought were its precursors before the First World War, and then to carry his computation forward as far as 1956.[100] Italy, however, played no serious part in his analysis and, indeed, he was rather more preoccupied by what he regarded as counter-revolutionary forces in the USA than by Benito Mussolini.

Another who, possessing a very different ideological perspective from that of Poulantzas and Mayer, sought in the 1970s to theorise fascism was the Yale-based sociologist Juan Linz. He started with the practical. Much about fascism, he averred, was decided by the simple fact that it was an intellectual 'latecomer', seeking authority when a modern left–right party system had already crystallised.[101] Prefiguring to a considerable degree post-1945 'catch-all' parties (Linz mentioned here Christian Democrat

96 N. Poulantzas, *Fascism and dictatorship*, pp. 165–7.
97 N. Poulantzas, *Fascism and dictatorship*, pp. 281–2, 357–8. Poulantzas also worried that the ideology could reappear, but was very vague about how, all the more because he emphasised the chameleon behaviour endemic in politics.
98 For more on his life in history, see R. J. B. Bosworth, *Explaining Auschwitz and Hiroshima*, pp. 90–3.
99 A. J. Mayer, 'The lower middle class as a historical problem', *Journal of Modern History*, 47, 1975, pp. 409–36.
100 A. J. Mayer, *Dynamics of counter-revolution in Europe, 1870–1956: an analytic framework*, New York, 1971, pp. 6–7.
101 J. J. Linz, 'Some notes towards a comparative study of fascism in sociological historical perspective', in W. Laqueur (ed.), *Fascism: a reader's guide: analyses, interpretations, bibliography*, Harmondsworth, 1979, pp. 14–16. This collection of essays was first published in 1976. In his preface, Laqueur argued that it was best to talk about fascisms (p. 7). For Linz's views, cf. also J. J. Linz, 'Political space and fascism as a latecomer', in S. U. Larsen *et al.* (eds), *Who were the fascists*, pp. 153–91.

movements), fascist parties often found eventual support from social groups which had not been at the heart of their initial appeal. Their 'anti-ness' (they were against socialism, liberalism, parliament, the Church, conservatives, the bourgeoisie) was significant and typical.[102] But the fascist movements' style and campaigning techniques were also crucial, notably in attracting students, youth of all classes and demobilised officers. According to Linz, fascism, aiming at 'a plebiscitarian mobilization of the masses', spread successfully from Italy, possessed its own 'historic era' and constituted a genuine ideology.[103]

However, the most remarkable attempt during the 1970s to place Fascist Italy comparatively was Charles Maier's guilefully entitled book *Recasting bourgeois Europe*. Examining socio-economic 'stabilization' and its political concomitants, Maier drew an unfamiliar comparison between Fascist Italy, Republican France and Weimar Germany. Marshalling a wealth of detail behind his case, Maier examined the tenacious way in which the middle class defended its 'social hegemony', despite what had seemed the likelihood of its imminent overthrow in the age of the masses.[104] This trick was played using the device of 'corporatism', that is, the subtraction of power from both parliaments and the bureaucracy, and the simultaneous weakening of civic liberty, in favour of such organised socio-economic forces as big business and big unions. Already by 1914, Maier averred, Weber was a more acute theorist of these 'emerging structures of power' than was Marx.[105] The First World War accelerated 'the integration of organized labor into a bargaining system supervised by the state'.[106] Although national differences were obvious, after the war the most powerful pattern was indeed the re-affirmation of 'corporatism', and it would similarly remain the most cherished conservative ambition following 1945. In Maier's view the 1920s thus became the most important decade of the century; these years witnessed 'capitalist restructuring and renovation', the emergence on the political stage of a new cast of players, and the re-forging of the bourgeois order in a fresh and lasting way.[107]

When Maier looked specifically at Italy, he found élites potentially betrayed by their own weakness in organisation and therefore needing 'political coercion' all the more in order to re-impose their influence. None the less, he argued, Italy did not behave in a way radically different from its neighbours. 'A world-wide Thermidor'[108] occurred in 1920 and was present

102 J. J. Linz, 'Some notes towards a comparative study of fascism, p. 29.
103 J. J. Linz, 'Some notes towards a comparative study of fascism', p. 26.
104 C. Maier, *Recasting bourgeois Europe: stabilization in France, Germany, and Italy in the decade after World War I*, Princeton, 1975, p. 3.
105 C. Maier, *Recasting bourgeois Europe*, p. 10.
106 C. Maier, *Recasting bourgeois Europe*, p. 11.
107 C. Maier, *Recasting bourgeois Europe*, pp. 14–15.
108 C. Maier, *Recasting bourgeois Europe*, p. 136.

in Italy, too, except that there the bourgeois recovery was not recognised when it had, in fact, happened.[109] Thus, the Fascist 'seizure of power' was certainly flawed and even unnecessary: 'With the surrender of real electoral competition, the political center in Italy ended an ineffective search for stability and influence through parliamentary representation. But nothing was given up save liberty.'[110] In Maier's brilliant and provocative analysis, the 'flankers' (as he literally translated *fiancheggiatori*) were to prove, at least by implication, a rather more important force in the Fascist regime than were the Fascists.

According to Maier, therefore, neither the Fascist acquisition of the Prime Ministership in October 1922 nor the declaration of the dictatorship in January 1925 wrenched time out of joint. 'Mussolini's Italy' was a recognisable place: 'Fascism did not suppress the causes of capitalist strife and class rivalry; it encouraged the centralization and coordination of that conflict such as was developing in other societies.' Moreover, Fascism 'did not particularly hasten the technological modernization of industry, but it did hasten its modernization in terms of corporate organization'. 'The Italian system', he added, 'was designed to consolidate the power of a ruling group supposedly independent of the powerful forces contending in the marketplace.... In actuality, the Fascist regime remained in a reciprocal and symbiotic relationship with the old forces of order.' Yet there was also something troubling about Mussolini's dictatorship: 'It was actually a tragic caricature of ... [the new capitalist] system: rewarding the powerful, disciplining the weak, imposing by political duress and economic consolidation what other societies worked toward by market forces alone.'[111]

Regrettably, Maier did not take his study forward into the 1930s. None the less, he did discern important distinctions between Fascist Italy and Nazi Germany, which sprang from the different corporatist structures developed in each country. As he put it: 'Italian fascism substituted for prior organization in the political arena or marketplace; German Nazism arose in resentment against the organization [created during the Weimar Republic] that seemed to dominate.' Nazism, indeed, reflected 'a grass-roots rebellion against the capitalist marketplace', while 'Italian fascism [merely] testified to the pre-industrial formation of the Italian élite.'[112] In this analysis, generic fascism was left as certainly a slippery and perhaps a meaningless concept. Nazism, by contrast, held its status as the common enemy of liberal capitalist humankind.

It was thus all the more appropriate that two decades of research into a model of fascism should, in 1979, be given a severe examination by the

109 C. Maier, *Recasting bourgeois Europe*, p. 173.
110 C. Maier, *Recasting bourgeois Europe*, p. 350.
111 C. Maier, *Recasting bourgeois Europe*, p. 577.
112 C. Maier, *Recasting bourgeois Europe*, p. 592.

acerbic Gilbert Allardyce and come out with a failing grade. As far as
Allardyce was concerned, historians had 'agreed to use the word [fascism]
without agreeing on how to define it'.[113] After flirting with the 'modest
proposal' that usage of the term be 'banned' altogether,[114] Allardyce
expressed the hope that the passion to formulate a definition of generic
fascism could be 'cooled'.[115] There was no need, he proclaimed, even to
glance at Marxist versions, given their evident absurdity and bias,[116] and
non-Marxists were hardly more convincing. 'The word *fascismo* had no
meaning beyond Italy'; it was absurd to think that nationalists of the world
could be united. So, in general, he declared reprovingly, 'The changing
interpretations of fascism reflect the intellectual illusions of the periods that
produce them.'[117] Without pausing to explain how he himself might be
exempt from this generalisation, Allardyce pressed on eagerly with his
demolition. The model of totalitarianism, modernisation theory, intellectual
and cultural histories treating Fascism as a genuine ideology – none of these
assisted understanding. As for psychological approaches to the subject, they
received an inevitable short shrift: despite efforts to locate fascism's 'source
in those areas of the personality most inaccessible to empirical analysis', any
sensible onlooker should accept that fascism did not compose 'a mental
category'.[118]

Allardyce had one other important message. Nazi Germany was a 'thing
apart'.[119] To use it historiographically was thus almost always a cheap shot.
'Nothing does more to demonize European "fascists" than to make them all
Nazis at birth.' 'Europe could probably have lived with Italian fascism',
Allardyce surmised, but Nazism was simply intolerable. Therefore,
Allardyce concluded, 'the time has come to recognize ... that the Hitler
regime involves problems too aberrant and peculiar to provide us with
conclusions for interpreting movements in other nations. Hard cases make
bad law.'[120]

Both in tone and content, and therefore in his implicit and explicit
messages, Allardyce was heralding the new conservatism which was
taking over political and cultural life throughout the globe (and duly
reflecting the intellectual beliefs or illusions of his own time). With the
onset of the 'second Cold War' in the 1980s came the revival and
domination of the model of totalitarianism. Historiographically, any

113 G. Allardyce, 'What fascism is not: thoughts on the deflation of a concept', *American Historical Review*, 84, 1979, p. 367.
114 G. Allardyce, 'What fascism is not', p. 367.
115 G. Allardyce, 'What fascism is not', p. 369.
116 Though he took evident pleasure in demolishing a 'left-footed' Poulantzas, 'crackling with the barricades spirit of 1968', in a footnote. G. Allardyce, 'What fascism is not', p. 369, n. 5.
117 G. Allardyce, 'What fascism is not', p. 370.
118 G. Allardyce, 'What fascism is not', p. 385.
119 G. Allardyce, 'What fascism is not', p. 383.
120 G. Allardyce, 'What fascism is not', p. 377.

discussion of the model of fascism was muted by the *Historikerstreit* in West Germany, in which conservatives, led by Ernst Nolte, sought to pass the blame for Nazism to the USSR and the triumph of the De Feliceans in Italy, which saw Fascism exempted from any connection with or responsibility for Nazism. When De Felice first announced in 1987 that anti-Fascism had lost its power to discriminate between what assisted a civic sense and what did not, he also spoke very much in the spirit of the moment – in his eyes and those of his friends, Italian communists could never shake off the original sin of alleged totalitarian views even while, paradoxically, Italian Fascists should not be upbraided too strongly for their version of totalitarianism. It was no wonder that as, with increasing depression, he sought to remain a sophisticated Marxist, Tim Mason now wondered 'whatever [had] happened to [the model of] "fascism"'?[121]

Politically, of course, the decade culminated with the victory of the USA and liberal capitalism in the long-running battle with the USSR and its revolution. This was the triumph which the pro-market political scientist Francis Fukuyama celebrated as marking the 'end of history'.[122] In his view, ideological conflicts about past, present or future had been rendered vain because the market and its most comfortable ideology had vanquished all their opponents, be they of left or right. The alternative seemed to be postmodernist relativism, in which seeking a model of fascism was presumably reduced merely to one game among others, an activity lacking any possible ethical or practical guidance, as silly or as sensible as studying communism, or duelling, or Aztec religion, or baseball premiers. In the new world order of the 1990s history, at best, was to be reduced to a heritage park, in which the people could play at will; at worst, under a total liberal hegemony, history would be left merely to parrot the liberal answer to all problems in the past. In either case, as a discipline history's power seemed utterly lost.

And yet, despite such pronouncements and prophesies, discussion of the meaning of generic fascism has continued. Given the depression and confusion of the left, it was predictable that the major participants should be influenced by George Mosse and his never-abandoned campaign to establish that fascist ideas, however obnoxious, were as serious and consistent as any others. The most lively new search for a model of fascism was conducted by Roger Griffin, who urged that it arose as 'a palingenetic form of populist ultra-nationalism'.[123] When he talked about Italy, Griffin acknowledged the influence of Emilio Gentile and A. J. Gregor[124] in helping

121 T. Mason, *Nazism, Fascism and the working class: essays*, ed. J. Caplan, Cambridge, 1995, pp. 323–31.
122 For his fullest summary, see F. Fukuyama, *The end of history and the last man*, London, 1992.
123 R. Griffin, *The nature of fascism*, London, 1991, p. 44.
124 R. Griffin (ed.), *Fascism*, Oxford, 1995, p. 2. His debt, which was sometimes also a critical debt, he noted, extended to Mosse, Nolte and Zeev Sternhell, a productive historian of French fascism, as well as to his immediate competitors, Roger Eatwell and Stanley Payne.

him arrive at his view that fascism was an inter-class movement whose ideas were already brewing in the crisis of the pre-1914 period (and would extend past 1945). Griffin brought some of the concepts of postmodernism to the elucidation of a 'fascist minimum', emphasising, like Gentile and Mosse, the power of 'myth' as a mobilising force.[125] Fascists thus were likely to be 'spoken' by their ideas, especially those about the regeneration of the nation and the recovered virility of the 'new man'. When fascists talked about a 'new order', they meant it.

In its other aspects Griffin's model merely replicated the accustomed liberal view. Fascism was anti-liberal and anti-conservative at its very base, and any inter-war alliances with the old order were 'forced'.[126] Though undoubtedly anti-Marxist and anti-Bolshevik, Griffin added, fascism had by no means sloughed off many socialist 'truths', being committed in its way to welfare and to the notion of a managed economy subject to an interfering state. By definition it had 'no specific class basis'.[127] It was racist, but not always anti-Semitic. It was anti-cosmopolitan, but could imagine a fascist International. However, Griffin's greatest interest seemed to lie in the paraphernalia of fascism, in its milking of charisma, and, above all, in the methods by which the ideology was marketed.

Rather more laboured than Griffin in their reformulations were Roger Eatwell and Stanley Payne. Eatwell was another to urge that fascist ideas should be reviewed seriously and 'objectively'.[128] In his understanding, fascism turned out to be 'a form of thought which preaches the need for social rebirth in order to forge a *holistic national radical* Third Way [sic]'.[129] It still existed.

For his part, Payne preferred a cumbersome 'retrodictive theory of fascism', whose principal 'elements' were four cultural, eight political, four social, two economic and two international 'factors'[130] (thus prompting a tired reader to recall Georges Clemenceau's remark about Woodrow Wilson's Fourteen Points: '*Le Bon Dieu* had only ten').[131] If his overall theorising was unconvincing, Payne none the less was of importance to a student of Italian Fascism because he was anxious to argue that the Italian movement was the first and, in many ways, the most typical of the varieties of fascism, and he even stated that Italy remained 'the chief homeland of neo-fascism' after 1945.[132] Whatever else Payne thought, he viewed Italian history as something that mattered. Given his background, it was predictable that Payne should look for meaning in a 'Latin' fascism. After

125 R. Griffin (ed.), *Fascism*, p. 3.
126 R. Griffin (ed.), *Fascism*, p. 4.
127 R. Griffin (ed.), *Fascism*, p. 7.
128 R. Eatwell, *Fascism: a history*, London, 1995, pp. xvii–xviii.
129 R. Eatwell, *Fascism: a history*, p. 11.
130 S. G. Payne, *A history of fascism, 1914–1945*, Madison, Wisc., 1995, p. 489.
131 Back in the 1970s, Kitchen had stuck to this god-like figure in his final model. M. Kitchen, *Fascism*, pp. 83–7.
132 S. G. Payne, *A history of fascism*, p. 502.

all, he had had a long and distinguished career as a historian of Spain, adopting a conservative stance on many of the highly disputed and ideologically charged issues surrounding that nation's Civil War.[133] Accepting that some sort of fascism had indeed appeared in Spain, Payne, rather like those historians who saw in the sins of Italian socialism a major explanation for Mussolini's rise to power, none the less spent much time denying or belittling the virtue of the Spanish Republic[134] and expressing his dislike of 'Leftist extremism'.[135]

With scholarly interests inclining him to the view that the 'third face' of fascism was located in Spain, Payne offered a brief typology of generic fascism as early as 1980.[136] Fifteen years later he extended this initial foray, endeavouring to write a history of all the fascisms – he now tabulated the existence of tan shirts in Lebanon and white, grey and iron shirts in Syria.[137] To be sure, in this new, more theoretically sophisticated work, he found it hard not to engage in a curmudgeonly political correctness of the right – Saddam Hussein, he averred, is the closest to a Hitler in the Third World; fascists pioneered environmentalism.[138] Similarly, despite his disagreement with the model of totalitarianism, Payne reiterated his beliefs that 'Hitlerian National Socialism more nearly paralleled Russian communism than has any other non-Communist system', and that the Soviet state was the most murderous of them all.[139] Predictably, too, when he acknowledged his intellectual debts, they were to Mosse (to whom his book was dedicated), Linz, Gentile, Gregor and De Felice.[140] Payne even praised the tendentious work of Rosaria Quartararo as 'the best general treatment of Italian [foreign] policy in the 1930s'.[141]

For all this commitment to an academic school and to a political cause, Payne did have some sensible things to say about Italian Fascism. Perhaps he exaggerated the influence of pre-1914 dissident intellectuals – it is hard to know what to make of his image of the Futurists as 'metaphysical motorcycle riders'[142] – yet he was right to see Mussolini as always 'élitist and anti-parliamentarian'[143] and thus never more than an unorthodox socialist

---

133 See e.g. S. G. Payne, *Falange: a history of Spanish fascism*, Stanford, Calif., 1961; *Franco's Spain*, London, 1968; *The Spanish revolution*, London, 1970. He has also published many articles in the *Journal of Contemporary History* and serves on its editorial board.

134 One of his targets was the left-democrat US historian Gabriel Jackson. See his memoirs, G. Jackson, *Historian's quest*, New York, 1969 and e.g. his prize-winning *The Spanish republic and the Civil War 1931–1939*, Princeton, 1969.

135 S. G. Payne, *The Spanish revolution*, p. iv.

136 S. G. Payne, *Fascism: comparison and definition*, Madison, Wisc., 1980; cf. also S. G. Payne, 'Fascism in Western Europe', in W. Laqueur (ed.), *Fascism: a reader's guide*, pp. 300–21.

137 S. G. Payne, *A history of fascism*, p. 352.

138 S. G. Payne, *A history of fascism*, pp. 33, 204, 478, 517.

139 S. G. Payne, *A history of fascism*, p. 211.

140 S. G. Payne, *A history of fascism*, p. xiii.

141 S. G. Payne, *A history of fascism*, p. 232, n. 72.

142 S. G. Payne, *A history of fascism*, p. 63.

143 S. G. Payne, *A history of fascism*, p. 83.

at best. Similarly, it was sensible of him to remember that Italy's course was directed to a considerable degree by its 'latecomers' history' (as Linz had doubtless told him). When he examined the trajectory of the Fascist regime, he was again convincing in some of his interpretations. After 1922 Fascism, in Payne's reckoning, was marked more by a 'dictatorship over the party' than by a dictatorship 'of the party'; and, despite its ambitions, Mussolini's regime never became 'structurally totalitarian'. Having differentiated his interpretation from that of Gentile, Payne also avoided the wilder recent assessments of Italy's effort in the Second World War. Already in 1938–9, he stated, the regime was losing touch with that 'public opinion' to which the *Duce* had been better attuned in the 1920s.[144] After a feeble war effort, marked by corruption, incompetence and bureaucratism, Mussolini, at Salò, was reduced to being a 'pitiful puppet'.[145] All in all, Payne's Fascist Italy is closer to that of Chabod, for example, than the one delineated by the more enthusiastic of the present revisionists.

With its somewhat traditional slant on the history of Italian Fascism, its view of the regime as one which had its imitators but was itself very much sprung from the humus of Italian political and social history rather than being a replica of any other movement, Payne's book provides a suitable terminus for this survey of Italy's place within the various models of generic fascism. At the beginning of this chapter I warned that Italy would be likely to be given a secondary rank in much of the model-building. In the review which has followed, it has become clear how frequently the modellers have been aiming above all either to explain Nazism, or to explain it away. It has been obvious, too, as Roger Griffin wisely noticed,[146] that any model-building, just like any comparative history, will by definition be approximate.

The proper reponse to this situation, however, is not to abandon both models and comparison – every single word is, after all, itself a model, inevitably existing as a 'process and not a thing' in a comparative setting. The great virtue of model-building is that it raises questions which historians can then ask in order to chart a path of understanding through the endless morass of 'factual' evidence. In their ability to provoke doubt and debate, almost all the models have something of value in them. How, for example, can either Italian Fascism or the more generic version be read without some sense of élite fears of the working class and of what, after 1917, seemed for a while to be a working-class revolution? Only a purblind and recalcitrant anti-Marxist will want to think about fascism, or the history of the twentieth century, without some reference to class and its

144 S. G. Payne, *A history of fascism*, p. 243.
145 S. G. Payne, *A history of fascism*, pp. 382–91, 436.
146 R. Griffin (ed.), *Fascism*, p. 2.

discontents.[147] Anti-fascist theorising is also important in urging commentators not to forget that fascism, as it was practised in Italy (and elsewhere), was a tyranny. Despite their penchant for a certain sort of welfare and therefore their rejection in the final analysis of the complete Social Darwinism of the market, neither the Italian nor other forms of fascism merit nostalgia or revival.

Equally, the liberal models of fascism can raise questions worth asking. Given the sexist nature of Italian Fascism and its efforts to construct or endorse an especially virile Fascist new man, the sexual habits of Italian men and women, and the expectations of the family (and the Church) deserve further examination, and in this regard a fully historicised appraisal of the psychologies of Italians may pay dividends. Similarly, even if the Fascist economic achievement was, by most measurements, modest, especially compared with those of the Giolittian era before and the Republican one to follow, a kind of 'modernisation' was indeed reaching Italy in the Fascist years, and, given that the movement led by Mussolini was in power for a generation, it is natural that an Italian view of modernity should carry some Fascist gloss. Such an understanding deserves exploration and analysis. Mosse and Gentile are right, too, when they say that Fascism possessed a political culture and sparked its own intellectuals, even if it is not so clear that the ideology they debated was 'fascinating'. On this as other occasions, the culturalist school could do far more to trace the complex effects of the meeting, both 'real' and imagined, between the ideas of intellectuals and those of the populace at large. Only then will it be possible better to comprehend the numerous, fluctuating and contradictory meanings of Fascist ideas and Fascist paraphernalia and their consequences. None the less, the teasing-out of the meaning of the cultures of Fascist Italy indeed deserves support.

In sum, the process of theorising about generic fascism, and applying the resultant theories to the history of Italian Fascism, has not constituted a fruitless exercise. Rather, so long as it is thought worthwhile to seek an explanation of 'Auschwitz', the 'barbarisation of warfare on the Eastern Front', and the 'long Second World War' which preceded, accompanied and, sometimes, outlasted these terrible events, and to examine the Italian role in them, historians and other social scientists courageous or foolhardy enough to build models of fascism should be encouraged to continue. Historians who, by contrast, prefer the task of the 'archive rat', and that of describing

147 This is also the reason why the most perceptive, if inevitably flawed, general history of this century so far to be published is E. Hobsbawm, *Age of extremes: the short twentieth century 1914–1991*, London, 1994. Hobsbawm agrees that Nazism was what made fascism really significant historically, while acknowledging the primacy of the Italian movement and Mussolini's influence on Hitler (pp. 116–17). He puts the sophisticated Marxist line that fascism was hostile to liberal civilisation in general, including democratic socialism, and that it was assisted by many conservative and middle-class fellow-travellers, who, before and thereafter, preferred liberal ideas.

'what actually happened', will need the stimulation and enlightenment that sometimes results from it. After all, in order to have a future as a discipline and to give the present and future a useful past, history must perpetually engage in a quest for new questions and for contestable answers.

Conclusion

It is now half a century since the Dutch liberal historian Pieter Geyl published *Napoleon: for and against*, a fundamental study of the 'myth' of the emperor who, at least for believers in Great Men, was either the 'heir' or the 'destroyer' of the French Revolution.[1] Though itself, of course, a period piece, Geyl's book marked a crucial moment in the development of historical understanding as it demonstrated how, for 150 years, historians had crafted rival interpretations of Napoleon which both elucidated the era being studied and the moment at which the historical text was written. But the full relationship between current times and history was not just a tale of 'anachronism', that is, of the preoccupations of the moment being 'answered' and coloured by present-centred explorations of the past. For, even as the present created or revived the past, contemporary society was simultaneously the product of the past, unimaginable without the nourishment which it had gained from its historical roots. If Geyl's study were to be accepted, then the Rankean verities of the academic discipline of history had lost their sway. Historians deceived themselves if they believed that, with the weight of scholarship and the denial of partisanship, they could empathetically comprehend the past on its own terms and recount 'what actually happened'. In future any diagram of history must chart movement, not stasis. Historical studies should doubtless aim at 'accuracy' and be sceptical towards the biases of the period under study, but the results of research joined a never-ending process in which there were no final solutions (apart from death), and in which the historian should be conscious less of relating the truth than of mounting a case in a democratic debate.

Napoleon: for and against remains a useful survey of both the history of Napoleon and of French culture and politics since 1815. However, by now perhaps its greatest utility is to be a book of its time, a source for the understanding of a society which had just experienced 'Auschwitz' and had

1 P. Geyl, *Napoleon: for and against*, London, 1949.

begun to reckon with it. Had not Geyl worked on his book's sentences while, a Dutch resister (of not altogether admirable motivation), he was a prisoner of the Nazis at Buchenwald?[2] Was *Napoleon: for and against* not the book of his individual 'long' Second World War? Did not Geyl search for means to reaffirm the discipline of history and, simultaneously, seek to rediscover a continuing path for human history, so ruptured by the horrors which Europe and the world had endured or inflicted in the death camps, on the Eastern front, at Nanking and Hiroshima, and on many another front of the varied Second World Wars? Should Geyl be believed, after these terrible experiences knowledge must become meeker, more fluid and less stable than in the past, and this new modesty was all the more necessary for a world which would not want to return to the tyrannous certainties of Nazi–fascism, certainly those involving 'race'.

In this book I have in some ways sought to replicate Geyl's work, with my focus transferred from Napoleon[3] to the history of Italian Fascism. Enlarging on a comment by historian Massimo Salvadori that 'a history of the interpretations of Fascism would run in strict parallel with the history of political and civic consciousness' in Italy,[4] I have narrated the various ways in which Fascism has been historicised. Under the regime itself it was natural for the new doctrine to be given a historical setting and a historical explanation. Fascists spoke of their 'revolution', but denied its full novelty by tracing a descent from the better part of the Risorgimento, while, for more nakedly propagandist reasons, finding antecedents in the history of classical Rome, in the corporate life of the Middle Ages and in the virile creativity of the Renaissance. This living contact with the past, it was alleged, would enhance the prospect that Fascism could locate a 'third way' between liberal capitalism and Marxist socialism, and drive Italy to its own special modernity. As Mussolini announced in November 1933, with characteristic bravado, 'Today we can affirm that the mode of capitalist production is overcome and with it the theory of economic liberalism which has both illuminated capitalism and offered an apologia for it'[5] (even if, only a few years later, he was more disarming when he told a leading Italian businessman, 'An economic question has never stopped the march of history').[6]

---

2 For the setting, see R. J. B. Bosworth, *Explaining Auschwitz and Hiroshima: history writing and the Second World War 1945–1990*, London, 1993, pp. 11–15.
3 It is predictable that Geyl has had his successors in the sophisticated historiography of modern France. See e.g. R. Gildea, *The past in French history*, New Haven, 1994, an account of many of the histories which course quite publicly through French life. Unfortunately, there is no equivalent study of the relationship between history and the Italians.
4 M. Salvadori in J. Jacobelli, *Il Fascismo e gli storici oggi*, Bari, 1988, p. 92.
5 B. Mussolini, *Opera omnia*, ed. E. and D. Susmel, Florence, 1958, xxvi, pp. 86–96.
6 Quoted by R. De Felice, *Mussolini il duce: II. Lo stato totalitario 1936–1940*, Turin, 1981, p. 266. The year was 1937; his interlocutor was Ettore Conti.

While Fascists sketched their own history (and argued about it and contradicted themselves), anti-Fascists worked at alternative interpretations. Prominent among them were Marxists. They needed to understand Fascism because followers of the socialist and communist parties had been the most immediate victims of Mussolini's rise to power; and because they remained the partisans of another, better – to them, the only – revolution: that under way in the USSR. For Marxists, Fascism, whatever else it might be, could not constitute a revolution. Rather, an easy syllogism ran, Fascism repressed socialists and capitalism was the pre-destined enemy of socialism, therefore Fascists must, whether knowingly or not, be the agents of capital, landowners, industry, and all those elements of present wealth, power and status who were doomed to historical defeat when the proletariat came into its own. In the Marxist analysis, Fascism was reactionary in its final purpose, and inevitably drew on a class base among those forces, like the petite bourgeoisie, which were trying to delay the victory of genuine social revolution. Fascists were therefore numbered with those who transgressed against 'history'. Their wickedness knew no bounds; Fascism meant war and the policy of racial extermination. Mussolini's regime would not ally with that of Hitler by accident; rather, the two 'fascist' states were conjoined inevitably, and each bore the responsibility for the other's crimes. In this interpretation of the twentieth century the basilear social, political and cultural distinction was that between fascists and anti-fascists. In the final analysis, it was a simple split between good and evil.

Though, with the occasional exception, Marxists remained the most visceral of anti-Fascists, liberals, Catholics and even conservatives were to unite in the great coalition which would win the Second World War against Nazi–fascism. For these non-Marxist anti-Fascists, too, the critical analysis of Fascism became an important activity. Headed by the towering figure of Croce, liberals denied the Marxist view that Fascism sprang from only one segment of society, and asserted instead that it was in its very nature an inter-class movement, appealing especially to the young and to those hardened by their endurance of the First World War. For theorists like Croce himself, who saw little wrong with pre-Fascist Liberal Italy, Fascism was also in no sense the 'revelation' of Italian history. It was not the product of the Risorgimento, national (*rivoluzione nazionale*) or 'missing' (*rivoluzione mancata*), or of the failings and injustices of Italian state and society, but rather a specific sickness brought on by the First World War and the Russian Revolution. Viewed retrospectively, it was a momentary contagion, and signalled but a parenthesis in the nation's positive history. It was both a chronological and a geographical accident, and, once cured, would not recur.

The immediate breakup of the wartime coalition in 1945 and its replacement by the Cold War offered the chance for a different intellectual alliance, too. Non-Marxist anti-Fascists clustered by the 1950s around the

model of totalitarianism which countered the model of fascism with the idea
that the real litmus test of human worth did not so much separate fascists
and anti-fascists as totalitarians and anti-totalitarians. Now conservatives
who believed that, by freeing the masses from their allegiance to God, the
world had fallen into temptation in the Enlightenment and French
Revolution and unleashed a flood of human sin, could unite with liberals
who were more optimistic about the benefits of capitalism, science,
parliamentary democracy and modernisation. In this understanding, the
Ribbentrop–Molotov pact marrying Stalin and Hitler was the most 'real'
event of the twentieth century. It was the way history ought to have gone,
and would go again should there be any appeasement of communists and
their fellow-travellers in the contemporary world. By this interpretation,
Italian Fascism, despite being Nazism's lasting ally, was a lesser evil indeed,
and Mussolini's regime may even have possessed good aspects. As Clare
Booth Luce, the virulently anti-Communist US ambassador to Italy in the
1950s, would put it, 'Mussolini's "corporate state" made some welcome
and much-needed reforms and, in its initial days, revived a sense of
individual hope and public purpose in the new nation', a memory that was
all the better, given the present 'murky' political circumstances in a country
burdened by too large a Communist party, and one too inclined to grow.[7]

The American ambassador's comment is a reminder that the hub of this
book is its account of the interpretion of Fascism and anti-Fascism since
1945. Here a number of processes have been made plain. One is a change
in the discipline of history itself. Put crudely, the 1950s were a decade of
the writing of diplomatic and political studies in which the agents of
history were Great Men (including Mussolini). From the early 1960s, this
approach was increasingly challenged by social historians who, still
reflecting the myths of the People's War, preferred to study the people
themselves, the 'working class', women, children and any with a
'subaltern' place in the structure of formal power (often social historians
found 'agency' being exercised by people who seemed at first sight the
victims of those with official authority). In the history of Fascism,
Mussolini would never disappear; but now it was possible to learn about
the Fascisms of the provinces and, as research proceeded, in a host of
social groupings. Now and hereafter, it became less natural to talk about
'Mussolini's Italy' and more sensible to review 'an Italian dictatorship'.

From the 1980s, however, social history in turn found its intellectual
empire under threat, this time from cultural historians who began, in some
way, to reflect the 'linguistic turn' associated with Michel Foucault and
other French critical theorists. They were thought to preach that 'discourse'
conditioned and even controlled human society, and that any human
experience was a construction. Often self-consciously radical, the new

---

7 C. B. Luce, 'Italy after one hundred years', *Foreign Affairs*, 39, January 1961, p. 223. She
   did add that Fascism had, eventually, betrayed its early promise.

cultural historians argued that social historians had fallen short of disclosing the hidden history of the 'other', and therefore had been remiss in helping the most socially deprived to obtain ownership of their particular histories. On occasion, it was said, social history had retained an 'imperialist' side, since its practitioners privileged written sources and rescued from the enormous condescension of posterity only the most visible and activist of the poor.

However, the new cultural history had problems, too. Ironically, even as they declared their intention to let every voice be heard,[8] cultural historians were often methodological conservatives, in their fashion neo-Rankeans. Borrowing from anthropologist Clifford Geertz the idea of 'thick description', they sometimes wrote as though the task of the historian, once more a master of empathy, was merely to let the 'other' speak for itself. If so, cultural history was to be a history with the history left out, in the sense that individual historians were no longer obliged self-consciously to advance their own critical (if imperfect) views of the subject which they were studying.

In the case of Italian Fascism, matters were still more perplexing, because the version of cultural history of Mussolini's regime which has become fashionable in the last decade usually concentrates on high culture and its intellectual makers. Claiming both novelty and objectivity, Emilio Gentile and his numerous American associates describe the 'fascination' of Fascist culture in its own words as they ponder what they think is its unique 'sacralization' of politics, its important furthering of the processes of the nationalisation of the masses, and therefore the genuineness of Fascism's claims to have forged a totalitarian state and society. As I have repeatedly suggested in this book, however, not everyone is convinced by this interpretation, especially because these culturalist historians often ignore both the manifold popular cultures of the Italies and the world-ranging popular culture of consumerism sallying forth triumphantly from Madison Avenue and the other centres of American capitalism.

Of course, methodological fashion (and its political context) have not been the only variables influencing the writing of the history of Italian Fascism since 1945. Rather, this book has indicated over and over again how intimately historical interpretation is directly related to changes in contemporary politics and society. Again set out schematically, the historiography of Fascism can be split into four phases.[9] Until 1960 the

8 Here there was a tremendous potential contradiction. Culturalist and other postmodernist historians declared worthily that their sensitivity would allow Aztecs, Australian Aboriginals and other 'native' peoples, lesbians and a variety of excluded subjects to be heard on their own terms. It is hard to see, however, why an absolute relativism should not extend this opportunity to SS guards, serial killers and religious fundamentalists.

9 Once again French scholarship provides a fascinating if flawed model here in a way that no historian of Italy can match. See H. Rousso, *Le syndrome de Vichy (1944–198 . . .)*, Paris, 1987, available in English as *The Vichy syndrome: history and memory in France since 1944*, Cambridge, Mass., 1991.

Fascist past, in most formal history writing as well as in film, literature and the other places in which the past is recounted, was met, after the initial preoccupations and excitations of 1945–8, with 'silence', a forgetting and an obscuring of the regime and its disasters. The 1950s were, after all, the decade of anti-Communism in which, in the eyes of the governing classes of the 'West', the need to repel Stalin and the ghost of Lenin outweighed all other matters.

The Tambroni affair of the summer of 1960 marked a neat symbolic break from this first era. With the rejection of Tambroni's public opening to the neo-fascist right, Italians, and foreigners whose attention chance or interest had fixed on Italy, began to argue about Fascism. For a while their debate was courteous and lacking in passion – by 1968, few disagreed with a generic understanding that Mussolini had been a sawdust Caesar and his regime a corrupt and incompetent tyranny, in which, however, evil ambition had been conditioned by practical failure. After 1968 a new phase opened, and the national political disputation intensified as communists and other anti-Fascists knocked more insistently than they had done in the past at the door of the *stanza dei bottoni* (the control room), as contemporary cliché denominated the presumed site of power. In parallel, historical debate quickened and historical interpretation grew more stark. Now anti-Fascist historians played up the murderousness of the regime, while also often tracing its connection with the injustices which were already apparent in its Liberal predecessor (and which often evidently continued in its Christian Democrat successor). Even Aldo Moro, borrowing, in characteristic way, a PCI slogan, could be heard urging meaningfully: 'The Resistance comes from afar and is going a long way.'[10] In the mid-1970s resisting seemed a praiseworthy activity at any time, and Fascism a form of evil not altogether overthrown in 1945. Now social history and structural accounts united in historiographical compromise to proclaim that Mussolini's regime had been the 'revelation' of national history. Now in so re/presenting an uncomfortable past, anti-Fascist history writing promised an uncomfortable future, at least for those who preferred the status quo.

Radical political rhetoric and radical history writing did not pass uncontested, however. Rather, Renzo De Felice emerged to be the historiographical chief of what would turn into the anti-anti-Fascist cause in Italy. Indeed, the 'De Felice affair', that controversy prompted by the historian's interview with Michael Ledeen and the volume of his biography of Mussolini concentrating on the 'years of consensus' from 1929 to 1936, coincided with the political 'crisis of the Italian crisis', running from the divorce referendum of 1974 to the murder of Aldo Moro by the Red Brigades in 1978. Assisted by his powerful conservative backers both within Italy and in the United States, and by his own remarkable research labours, De Felice won victory after victory, whether intellectual or practical, and

10 A. Moro, *L'intelligenza e gli avvenimenti: testi 1959–1978*, Milan, 1979, p. 243.

whether based on his interpretation of Fascism or on his deployment of academic patronage. By his death in 1996 De Felice had not, it was true, liquidated all his opponents in the Italian academic world – those who defined themselves as anti-Fascists retained some influence and coherence – but the conservative historian enjoyed an international reputation without challenge, and was widely esteemed as the expert on the Fascist era.

The story of De Felice's rise to historiographical power has its odd aspects, however. Though his productivity cannot be denied, his skills in interpretation are open to greater challenge, and it often seems necessary to interpret him (and to write his history) before comprehending his version of Fascism. As once perhaps by Ledeen, and certainly in his declining years, De Felice was open to capture by the forces of the political right, who read him in their own way. By 1996, De Felice seemed less important for a reckoning with that *Duce* whose biography he would never complete than as an aide to those political elements in Italy who wanted a stronger (more presidential and 'Gaullist') state and, perhaps anachronistically as their country made ready to enter Europe, a more committed nation. For these more rightward-leaning De Feliceans, the history of Fascism now signified little except that it was a period in which some advance towards 'modernity' had occurred, and in which a modicum of genuine patriotism still moved the masses. For this faction of the Italian historical profession the ethical spotlight had switched to the anti-Fascists, to their hidden crimes and to the allegedly destructive legacy they had left to the 'First Republic', in which fealty to a party overbore duty to the nation.

This anti-anti-Fascist stance had an evident utility for those who favoured the 'virtual politics' of Silvio Berlusconi, or looked to Gianfranco Fini and his 'post-fascists' and the final building of a genuine Italian conservative party. Better still, it diverted the glare of media attention from attitudes and behaviour in the 1980s, when in Italy, too, greed had been good for those who had hailed the leadership of the Socialist and anti-Communist Prime Minister, Bettino Craxi. If anti-Fascism and its past were the canker at the heart of Italy, then the responsibility of Craxian Italy for paving the way to *Tangentopoli* could be denied. If the Republic had been flawed in its first creation, then there was no need to ponder its most recent past.

Of course, most academic history was not so cynical and manipulative in its motivation and purpose. Moreover, although De Felice, Gentile and their friends had, by the flaunted 'objectivity' of their researches, blunted the ethical thrust of the anti-Fascist historiography of Fascism, they had not ended debate about Mussolini and his regime. Rather, as I have repeatedly shown in this book, histories continue to be written which aim to increase our understanding of the texture of life under the Fascist dictatorship, as well as continuing to assert that Fascism mattered, matters and will go on mattering.

Current discussion may be less animated than it was a generation ago.

After all, the collapse of communism has very likely ended the 'short twentieth century', and made the 1990s a decade of transition in which the road to the future (unless it be that mapped with such naïve confidence by Fukuyama) and therefore the path to the past are particularly obscure. As a result, the discipline of history is embattled in Italy, as in other parts of the world. None the less, history, despite some defeats, remains an inescapable subject; humankind is still possessed by it.

Perhaps the best hope is that the discipline of history and its natural allies in the humanities will go on arguing about Mussolini, Fascism and the Italian dictatorship, as about other ethically significant bygone eras. In 1931 Carlo Scorza, secretary of GUF (*Gruppi universitari fascisti*), the Fascist party organisation for university youth, was insecure about Fascist cultural hegemony:

> The masses in the universities are not yet what the Duce wants. . . . Among university students those furthest from us are students of Jurisprudence [where history was frequently studied], Literature, Philosophy: the abstract subjects. Those closest to us are, on the other hand, students of Medicine and Engineering, the exact subjects.[11]

It is a pleasing anecdote to close a study of the historiography of Fascism. Despite the pressure of their Italian dictatorship, even in the 1930s, it seems, some young students of history preferred questions to answers. In the next millennium, too, human freedom will again depend on the preservation of human inexactitude and on our ability to keep finding rival viewpoints about what that abstract concept, 'human freedom', might mean.

---

11 Quoted by M. A. Ledeen, *Universal Fascism: the theory and practice of the Fascist International, 1928–1936*, New York, 1972, pp. 11–12.

Select Bibliography

This bibliography is essentially restricted to English-language material. The only exception is where crucial Italian works of the last couple of decades have been listed. For Italian material, at least as published before the 1990s, see further R. De Felice (ed.), *Bibliografia orientativa del fascismo* (Rome, Bonacci, 1991). For a survey of the general historiography of Italy, see J. A. Davis, 'Modern Italy – changing perspectives since 1945', in M. Bentley (ed.), *Companion to historiography* (Routledge, London, 1996), and the less discriminating, F. Mazzonis (ed.), *L'Italia contemporanea e la storiografia internazionale* (Marsilio, Venice, 1995). Of Italian scholarly journals, the ones which most regularly addressed issues concerning Fascism were *Passato e Presente*, *Storia contemporanea*, and *Rivista di storia contemporanea*. They came from different and rival ideological perspectives, but in the mid-1990s the last two ceased publication.

General histories of Italy

Absalom, R. *Italy since 1800: a nation in the balance?* (London, Longman, 1995).

Bosworth, R. J. B. *Italy and the wider world 1860–1960* (London, Routledge, 1996).

Clark, M. *Modern Italy 1871–1982* (London, Longman, 1984; rev. ed., 1996).

Clough, S. B. *The economic history of modern Italy* (New York, Columbia University Press, 1964).

Di Scala, S. *Italy: from revolution to republic, 1700 to the present* (Boulder, Colo., Westview Press, 1995).

Procacci, G. *History of the Italian people* (London, Weidenfeld and Nicolson, 1970).

Sereni, E. *History of the Italian agricultural landscape* (Princeton University Press, 1997).

Seton-Watson, C. *Italy from Liberalism to Fascism: 1870–1925* (London, Methuen, 1967).

Smith, D. Mack *Italy: a modern history* (rev. ed., Ann Arbor, University of Michigan Press, 1969).

Zamagni, V. *The economic history of Italy 1860–1990* (Oxford, Clarendon, 1993).

General studies of fascism

Allardyce, G. 'What fascism is not: thoughts on the deflation of a concept', *American Historical Review*, 84 (1979).

Bessel, R. (ed.), *Fascist Italy and Nazi Germany: comparisons and contrasts* (Cambridge University Press, 1996).

Blinkhorn, M. (ed.), *Fascists and conservatives: the Radical Right and the establishment in twentieth-century Europe* (London, Unwin Hyman, 1990).

Bosworth, R. J. B. *Explaining Auschwitz and Hiroshima: history writing and the Second World War 1945–1990* (London, Routledge, 1993).

Cammett, J. M. 'Communist theories of Fascism 1920–1935', *Science and Society*, 31 (1967).

Carsten, F. L. *The rise of fascism* (London, Batsford, 1967).

Cassels, A. *Fascism* (Arlington Heights, Ill., Harlan Davidson, 1975).

Ceplair, L. *Under the shadow of war: Fascism, Anti-Fascism, and Marxists, 1918–1939* (New York, 1987).

De Grand, A. J. *Fascist Italy and Nazi Germany: the 'fascist' style of rule* (London, Routledge, 1995).

Eatwell, R. *Fascism: a history* (London, Chatto and Windus, 1995).

Golsan, R. J. (ed.), *Fascism, aesthetics, and culture* (Hanover, University of New England Press, 1992).

Gregor, A. J. *The ideology of fascism: the rationale of totalitarianism* (New York, Free Press, 1969).

Gregor, A. J. *The Fascist 'persuasion' in radical politics* (Princeton University Press, 1974).

Gregor, A. J. *Interpretations of fascism* (Morristown, NJ, General Learning Press, 1974).

Griffin, R. *The nature of fascism* (London, Pinter, 1991).

Griffin, R. (ed.), *Fascism* (Oxford, 1995).

Griffin, R. (ed.), *International fascism: theories, causes and the new consensus* (London, Arnold, 1998).

Guerin, D. *Fascism and Big Business* (New York, Anchor, 1973; first published 1934).

Hamilton, A. *The appeal of fascism: a study of the intellectuals and fascism 1919–1945* (London, A. Blond, 1971).

Hayes, P. M. *Fascism* (London, George Allen and Unwin, 1973).

Kitchen, M. *Fascism* (London, Macmillan, 1976).

Laqueur, W. *Fascism: a reader's guide: analysis, interpretations, biblio-graphy* (Harmondsworth, Penguin, 1979).

Laqueur, W. *Fascism: past, present and future* (Oxford University Press, 1996).

Larsen, S. U. *et al.* (eds), *Who were the fascists: social roots of European fascism* (Bergen, Universitätsforlaget, 1980).

Lubasz, H. (ed.), *Fascism: three major regimes* (New York, J. Wiley, 1973).

Maier, C. S. *Recasting bourgeois Europe: stabilization in France, Germany, and Italy in the decade after World War I* (Princeton University Press, 1975).

Mason, T. *Nazism, Fascism and the working class* (Cambridge University Press, 1995).

Nolte, E. *Three faces of fascism: Action Française, Italian Fascism, National Socialism* (New York, Mentor, 1969).

Payne, S. G. *A history of fascism, 1914–1945* (Madison, University of Wisconsin Press, 1995).

Poulantzas, N. *Fascism and dictatorship: the Third International and the problem of fascism* (London, NLB, 1974).

Talmon, J. L. *The myth of the nation and the vision of the revolution: the origins of ideological polarisation in the twentieth century* (London, Secker and Warburg, 1981).

Turner, H. A. (ed.), *Reappraisals of fascism* (New York, New Viewpoints, 1975).

Turner, S. P. and Käsler, D. (eds), *Sociology responds to fascism* (London, Routledge, 1992).

Weber, E. 'Revolution? Counterrevolution? What revolution?', *Journal of Contemporary History*, 9 (1974).

Weiss, J. L. *The fascist tradition: radical right-wing extremism in modern Europe* (New York, Harper and Row, 1967).

Woolf, S. J. (ed.), *The nature of fascism* (London, Weidenfeld and Nicolson, 1968).

Woolf, S. J. (ed.), *Fascism in Europe* (London, Methuen, 1981).

General studies of Italian Fascism

Cannistraro, P. V. *Historical dictionary of Fascist Italy* (Westport, Conn., Greenwood Press, 1982).

Carocci, G. *Italian Fascism* (Harmondsworth, Penguin, 1975).

Cassels, A. *Fascist Italy* (London, Routledge and Kegan Paul, 1969).

Chabod, F. *A history of Italian Fascism* (London, Weidenfeld and Nicolson, 1963).

De Felice, R. *Mussolini* (Turin, Einaudi, 1965–97). This biography, which includes a posthumously published volume but was never fully completed, is composed of *Mussolini il rivoluzionario 1883–1920*

(1965); *Mussolini il fascista 1: La conquista del potere 1921–5* (1966), 2: *L'organizzazione dello stato fascista, 1925–1929* (1968); *Mussolini il duce 1: Gli anni del consenso, 1929–1936* (1974), 2: *Lo stato totalitario 1936–1940* (1981); *Mussolini l'alleato 1940–1945 1: L'Italia in guerra 1940–1943* (2 vols., 1990); *Mussolini l'alleato 1940–1945 2: La guerra civile 1943–1945* (1997).

De Felice, R. *Le interpretazioni del fascismo* (Bari, Laterza, 1971).

De Felice, R. *Intervista sul fascismo* (Bari, Laterza, 1975; rev. ed., 1997).

De Felice, R. (ed.), *Antologia sul fascismo: il giudizio storico* (Bari, Laterza, 1976).

De Felice, R. (ed.), *Antologia sul fascismo: il giudizio politico* (Bari, Laterza, 1976).

De Felice, R. *Fascism: an informal introduction to its theory and practice* (New Brunswick, NJ, Transaction books, 1977).

De Felice, R. *Interpretations of fascism* (Cambridge, Mass., Harvard University Press, 1977).

De Felice, R. *Autobiografia del Fascismo: antologia di testi fascisti, 1919–1945* (Bergamo, Minerva Italica, 1978).

De Felice, R. 'Italian historiography since the Second World War', in R. J. B. Bosworth and G. Cresciani (eds), *Altro Polo: a volume of Italian studies* (Sydney, F. May Foundation, 1979).

De Felice, R. 'Italian Fascism and the middle classes', in S. U. Larsen *et al.* (eds), *Who were the Fascists: social roots of European Fascism* (Bergen, Universitätsforlaget, 1980).

De Felice, R. and Goglia, L. *Storia fotografica del fascismo* (Bari, Laterza, 1982).

De Felice, R. and Goglia, L. *Mussolini il mito* (Bari, Laterza, 1983).

De Felice, R. (ed.), *Futurismo, cultura e politica* (Turin, Fondazione Agnelli, 1988).

De Felice, R. *Rosso e nero* (Milan, Baldini and Castaldi, 1995).

De Felice, R. *Fascismo, antifascismo, nazione: note e ricerche* (Rome, Bonacci, 1996).

De Grand, A. J. *Italian Fascism: its origins and development* (Lincoln, University of Nebraska Press, 1982).

Forgacs, D. *Rethinking Italian Fascism: capitalism, populism and culture* (London, Lawrence and Wishart, 1986).

Gramsci, A. *The modern prince and other writings* (New York, International, 1959).

Gramsci, A. *Selections from the prison notebooks* (London, Lawrence and Wishart, 1971).

Gramsci, A. *Letters from prison* (New York, Harper and Row, 1973).

Gramsci, A. *Selections from political writings (1921–1926)* (London, Lawrence and Wishart, 1978).

Gramsci, A. *Selections from cultural writings* (London, Lawrence and Wishart, 1985).

Gramsci, A. *Pre-prison writings* (Cambridge University Press, 1994).

Gregor, A. J. *Italian Fascism and developmental dictatorship* (Princeton University Press, 1979).

Halperin, S. W. (ed.), *Mussolini and Italian Fascism* (New York, Van Nostrand, 1964).

Morgan, P. *Italian Fascism 1919–1945* (New York, St. Martins Press, 1995).

Ridley, J. *Mussolini* (London, Constable, 1997).

Smith, D. Mack 'Mussolini: artist in propaganda', *History Today*, 9 (1959).

Smith, D. Mack, *Mussolini* (London, Weidenfeld and Nicolson, 1981).

Tannenbaum, E. R. *Fascism in Italy: society and culture 1922–1945* (London, Allen Lane, 1973).

Tasca, A. *The rise of Italian Fascism 1918–1922* (New York, H. Fertig reprint, 1966).

Togliatti, P. *Lectures on Fascism* (London, Lawrence and Wishart, 1976).

Vajda, M. *Fascism as a mass movement* (London, Allison and Busby, 1976).

Whittam, J. *Fascist Italy* (Manchester University Press, 1995).

Wiskemann, E. *Fascism in Italy* (London, Macmillan, 1969).

Monographs on Italian Fascism

Absalom, R. *A strange alliance: aspects of escape and survival in Italy 1943–45* (Florence, Olschki, 1991).

Absalom, R. 'Hiding history: the Allies, the Resistance and the others in occupied Italy 1943–1945', *Historical Journal*, 38 (1995).

Adamson, W. L. 'Fascism and culture: avant-gardes and secular religion in the Italian case', *Journal of Contemporary History*, 24 (1989).

Adamson, W. L. 'Modernism and Fascism: the politics of culture in Italy, 1903–1922', *American Historical Review*, 95 (1990).

Adamson, W. L. 'The language of opposition in early twentieth-century Italy: rhetorical continuities between pre-war Florentine avant-gardism and Mussolini's Fascism', *Journal of Modern History*, 64 (1992).

Adamson, W. L. 'The culture of Italian Fascism and the Fascist crisis of modernity: the case of *Il Selvaggio*', *Journal of Contemporary History*, 30 (1995).

Adler, F. H. *Italian industrialists from Liberalism to Fascism: the political development of the industrial bourgeoisie, 1906–1934* (Cambridge University Press, 1995).

Amendola, G. *Intervista sull'antifascismo* (Bari, Laterza, 1976).

Aquarone, A. *L'organizzazione dello stato totalitario* (Turin, Einaudi, 1965).

Aquarone, A. 'Italy: the crisis of the corporative economy', *Journal of Contemporary History*, 4 (1969).

Arlacchi, P. *Mafia, peasants and great states: society in traditional Calabria* (Cambridge University Press, 1983).

Arnaldi, G. *et al.*, *Incontro con gli storici* (Bari, Laterza, 1986).

Asante, S. K. B. *Pan-African protest: West Africa and the Italo-Ethiopian crisis, 1934–1941* (London, Longmans, 1977).

Azzi, S. C. 'The historiography of Fascist foreign policy', *Historical Journal*, 36 (1993).

Baer, G. W. *The coming of the Italo-Ethiopian war* (Cambridge, Mass., Harvard University Press, 1967).

Baer, G. W. *Test case: Italy, Ethiopia and the League of Nations* (Stanford, Calif., Hoover Institution Press, 1976).

Barbagli, M. *Educating for unemployment: politics, labor markets and the school system – Italy, 1859–1973* (New York, Columbia University Press, 1982).

Barros, J. *The Corfu incident of 1923: Mussolini and the League of Nations* (Princeton University Press, 1965).

Ben-Ghiat, R. 'Fascism, writing, and memory: the realist aesthetic in Italy, 1930–1950', *Journal of Modern History*, 67 (1995).

Ben-Ghiat, R. 'Italian Fascism and the aesthetics of the "third way"', *Journal of Contemporary History*, 31 (1996).

Berezin, M. *Making the Fascist self: the political culture of interwar Italy* (Ithaca, NY, Cornell University Press, 1997).

Bernardini, G. 'The origins and development of anti-Semitism in Fascist Italy', *Journal of Modern History*, 49 (1977).

Binchy, D. A. *Church and state in Fascist Italy* (London, Oxford University Press, 1970).

Blatt, J. 'The battle of Turin, 1933–1936: Carlo Rosselli, Giustizia e Libertà, OVRA and the origins of Mussolini's anti-Semitic campaign', *Journal of Modern Italian Studies*, 1 (1995).

Bosworth, R. 'Italian foreign policy and its historiography', in R. Bosworth and G. Rizzo (eds), *Altro Polo: intellectuals and their ideas in contemporary Italy* (Sydney, F. May Foundation, 1983).

Bosworth, R. 'Italy's historians and the myth of Fascism' in R. Langhorne (ed.), *Diplomacy and intelligence during the Second World War: essays in honour of F. H. Hinsley* (Cambridge University Press, 1985).

Bosworth, R. 'Bernardo Bertolucci, *1900* and the myth of Fascism', *European History Quarterly*, 19 (1989).

Bosworth, R. J. B. and Romano, S. (eds), *La politica estera italiana (1860–1985)* (Bologna, Il Mulino, 1991).

Bosworth, R. and M. *Fremantle's Italy* (Rome, Gruppo Editoriale Internazionale, 1993).

Bosworth, R. J. B. 'Tourist planning in Fascist Italy and the limits of a totalitarian culture', *Contemporary European History*, 6 (1997).

Bosworth, R. J. B. 'The *Touring Club Italiano* and the nationalisation of the Italian bourgeoisie', *European History Quarterly*, 27 (1997).

Braun, E. 'Expressionism as Fascist aesthetic', *Journal of Contemporary History*, 31 (1996).

Brunetta, G. P. 'The conversion of the Italian cinema to fascism in the 1920s', *Journal of Italian History*, 1 (1978).

Bruzzone, A. M. 'Women in the Italian Resistance', in P. Thompson (ed.), *Our common history: the transformation of Europe* (London, Pluto Press, 1982).

Burgwyn, H. J. 'Conflict or rapprochement? Grandi confronts France and its protégé Yugoslavia: 1929–1932', *Storia delle relazioni internazionali*, 3 (1987).

Burgwyn, H. J. *Italian foreign policy in the interwar period 1918–1940* (Westport, Conn., Praeger, 1997).

Cammett, J. M. *Antonio Gramsci and the origins of Italian communism* (Stanford University Press, 1967).

Cannistraro, P. V. 'Mussolini's cultural revolution: Fascist or Nationalist?', *Journal of Contemporary History*, 7 (1972).

Cannistraro, P. V. *La fabbrica del consenso: fascismo e mass media* (Bari, Laterza, 1975).

Cannistraro, P. V. 'Fascism and Italian-Americans in Detroit', *International Migration Review*, 9 (1975).

Cannistraro, P. V. and Rosoli, G. 'Fascist emigration policy in the 1920s: an interpretative framework', *International Migration Review*, 13 (1979).

Cannistraro, P. V. and Sullivan, B. R. *Il Duce's other woman* (New York, William Morrow, 1993).

Cardoza, A. L. *Agrarian elites and Italian fascism: the province of Bologna 1901–1926* (Princeton University Press, 1982).

Caracciolo, N. *Uncertain refuge: Italy and the Jews during the Holocaust* (Urbana, University of Illinois Press, 1995).

Carpi, D. *Between Mussolini and Hitler: the Jews and the Italian authorities in France and Tunisia* (Hanover, Brandeis University Press, 1994).

Carrié, R. Albrecht-, *Italy at the Paris Peace Conference* (Hamden, Conn., Archon, 1966).

Cassels, A. *Mussolini's early diplomacy* (Princeton University Press, 1970).

Cassels, A. *et al.* 'A conversation with Denis Mack Smith', *Canadian Journal of Italian Studies*, 5–6 (1982).

Chadwick, O. 'Bastianini and the weakening of the Fascist will to fight the Second World War', in T. C. W. Blanning and D. Cannadine (eds), *History and biography: essays in honour of Derek Beales* (Cambridge University Press, 1996).

Chapman, C. G. *Milocca: a Sicilian village* (London, George Allen and Unwin, 1973).

Cicioni, M. *Primo Levi: bridges of knowledge* (Oxford, 1995).

Clark, M. *Antonio Gramsci and the revolution that failed* (New Haven, Yale University Press, 1977).

Clark, M. 'Italian Squadrismo and contemporary vigilantism', *European History Quarterly*, 18 (1988).

Clarke, J. Calvitt III, *Russia and Italy against Hitler: the Bolshevik-Fascist rapprochement of the 1930s* (Westport, Conn., Greenwood Press, 1991).

Cliadakis, H. 'Neutrality and war in Italian policy 1939–40', *Journal of Contemporary History*, 9 (1974).

Cohen, J. S. 'The 1927 revaluation of the lira: a study in political economy', *Economic History Review*, 25 (1972).

Cohen, J. S. 'Was Italian fascism a developmental dictatorship? some evidence to the contrary', *Economic History Review*, 41 (1988).

Colarizi, S. *L'opinione degli italiani sotto il regime 1929–1943* (Bari, Laterza, 1991).

Corner, P. *Fascism in Ferrara 1915–1925* (London, Oxford University Press, 1975).

Corner, P. 'Women in Fascist Italy: Changing family roles in the transition from an agricultural to an industrial society', *European History Quarterly*, 23 (1993).

Coverdale, J. F. *Italian intervention in the Spanish Civil War* (Princeton University Press, 1975).

Cresciani, G. *Fascism, Anti-Fascism and Italians in Australia* (Canberra, ANU Press, 1980).

Cunsolo, R. S. *Modern Italian nationalism: from its origins to World War II* (New York, Krieger, 1990)

Deakin, F. W. *The brutal friendship* (London, Weidenfeld and Nicolson, 1962).

Davis, J. A. (ed.), *Gramsci and Italy's passive revolution* (London, Croom Helm, 1979).

Davis, J. A. 'Remapping Italy's path to the twentieth century', *Journal of Modern History*, 66 (1994).

De Felice, R. *Storia degli ebrei sotto il fascismo* (Turin, Einaudi, 1961; 4th rev. ed., 1988).

De Felice, R. *Jews in an Arab land: Libya 1835–1970* (Austin, University of Texas Press, 1985).

De Felice, R. 'Fascism and culture in Italy: outlines for further study', *Stanford Italian Review*, 8 (1990).

De Giorgio, M. 'Women's history in Italy (nineteenth and twentieth centuries)', *Journal of Modern Italian Studies*, 1 (1996).

De Grand, A. J. 'Curzio Malaparte: the illusion of the Fascist revolution', *Journal of Contemporary History*, 7 (1972).

De Grand, A. J. *The Italian Nationalist Association and the rise of Fascism in Italy* (Lincoln, University of Nebraska Press, 1978).

De Grand, A. J. 'Cracks in the facade: the failure of Fascist totalitarianism in Italy 1935–9', *European History Quarterly*, 21 (1991).

De Grazia, V. *The culture of consent: mass organisation of leisure in Fascist Italy* (Cambridge University Press, 1981).

De Grazia, V. *How Fascism ruled women: Italy 1922–1945* (Berkeley, University of California Press, 1992).

Del Boca, A. *The Ethiopian war 1935–1941* (University of Chicago Press, 1969).

Delzell, C. F. *Mussolini's enemies: the Italian Anti-Fascist Resistance* (Princeton University Press, 1961).

Diggins, J. P. *Mussolini and Fascism: the view from America* (Princeton University Press, 1972).

Domenico, R. P. *Italian fascists on trial, 1943–1948* (Chapel Hill, University of North Carolina Press, 1991).

Doordan, D. *Building modern Italy: Italian architecture 1914–1936* (Princeton University Press, 1988).

Doumanis, N. and Pappas, N. G. 'Grand history in small places: social protest on Castelorizo (1934)', *Journal of Modern Greek Studies*, 15 (1997).

Doumanis, N. *Myth and memory in the Mediterranean: remembering Fascism's empire* (London, 1997).

Duggan, C. *Fascism and the Mafia* (New Haven, Yale University Press, 1989).

Eley, G. 'Reading Gramsci in English: observations on the reception of Antonio Gramsci in the English-speaking world 1957–82', *European History Quarterly*, 14 (1984).

Ellwood, D. W. *Italy 1943–1945* (Leicester University Press, 1985).

Falasca-Zamponi, S. *Fascist spectacle: the aesthetics of power in Mussolini's Italy* (Berkeley, California University Press, 1997).

Femia, J. V. *Gramsci's political thought: hegemony, consciousness and the revolutionary process* (Oxford, Clarendon, 1981).

Fogu, C. 'Fascism and *historic* representation: the 1932 Garibaldinian celebrations', *Journal of Contemporary History*, 31 (1996).

Fogu, C. '*Il Duce taumaturgo*: modernist rhetorics in Fascist representations of history', *Representations*, 57 (1997).

Forgacs, D. *Italian culture in the industrial era 1880–1980: cultural industries, politics and the public* (Manchester University Press, 1990).

Fornari, H. *Mussolini's gadfly: Roberto Farinacci* (Nashville, Vanderbildt University Press, 1971).

Forsyth, D. J. *The crisis of Liberal Italy: monetary and financial policy, 1914–1922* (Cambridge University Press, 1993).

Fraddosio, M. 'The Fallen Hero: the myth of Mussolini and Fascist women in the Italian Social Republic (1943–5)', *Journal of Contemporary History*, 31 (1996).

Fuller, M. 'Wherever you go, there you are: Fascist plans for the colonial city of Addis Ababa and the colonizing suburb of EUR '42', *Journal of Contemporary History*, 31 (1996).

Gatt, A. 'Futurism, proto-Fascist Italian culture and the sources of Douhetism', *War and Society*, 15 (1997).

Gentile, E. *Le origini dell'ideologia fascista (1918–1925)* (Bari, Laterza, 1975).

Gentile, E. *Il mito dello stato dall'antigiolittismo al fascismo* (Bari, Laterza, 1982).

Gentile, E. 'The problem of the party in Italian Fascism', *Journal of Contemporary History*, 19 (1984).

Gentile, E. 'Fascism in Italian historiography: in search of an individual historical identity', *Journal of Contemporary History*, 21 (1986).

Gentile, E. *Storia del Partito Fascista 1919–1922: movimento e milizia* (Bari, Laterza, 1989).

Gentile, E. 'Fascism as political religion', *Journal of Contemporary History*, 25 (1990).

Gentile, E. 'Impending modernity: Fascism and the ambivalent image of the United States', *Journal of Contemporary History*, 28 (1993).

Gentile, E. *Il culto del littorio: la sacralizzazione della politica nell'Italia fascista* (Bari, Laterza, 1993).

Gentile, E. *La via italiana al totalitarismo: il partito e lo stato nel regime fascista* (Rome, La Nuova Italia Scientifica, 1995).

Gentile, E., *The sacralization of politics in Fascist Italy* (Cambridge, Mass., Harvard University Press, 1996).

Gentile, E. 'Renzo De Felice: a tribute', *Journal of Contemporary History*, 32 (1997).

Germino, D. L. *The Italian Fascist Party in power: a study in totalitarian rule* (Minneapolis, University of Minnesota Press, 1959).

Germino, D. L. *Antonio Gramsci: architect of a new politics* (Baton Rouge, Louisiana University Press, 1990).

Ginsborg, P. *A history of contemporary Italy: society and politics 1943–1988* (Harmondsworth, 1988).

Ghirardo, D. *Building new communities: New Deal America and Fascist Italy* (Princeton University Press, 1989).

Ghirardo, D. '*Città fascista*: surveillance and spectacle', *Journal of Contemporary History*, 31 (1996).

Goglia, L. *Storia fotografica dell'impero fascista 1935–1941* (Bari, Laterza, 1985).

Gregor, A. J. 'Professor Renzo De Felice and the Fascist phenomenon', *World Politics*, 30 (1978).

Gregor, A. J. *Young Mussolini and the intellectual origins of Fascism* (Berkeley, University of California Press, 1979).

Gumbrecht, H. U. '*I redentori della vittoria*: on Fiume's place in the genealogy of Fascism', *Journal of Contemporary History*, 31 (1996).

Harney, R. *From the shores of hardship: Italians in Canada* (Welland, Ont., Editions Soleil, 1993).

Hay, J. *Popular film culture in Fascist Italy: the passing of the 'Rex'* (Bloomington, Indiana University Press, 1987).

Hughes, H. S. *Prisoners of hope: the silver age of the Italian Jews 1924–1974* (Cambridge, Mass., Harvard University Press, 1983).

Ignazi, P. *Il polo escluso: profilo del Movimento Sociale Italiano* (Bologna, Il Mulino, 1989).

Ipsen, C. *Dictating demography: the problem of population in Fascist Italy* (Cambridge University Press, 1996).

Jacobelli, J. *Il fascismo e gli storici oggi* (Bari, Laterza, 1988).

Joll, J. *Gramsci* (Glasgow, Fontana, 1977).

Joseph, R. 'The Martignoni affair: how a Swiss politician deceived Mussolini', *Journal of Contemporary History*, 9 (1974).

Kelikian, A. A. *Town and country under Fascism: the transformation of Brescia 1915–26* (Oxford, Clarendon, 1986).

Kent, P. C. *The Pope and the Duce: the international impact of the Lateran Agreements* (London, Macmillan, 1981).

Kent, P. C. 'Italy in the aftermath of the First World War', *International History Review*, 8 (1986).

Kent, P. C. 'A tale of two Popes: Pius XI and Pius XII and the Rome–Berlin Axis', *Journal of Contemporary History*, 23 (1988).

Kent, P. C. 'Between Rome and London: Pius XI, the Catholic Church and the Abyssinian crisis of 1935–1936', *International History Review*, 11 (1989).

Knox, M. *Mussolini unleashed 1939–1941: politics and strategy in Fascist Italy's last war* (Cambridge University Press, 1982).

Knox, M. 'Fascist Italy assesses its enemies' in E. R. May (ed.), *Knowing one's enemies: intelligence assessment before the two world wars* (Princeton University Press, 1984).

Knox, M. 'Conquest, foreign and domestic, in Fascist Italy and Nazi Germany', *Journal of Modern History*, 56 (1984).

Knox, M. 'I testi "aggiustati" dei discorsi segreti di Grandi', *Passato e Presente*, 13 (1987).

Knox, M. 'The Fascist regime, its foreign policy and its wars: an anti-anti-Fascist orthodoxy?' *Contemporary European History*, 4 (1995).

Koon, T. H. *Believe, obey, fight: political socialization of youth in Fascist Italy 1922–1943* (Chapel Hill, University of North Carolina Press, 1985).

Lamb, R. *Mussolini and the British* (London, J. Murray, 1997).

Landy, M. *Fascism in film: the Italian commercial cinema, 1931–1943* (Princeton University Press, 1986).

Larebo, H. M. *The building of an empire: Italian land policy and practice in Ethiopia 1935–41* (Oxford University Press, 1994).

Lears, T. Jackson, 'The concept of cultural hegemony: problems and possibilities', *American Historical Review*, 90 (1985).

Ledeen, M. 'Italian Fascism and youth', *Journal of Contemporary History*, 4 (1969).

Ledeen, M. *Universal Fascism: the theory and practice of the Fascist international, 1928–1936* (New York, H. Fertig, 1972).

Ledeen, M. 'The evolution of Italian Fascist Antisemitism', *Jewish Social Studies*, 37 (1975).

Ledeen, M. 'Renzo De Felice and the controversy over Italian Fascism', *Journal of Contemporary History*, 11 (1976).

Ledeen, M. *The first Duce: D'Annunzio at Fiume* (Baltimore, Johns Hopkins Press, 1977).

Lepschy, G. C. 'The language of Mussolini', *Journal of Italian History*, 1 (1978).

Linsenmeyer, W. S. 'Italian peace feelers before the fall of Mussolini', *Journal of Contemporary History*, 16 (1981).

Lowe, C. J. and Marzari, F. *Italian foreign policy, 1870–1940* (London, Routledge and Kegan Paul, 1975).

Lyttelton, A. 'Fascism in Italy: the first wave', *Journal of Contemporary History*, 1 (1966).

Lyttelton, A. *The seizure of power: Fascism in Italy 1919–1929* (London, Weidenfeld and Nicolson, 1973).

Macartney, M. H. H. *One man alone: the history of Mussolini and the Axis* (London, Chatto and Windus, 1944).

MacDonald, C. A. 'Radio Bari: Italian wireless propaganda in the Middle East and British countermanoeuvres 1934–38', *Middle Eastern Studies*, 13 (1977).

Marks, S. 'Mussolini and Locarno: Fascist foreign policy in microcosm', *Journal of Contemporary History*, 14 (1979).

Marzari, F. 'Projects for an Italian-led Balkan bloc of neutrals, September–December 1939', *Historical Journal*, 13 (1970).

Mason, T. 'The great economic history show', *History Workshop*, 21 (1986).

Mason, T. 'Italy and modernization: a montage', *History Workshop*, 25 (1988).

Melograni, P. 'The cult of the Duce in Mussolini's Italy', *Journal of Contemporary History*, 11 (1976).

Michaelis, M. *Mussolini and the Jews: German-Italian relations and the Jewish question in Italy 1922–1945* (Oxford, Clarendon, 1978).

Michaelis, M. 'Fascism, totalitarianism and the Holocaust: reflections on current interpretations of National Socialist Anti-Semitism', *European History Quarterly*, 19 (1989).

Miller, J. E. *The United States and Italy 1940–1950: the politics and diplomacy of stabilization* (Chapel Hill, University of North Carolina University Press, 1986).

Missori, M. *Gerarchi e statuti del PNF: Gran consiglio, Direttorio nazionale, federazioni provinciali: quadri e biografie* (Rome, Bonacci, 1986).

Mockler, A. *Haile Selassie's war: the Italian–Ethiopian campaign 1935–1941* (New York, Random House, 1984).

Molony, J. N. *The emergence of political catholicism in Italy: 'partito popolare' 1919–1926* (London, Croom Helm, 1977).

Morris, J. *The political economy of shopkeeping in Milan 1886–1922* (Cambridge University Press, 1993).

Morris, J. 'Retailers, Fascism, and the origins of the social protection of shopkeepers in Italy', *Contemporary European History*, 5 (1996).

Mosse, G. L. 'The political culture of Italian Futurism: a general perspective', *Journal of Contemporary History*, 25 (1990).

Mosse, G. 'Fascist aesthetics and society: some considerations', *Journal of Contemporary History*, 31 (1996).

Negash, T. *Italian colonialism in Eritrea, 1882–1941: policies, practice and impact* (Uppsala, Almquist and Wiksell, 1987).

Noether, E. P. 'Italian intellectuals under Fascism', *Journal of Modern History*, 43 (1971).

O'Brien, A. C. 'Italian youth in conflict: Catholic Action and Fascist Italy, 1929–1931', *Catholic Historical Review*, 68 (1982).

Painter, B. W. 'Renzo De Felice and the historiography of Italian Fascism', *American Historical Review*, 95 (1990).

Passerini, L. 'Italian working class culture between the wars: consensus to Fascism and work ideology', *International Journal of Oral History*, 1 (1980).

Passerini, L. 'Work ideology and working class attitudes to Fascism', in P. Thompson (ed.), *Our common history: the transformation of Europe* (London, Pluto Press, 1982).

Passerini, L. *Fascism in popular memory: the cultural experience of the Turin working class* (Cambridge University Press, 1987).

Passerini, L. *Mussolini immaginario: storia di una biografia, 1915–1939* (Bari, Laterza, 1991).

Pavlowitch, S. K. 'The King who never was: an instance of Italian involvement in Croatia, 1941–3', *European Studies Review*, 8 (1978).

Pavone, C. *Una guerra civile: saggio storico sulla moralità nella Resistenza,* (Turin, Bollati Boringhieri, 1991).

Petracchi, G. 'Ideology and *Realpolitik*: Italian–Soviet relations 1917–1932', *Journal of Italian History*, 2 (1979).

Pickering-Iazzi, R. (ed.), *Mothers of invention: women, Italian Fascism and culture* (Minneapolis, University of Minnesota Press, 1995).

Pinkus, K. *Bodily regimes: Italian advertising under Fascism* (Minneapolis, University of Minnesota Press, 1997).

Pitkin, D. S. *The house that Giacomo built: history of an Italian family, 1898–1978* (Cambridge University Press, 1985).

Pollard, J. F. *The Vatican and Italian Fascism, 1929–32: a study in conflict* (Cambridge University Press, 1985).

Procacci, G. 'Italy: from interventionism to Fascism 1917–19', *Journal of Contemporary History*, 3 (1968).

Pugliese, S. G. 'Death in exile: the assassination of Carlo Rosselli', *Journal of Contemporary History*, 32 (1997).

Quazza, G. (ed.), *Storiografia e fascismo* (Milan, F. Angeli, 1985).

Reece, J. E. 'Fascism, the Mafia, and the emergence of Sicilian separatism (1919–1943)', *Journal of Modern History*, 45, 1973.

Renzi, W. A. 'Mussolini's sources of financial support, 1914–1915', *History*, 56 (1971).

Revelli, N. *La guerra dei poveri* (Turin, Einaudi, 1979).

Roberts, D. D. *The syndicalist tradition and Italian Fascism* (Manchester University Press, 1979).

Robertson, E. M. *Mussolini as empire builder: Europe and Africa, 1932–6* (London, Macmillan, 1977).

Robertson, E. M. 'Race as a factor in Mussolini's policy in Africa and Europe', *Journal of Contemporary History*, 23 (1988).

Rosengarten, F. *The Italian Anti-Fascist press (1919–1945): from the legal opposition press to the underground newspapers of World War II* (Cleveland, OH., Case Western Reserve University Press, 1968).

Roth, J. J. 'The roots of Italian Fascism', *Journal of Modern History*, 39 (1967).

Rusinow, D. L. *Italy's Austrian heritage, 1919–1946* (Oxford, Clarendon, 1969).

Sachs, H. *Music in Fascist Italy* (New York, W.W. Norton, 1988).

Sadkovich, J. J. 'Aircraft carriers and the Mediterranean 1940–1943: rethinking the obvious', *Aerospace Historian*, 34 (1987).

Sadlovich, J. J. *Italian support for Croatian separatism 1927–1937* (New York, Garland publishing, 1987).

Sadkovich, J. J. 'Understanding defeat: reappraising Italy's role in World War II', *Journal of Contemporary History*, 24 (1989).

Sadkovich, J. J. 'Of myths and men: Rommel and the Italians in North Africa', *International History Review*, 13 (1991).

Sadkovich, J. J. 'The Italo–Greek war in context: Italian priorities and Axis diplomacy', *Journal of Contemporary History*, 28 (1993).

Sadkovich, J. J. 'Italian morale during the Italo–Greek war of 1940–1941', *War and Society*, 12 (1994).

Sadkovich, J. J. *The Italian navy in World War II* (Westport, Conn., Greenwood Press, 1994).

Salvati, M. *Il regime e gli impiegati: la nazionalizzazione piccolo-borghese nel ventennio fascista* (Bari, Laterza, 1992).

Salvemini, G. 'Pietro Badoglio's role in the Second World War', *Journal of Modern History*, 21 (1949).

Salvemini, G. 'Economic conditions in Italy, 1919–1922', *Journal of Modern History*, 23 (1951).

Salvemini, G. *Prelude to World War II* (London, Gollancz, 1953).

Santoro, C. M. *La politica estera di una media potenza: L'Italia dall'Unità ad oggi* (Bologna, Il Mulino, 1991).

Sarti, R. 'Fascist modernization in Italy: traditional or revolutionary?', *American Historical Review*, 75 (1970).

Sarti, R. 'Mussolini and the Italian industrial leadership in the battle of the lira 1925–1927', *Past and Present*, 47 (1970).

Sarti, R. *Fascism and the industrial leadership in Italy, 1919–1940: a study in the expansion of private power under Fascism* (Berkeley, University of California Press, 1971).

Sarti, R. (ed.), *The Ax within: Italian fascism in action* (New York, New Viewpoints, 1974).

Sbacchi, A. *Ethiopia under Mussolini: Fascism and the colonial experience* (London, Zed books, 1985).

Schnapp, J. T. 'Epic demonstrations: Fascist modernity and the 1932 Exhibition of the Fascist Revolution', in R. J. Golsan (ed.), *Fascism, aesthetics, and culture* (Hanover, University of New England Press, 1992).

Schnapp, J. T. '*18BL*: Fascist mass spectacle', *Representations*, 43 (1993).

Schnapp, J. T. 'Fascinating Fascism', *Journal of Contemporary History*, 31 (1996).

Schnapp, J. T. *Staging fascism: 18BL and the theater of masses for masses* (Stanford University Press, 1996).

Scriba, F. 'The sacralization of the Roman past in Mussolini's Italy: Erudition, aesthetics and religion in the exhibition of Augustus' bimillenary in 1937–38', *Storia della storiografia*, 30 (1996).

Segrè, C. G. 'Italo Balbo and the colonization of Libya', *Journal of Contemporary History*, 7 (1972).

Segrè, C. G. *Fourth shore: the Italian colonization of Libya* (University of Chicago Press, 1974).

Segrè, C. G. 'Douhet in Italy: prophet without honour?' *Aerospace Historian*, 26 (1979).

Segrè, C. G. *Italo Balbo: a Fascist life* (Berkeley, University of California Press, 1987).

Serneri, S. Neri, 'A past to be thrown away? Politics and history in the Italian Resistance', *Contemporary European History*, 4 (1995).

Settembrini, D. 'Mussolini and the legacy of revolutionary socialism', *Journal of Contemporary History*, 11 (1976).

Shorrock, W. I. 'France and the rise of Fascism in Italy, 1919–23', *Journal of Contemporary History*, 10, 1975.

Shorrock, W. I. *From ally to enemy: the enigma of Fascist Italy in French diplomacy, 1920–1940* (Kent, OH., Kent State University Press, 1988).

Sluga, G. A. 'The Risiera di San Sabba: Fascism, anti-Fascism, and Italian nationalism', *Journal of Modern Italian Studies*, 1 (1996).

Smith, D. Mack, 'Benedetto Croce: history and politics', *Journal of Contemporary History*, 8 (1973).

Smith, D. Mack, 'Anti-British propaganda in Fascist Italy', in *Inghilterra e Italia nel 1900: atti del convegno di Bagni di Lucca ottobre 1972* (Florence, Nuova Italia, 1973).

Smith, D. Mack, *Mussolini's Roman Empire* (London, Longmans, 1976).

Smith, D. Mack, *Italy and its monarchy* (New Haven, Yale University Press, 1989).

Smith, D. Mack, 'Documentary falsification and Italian biography', in

T. C. W. Blanning and D. Cannadine (eds), *History and biography: essays in honour of Derek Beales* (Cambridge University Press, 1996).

Smyth, H. McG. *Secrets of the Fascist era: how Uncle Sam obtained some of the top-level documents of Mussolini's period* (Carbondale, Southern Illinois University Press, 1975).

Snowden, F. M. *Violence and the great estates in the south of Italy: Apulia, 1900–1922* (Cambridge University Press, 1986).

Snowden, F. M. *The Fascist revolution in Tuscany 1919–1922* (Cambridge University Press, 1989).

Spriano, P. *The occupation of the factories: Italy 1920* (London, Pluto Press, 1975).

Spriano, P. *Antonio Gramsci and the party: the prison years* (London, Lawrence and Wishart, 1979).

Stafford, P. 'The Chamberlain–Halifax visit to Rome: a reappraisal', *English Historical Review*, 98 (1983).

Steinberg, J. *All or nothing: the Axis and the Holocaust 1941–3* (London, Routledge, 1990).

Stille, A. *Benevolence and betrayal: five Italian Jewish families under Fascism* (New York, Penguin, 1993).

Stone, M. 'Staging Fascism: the exhibition of the Fascist revolution', *Journal of Contemporary History*, 28 (1993).

Sullivan, B. R. 'A fleet in being: the rise and fall of Italian sea power, 1861–1943', *International History Review*, 10, (1988).

Tannenbaum, E. R. 'The goals of Italian Fascism', *American Historical Review*, 74 (1969).

Thompson, D. *State control in Fascist Italy: culture and conformity 1925–1943* (Manchester University Press, 1991).

Tinghino, J. J. *Edmondo Rossoni: from revolutionary syndicalism to Fascism* (New York, P. Lang, 1991).

Toscano, M. *The origins of the Pact of Steel* (Baltimore, J. Hopkins University Press, 1967).

Tranfaglia, N. *L'Italia unita nella storiografia del secondo dopoguerra* (Milan, Feltrinelli, 1980).

Tranfaglia, N. 'Fascismo e mass media: dall'intervista di De Felice agli sceneggiati televisivi', *Passato e Presente*, 3 (1983).

Tranfaglia, N. *Labirinto italiano: radici storiche e nuove contraddizioni* (Turin, Celid, 1984).

Tranfaglia, N. *Un passato scomodo: fascismo e postfascismo* (Bari, Laterza, 1996).

Trifkovic, S. 'Rivalry between Germany and Italy in Croatia 1942–1943', *Historical Journal*, 36 (1993).

Urban, G. R. (ed.), *Eurocommunism: its roots and future in Italy and elsewhere* (London, Temple-Smith, 1978).

Vanek, W. M. 'Piero Gobetti and the crisis of the "prima dopoguerra"', *Journal of Modern History*, 37 (1965).

Varsori, A. 'Italy, Britain and the problem of a separate peace during the Second World War', *Journal of Italian History*, 1 (1978).

Verna, F. P. 'Notes on Italian rule in Dalmatia under Bastianini, 1941–1943', *International History Review*, 12 (1990).

Villari, L. *The Liberation of Italy, 1943–1947* (Appleton, Wisc., C. Nelson, 1959).

Visser, R. 'Fascist doctrine and the cult of *romanità*', *Journal of Contemporary History*, 27 (1992).

Vivarelli, R. *Il dopoguerra in Italia e l'avvento del fascismo (1918–1922), vol. 1: dalla fine della guerra all'impresa di Fiume* (Naples, Istituto italiano per gli studi storici, 1967).

Vivarelli, R. *Storia delle origini del fascismo: l'Italia dalla grande guerra alla marcia su Roma* (Bologna, Il Mulino, 1991).

Vivarelli, R. 'Interpretations of the origins of Fascism', *Journal of Modern History*, 63 (1991).

Von Henneberg, K. 'Imperial uncertainties: architectural syncretism and improvisation in Fascist colonial Libya', *Journal of Contemporary History*, 31 (1996).

Walston, J. 'History and memory of the Italian concentration camps', *Historical Journal*, 40 (1997).

Wanrooij, B. '*Il Bo* 1935–1944: Italian students between Fascism and Anti-Fascism', *Risorgimento*, 3 (1982).

Wanrooij, B. 'The rise and fall of Italian Fascism as a generational conflict', *Journal of Contemporary History*, 22 (1987).

Ward, D. *Antifascisms: cultural politics in Italy 1943–46: Benedetto Croce and the liberals, Carlo Levi and the 'Actionists'* (Madison, Wisc., Farleigh Dickinson University Press, 1996).

Whittam, J. R. 'Drawing the line: Britain and the emergence of the Trieste question 1941–May 1945', *English Historical Review*, 106 (1991).

Williams, G. A. *Proletarian order: Antonio Gramsci, factory councils and the origins of Italian communism 1911–1921* (London, Pluto Press, 1975).

Williams G. L. *Fascist thought and totalitarianism in Italy's secondary schools: theory and practice 1922–1943* (New York, P. Lang, 1994).

Willson, P. R. *The clockwork factory: women and work in Fascist Italy* (Oxford University Press, 1993).

Willson, P. R. 'Flowers for the doctor: pro-natalism and abortion in Fascist Milan', *Modern Italy*, 1 (1996).

Wiskemann, E. *The Rome–Berlin Axis* (London, Oxford University Press, 1949).

Woolf, S. J. 'Mussolini as revolutionary', *Journal of Contemporary History*, 1 (1966).

Zamagni, V. 'The rich in a late industrializer: the case of Italy, 1800–1945', in W. D. Rubinstein (ed.), *Wealth and the wealthy in the modern world* (London, Croom Helm, 1980).

Zapponi, N. 'Fascism in Italian historiography 1986–93: a fading national identity', *Journal of Contemporary History*, 29 (1994).

Zucchi, J. E. *Italians in Toronto: development of a national identity, 1875–1935* (Kingston, Ont., McGill-Queen's University Press, 1988).

Zuccotti, S. *The Italians and the Holocaust* (New York, Basic Books, 1987).

Autobiographies and other primary sources, including major contemporary studies of Fascism

Agnelli, S. *We always wore sailor suits* (London, Weidenfeld and Nicolson, 1975).

Alfieri, D. *Dictators face to face* (London, Elek, 1954).

Badoglio, P. *The war in Abyssinia* (London, Methuen, 1937).

Badoglio, P. *Italy in the Second World War: memories and documents* (London, Oxford University Press, 1948).

Bonomi, I. *From socialism to Fascism: a study of contemporary Italy* (London, M. Hopkinson, 1924).

Chamberlain, L. (ed.), *The Futurist cookbook* (London, Trefoil publications, 1989).

Ciano, G. *Diary 1937–8* (London, Methuen, 1952).

Ciano, G. *Diary 1939–43* (London, Heinemann, 1947).

Ciano, G. *Diplomatic papers* (London, Odhams, 1948).

De Bono, *Anno XIIII: the conquest of an empire* (London, Cresset, 1937).

Delzell, C. F. (ed.), *Mediterranean fascism, 1919–1945* (New York, Harper and Row, 1970).

Finer, S. H. *Mussolini's Italy* (London, Gollancz, 1935).

Hood, S. *Carlino* (Manchester, Carcanet, 1985).

Kemechey, L. *Il Duce: the life and work of Benito Mussolini* (London, Williams and Norgate, 1930).

Levi, C. *Christ stopped at Eboli* (London, Cassell, 1948; film version, directed by F. Rosi, 1979).

Levi, P. *If this is a man* (Harmondsworth, Penguin, 1979).

Ludwig, E. 'Mussolini: the Italian autocrat', in his *Leaders of Europe* (London, Nicholson, 1934).

Lussu, E. *Sardinian brigade* (New York, Grove Press, 1970).

Lussu, E. *Enter Mussolini* (London, Methuen, 1936).

Lyttelton, A. (ed.), *Italian fascisms from Pareto to Gentile* (London, Cape, 1973).

Matteotti, G. *The 'Fascisti' exposed: a year of Fascist domination* (New York, H. Fertig reprint, 1969).

Megaro, G. *Mussolini in the making* (London, George Allen and Unwin, 1938).

Monelli, P. *Mussolini: an intimate life* (London, Thames and Hudson, 1953).

Moore, M. *Fourth shore: Italy's mass colonization of Libya* (London, Routledge, 1940).

Mussolini, B. 'The political and social doctrine of Fascism', *Political Quarterly*, 4 (1933).

Mussolini, B. *Memoirs, 1942–1943 with documents relating to the period* (New York, H. Fertig reprint, 1975).

Mussolini, B. *The corporate state* (New York, H. Fertig reprint, 1975).

Mussolini, R. *My life with Mussolini* (London, R. Hale, 1959).

Mussolini, R. *The real Mussolini* (Farnborough, Saxon House, 1973).

Mussolini, V. *Mussolini: the tragic women in his life* (London, NEL, 1973).

Nenni, P. *Ten years of tyranny in Italy* (London, George Allen & Unwin, 1932).

Newby, E. *Love and war in the Apennines* (London, Hodder & Stoughton, 1971).

Newby, W. *Peace and war: growing up in Fascist Italy* (London, Collins, 1991).

Nitti, F. F. *Escape* (New York, Putnam's, 1930).

Passerini, L. *Autobiography of a Generation: Italy, 1968* (Hanover, Wesleyan University Press, 1996).

Pesce, G. *And no quarter: an Italian partisan in World War II* (Athens, Ohio University Press, 1972).

Pound, E. *Jefferson and/or Mussolini: 'l'idea statale': Fascism as I have seen it* (London, Nott, 1935).

Quaranta di San Severino, B. *Mussolini as revealed in his political speeches* (London, Dent, 1923).

Salvadori, M. *The labour and the wounds: a personal chronicle of one man's fight for freedom* (London, Pall Mall Press, 1958).

Salvemini, G. *The Fascist dictatorship in Italy* (New York, Holt, 1927).

Salvemini, G. *Under the axe of Fascism* (London, Gollancz, 1936).

Salvemini, G. *Italian Fascism* (London, Gollancz, 1938).

Salvemini, G. and La Piana, G. *What to do with Italy* (London, Gollancz, 1943).

Salvemini, G. *Italian fascist activities in the United States* (New York, Centre for Migration Studies, 1977).

Sarfatti, M. *The life of Benito Mussolini* (London, T. Butterworth, 1934).

Schneider, H. W. *Making the Fascist state* (New York, Oxford University Press, 1928).

Schneider, H. W. and Clough, S. B. *Making Fascists* (University of Chicago Press, 1929).

Segre, D.V. *Memoirs of a fortunate Jew: an Italian story* (London, Paladin, 1987).

Seldes, G. *Sawdust Caesar: the untold history of Mussolini and Fascism* (London, Barker, 1936).

Sforza, C. *European dictatorships* (New York, Freeport, 1931).

Sillani, T. (ed.), *What is Fascism and why?* (London, Benn, 1931).

Silone, I. *The school for dictators* (London, Cape, 1939).

Sturzo, L. *Italy and 'Fascismo'* (London, Faber, 1926).

Sturzo, L. *Italy and the new world order* (London, MacDonald, 1944).

Villari, L. *The Fascist experiment* (London, Faber and Gwyer, 1926).

Villari, L. *The expansion of Italy* (London, Faber, 1930).

Villari, L. 'The economics of Fascism' in G. S. Counts *et al.*, *Bolshevism, Fascism and Capitalism: an account of the three economic systems* (New Haven, Yale University Press, 1932).

Villari, L. *On the roads to Rome* (London, Maclehone, 1932).

Villari, L. *The war on the Italian front* (London, Coledan-Sanderson, 1932).

Welk, W. G. *Fascist economic policy: an analysis of Italy's economic experiment* (Cambridge, Mass., Harvard University Press, 1938).

Film and literary explorations of Italian Fascism: some major examples

Bassani, G. *The Garden of the Finzi-Continis* (Harmondsworth, 1969; film version directed by V. De Sica, 1970).

Bertolucci, B. *The Spider's Strategem* (film, 1970).

Bertolucci, B. *1900* (film, 1976).

Brancati, V. *Bell'Antonio* (London, Harvill, 1993).

D'Annunzio, G. *The Flame* (London, Quartet, 1991).

Fellini, F. *Amarcord* (film, 1972).

Gadda, C. E. *That awful mess on the Via Merulana* (London, Encounter, 1985).

Leto, M. *La Villeggiatura* (film, 1973).

Malaparte, C. *The Skin* (London, A. Redman, 1952; film version directed by L. Cavani, 1981).

Morante, E. *History: a novel* (Harmondsworth, Penguin, 1980).

Moravia, A. *The Time of indifference* (Harmondsworth, Penguin, 1970).

Moravia, A. *The Conformist* (London, Secker & Warburg, 1952; film version directed by B. Bertolucci, 1970).

Mussolini, B. *The Cardinal's mistress* (London, Cassell, 1929).

Pasolini, P. P. *Salò o le 120 giornate di Sodoma* (film, 1975).

Pratolini, V. *A Tale of poor lovers* (London, Hamish Hamilton, 1949).

Rimanelli, G. *The Day of the lion* (London, Heinemann, 1956).

Rossellini, R. *The war trilogy: Rome: open city, Paisan, Germany – Year Zero* (New York, Grossman, 1973).

Rossellini, R. *Il generale della Rovere* (film, 1959).

Silone, I. *Fontamara* (London, Methuen, 1934; film version directed by C. Lizzani, 1980).

Taviani, V and P. *The Night of the shooting stars* (film, 1983)

Thomas di Giovanni, N. *1900* (Glasgow, Fontana, 1977).

Vancini, F. *La lunga notte del '43* (film, based on Bassani short story, 1960).

Vancini, F. *Il Delitto Matteotti* (film, 1971).

Vittorini, E. *Conversations in Sicily* (Penguin, Harmondsworth, 1961).

Wertmüller, L. *Love and anarchy* (film, 1974).

Wertmüller, L. *Seven Beauties* (film, 1975).

There are many dictionaries of Italian film. See e.g. R. Chiti (ed.), *Dizionario del cinema italiano* (4 vols., Rome, 1991–6).

The lyrics of Fascist songs and a discography are available in A. V. Savona and M. L. Straniero (eds), *Canti dell'Italia fascista (1919–1945)* (Milan, Garzanti, 1979).

Index

Printed in the United Kingdom
by Lightning Source UK Ltd.
9472500001B